**Third Edition**

# Reading Specialists
## <u>and</u> Literacy Coaches
## <u>in the</u> Real World

**Third Edition**

# Reading Specialists and Literacy Coaches in the Real World

## MaryEllen Vogt

*California State University, Long Beach*

## Brenda A. Shearer

*University of Wisconsin Oshkosh*

WAVELAND
PRESS, INC.
Long Grove, Illinois

For information about this book, contact:
Waveland Press, Inc.
4180 IL Route 83, Suite 101
Long Grove, IL 60047-9580
(847) 634-0081
info@waveland.com
www.waveland.com

10-digit ISBN 1-4786-3297-6
13-digit ISBN 978-1-4786-3297-9

To Karlin, a talented and dedicated reading specialist,
who makes her mother very proud.
MEV

To Jessica, Ann, Claudia, Brianna, Lydia, Pat, and wise women everywhere;
and to Michael, with love.
BAS


And to our dear friend, Dr. Martha Rapp Ruddell (Marty), for her profound
influence on our lives and our careers.
MEV and BAS

Between the time *Reading Specialists and Literacy Coaches in the Real World* by Vogt and Shearer was originally published and this 2016 Waveland Press, Inc. reissue, two organizations implemented name changes. The International Reading Association (IRA) is now the International Literacy Association (ILA). The National Reading Conference (NRC) is now the Literacy Research Association (LRA).

If you have any questions, please communicate with the publisher. Contact information for Waveland Press, Inc. is on the copyright page of this book.

# About the Authors

**MaryEllen Vogt** is Distinguished Professor Emerita of Education at California State University, Long Beach. Dr. Vogt has been a classroom teacher, reading specialist, special education specialist, curriculum coordinator, and university teacher educator. She received her doctorate from the University of California, Berkeley, and is a coauthor of fifteen books, including *Making Content Comprehensible for Elementary English Learners: The SIOP® Model* (2010), *Making Content Comprehensible for Secondary English Learners: The SIOP® Model* (2010), and *Response to Intervention (RtI) and English Learners: Making It Happen* (2011). Her research interests include improving comprehension in the content areas, teacher change and development, and content literacy and language acquisition for English learners. Dr. Vogt was inducted into the California Reading Hall of Fame, received her university's Distinguished Faculty Teaching Award, and served as President of the International Reading Association in 2004–2005. She lives in the Lake Tahoe area with her husband, Keith.

**Brenda A. Shearer,** Professor Emerita of Reading Education at the University of Wisconsin Oshkosh, has over thirty years of experience as a teacher, reading specialist, professor, and researcher in urban and rural Wisconsin. She received her doctorate in Curriculum and Instruction from the University of Minnesota and was named Outstanding Faculty Member in the College of Education at the University of Wisconsin—River Falls. Dr. Shearer is past president of the Wisconsin State Reading Association and maintains an active publication, presentation, and research agenda. Her scholarly works include numerous textbook chapters and articles in *The Reading Teacher, Journal of Educational Psychology, Journal of Adolescent and Adult Literacy, NRC Yearbook,* and other professional journals. Dr. Shearer's interests focus on the changing roles of reading professionals, adolescent literacy, and effective literacy intervention programs and practices. She lives in the Blue Ridge Mountains of western North Carolina with her husband, Michael.

# Contents

**PART III** • *Reading Specialists and Literacy Coaches: Leading Principled Practice*

**6** *Differentiating Instruction to Meet Learners' Needs: Framing Literacy Intervention*    **112**

**12**     *Moving the Field Forward as Leaders
and Literacy Advocates*     **239**

# *Preface*

Welcome to the *real* world of reading specialists and literacy coaches! You are about to join a unique group of educators—those who care passionately about reading and writing, and about ensuring that all children, adolescents, and adults read and write well enough not just to survive, but to thrive, in their lives and in their work. You are fortunate to be in a position, as highly educated, knowledgeable, and skilled literacy professionals, to support them in this journey. And although we reading specialists and literacy coaches are comparatively few in number, individually and collectively we hold tremendous potential for shaping our world.

The traditional role of the reading specialist has changed significantly, in part because of districts scrambling to meet federally mandated standards associated with No Child Left Behind/ESEA or face sanctions that include a possible loss of desperately needed funding. When the first edition of this book was released in late 2002, we barely mentioned *literacy coaches*. We never could have guessed the number who would be working in classrooms today. And it would have been unimaginable to us that they would be joining forces with middle and secondary educators. Since then, the title of *literacy coach* has expanded to include *reading coach* and *instructional coach*. We now find that those called reading specialists and those called literacy coaches often assume many or all of the same responsibilities. However, their job descriptions continue to vary significantly from school to school and from district to district. We worked hard in the previous edition to "nail down," once and for all, the differences between reading specialists and literacy coaches. Fortunately, we have grown some since then. We are no longer preoccupied with labels. We just want to make sure that the most knowledgeable, qualified, credentialed reading professionals are working with the students who need them the most. Professional organizations have worked side by side with reading professionals in the field to support increased accountability and to promote certification standards. Today, this is the *real* world of the reading specialist and literacy coach.

As students, professors, and authors, we've scrutinized textbooks for years. Experience tells us that after most of us read a text, we rarely open it again. That is why, this time, we decided to take a different approach. Times have changed and so must we. Rather than taking you from your world and into academia, we wrote this book to send you out into the *real world,* where you live and teach. We have developed a companion website to support this edition of our text. This has given us a great deal of flexibility that we've never had before. We can expand on definitions and update and reinforce information in ways that are much less space-constrained, yet carefully tied to the book. We don't have all the answers, but we certainly have the questions—many of the same ones you do—and we know where to look for answers. In each chapter, we provide a substantial common base of information—things we believe reading professionals need to know. But we also recognize that each of you is different. So we include a number of "Beyond the Book" opportunities; new projects for portfolios, professional development, and self-assessment; and links that will lead you far beyond anything our book alone could provide. Thus, you have the opportunity to put your thumbprint on the content of this course of study if you so choose. We believe this stance is far more congruent with the way all of us seek and use information today. Think of our book as an extremely comprehensive homepage with great information and practical "how to" advice. You could stop right there (and use the book as a traditional text) or follow a link to an avenue of information that addresses a need or piques your interest. In a way, this edition of our book can be compared to a hybrid car. We like to think of it as our "hybrid text"—one vehicle with a choice of how to proceed.

We hope you will find this book both scholarly and practical. We provide an overview of the historical, political, and social forces that shape evidence-based practice, and honor cultural and linguistic contexts. We guide you through the process of school reform as you conduct a needs assessment and create a two-year plan. We explore the expanded roles and responsibilities of reading professionals and incorporate the significant developments in intervention, assessment, professional development, and adolescent literacy and their impact on instructional practice. Our companion website for this edition is closely tied to the book. You can still use this book as a stand-alone resource, but we are hoping you won't.

## *What's New in this Edition*

Changes in the roles of literacy professionals related to assessment and professional development, new insights into literacy processes, a number of mandates from government and professional organizations, new standards in assessment, the proliferation of RtI, advances in technology and its instructional uses, widespread interest and research in adolescent literacy and literacy for English learners are among the many developments that required substantial revision of this book.

The challenge was to retain its philosophy, all of its effective features, and the basic tone and structure of the text, while revising and updating large sections in many of the chapters. We think we have accomplished this. Our aim was to present current, substantive information on the various topics and then to provide readers with a list of additional tools including web sources, professional materials, and research articles beyond the book that can be used for further reading and investigation. We think this is exactly what a textbook ought to be in the 2010s. Web resources are a large part of a reading professional's life and the book reflects this, yet stands on its own as a basic and comprehensive source of information, one that we hope reading specialists and literacy coaches will keep on the desk and within reach.

Among the features included in the new edition of *Reading Specialists and Literacy Coaches in the* Real *World* are:

- **A Companion Website.** One of the new features we hope you will find especially useful is our companion website. Although it is closely tied to the content and activities in the book, this feature allows us to extend that information and direct you to specific resources and projects related to the text and to your goals. Both professors and master's degree candidates will find the chapter alignment with the most current standards for reading professionals very attractive for accreditation and professional development. The site includes a glossary of key concepts and other related vocabulary for each chapter. It also allows us to update information periodically, incorporate new features, provide several organizers, and tie all of these elements directly to specific portions of the text. An icon in the margin of the text indicates that related information is available on the companion website (waveland.com/Extra_Material/32979/).

- **New Chapter on the Roles of Literacy Professionals.** Much has changed in recent years in the world of the reading specialist and literacy coach. Chapter 2 reflects this. Special emphasis is devoted to intervention, RtI, assessment, and professional development. We created a matrix to guide you through the elements that characterize the various professional roles, and we discuss the evolving responsibilities of the *reading coach* and *instructional coach*. We also updated the six models of literacy coaching. We hope that, whatever your title, you will find professional support here.

- **Needs Assessment and Two-Year Plan.** Based on your feedback and our experiences teaching literacy leadership and supervision classes, we streamlined the process for developing the needs assessment and two-year plan. We believe they are both very important. However, we recognize that even reading specialists strive to have real lives in the real world. Therefore, we hope that you will find the processes doable and relevant, given your many other responsibilities.

- **Beyond the Book.** We eliminated some of the "Other Voices" in favor of a new feature called "Beyond the Book" which highlights a focus issue for each chapter and in some way links it to the outside world. These exercises require you to explore ways in which issues "play out" in the real world. They might incorporate an information search, a jigsaw technique, one of the group activities found throughout the book, or some other exercise that connects the text to your knowledge and experience.

- **Graphic Organizers and Learning Goals.** In order to help focus your reading, each chapter begins with a graphic overview of the content. We also provide a number of learning goals that identify what we hope you will know and be able to do after reading the chapter. Many of these have been revised to reflect the new content in this book. We encourage you to think about a personal learning goal for each chapter: What would you like to learn or explore in greater depth? Which idea or activity would you like to try in your classroom?

- **Chapter Vignettes.** We use a real-world vignette to introduce each chapter, and we revisit the vignette frequently, affording you the opportunity to reflect on real-world solutions. The vignettes are based on our knowledge of situations encountered by reading specialists and literacy coaches. A number of them are new or revised to address current issues. We believe they will be particularly useful in challenging your thinking and problem-solving skills as you prepare to be reading specialists and literacy coaches.

- **Portfolio and Self-Assessment Projects.** Many of you are enrolled in graduate programs that require course and/or program portfolios. Some of you are also pursuing

National Board Certification. Therefore, we offer several ideas that you may wish to incorporate into your personal literacy portfolios. This resource has been updated to accommodate the increased focus on professional development and self-assessment. We are especially pleased that our companion website enables us to offer additional project ideas linked to each chapter.

- **Recommended Readings.** This feature has been retitled "Recommended Readings: Suggestions for Book Clubs, Study Groups, and Professional Development." Each chapter concludes with a list of annotated resources and references that extend its content. We recognize that reading specialists and literacy coaches are assuming leadership of professional development programs and are often asked for suggestions for book clubs and study groups. Therefore, in addition to the professional and scholarly publications you are accustomed to finding in this section, we included selections relevant to practitioners and suitable for use in professional development. We hope you will take a look at some of these.

- **Multiliteracies: Linking Home, School, and Community.** Historically, schools have defined language and literacy practices in rather narrow ways, privileging certain literacies above, or to the exclusion of, others. When we broaden our definitions to include the new ways in which people convey meaning—for example, symbolically, through pop culture, texting, Facebook, blogs, or other Web 2.0 venues—we can then provide and develop resources that connect to the lives of our students. In this new edition, we demonstrate that we need not alter the goals of literacy relative to standards or abandon our responsibility to prepare our students to function within existing structures. Instead, we can use these multiple literacies within our existing structures to meet the goals of the home, school, district, and community.

- **Our Own Voices as Authors.** Reading involves interactions between the reader and the author. Therefore, we drop the masks generally used in textbook writing and use the first person, presenting our own opinions and biases. Note, however, that we also ground our writing in research and theory. Our approach to writing this book illustrates how we continue to question our work and our world as we seek answers related to literacy and teaching.

## Organization of the Book

The third edition of *Reading Specialists and Literacy Coaches in the* Real *World* is organized into four parts, based on the roles and responsibilities of today's reading professionals. Each part represents a different domain (way of thinking or acting) in which reading specialists and literacy coaches operate.

### Part I: Reading Specialists and Literacy Coaches: Honoring the Past, Shaping the Future

Part I recognizes the substantive knowledge base that undergirds today's practice by tracing the history of literacy pedagogy and the evolution of the reading professional.

***Chapter 1: Examining the Historical Context for Teaching Reading.*** Chapter 1 has been updated to provide an historical perspective that includes the impact of recent events. It examines:

- Trends and advances in literacy research and classroom practice.
- The implications of legislation related to education, including changes in mandates and standards.
- The case for principled practice (new term) and research-based and evidence-based practice.

***Chapter 2: Serving as an Elementary, Secondary, or District-Level Reading Specialist or Literacy Coach.*** Formerly Chapter 10, this chapter underwent substantial revision to reflect the sweeping changes in roles and qualifications of coaches and reading specialists. It includes:

- A detailed role matrix for reading specialists and literacy coaches, aligned with current professional standards.
- The six models of literacy coaching.
- The latest research on the "value-added" effectiveness of literacy coaches for school improvement.
- New titles and responsibilities for literacy coaches, including *reading coaches* and *instructional coaches* in middle and high schools.

## Part II: Reading Specialists and Literacy Coaches: Leading a Collaborative Vision

This section supports literacy coaches and reading specialists in creating and leading dynamic, collaborative school literacy programs.

***Chapter 3: Forming a Literacy Team and Creating a Literacy Vision.*** Chapter 3 (formerly Chapter 2) remains focused on the processes of forming an effective literacy team and creating a vision statement. It also explores:

- Issues of culture and community.
- The core standards movement and current resources.
- New collaborative models for problem-solving.

***Chapter 4: Determining a School's Literacy Needs and Developing a Plan.*** Although the information in this chapter (formerly Chapter 3) has been streamlined, it continues to provide guidance in:

- The step-by-step processes of conducting a needs assessment and creating a two-year plan.
- New resources and research to support effective collaboration for school improvement.

***Chapter 5: Matching Context to Students: Assessment as Inquiry.*** Formerly Chapter 4, this chapter remains grounded in the Contextualized Assessment Model and continues to employ a case study to illustrate the principles of assessment. It contains a great deal of new information on:

- *Screening, diagnosis, progress monitoring*, and *outcome* assessments.
- Instructions for selecting appropriate assessment instruments for different purposes.
- Enhanced guidance on establishing schoolwide and districtwide assessment programs.
- The impact of the 2009 IRA/NCTE Standards for the Assessment of Reading and Writing.

## Part III: Reading Specialists and Literacy Coaches: Leading Principled Practice

The chapters in this section address the heart of the reading educator's mission: securing for every child the level of literacy proficiency necessary for success in school and in life.

***Chapter 6: Differentiating Instruction to Meet Learners' Needs: Framing Literacy Intervention.*** Chapter 6 (formerly Chapter 5) has been revised to align with new paradigms for literacy intervention and their impact on the roles and responsibilities of reading professionals. It includes:

- In-depth discussion of multitiered intervention models (such as RtI) at the early childhood, elementary, middle school, and secondary levels.
- Examples of successful programs.
- Evidence for what works in intervention models, regardless of their structure.

***Chapter 7: Language and Literacy Development for English Learners.*** Formerly Chapter 6, this chapter reflects the substantial progress made in what we know about instruction for English learners. It includes:

- Practical approaches to addressing the rapidly increasing language diversity in today's schools.
- Explicit guidance on practices proven to facilitate the acquisition of literacy for English learners, especially with regard to academic language.
- The powerful effect of sheltered English instruction (the SIOP® Model) on literacy and learning for English learners.

***Chapter 8: Implementing a Comprehensive Literacy Program in the Elementary School.*** Based on feedback that those who use this book already have considerable knowledge and experience in elementary literacy, we changed the focus of this chapter (formerly Chapter 7) from explaining elementary methods to connecting reading professionals to websites, research, and resources. We adopted an issues-oriented perspective. The chapter provides:

- Updated information on evidence-based practices.
- Increased support for reading specialists and literacy coaches as they assume greater responsibility for creating and leading professional development workshops and study groups.
- Exploration of ways technology can support elementary students' literacy acquisition.
- A comprehensive matrix that illustrates effective practices, the research that supports them, and their classroom applications.

***Chapter 9: Implementing a Comprehensive Literacy Program in Middle and Secondary Schools.*** Formerly Chapter 8, this chapter is particularly designed to meet the needs of those familiar with adolescent literacy practices *and* those whose experience with older students is more limited. It has been revised to reflect:

- The significant changes that have transformed adolescent literacy and the roles of literacy professionals.
- Legislative initiatives, standards, and intervention models.
- Uses of new literacies and technologies.
- A comprehensive matrix that illustrates effective practices, the research that supports them, and their classroom applications.
- Increased emphasis on current research and groundbreaking publications.

***Chapter 10: Selecting and Evaluating Instructional Materials and Technology Resources.*** Although we continue to guide the textbook adoption process, we have shifted our emphasis to include:

- Teachers' knowledge and use of instructional technology to enhance students' learning.
- Selection of instructional materials and issues related to leveling books.
- A textbook adoption survey that will be an especially helpful tool for literacy specialists and teachers.

## Part IV: Reading Specialists and Literacy Coaches: Leading Growth and Change

This section reflects the pivotal role of the reading specialist and literacy coach in professional development and advocacy. It also addresses the growing link between school and community with regard to adult and family literacy initiatives.

***Chapter 11: Planning and Implementing Multidimensional Professional Development.*** This is another area in which the role of the reading specialist has changed a great deal. The chapter has been revised to provide substantive support for leadership in professional development. It includes new information related to:

- The use of the needs assessment and two-year plan to develop a sustained, multifaceted professional development program.
- The role of the literacy professional in coaching, mentoring, providing peer support, leading study groups, conducting workshops, and engaging in self-evaluation.

*Chapter 12: Moving the Field Forward as Leaders and Literacy Advocates.* Chapter 12 combines updated information from Chapters 12 and 13 in the previous edition. It includes:

- New resources and links to information for literacy professionals as they assume the roles of leaders and literacy advocates.
- Valuable resources and information related to adult and family literacy programs.

## Acknowledgments

We express appreciation to our former and current graduate students who have helped us with this book, both in terms of their critiques of manuscripts we've used in our supervision and leadership classes and in their willingness to test our ideas. They've also shared case problems that helped focus our vignettes, as well as their needs assessments, two-year plans, and literacy assessment profiles that were completed for course requirements.

We acknowledge and express gratitude to Claudia Reinbold for her assistance in preparing the manuscript for publication and to our colleagues who served as reviewers: Amy Cooper, Wilshire Park Elementary School; Joyce C. Fine, Florida International University; Donna Schweitzer, Forwood Elementary School; Allie Smith, Wilshire Park Elementary School; and Dr. Betty Wells Brown, UNC Pembroke, School of Education. Your comments and suggestions for this revision were helpful, on target, and valued.

To our families, we are so thankful that you put up with us while we were writing—often in our jammies well into the afternoon. Your support of our work is appreciated more than you realize!

■ *Author's Note: MaryEllen* I want to offer grateful acknowledgment to Brenda Shearer for taking the lead for the third edition of this book. Brenda's keen eye for what is current, her professionalism, and her "spot on" ability to identify sources and trends in our field are greatly appreciated.

## Welcome to the World of Reading Specialists and Literacy Coaches

Finally, we'd like to welcome you to our exciting, rewarding, challenging, stimulating and ever-changing profession. As a reading specialist or literacy coach you will never be bored or without something that needs to be done. You'll find yourself worrying in the middle of the night about kids' reading problems, instructional materials, and that new teacher who needs your help. At times, you may question yourself and your ability to perform all the responsibilities required of you. And you may quickly learn to avoid any conversation about reading, reading problems, and the latest trends in reading while flying on an airplane or attending a social event, because you'll quickly be targeted as someone who has the knowledge and information that others want to discuss. Also, some of you may be in districts where reading specialists or literacy coaches are few and far between, and you may never work in a room that has the title "Reading Specialist" or "Literacy Coach" on the door. But, remember—once you are a reading professional, you'll always be one. No matter how many responsibilities you have or how many degrees you earn, you will find your greatest reward still comes in that "just right" teachable moment, one student at a time, and one teacher at a time. How fortunate, indeed. Welcome aboard!

MEV and BAS

# 1

# *Examining the Historical Context for Teaching Reading*

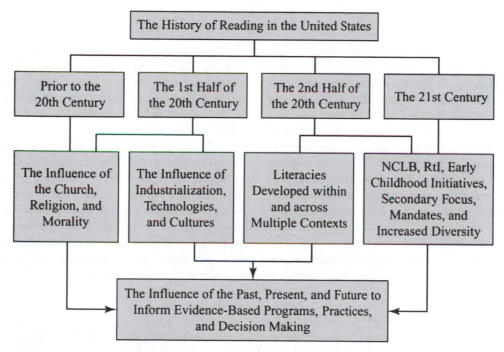

**FIGURE 1.1**  *Chapter Overview*

## *Learning Goals*

After reading, discussing, and engaging in activities related to this chapter, you will be able to:

1. Relate the history of reading instruction to your own development as a reader.
2. Explain why reading specialists and literacy coaches need to understand the influences of methods and approaches to teaching reading that have been used in the United States.

3. Define and describe historical terminology, methods, and materials used for teaching reading in the United States.

4. Explain what is meant by evidence-based practice and programs and describe how reading specialists and literacy coaches can foster such practices.

5. *Personal Learning Goal:* In a three-minute brainstorming session, share what you know about the history of reading instruction. Write a goal or a question that reflects something you want to learn about this topic. Share this with others in your group.

## Standards for Reading Professionals

This chapter provides focused support for current IRA Standards for Reading Professionals. See our companion website (waveland.com/Extra_Material/32979/) for a complete listing of the standards that align with this chapter.

### Vignette

Barbara Johnson has recently been hired as her district's reading coordinator. She is responsible for overseeing the literacy instructional programs in the twenty-four elementary and middle schools in the district. For the past five years, she has served as her school's reading specialist. Her supervisor, the assistant superintendent for curriculum and instruction, has expressed concern about the district's lack of a cohesive reading program for the elementary grades, and he has been pushing Barbara to "get teachers on the same page for reading."

The community has experienced a gradual increase in the number of English language learners over the past ten years, as well as a number of new teachers. District standardized test scores have dipped in comparison to comparable districts in the state, and teachers, administrators, parents, and the school board have all expressed concern about achieving adequate yearly progress.

There are currently several integrated reading series in use in the elementary grades, as well as supplemental programs for teaching phonics and spelling. Although teachers use a Readers/Writers Workshop approach, there is little agreement about its structure. Some upper-grade teachers have chosen to use class sets of chapter books for their reading instruction rather than any commercial reading series.

### Thinking Points

1. What do you suspect are the underlying issues Barbara may want to investigate?
2. Which issue should she address first?

### Expanding the Vignette: Exploring the Issues

Barbara decided that her first step was to meet with teachers and reading specialists at each of the twenty-four schools. Almost immediately she became aware of the strong prejudices some teachers held in favor of the reading approaches they were currently using. She frequently heard comments from veteran teachers, such as: "I've been doing this for years, and my students all became readers. Why should I think about changing how I teach?" "Look, reading programs and approaches come and go, and we just jump on any bandwagon that comes along. Yes, I teach *phonics, and, yes, I teach comprehension. I've been through all the phases and I've seen all the trends. What I've learned is that what I use to teach reading isn't nearly as important as how I teach it."*

*However, several new teachers expressed concerns, such as: "I'm just trying to figure out what I'm doing. At the university, my professors said I should be teaching in a particular way, but I don't see the teachers at my school doing that.*

*I don't know what to do or what I should use. I just want to survive this school year."*

*Barbara felt overwhelmed after discussing these issues with the teachers and reading specialists throughout her district. They seemed surprised when asked if there was a research base for why they taught as they did. She knew the assistant superintendent was expecting a plan of action, and she knew he wanted it immediately. However, she didn't know where to begin.*

### Thinking Points

1. What additional issues and questions have you identified in the vignette?
2. What are some short-term suggestions you would give Barbara?
3. What long-term measures should Barbara consider, given the district policies and the teachers with whom she is working?
4. What are some proactive measures a reading specialist or coach, either at the school or district level, could take to avoid the problems you identified?

Keep your answers to these questions in mind as you read. We will revisit the vignette at the end of this chapter.

What Barbara is experiencing is not uncommon. She works in a district in which the reading program is loosely defined. Consequently, teachers are all doing what they *believe* works best, based on their experience, resources, and student population. As an experienced reading specialist and teacher, she, too, has used a number of innovative approaches, materials, and trends. However, she has also seen these same approaches and materials fall into disfavor and disappear when the new tidal wave of methods and instructional resources hits. How can Barbara lead the teachers toward an investigation of practices that are evidence based?

## *Why Change?*

We find it amazing that between the two of us, we have over seventy years of teaching experience, and during this time, we've survived a variety of trends and approaches. Throughout, we've adjusted our instruction, learned new methods, and adapted to "the latest."

Although we "old-timers" like to say "kids don't change," the reality is that they *do* change. Society changes, the school population changes, parents change, teachers change, and reading curriculum changes. It's part of the teacher's life—and the more reading specialists understand the change process, including what's come before, the better able we are to make sound instructional decisions about what children and adolescents need to become proficient readers and writers in a complex world.

In this chapter we provide an historical synopsis of some of the approaches and methods that have been used for teaching reading during the twentieth century and into the twenty-first. We attempt to situate them in the political, cultural, social, and historical contexts that shaped them. Think about how you learned to read. If you and your parents share your memories, you will most likely discover that their memories of learning to read are different from yours. If you are a "seasoned" teacher and have taught for twenty to thirty years, you have probably gone through at least three major cycles in reading instructional approaches and materials. In the following section, we'll explore some of these and how theory, research, political, and sociocultural factors have influenced the methods, approaches, and materials used in schools. We will also investigate how responsible educators use evidence to inform their decision making.

## Exploring Reading Instruction over Time

*Tears must be shed—by tender little creatures liable to so many accidents and diseases;*
*Tears must be shed—by eager little creatures so often refused desired toys;*
*Tears must be shed—by affectionate little creatures, forced to part from a charming playmate;*
*But tears need not be shed—by little creatures, ignorant and playful*
*though they be, while learning to read.*

—*Reading without Tears*, Preface, p. vii

Some time ago, one of our graduate students shared a rare, old book his grandmother had stored in her attic. The book was written for teachers and was an early attempt at providing methodology instruction for teaching children to read. The title of the book is *Reading without Tears: A Pleasant Mode of Learning to Read.* Although the book doesn't include the author's name, we have discovered via the Internet that the author of the old volume was Favell Lee Mortimer. There is no publication date given, but on the inside cover of the book in beautiful old penmanship is the following: "Harriet Ely, July 3, 1867." Was Harriet a reading teacher? A principal? A mother or grandmother who wanted to help her children or grandchildren learn to read? In the opening section, the author of this book suggests that the act of teaching reading should occur only under certain conditions:

> Only let them not begin too soon (never before four, sometimes not till five); only—let not the lessons be too long; and only—let them be omitted altogether, when the little learners are sick, though only from a cold; or when they are wearied from walking or playing; or when they are excited by promised pleasures. . . . (*Reading without Tears*, p. vii)

From the title of this book, and from the author's expressed concerns, it appears that when this book was written, certainly before 1867, there were reading methods that brought young children to tears. We wonder about the reading instructional approaches that have come and gone during our own teaching careers, and which, if any, have evoked frustration to the point of eliciting children's (and sometimes teachers') tears.

The suggested approach in *Reading without Tears* relies heavily on phonics and the gradual introduction of sound–letter correspondences. For example, the first lesson after introducing the alphabet consists of simple phonetically regular sentences in large, dark type (see Figure 1.2). The remainder of the old text includes gradually more difficult sentences

WITHOUT TEARS.

*It is suggested that* COLOURING *the letters would render them more attractive, and distinguish them better from the pictures. They might be coloured by degrees, as a reward to the little pupil for remembering their names.*

A *has an acorn.* B *has a butterfly.* C *has a cow.* D *has a dog.*

E *has an eel.* F *has a fish.* G *has a goat.* H *has a horse.*

I *has ivy.* J *has a jug.* K *has a kettle.* L *has a lamb.*

READING WITHOUT TEARS. 3

A cat is in my hat
A rat is in my hat
A bat is in my hat

My cat is on the mat
My hat is on the mat
My rat is on the mat
My bat is on the mat

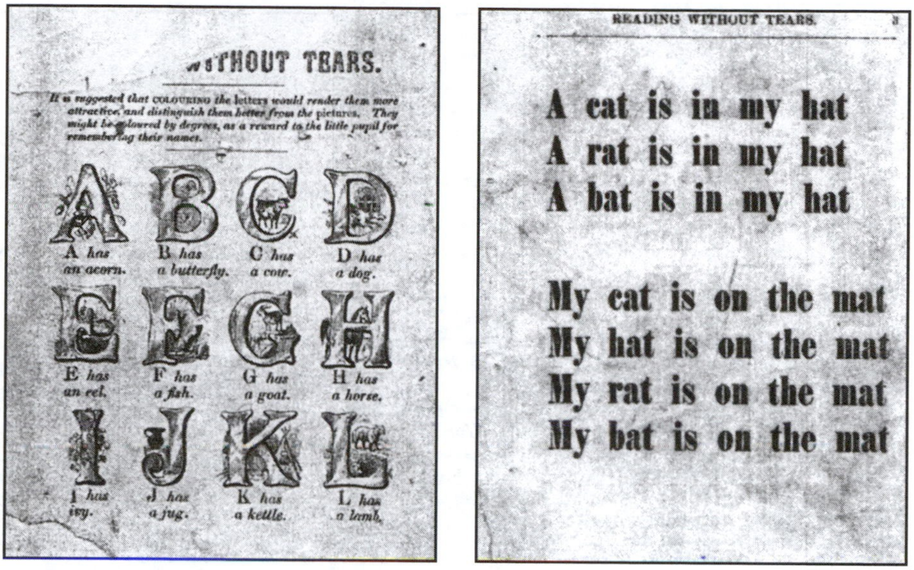

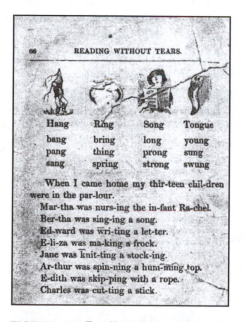

**FIGURE 1.2 Reading without Tears:** ***The Alphabet and First Story***

that carry more meaning. Note the complexity of the sentences that are found in Figure 1.3 (midway through the book) and then in Figure 1.4 (see page 6), the final story of the book, "The Beggar Boy."

66 READING WITHOUT TEARS.

| Hang | Ring | Song | Tongue |
|---|---|---|---|
| bang | bring | long | young |
| pang | thing | prong | sung |
| sang | spring | strong | swung |

When I came home my thir-teen chil-dren were in the par-lour.
Mar-tha was nurs-ing the in-fant Ra-chel.
Ber-tha was sing-ing a song.
Ed-ward was wri-ting a let-ter.
E-li-za was ma-king a frock.
Jane was knit-ting a stock-ing.
Ar-thur was spin-ning a hum-ming top.
E-dith was skip-ping with a rope.
Charles was cut-ting a stick.

**FIGURE 1.3 Reading without Tears:** ***page 66***

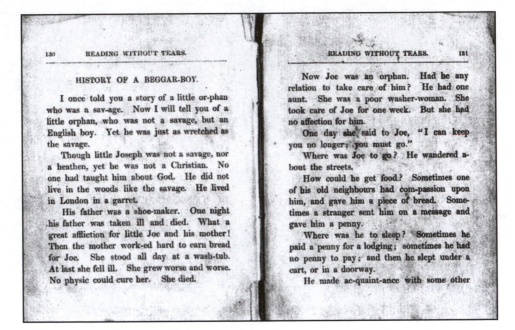

FIGURE 1.4    **Reading without Tears:** *"The Beggar Boy," page 130*

The methods suggested in this 140+ year-old book parallel many of those recommended today, and they demonstrate that the search for the most effective ways to teach children to read has preoccupied reading teachers and specialists for a long time.

## The Early Years of the United States

The earliest "textbook" used in the Jamestown settlement in 1607 was the Horn Book, a paddle-shaped piece of wood with a transparent sheet of animal horn that protected the alphabet and verses written on the wood (Ruddell, 2006). Later, *The New England Primer* (1790–1850) was published, with grim admonitions for children to behave themselves or suffer the consequences. This early textbook included the alphabet, verses, rhymes, and stories, such as the following:

> *In the burying place may see*
> *Graves shorter there than I;*
> *From Death's arrest no age is free,*
> *Young children too may die.*
> *My god, may such an awful sight,*
> *Awakening be to me!*
> *Oh! That by early grace I might*
> *For Death prepared be.*

Religious and patriotic views dominated instruction in the country from 1607 to 1840. The instructional emphasis was on knowledge of the alphabet, recitation, memorization of Bible verses, spelling bees, oral reading, and elocution. Teachers were most often highly moral men who could read and write (Ruddell, 2006).

In the mid and late 1800s, the Civil War, Gold Rush, westward expansion, and industrial revolution increased the need for an educated populace. In 1841, Rev. William Holmes McGuffey published the first *McGuffey Reader* with fifty-five lessons that introduced a strict ethical code that required children to be prompt, good, kind, honest, and truthful. The first two readers focused on alphabet knowledge, phonics, syllables, and sight words, and the stories were written at increasingly difficult reading levels with some comprehension questions. The second reader included 85 lessons with 160 pages that outlined history, biology, astronomy, zoology, and botany, along with table manners and attitudes toward God, teachers, parents, and the poor. In all, there were six readers, with the third through sixth intended for what would be today's middle and secondary students. The sixth was published in 1885, with 186 selections that quoted great authors such as Longfellow, Shakespeare, and Dickens (Payne, 2001). The "eclectic" readers (so-called because they included selections from a variety of sources) were very moralistic and presented a picture of a white Protestant America (see Figure 1.5).

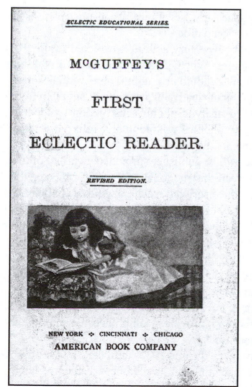

**FIGURE 1.5    McGuffey Reader** *Excerpt*

### The First Half of the Twentieth Century

In 1908, E. B. Huey published *The Psychology and Pedagogy of Reading,* an influential and progressive text that examined the reading process using the scientific method (Huey, 1908/1968). At about this time, universal education in the United States was gaining momentum with an enormous increase in those attending school, and with the support of federal and state legislatures. However, as waves of immigrants from Western Europe were landing on Ellis Island, children of immigrants, descendants of former slaves, and the sons and daughters of the poor continued to labor in factories, fields, and sweatshops, with little access to formal education.

In the schools, reading for information and commerce replaced the primary purpose of reading during the eighteenth and nineteenth centuries, which was reading the Bible. As the United States entered World War I, the armed forces needed to identify young men who demonstrated leadership. Because this had to be accomplished rapidly, the decision was made to use newly developed "scientific testing." The intent was to identify both the "leaders" and the "followers." The result was the country's first large-scale testing program (Ruddell, 2005) and the development of a constellation of instruments, a number of which, though revised, are still in use today. Thorndike's 1917 measure of reading comprehension, which he described as ability in reading, Binet's IQ test, and Gray's (1915) *Standardized Oral Reading Paragraphs* are among the early "scientifically constructed" tests that attempted to measure complex cognitive abilities and processes.

During the first half of the twentieth century, educators explored a variety of approaches for teaching reading, including phonics. Whether to teach phonics was not argued; what was debated was when and how phonics should be taught. There were those who advocated for synthetic phonics instruction (students learn the parts and blend them into words), and there were those who recommended analytic phonics instruction (students learn words and then analyze the parts). Analytic phonics was popularly referred to as a "look–say" approach, later to be skewered in the popular press.

In the late 1930s through the 1960s, publishers provided a variety of leveled readers that were used to teach children to read. Instructional approaches reflected the dominance of behaviorism and the quest to produce scripted teachers' guides. Remember that during the first half of the century, the majority of teachers received less than two years of preparation in regional "Normal Schools." The leveled readers also reflected the work of researchers such as Thorndike (1921) and Dolch (1942), who identified the words most frequently used in books. Publishers then produced children's "readers" with stories written according to these word lists. The resulting books included contrived stories with carefully controlled vocabulary, and sight words that were frequently repeated so that a child eventually achieved independence in reading them. Nila Banton Smith's (1935) *American Reading Instruction* and her second edition (1965) provide a comprehensive and fascinating examination of literacy instruction in those times.

Throughout the United States, from the mid 1930s until the 1980s, millions of children came to know a "typical" American family and its members: Father, Mother, Dick, Jane, Sally, and, of course, their pets, Puff and Spot (see Figures 1.6 and 1.7 opposite and 1.8 on page 10). If children were not reading about Dick and Jane, they most likely were reading in other books about Alice and Jerry, Ann and David, or Janet and Mark, all of whom lived in

**Spot and Little Rabbit**

Here is Spot.

He is not happy.

He wants to find Dick.

He wants some fun.

"Bow-wow," said Spot.

"I will look for Dick."

9

**FIGURE 1.6** *Dick and Jane: 1935*

*Source:* Reprinted with permission of SRA/Scott Foresman.

Dick said, "See Puff.

Puff can play.

Puff can run and jump."

Jane said, "Oh, oh.

Spot can not play.

Spot can not run.

Spot can not jump.

Spot is funny."

**FIGURE 1.7** *Dick and Jane: 1945*

*Source:* Reprinted with permission of SRA/Scott Foresman.

white, middle-class families and communities like Dick and Jane's. The homogenization of American culture and the resulting lack of diversity in some of the early readers characterized the instructional materials that were used in classrooms for over forty years. Later editions of this series included illustrations of children of different ethnicities. These were portrayed as classmates, neighbors, and friends of Dick, Jane, and Sally, or their counterparts in the other readers.

## The Second Half of the Twentieth Century

During World War II, educators and the public discovered once again that many soldiers were unable to read well enough to comprehend training manuals and other related texts. The advent of content area reading—teaching students how to read informational and expository texts—was a direct result. Post–World War II was a time of increased prosperity and political conservatism as the United States entered the Cold War. Along with the growing nationalism during the two World Wars and the notion of the United States as the melting pot, immigrant and Native American children were strongly encouraged to assimilate,

**FIGURE 1.8**     *Dick and Jane: 1962*

*Source:* Reprinted with permission of SRA/Scott Foresman.

often losing most of their cultural heritage in one generation. When the Russians launched *Sputnik,* the "Race for Space" brought millions of dollars to the task of reforming the science, mathematics, and reading programs in schools. Laws were passed to increase the age of mandatory school attendance. Although the United States offered "education to all," many inequities remained in the quality of education for the rich and poor, particularly in racially segregated schools.

During this time, phonics was taught in many schools, and debate continued about the best approach, synthetic or analytic. Rudolph Flesch's (1955) famous publication *Why Johnny Can't Read* mobilized proponents of synthetic phonics, including many parents throughout the country. Then, the publication of the book *Learning to Read: The Great Debate* (Chall, 1967) divided reading professionals into two camps: those advocating synthetic phonics and those advocating more holistic and analytic methods of phonics instruction. The First Grade Studies (Bond & Dykstra, 1967a, 1967b; reprinted in *Reading Research Quarterly,* 1997) attempted to answer the question about the most effective way to teach reading, once and for all. Guy Bond and Robert Dykstra, and their colleagues involved in the First Grade Studies, concluded that no one method was so much more effective in all situations that it should be considered the one best method for teaching reading. Unfortunately, both sides interpreted the findings to support their positions on phonics. According to Bob Dykstra, "Reading educators all over the country were telling their audiences that the most important conclusion of this research was that the teacher is the most important element in the instructional situation. Although this may well be true and is a 'feel good' thing to say, it was not a conclusion we reached, nor that the data support" (Shearer, 2001, p. 2).

In response to perceived concerns about a lack of phonics instruction, some researchers during the 1960s and 1970s became very interested in examining the linguistic foundations of the reading process. From their work came new approaches, including programmed reading with its sequential lessons in workbooks, cards, and worksheets (Sullivan & Buchanan, 1963), reading machines (e.g., the language master and tachistoscope), color-coded text, scripted teacher's guides (see Figure 1.9), and the Linguistic Approach, advocated by linguists interested in studying how "talk" is translated into reading (Fries, 1963). The intent of these methods and programs was to provide beginning readers with consistency, explicit instruction, a

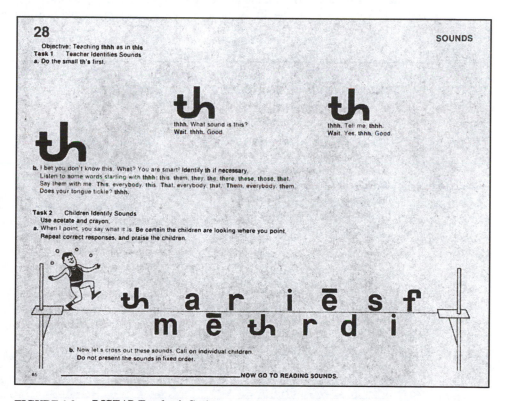

**FIGURE 1.9    *DISTAR Teacher's Script***

*Source:* S. Engelmann and E. C. Burner, *Distar Reading I, An Instructional System.* Copyright © 1969 by Science Research Associates. Reprinted with permission of McGraw-Hill Educators.

great deal of practice in decoding, and the gradual introduction of texts that contained the specific linguistic elements that were being taught.

One of the most interesting experiments implemented during the 1960s and early 1970s was the Initial Teaching Alphabet (i/t/a) (Downing, 1962; Mazurkiewicz & Tanyzer, 1966). The i/t/a alphabet was originally called the Augmented Roman Alphabet, and it consisted of forty-four lowercase characters, twenty-four of them conventional letters. Each symbol in i/t/a, according to Sir James Pitman who created the alphabet, had one phonic meaning. For example, the two sounds of the *th* digraph, as in *the* (voiced) and in *thistle* (voiceless) had two distinctive symbols. The purpose of i/t/a was to provide children with a phonetically regular alphabet so that they could quickly learn to read i/t/a stories, with the goal of eventually transferring their developing reading skills to conventional English. Children's books were written with i/t/a (see Figure 1.10), and, not surprisingly, though the students learned to read these books, many had difficulty later when they attempted to read conventional texts.

During the 1960s, a social, political, cultural, and moral revolution was occurring outside the walls of schools. The Beatles changed the music, clothing, and culture of the students, the Vietnam War polarized the nation, marijuana and LSD began to show up in even the most rural schools, and television brought the Civil Rights movement and "The War" into every home. University attendance exploded as large numbers of white students

**FIGURE 1.10**   *Initial Teaching Alphabet Text*

*Source:* Reprinted from M. Miller, *The Trick,* 1966, Initial Teaching Alphabet Publications, Inc.

and a small, but increasing, number of students from various racial and ethnic groups took their seats as "first generation college students," many to avoid the draft. In general, the public schools seemed oblivious to these social and moral phenomena, continuing to ask the same pedagogical questions, independently of the context of the times.

As teachers began to place a greater emphasis on phonics and decoding, many found their students were not developing proficient comprehension. As with phonics, a discrete list of comprehension skills was identified and it was recommended that the skills be taught and that students practice them frequently through a variety of skills exercises (Clymer, 1963). Among these comprehension skills were finding the main idea and supporting details, sequencing, drawing conclusions, making generalizations, comparing and contrasting, and identifying cause-and-effect relationships.

The primary instructional materials during the 1970s and 1980s were basal reading programs and they included leveled readers, phonics activities, and a great deal of comprehension skill practice, usually found on the pages of the accompanying workbooks. The programs also included highly structured, detailed teacher's guides, with different lesson plans for each of the three instructional groups (high, average, low). The fallout from the political and cultural revolution of the earlier decade fostered an attitude of conservatism that was manifested in instructional materials designed for schools.

However, as with the other approaches and methods that had been used over the decades, problems such as the following appeared.

1. Because reading instruction took place in ability groups, there were built-in advantages for capable readers, who were exposed to far more vocabulary in the "high" group reading books than in the books assigned to the "low" groups. Over the years of elementary school, therefore, the "rich got richer, and the poor got poorer" (Stanovich, 1986).
2. The contrived texts, for the most part, contained stories (with very little informational text) that reflected little or no diversity in characters, families, and cultures.
3. The teachers' guides and workbooks included end-of-story questions and activities that kept students busy, but they simply tested, rather than taught, comprehension. Once again, the methods and materials for teaching fell into disfavor.

During the next two decades (1980s, 1990s), theorists and researchers from across the fields of psychology, linguistics, and education explored how readers think about text, how they make connections while they read, and how they ultimately construct meaning. Educators' conversations about reading methods and materials included references to schema formation, the influence on meaning-making of prior knowledge and experience (Anderson & Pearson, 1984); transactional theory, the view that meaning is constructed through an active interchange of ideas within a particular context, as with reader and text (Rosenblatt, 1978); and scaffolding, how learners benefit from the assistance of more experienced individuals, and how they eventually gain independence when that support is gradually lessened (Bruner, 1983; Vygotsky, 1978). Instead of focusing on the finite skills that readers develop, educators began talking about how to build students' backgrounds, promote concept formation, instill joy and delight in reading, and forge connections among the language processes of reading, writing, listening, and speaking.

Also during the early 1980s, computers began to be used in the schools, mostly for drill and practice and for teaching students to learn to write basic computer programs. Remember, at that time, people actually believed that computer users would have to write their own programs! Not surprisingly, in the early stages of computer use, teachers lacked the time, training, and technical support to help students, and software was comparatively unsophisticated.

At the time, linguistics, psychology, and research on the writing process were fostering more holistic instructional approaches (Calkins, 1983; Cambourne, 1988; Goodman, 1986). An amazing grassroots movement, led by classroom teachers, ushered in a new theoretical perspective that swept the nation and evolved into what was eventually called "whole language." For about a ten-year period in the United States (mid 1980s to the mid 1990s), there was a decreased emphasis on teaching discrete skills, whether phonics/decoding or comprehension. The 1985 publication of *Becoming a Nation of Readers* (Anderson, Hiebert, Scott, & Wilkinson, 1985) supported this shift in pedagogy. Instructional materials for reading included literature, with a wide variety of unadapted texts, stories, and books that were not contrived and that had not been controlled for vocabulary difficulty or readability.

As you might have guessed by now, once again, reading approaches and materials came under intense scrutiny. This time, the changes were propelled by a number of factors, including:

1. The low reading performance of students as measured by standardized tests in states where more holistic teaching approaches were used;
2. A series of federally funded research studies that revealed that, for most children, learning to read is not a "natural" process; that for most children, identifying, blending, and segmenting sounds in words appears to be an important predictor of eventual reading achievement; that these same children appear to benefit from explicit phonics instruction; that many children need practice in reading texts with a high percentage of decodable words; and that young children who have difficulty learning to read benefit from early, intensive reading intervention (Adams, 1990; National Reading Panel, 2000; Snow, Burns, & Griffin, 1998); and
3. The huge influx of immigrant children in states such as California, Texas, Arizona, and Florida whose home language was other than English.

These factors collectively had an enormous impact on reading instruction toward the end of the 1990s. In the next section, we look at what's to come in the twenty-first century.

## BEYOND THE BOOK

### Chapter 1 Focus Issue: Why Do You Teach the Way You Do?
- How did your teacher preparation program shape your knowledge base and philosophy as a beginning teacher of reading and writing?
- In what ways did the unique social culture of the school and surrounding community influence and shape your emerging beliefs and practices?
- How have your views been influenced or supported by colleagues, literacy professionals, and administrators?

- How have professional development, professional affiliations (such as International Reading Association [IRA] membership or attendance at conferences), journal subscriptions, and/or professional service changed you as a literacy educator?
- How have outside forces such as the economy, NCLB, RtI, and now, Race to the Top performance mandates, changing student and professional standards, and other factors altered the way you teach?

## Teaching Reading in the Twenty-First Century

At the beginning of the century, many classrooms were dynamic and process-oriented in their approach to reading and writing. Although the workshop approach to literacy had been around for years (Atwell, 1998; 2007), a new generation of educators adapted it to reflect a more focused and goal-oriented view of instruction (Dorn & Soffos, 2005; Serafini, 2001). This was in part a response to more rigid standards and testing requirements, but also a result of better understandings about the interrelated nature of language processes (reading, writing, speaking, listening, representing). By the end of the 1990s, we witnessed the widespread use of Six Trait Writing (Culham, 2003) and other approaches that attempted to make visible the writer's in-process thinking and provide the student with a structure for cognitive self-assessment. Although many teachers still engaged in variations of Daily Oral Language (Byers, 2001), which included the use of sentences with errors or missing elements written on the board to teach grammar and spelling, classrooms across the nation were also embracing literature circles (Daniels, 2002) and recognizing the role of scaffolding student-to-student interaction as a powerful way to improve comprehension and develop critical language skills (Echevarria, Vogt, & Short, 2008; Shearer, Ruddell, & Vogt, 2001). Guided reading described the teacher's role as that of cognitive coach (Dorn, French, & Jones, 1998) and became a widely used model for instruction (Fountas & Pinnell, 1996; Opitz & Ford, 2001). Guided reading proponents favored what was commonly called a *balanced literacy approach*, a comprehensive literacy program characterized by the use of authentic texts and explicit skill instruction. In such an approach, responsibility for implementing strategies was gradually shifted from teacher to student as a skill or strategy was acquired. Although books were often leveled, students were grouped in flexible, creative, and nonstatic ways. Rather than establishing fixed reading groups, teachers varied the way they grouped students, at times working with the whole class or calling together groups of various sizes for work on a particular skill or strategy (Caldwell & Ford, 2002; Opitz & Ford, 2008; Mosteller, Light, & Sachs, 1996). Proponents of flexible grouping were responding to the growing body of research related to the harmful effects of practices such as round robin reading and fixed ability grouping (Caldwell & Ford, 2002; Worthy, Broaddus, & Ivey, 2001). Moreover, there was an emphasis, even in the primary grades, on the fostering of critical literacy (McLaughlin & DeVoogd, 2004a; Van Sluys, Lewison, & Seely-Flint, 2006). Technology was no longer a stranger in the classroom, and teachers moved beyond the primitive use of computers for drill and fill tutorials into using technology as a truly innovative and socially driven means for teaching and learning that challenged previous assumptions about literacy's forms and purposes.

Several highly influential documents were published in the late 1990s and early 2000s. They were widely disseminated, not only to educators and administrators, but also to national and state legislators and other policymakers. These included substantial research syntheses of studies related to reading/language arts. The Report of the National Reading Panel (NRP, 2000), the Report of the Committee on Reading Disabilities (Snow, Burns, & Griffin, 1998), and the series of reports of the Center for the Improvement of Early Reading Achievement (CIERA) had a powerful influence on the literacy research agenda at the beginning of the 2000s.

Major findings from these reports identified five areas that the Panel believed had a sufficient amount of scientifically-based research on which to draw conclusions: comprehension, fluency, phonemic awareness, phonics, and word meaning/vocabulary. In the mid 2000s, the National Literacy Panel on Language Minority Children and Youth (NLP) published their findings about literacy instruction for language minority students (August & Shanahan, 2008), and the Institute for Education Sciences of the U.S. Department of Education issued recommendations for literacy and language instruction for English learners in the elementary grades (Gersten, Baker, Shanahan, Linan-Thompson, Collins, & Scarcella, 2007). These important documents reinforced and extended the findings and recommendations of the NRP and CIERA reports.

Major findings from these reports include:

- Assessment must be continual, ongoing, dynamic, and inextricably linked to instruction.
- For most children, learning to read is not a natural process and must include explicit, systematic instruction in phonics as well as instruction in specific comprehension skills and strategies.
- Reading and writing are highly interrelated, especially in early stages.
- Adolescents need to spend more time writing and reading high-quality literature.
- Motivation can be enhanced and assessed.
- Children not reaching benchmarks can benefit from thirty minutes a day of intensive intervention in addition to regular classroom instruction.
- Teachers should actively seek connections between home and school literacies.

Despite the fact that the National Reading Panel Report and other federally funded reports were embraced by legislators and the press and served as catalysts for numerous reform efforts throughout the country, there were also thoughtful, scholarly, and highly critical responses to them (Cunningham, 2001; Purcell-Gates, 2000). These suggested that the National Reading Panel Report had serious flaws. Chief among them were that the methods used by the panel for selecting research studies to analyze were limited.

The conversations about how research should be conducted continue today. Topics include methodologies that are or are not appropriate for particular research questions; the role of large-scale, empirical studies of children using control and experimental groups; and the place of qualitative studies, including case study and ethnography (see Dillon, 2005; Hinchman, 2005; Steinkuehler, Black, & Clinton, 2005; Tobin, 2005). At the time of this writing, the Institute for Educational Sciences (IES) within the U.S. Department of Education (USDE) has indicated that there will be a more flexible approach to educational research design within the Obama administration. The changes recommended by IES remain to be seen, but it is our hope that researchers will be able to employ the full range of research methodologies to answer the pressing educational questions in our field.

During the early and mid 2000s, many U.S. schools worked diligently to meet the requirements of the historic, bipartisan, federal legislation titled No Child Left Behind (NCLB), which was a major component of the reauthorized Elementary and Secondary Education Act (ESEA) of 2001. Signed into law in early 2002, NCLB and the accompanying Reading First initiative:

- Significantly increased the amount of federal funding for improving reading instruction in the early grades. Participating schools had to provide detailed descriptions of their methods to ensure that they were using "scientifically-based reading instruction."
- Required that teachers engage in systematic instruction and assessment of children's phonemic awareness, phonics, vocabulary, fluency, and comprehension. Schools that did not meet the Department of Education's criteria for "adequate yearly progress" were expected to engage in systematic improvements in order to meet children's literacy needs or face sanctions.
- Required that reading instruction must be based on "what works." Who and what determines "what works" was a major question in the mid 2000s. The point on which everyone seemed to agree was that we needed to keep seeking more effective ways to help all children achieve literacy (Allington & Walmsley, 2007).

In 2004, the reauthorization of the Individuals with Disabilities Education Act (IDEA) gave rise to a general education initiative called Response to Intervention (RtI). Designed to reduce the number of students placed in special education, RtI seeks to identify and address the needs of struggling readers before they fail. Components of RtI include:

- High-quality (research-based) classroom instruction;
- Periodic screening of all students to identify those in need of support;
- Careful monitoring of student learning;
- Targeted differentiated instruction; and
- Increasing intensity in the levels of support provided to struggling readers.

RtI is often, but not always, implemented in a three-tiered model. (See Chapter 6 for a complete discussion of the reading professional's role in implementing RtI.)

In 2005, a new grant program was authorized under Title I and No Child Left Behind. Called Striving Readers, the program intended to raise the reading achievement levels of middle and high school-aged students in Title I eligible schools. The project's components include:

- Professional development for teachers across subject areas;
- Targeted intervention for struggling readers; and
- Rigorous project evaluation.

The release of *Reading Next: A Vision for Action and Research in Middle and High School Literacy* (Biancarosa & Snow, 2004) had a powerful impact on adolescent literacy programs. Revised in 2006, it outlined fifteen key elements for adolescent literacy intervention.

Shortly thereafter, a number of educators began to envision the use of the RtI model with struggling adolescent readers. To fulfill the requirements of both Reading First and Striving Readers and to meet students' literacy needs, it became readily apparent that many more reading specialists and literacy coaches would be needed (Shanklin, 2007). In the decade before the economic downturn of 2008–2009, the number of K–12 literacy coaches increased considerably, even though there were few agreed-on roles and responsibilities for these newly created positions in the nation's schools (Bean, Cassidy, Grumet, Shelton, & Wallis, 2002; Walpole & Blamey, 2008).

One of the quiet revolutions that occurred in the first decade of the millennium was the unprecedented growth of pre-kindergarten programs (Maeroff, 2006). According to a *New York Times* report released by Rutgers Early Childhood Professor Steven Barnett (2009), in the six years between 2002 and 2008, enrollment in pre-school rose to 1.1 million, and spending on early childhood programs nearly doubled, from $2.4 billion to $4.6 billion. (See http://www.nytimes.com/2009/04/08/education/08school.html?r=1&ref=us.)

The International Reading Association and other literacy-related entities strove to maintain a "seat at the table" in Washington, working hard to improve the efficacy of NCLB, while voicing a number of continued concerns about the nature of evidence, methodology, and "best practice." In *A Call to Action and a Framework for Change: IRA's Position on NCLB Reform*, posted on the reading.org website (www.reading.org/resources/issues/focus_nclb.html), the organization urged that the following items be added to the five essential elements of effective reading: classroom organization, differentiated instruction, expert intensive tutoring, motivation and student engagement, writing, and oral language.

With stimulus money available and all the attention paid to professional development, it came as no surprise when, late in 2009, the Obama administration announced that it would be introducing the new Literacy Education for All, Results for the Nation (LEARN) Act proposal to Congress. LEARN sought to provide funds for professional development efforts for K–12 teachers in high-poverty and low-achieving states.

### Change and Challenge

As the 2007 target date for the Reauthorization of NCLB/ESEA came and went, the war in Iraq and growing conflict in Afghanistan continued to strain the federal budget. One of the factors that stalled the reauthorization process was the perceived failure of the government to devote the kinds of money necessary to enable schools to meet the demands of NCLB. As discussion on NCLB continued, many legislators sought to reconnect NCLB to its earlier label, the Elementary and Secondary Education Act (ESEA). Although both political parties promised to put educational reform at the forefront, by the time Barack Obama assumed the Presidency, the nation was in what many called the greatest recession since The Great Depression. A rapidly declining stock market, the bailout of financial institutions, the collapse of the housing market, and continued military conflict threatened to make educational reform less of a priority. Rising unemployment meant a greatly reduced tax base, on which schools relied. As families struggled to remain in their homes, many school districts across the nation were forced to cut teacher salaries and eliminate a number of teaching positions. Among the results were larger class sizes and an increasing need to find on-site ways to address professional development. Funds for professional development that involved travel virtually evaporated. Reading specialists who had never missed IRA conventions or their state reading conferences found that their districts simply had no funds available for these vital professional activities.

## Race to the Top: The New Template for ESEA

On March 10, 2009, President Obama delivered the first major education speech of his presidency, laying the foundation for restructuring the nation's educational system with the announcement of his "five pillars of educational reform."

- "Investing in early childhood initiatives," reframing Early Head Start and Head Start.
- "Encouraging better standards and assessments" by using testing itineraries that are more suitable for students and better aligned with the world in which they live.
- "Recruiting, preparing, and rewarding outstanding teachers" with incentives for a new generation of teachers and for new levels of excellence among all teachers.
- "Promoting innovation and excellence in America's schools" by modernizing the school calendar and the structure of the school day and supporting effective charter schools.
- "Providing every American with a quality higher education—whether it's college or technical training."

(See ED Review, March 13, 2009 at http://www.ed.gov/news/newsletters/edreview/2009/0313.html for links to the entire speech.)

Still, the government was grappling with the Reauthorization of NCLB/ESEA. Because of all the strong emotions surrounding NCLB/ESEA, legislators and educators were looking to reframe these titles and to address some of the concerns expressed by critics of the Act. On January 4, 2010, in hopes of signaling a sincere commitment to reform, an article in *Education Week* released by the U.S. Department of Education announced that "the new template" for NCLB/ESEA will be Race to the Top. It incorporates many of the ideas related in President Obama's earlier address. Once again, schools applying for funds under the Race to the Top initiative will have to meet stringent guidelines, such as tying teacher evaluations to student achievement on standardized tests, and being required to prove that the school's educational practices result in "value added," meaning they meet a certain criteria in terms of measurable gains on students' test scores. You can follow the developments related to NCLB/ESEA and Race to the Top on the *Education Week* website at http://www.edweek.org.

As schools battled to do more with less, many districts were able to benefit from the influx of $44 billion in the first round of money for schools from the federal stimulus package (www.ed.gov). This more than doubled the funding for education from the previous two years. Though not sufficient to cover local and state educational deficits, unprecedented funds were allocated to meet needs directly related to educational outcomes, such as hiring teachers and developing sustainable literacy programs.

Then, in 2009 and 2010, as part of the stimulus package under the American Recovery and Reinvestment Act (ARRA), the federal government implemented the Race to the Top initiative, releasing $4.35 billion in funds to support states implementing educational reforms. What made this initiative different was that one of its major goals was to ensure that as students progressed from grades 3–12, they were *on track for college* and *career ready* by the time they graduated from high school. Thus, assessments became a huge issue in the equation. Because states would be competing against one another for these funds, strict compliance with parameters on raising standards, improving teacher quality, and expanding the reach of charter schools *as defined by the federal government* was seen as a blessing by some and as coercion by others. For more information on Race to the Top and updates on its implementation, visit http://www2.ed.gov/programs/racetothetop/index.html.

In spite of all the wrangling over NCLB throughout the years, many positive and lasting changes have grown directly or indirectly out of the National Reading Panel's original work.

- America's long neglected middle and high school reading programs have come to the forefront, and content area teachers are (sometimes reluctantly) joining in the literacy quest.
- Another great victory for literacy is the shift from a focus on Reading First and Striving Readers to the widespread adoption of the Response to Intervention model. A term that originated in U.S. Legislature, Response to Intervention (RtI) is a model for intervention emphasizing prevention of reading failure and seeking to reduce the number of referrals to special education. (See Chapter 6 for further discussion of RtI.)
- Never before has there been such momentum to ensure that highly qualified professionals—anyone working with children, from paraprofessionals to administrators—are highly skilled and educated in literacy processes and practices.
- Never before have we seen such collaboration among educators across the country to engage in meaningful professional development.
- Universities have re-examined their programs to raise the competency levels of all those responsible for direct and indirect literacy instruction and to align with increasing professional standards.
- Schools are recognizing the importance of using substantive content area instruction as a vehicle for facilitating English language acquisition for students at all levels of proficiency. Practices that embody the Sheltered Instruction Observation Protocol (SIOP®) Model (Echevarria, Vogt, & Short, 2010a; Echevarria, Vogt, & Short, 2010b) are leading educators' thinking and transforming their practice as they implement these powerful and effective techniques to enhance both content learning and language proficiency in their English learners.

The impact of NCLB/ESEA, combined with the economic challenges that began in 2008 and 2009, changed our schools forever. Historically, the infrastructures of society, such as government programs, schools, and transportation, feel the impact of economic crises most keenly and their unwieldy structures make them slowest to recover. The 2010s find us in times of challenge and opportunity. It may take the next ten years to decipher the full effects of all that occurred in the past decade. No one can or should make light of the suffering of communities struggling to educate their children. However, these trials force us to examine our essence and rededicate ourselves as educators. While the debate continues about issues such as adoption of nationwide standards for students or what constitutes evidence-based instructional practice, we suggest that the debate is not a sign of a broken system. We sincerely believe that healthy debate is one of the best ways to remain focused on finding increasingly effective ways to improve our educational system and validate our hopes for our children.

### Thinking Points: What's Important to You?

Now that you have read our synthesis of the history of reading, the elements NCLB suggested as the most important aspects of literacy, and the Obama "five pillars,"

- Make a list of YOUR top five components of effective literacy instruction.
- What is the evidence base for these?
- Are there any items on your list that you are certain are research-based, but that you cannot support with data until you do some investigating?

Perhaps Barbara is like you. How can this exercise help Barbara relate to teachers' beliefs and practices?

## *Looking to the Future: The Case for Evidence-Based Decision Making and Principled Practice*

Because this chapter deals with past and present educational practice, and because so much continues to revolve around establishing a *research base* or *evidence base* for what we do, we think it is important to clarify what we mean by some of the terms that are often used to support our practices. In mid 2009, out of curiosity, we conducted a web search on bing.com using the designators *best practice in reading instruction*. Would you be surprised to know it called up 9,940,000 sites? Ask.com yielded links to 7,515,000 websites, while Google led us to a mere 1,440,000 sites. Is it any wonder that sincere educators who care so much about children are overwhelmed? We had similar results with the terms *evidence-based reading instruction*, well over a million links. Fortunately, the first link listed was to www.reading.org (IRA's website), with their thoughtful, powerful position statement entitled "What Is Evidence-Based Reading Instruction?" (IRA, 2004).

IRA (2004) defines *evidenced-based* instruction, sometimes called *scientifically-based* or *research-based* instruction, as a program or collection of instructional practices with a proven record of success—reliable, trustworthy, with valid evidence to suggest that, when used with a particular group of children, the result will be adequate gains in literacy achievement.

Although qualitative methods are expanding our research repertoire, traditionally, high-quality research is that which is:

- Objective—that the data would yield a similar interpretation regardless of the individual evaluator.
- Valid—that the task is important in order for the student to become proficient in reading.
- Reliable—data will be consistent if the test is given on a different day or by a different person.
- Systematic—data are collected according to rigorous design methodology or observation standards.
- Refereed—data are approved for publication by independent reviewers in the field.

One important distinction is the difference between *evidence-based programs* and *evidence-based practices*. If you are on a quest for the one right program, you will be disappointed. Nobody has come up with one that is best in all settings, for all students, in all situations. However, there are programs that may be highly suitable for the majority of students in your social and cultural setting. More important, there are "just right" practices, or combinations of practices, with evidence to back them, that make them "just right" for your students. Evidence-based practices are generally ones proven to enhance literacy proficiency no matter what the program.

### Principled Practice

Rather than continue the argument about what constitutes *research* and *evidence*, we advocate the notion of implementing *principled practice*, because we feel it is a more inclusive term (see Figure 1.11). We define *principled practice* as follows:

> **Principled practice** encompasses the instructional strategies, methods, materials, and activities used by teachers based on their knowledge of research **and** their experience-based beliefs about what works with their students.

We believe that teachers who engage in principled practice neither slavishly follow a new idea, mandate, or practice based *solely* on claims of a research study or expert, nor reject a new idea *solely* because it involves a paradigm shift. Rather, they thoughtfully rely on a

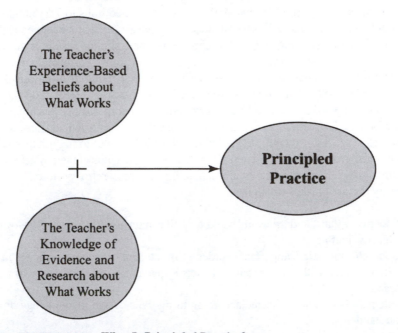

**FIGURE 1.11**   *What Is Principled Practice?*

body of evidence from several sources they deem credible. Then they weigh this evidence against their beliefs—what they know as experienced and knowledgeable educators—in order to develop their own *principled practice*. So when we use the terms evidence-based practice or research-based practice throughout this book, know that we are really talking about principled practice.

### Research as Principled Argument

Rather than using research as a bludgeon to manipulate and coerce, we suggest adopting Ian Wilkinson and David Bloome's (2008) definition of research as *principled argument*. They define research as *knowledge claims* linked to theory and evidence through a clear public chain of reasoning that constitutes a warrant to the claims (p. 7). Put simply, assuming the researchers provide access to their data, if you (a) follow the research path and the line of reasoning used, (b) explore the research base, (c) investigate the means and methods, and (d) look at the match between the design and its appropriateness to the question, is there a reason to believe the claims are warranted?

There are so many important questions about what constitutes evidence. The good thing is that, as we (Brenda & MaryEllen) reflect on our last thirty-five years as educators, we are convinced that today's teachers are more savvy than ever before. As you read this book and explore the resources available to you, you will find considerable support for your boundless intellectual curiosity.

Here are some suggestions: Start with IRA; join, visit the website, subscribe to the journals, and share them. Become active in your local or state reading council. Rely on your reading specialists, literacy coaches, and fellow teachers. Attend conferences whenever possible. Join study groups and share with your peers. Be a skeptic, but one with a positive outlook. We hope to provide you with a wealth of support as you continue to find the kind of evidence you need to make informed, principled decisions on behalf of children and adolescents.

■ *Group Inquiry Activity* Think about the school in which you teach.

1. What do you see as the three most critical needs related to teaching reading/ language arts in your school?
2. What could a reading specialist or literacy coach do to help alleviate these needs? Share your identified needs with a small group.
3. How many of the concerns are related or similar? Discuss what each of you has suggested that a reading specialist or literacy coach could do to help with these concerns. How could you get started?

## Revisiting the Vignette

1. Reflect on reading specialist Barbara Johnson's dilemma described in the opening to this chapter. Are there any recommendations you would now modify based on what you learned in the chapter and through discussion with your peers?

2. Using what you have learned about the historical trends in reading instruction, how could Barbara and the teachers explore and implement evidence-based practice in the district's reading program? What steps should she take to begin this process?
3. How can Barbara reconcile the differences between the methods promoted by the university and those used by classroom teachers?

## Points to Remember

Since the inception of schools in the United States, educators have debated the best approaches for teaching children to read, and teachers have used a wide variety of methods and materials for teaching reading. Early in the country's history, children of the elite were taught the alphabet and sound–symbol relationships, and they learned to read didactic texts. Later, analytic and synthetic phonics approaches were adopted, with ongoing debates as to the efficacy of each. Basal reading series were used in nearly every school in the country for many years, and teachers grouped students for instruction according to their abilities and reading levels. More holistic and integrated methods of teaching reading appeared in the 1980s and 1990s, though they had fallen into disfavor by the end of the twentieth century. Federally funded research and national panel recommendations that were controversial and critically reviewed urged more explicit teaching of phonemic awareness, phonics, and fluency as well as vocabulary and comprehension. There is now general agreement that reading is a complex process involving the integration and thoughtful application of a variety of skills and strategies within a variety of social, political, cultural, and educational contexts.

Think back to the year 2000. There were so many new initiatives started in the first decade of the century that we never could have imagined back then. It will take a while before we know how things will work out with many of them. However, as reading professionals we are not passive spectators. We have a great deal invested in how these initiatives are implemented and we are the ones who will be shaping the future of literacy instruction. We are definitely up for the challenge.

We end this chapter with a quote from Harvey Graff's (2007) fascinating exploration of the history of reading in Western culture. We hope you will pause a moment to reflect on these words:

> Failure to appreciate the provenance of the past, of history, in the present and the possibilities for the future makes us its prisoners, bound to repeat the past, rather than to learn from it and break its bonds. (p. 12)

We couldn't agree more.

## Portfolio and Self-Assessment Projects

1. Interview a parent, grandparent, or other older person about how he or she learned to read. Ask about reading materials, instruction, or anything else that the person can remember about early literacy experiences. Share the responses during class.

2. Create a time line or other graphic organizer of the historical trends presented in this chapter. Relate them to current approaches and methods for teaching reading/language arts.

3. Create your own literacy history. Chronicle as many memories as you can about learning to read and write. Be sure to situate your experiences in pop culture and political/historical/social contexts. As you engage in this reflection, consider also your beliefs about students, teaching, and learning. What do you feel strongly about that's related to teaching reading (Dillon, 2000)? How did your family and community beliefs about the definitions, uses, and importance of literacy influence your development and beliefs? After you are finished, identify the communities and literacies present in your autobiography and compare them to those valued by schools. Write your literacy history or use another medium to convey your memories (i.e., create a picture book, poster, video, poem, or the like). Use the Literacy History Prompts in Appendix A (McLaughlin & Vogt, 1996) to jog your memories. Be sure to share your literacy history with others in your class; you'll be amazed at the power of this activity!

4. Make a case for items on your list of evidence-based practice. Keep a log of your inquiry path.

5. *Personal Goal:* Revisit the goal you set for yourself at the beginning of the chapter. Create a portfolio item that reflects what you have learned relative to your goal.

## Recommended Readings: Suggestions for Book Clubs, Study Groups, and Professional Development

Fresch, M. J. (2008). *An essential history of current reading practices.* Newark, DE: International Reading Association. This is a great resource to frame your thinking about evidence-based practice. The message is that it is essential for us to consider carefully the work of those who have gone before us. Researchers and classroom teachers will find it helpful and grounding.

Graff, H. J. (2007). *Literacy and historical development: A reader.* Carbondale: Southern Illinois University Press. This is a beautifully written, scholarly exploration of literacy's heritage and how social, cultural, and political contexts shaped its past and influence the present. Different from all the others in scope and conscience, it is a must read for any serious scholar of early literacy.

Kirp, D. L. (2007). *The sandbox investment: The pre-school movement and kids-first politics.* Cambridge, MA: Harvard University Press. This socially conscious historical perspective on the evolution of pre-school education examines the crippling effects of the disparities in opportunity afforded the rich and poor, yet clearly lives in the solution. Kirp argues that a good pre-school for all children is the smartest investment we can make for our future.

Smith, N. B. (2002). *American reading instruction* (4th ed.). Newark, DE: International Reading Association. Nila Banton Smith's groundbreaking history of reading was first published in 1935 and revised in 1965. It is one of the most widely recognized classics in the field. After her death in 1976, IRA paid tribute to her work by updating the book in 1986 and again in 2002. The latest edition spans the last quarter of the twentieth century and contains an eloquent prologue by P. David Pearson and an equally brilliant epilogue by Steven Stahl.

## Online Resources

### http://www.ed.gov/news/newsletters/index.html

This will link you to the U.S. government's official education website. Although there are many resources here, one that is particularly useful is the Newsletter, to which you can subscribe. It is an excellent way to keep current on important news and search the archives for valuable information.

### http://www.historyliteracy.org

This is the official website of the History of Literacy organization, part of IRA's History of Reading Special Interest Group (SIG). There are links to articles on numerous topics relating to historical aspects of literacy from its origins to the present.

The following position statements are on the IRA website: **www.reading.org** under the Research and Policy link:

International Reading Association. (2002). *What is evidence-based reading instruction?: A position statement of the International Reading Association.* International Reading Association, Newark: DE.

International Reading Association. *A call to action: A position statement of the International Reading Association.* International Reading Association, Newark: DE.

## Companion Website Resources

The following resources to support and extend your learning of this chapter can be found on our companion website (waveland.com/Extra_Material/32979/): key vocabulary, concepts, and other terms; extended examples; updated resources specifically tied to information in the chapter; related websites; and other support features.

# Serving as an Elementary, Secondary, or District-Level Reading Specialist or Literacy Coach

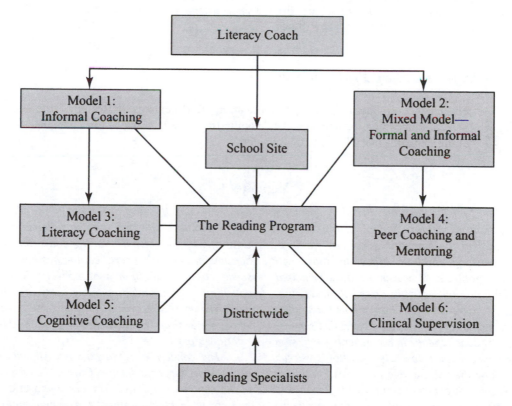

**FIGURE 2.1** *Chapter Overview*

## Learning Goals

After reading, discussing, and engaging in activities related to this chapter, you will be able to:

1. Understand the roles of the various educators engaged in literacy instruction in your school (reading teacher, literacy coach, reading specialist, educational support person [paraprofessional]), literacy team member, classroom teacher (pre-K–elementary; middle and high school). Develop a well-defined and fully operational job description for each. This should be done in collaboration with the professionals involved, and may include input from others, such as administrators and literacy team members.

2. List the qualifications of the individuals in your school who are currently in these positions. Compare their qualifications to the qualifications suggested in this chapter. Respond to the following statement, providing evidence for your assertions: *I am confident that fully qualified reading professionals are working with teachers and students in our school.*

3. Discuss the changes and challenges with regard to the roles of reading professionals and the steps that might be taken to address them.

4. Explain in detail the differences among those holding the titles literacy coach, reading coach, and instructional coach.

5. *Personal Learning Goal:* In a three-minute brainstorming session, share what you know about this topic. Write a goal or a question that reflects something you want to learn about the topic. Share this with others in your group.

## Standards for Reading Professionals

This chapter provides focused support for current IRA Standards for Reading Professionals. See our companion website (waveland.com/Extra_Material/32979/) for a complete listing of the standards that align with this chapter.

### Vignette

When hired for the position of reading specialist at Jefferson Elementary School, Caitlin Howard assumed that the majority of her day would be spent teaching children, especially those with reading problems. However, Caitlin's principal, Ed Tagliano, had recently attended an administrator's conference and returned home committed to having his school's reading specialist serve as a literacy coach to four new teachers at Jefferson. As the only reading specialist, Caitlin is worried about how she will be able to do this in addition to her teaching responsibilities. Jefferson Elementary, located in a rural area of the northeast, has 320 children and fourteen teachers, in addition to the reading specialist and special edu-

cation teacher. Because of the size of the school, the principal is the only on-site administrator. Caitlin, with her MA in reading education and her advanced reading certification, has had little specific preparation in the new models of literacy coaching, and is understandably leery of being perceived as a "supervisor" for the teachers with whom she's already established a good working relationship.

Her concern about this newly assigned role grows when the principal asks Caitlin to coach one of the new teachers, Alex. The previous week, Ed had spent an hour during the reading/language arts block in Alex's first-grade classroom. To Caitlin, he expressed concerns about Alex's *reading approach and suggested that she "get in there as soon as possible and see what Alex is doing with those kids." Caitlin trusts Ed's opinion,* *but instantly realizes she has a big problem. She and Ed have very different ideas about the role of a literacy coach.*

### Thinking Points

1. What can you identify as the primary tension in this vignette?
2. What do you think Caitlin should do at this point?
3. How should Caitlin respond to Ed, her principal?
4. How might she approach Alex, the new teacher?

## Expanding the Vignette: Exploring the Issues

*Caitlin spends a sleepless night. What should she say to Ed? She'll just have to sit down with him ASAP to clear things up. She and Ed have been working together for years and they have a great deal of mutual respect. Still, he is her boss, and if push comes to shove, she understands she'll be forced to observe Alex. She knows if teachers ever find out she is there to "report back to Ed," she might as well retire right now. She can already hear the doors slamming as she walks down the hall. Yes, she'll go in there first thing tomorrow. But what will she say? She thinks she knows what a reading coach should do, but she's not 100 percent sure.*

*At 6:30 A.M., Caitlin calls her best friend, Ann McGrath, an expert reading specialist in the neighboring district who has been serving as a literacy coach for the last three years.*

*Ann listens intently. She uses phrases such as, "Can you tell me a little more about that?" "How do you envision what you ought to be doing?" "What do you think Ed sees as your role here?" "Do you have a needs assessment?" (Caitlin isn't sure why Ann would want to know that!) At this point, Caitlin wants to cry. Finally she says, "Oh, Ann, just tell me what to do!" Ann sighs and tells her about six different models of literacy coaching. Caitlin's never heard of them. Ann explains that only Caitlin and Ed can decide what her new duties should be. But, once again, friendship prevails. Ann tells her to be sure to get to school before Ed. There she will find a fax explaining the six models of literacy coaching waiting for her. "Read it before you see Ed! Good luck! You'll be fine!" (Click!)*

### Thinking Points

1. Why is Ann asking so many questions?
2. Why might Ann have asked about a needs assessment?
3. What are some things that will help Caitlin and Ed resolve this issue?
4. How might reading about the six models help Caitlin?
5. What should she say to Ed?

Caitlin is fortunate to have Ann as her best friend. She is also fortunate to have an expert nearby. The reality is that most teachers have a few close friends or a professional network, sometimes comprised of colleagues they've met in local and state reading councils or in graduate classes. Think about the people in your professional circle. They are what Jim Gee (2004) would call your "affinity group," an association of individuals drawn together around a certain interest or a common goal. You speak the same language, both literally and figuratively, as you discuss issues surrounding reading processes and instruction. This is exactly the kind of relationship Caitlin wants to cultivate with the teachers she seeks to serve as a literacy coach.

Because our primary aim is to assist reading specialists and literacy coaches, we will focus the majority of our efforts on exploring these two roles, but we will also address, to a lesser extent, the roles of the other literacy professionals in our schools. It is imperative to recognize that specialists and coaches exist as members of collaborative teams working to meet school and district literacy goals. We are delighted that, increasingly, reading specialists and coaches are leading the adoption of collaborative approaches used by effective schools.

## Evolution of the Literacy Professional: Reading Specialists and Literacy Coaches

Although classroom teachers with special interest and expertise in reading instruction have long been part of the educational landscape, the kind of school or district reading specialists we know today have existed in large numbers only since the late 1960s and early 1970s. This phenomena corresponds to the widespread creation of graduate programs in education. With the proliferation of masters programs, particularly at state universities, an opportunity arose for focused study in the psychology and pedagogy of reading, and often, special certification related to reading and learning disabilities. But university programs are primarily responsive to needs. What were the needs that led to the formation of masters programs in reading?

### The Reading Specialist 1960–2000

By the late 1960s, schools were the beneficiaries of a tremendous infusion of funding for education. Initiatives of the Elementary and Secondary Education Act (ESEA) focused on establishing the following Entitlement Programs: Title I programs in high-poverty schools that target children with low achievement; federally funded Research and Development Centers; the creation of Centers and Regional Educational Laboratories; support for improving library resources; and programs to foster relationships between education and community organizations. Still, there were many children who were not becoming proficient readers.

In response, schools began using Title I funds to hire specially selected and (sometimes) specially trained teachers to work with youngsters experiencing reading difficulties. These teachers held a variety of titles: reading specialist, reading resource teacher, reading coordinator, or reading supervisor. They could be found fulfilling the following roles: resource person, advisor, in-service leader, investigator, diagnostician, evaluator, and instructor (Robinson & Rauch, 1965). They worked primarily in one school, providing diagnoses and remediation for students, usually in small-group pull-out programs. This model was sometimes referred to as "the closet model" because many clinicians worked in any extra space that existed in the school.

In 1986, the International Reading Association (IRA) identified five roles of the reading specialist: diagnostic/remedial specialist; developmental reading/study skills specialist; reading consultant/reading resource teacher; reading coordinator/supervisor; and reading professor. That list was shortened by IRA in 1992 to include only three primary responsibilities: teacher or clinician; consultant/coordinator; and teacher educator/researcher (Wepner & Seminoff, 1995).

By the end of the 1980s, during the Reagan Administration, the nation was in the grip of an economic recession. As a result, many reading specialist positions were downsized or eliminated. Students needing specialized assistance were referred for special education services, and many who did not qualify for special education were left without assistance. Those who were accepted were often taught by special educators with little advanced preparation in reading. It was a tough time for both reading educators and their students.

In 1996, the Executive Board of IRA appointed a Commission on the Role of the Reading Specialist to investigate the roles, responsibilities, and working conditions of reading teachers identified as Title I reading teacher, reading specialist, and reading supervisor/coordinator (Quatroche, Bean, & Hamilton, 1998, p. 4). The commission found, not surprisingly, that reading specialists' roles appeared to depend on context: with whom the specialist worked (classroom teachers with their own sets of expectations) and the setting and location of their work (school/district; pull-out/in-class).

The IRA Commission also found there is sparse research on whether there is a direct link between the work of reading specialists and a school's reading achievement. A number of studies examined successful literacy intervention and developmental reading programs, and concluded that "programs with the strongest backgrounds in the teaching of reading have the highest rates. Therefore, it appears critical that professionals with extensive knowledge of reading instruction be part of every classroom where there are students who need help learning to read" (Quatroche, Bean, & Hamilton, 1998, p. 18).

In an extensive survey of reading specialists, the IRA Commission found that reading specialists' primary roles in the 1990s included instruction (in-class, pull-out, and supporting classroom testing); serving as a resource (providing materials, ideas, and support to teachers, special educators, and other allied professionals); and administration (activities such as documenting and monitoring performance of students and completing reports) (Bean, Cassidy, Grumet, Shelton, & Wallis, 2002, p. 736). A majority of the responding reading specialists indicated that they believed they had a responsibility not only for struggling readers but also for schoolwide literacy improvement for all students. They also reported that recent changes in their jobs included an increasing amount of paperwork, more time spent serving as a resource to teachers, more planning with teachers, and more in-class instruction for students (p. 741).

During the late 1990s, as a result of flat and in some states decreased reading scores on the National Assessment of Educational Progress (NAEP), legislators came to realize what educators had suspected for some time: Many children and adolescents in the United States were not becoming proficient readers, those who could deal with the increasingly complex reading demands of a new century.

## The Reading Professional in the Twenty-First Century: Emergence of the Literacy Coach

As the new decade and century began, reading specialists (now often called reading/language arts specialists or literacy specialists) were in increasing demand in part because of the No Child Left Behind legislation of 2002 and the Reading First Initiative. University graduate programs in reading were experiencing unprecedented growth. The IRA Standards for the Preparation of Reading Specialists (IRA/NCATE) as well as most state standards for graduate programs in reading required that candidates have advanced study in the reading process, theory and research, assessment and diagnosis, intervention, curriculum, and instruction. Programs were also focusing on the preparation of literacy coaches, whose jobs included coaching, mentoring, serving as a resource; guiding professional development; supervising; selecting materials; implementing and evaluating reading programs; and professional development. Increasingly, in addition to the previously cited responsibilities, reading specialists were often required to provide reading and language instruction for English learners, as well as for students receiving special education services.

Schools dug in, working hard to meet the demands initiated by NCLB. School reform and literacy achievement were ubiquitous media topics. Then came Autumn 2008. Most teachers were too young to have experienced the impact of the 1980s recession on schools, but older educators were not surprised when—once again—many schools began to eliminate or downsize any supportive positions. And—once again—reading specialists and literacy coaches, whose education and experience made them *expensive* to their schools, saw their positions threatened.

Until the turn of the century, the term literacy coach was unknown. In fact, when our first edition was being written in 2002, we had very little information on which to draw for our limited discussion of literacy coaching. Now the reading specialist and literacy coach's jobs overlap a great deal.

One of the biggest developments for coaches came with the creation of The Literacy Coaching Clearinghouse (LLC), through the hard work of its first director, Nancy Shanklin. (See http://www.literacycoachingonline.org.) The site is a repository of research, collaboration, and most of all, tools for literacy coaches that are also useful to reading specialists. Originally, it was jointly sponsored by IRA and NCTE. At the time of this writing, it is sponsored by NCTE and can be accessed directly or through the NCTE website, www.ncte.org.

In a 2009 Literacy Coaching Collaborative brief, Melinda Mangin examined factors that influenced whether or not districts decided to hire literacy coaches. She reported that the number one factor influencing a district's decision *not to hire* literacy coaches was "limited finances." Districts reported that the decision *to hire* literacy coaches was most influenced by "state and national reform contexts" (Mangin, 2009). Having literacy coaches in the district was a way for schools to demonstrate their compliance with NCLB and Reading First directives. It was obvious to all that years of "drive-by" professional development failed to result in improved teaching or learning, much less school reform. Gradually, administrators began to see the promise of sustained, focused, long-term professional development that a literacy coach could provide.

School reform was a priority and schools were dedicated to promoting literacy, even with economic constraints. To justify investing in literacy coaches, schools needed research-based evidence that coaches made a "value-added" difference in students' reading scores, and as we will discover in this chapter, that evidence was beginning to materialize (Biancarosa, Bryk, & Dexter, 2008; Lapp, Fisher, Flood, & Frey, 2003).

## Thinking Point

The roles for reading professionals have certainly changed throughout the years. Some of the old roles may seem quaint, but they tell us a great deal about how we defined reading, how we defined ourselves, and how we viewed students and their needs. Look at the roles again: *study skills specialist, resource person, advisor, in-service leader, investigator, diagnostician, evaluator, and instructor* (Robinson & Rauch, 1965). How are they different from some of the terms we use today to describe reading specialists, and especially coaches, such as *literacy coach, instructional coach, mentor, peer teacher, collaborator, professional development facilitator, consultant?* What does this comparison tell us about our changing beliefs?

The subject of our first exploration in this chapter pertains to the roles and qualifications of the reading specialist. Next, we will focus on the literacy coach and the rapidly expanding roles, titles, qualifications, and ways in which these professionals are carving out a new path, especially at the middle and secondary levels. We will begin by discussing the various differences between school-site reading specialists and those that are districtwide reading specialists.

## BEYOND THE BOOK

### *Chapter 2 Focus Issue: Your Professional Affinity Group*

■ *Group Inquiry Activity* In your group, do a Think-Pair-Share (Lyman, 1981). Read each question out loud to the group. Reflect silently for one minute, then jot down your ideas for one minute. Finally, after each question, take two minutes to share the ideas you wrote.

1. Who are the three colleagues you would be most likely to call if you had a professional crisis?
2. What are the ways that these people interact with you?
3. How might these relationships inform your philosophy and orientation toward your role as a literacy coach?
4. With your group, create a Venn diagram, comparing and contrasting characteristics of your affinity group with characteristics of an effective literacy coach.

In the opening vignette for this chapter, Ann was actually modeling for Caitlin some of the most important qualities of a literacy coach and peer mentor. First of all, she *listened.* Next, she *asked questions,* not only to find out what Caitlin was thinking but also to help Caitlin articulate her thoughts. The last thing Ann did was to provide for Caitlin what she couldn't provide for herself, given the urgency of the problem. Had Ann done what most of us would have done—that is, jumped right in and attempted to solve the problem—she might have acted before she fully understood the facts. However, she never really did tell Caitlin what to do. Instead, Ann gave Caitlin the tools to solve her own problem. Such a response shows a friend and/or colleague that you respect her and have confidence in her abilities to handle and solve her own problems with a minimum of assistance. Both friends benefited from this exchange.

## School and District Roles of Literacy Coaches and Reading Specialists

It is helpful to begin our exploration by distinguishing between school-site and district-level literacy professionals (see Figures 2.2 and 2.3). Most often, the combined position of literacy coach/reading specialist is found exclusively in a school-site context. This is hardly a surprise, since coaches usually work in one-to-one collaboration with teachers or split the duties of literacy coach and reading specialist, spending part of their day with students. However, it is at the district level where the two jobs split. We find that the literacy professional is almost always a reading specialist whose focus is on a systemic, programmatic level. Although the roles will vary from district to district, and state to state, there are positions that resemble the following:

- *School-Site Literacy Coaches/Reading Specialists (Traditional Reading Specialist Model):* Primary responsibility is instruction of children who need additional support with literacy, sometimes as a part-time Title I teacher; as the only school reading professional, may spend very little time coaching, modeling, and co-teaching; is involved in curriculum design and implementation; often assesses new students or those experiencing difficulty; leads study groups and gives input regarding professional development; reports to the building principal.

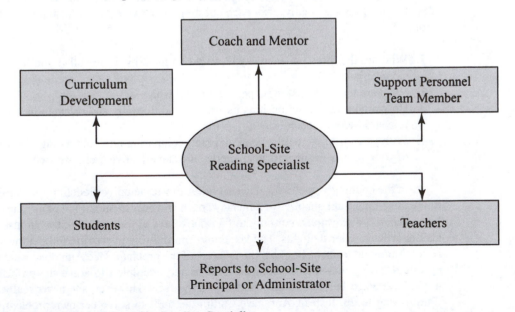

**FIGURE 2.2     *School-Site Reading Specialist***

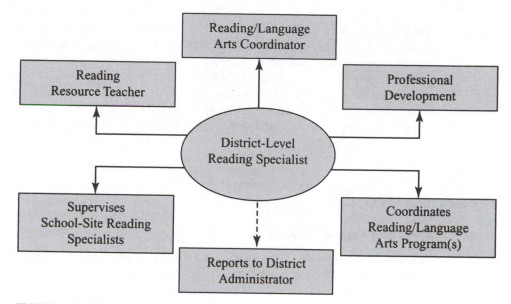

**FIGURE 2.3** *District-Level Reading Specialist*

- *School-Site Literacy Coaches/Reading Specialists (Traditional Team Model):* Works as a member of a team, alongside other reading professionals, paraprofessionals, and support personnel (including the counselor, speech clinician, special education team, curriculum coordinator, or assessment coordinator); coaches grade-level teams and facilitates peer coaching and cognitive coaching partnerships; reports to the building principal or other administrator who oversees support personnel.
- *School-Site Literacy Coaches/Reading Specialists (Literacy Coaching Model):* Primary responsibility is to support teachers and paraprofessionals in developing and meeting their own goals and those of the school; may help teachers design individual or group professional development plans; spends part of the time conferring, modeling, coaching, and observing; answers to building principal, supervisor, or curriculum coordinator.
- *District-Level Reading Resource Specialist:* Works as a reading resource teacher, with responsibilities for working with a variety of schools and staffs on implementation of effective literacy teaching practices and materials; reports to the assistant superintendent for curriculum, curriculum director, reading supervisor, or perhaps the superintendent.
- *District-Level Reading Specialist:* Supervises the work of school-site reading specialists and literacy coaches (but does not engage in formal evaluation procedures); reports to the curriculum or reading director, assistant superintendent, or superintendent.
- *District-Level Director of Reading or Reading Supervisor:* Is responsible for all reading/language arts instructional programs; oversees the adoption of instructional materials; supervises and formally evaluates all district reading specialists, literacy coaches, and paraprofessionals; reports to an assistant superintendent or superintendent.

It is obvious that the reading professional today must be highly educated (International Reading Association, 2006). The job descriptions we just examined contained dozens of roles and responsibilities. Some states are now requiring their reading specialists to obtain administrator licensure or other advanced certification. If you eventually intend to work at the district level, you might want to pursue advanced administrative certification.

If you are a literacy coach/reading specialist, your world holds exciting new challenges and opportunities. You are definitely in the right place at the right time. You are in demand because you have something the world needs. You have the knowledge and the passion to effect lasting change.

## The Reading Specialist

### Roles and Responsibilities

Category III of the International Reading Association's revised role definitions for reading specialists (IRA, 2007) defines the reading specialist as one who works with literacy learners at all levels from early childhood to adult education, especially students who are experiencing difficulties with reading. Many spend part of their time as literacy coaches or reading/literacy coaches, but they can also act as supervisors or coordinators of reading/literacy programs with related administrative duties. The Literacy Coaching Clearinghouse (2008) updated the definition of Reading Specialist to reflect IRA's new category III.

According to NCTE and IRA recommendations posted on the Literacy Coaching Clearinghouse (LLC) website, these are the primary roles a reading specialist might fulfill:

- *Working with struggling readers.* Since the 1970s, the primary responsibility of reading specialists has been to provide intensive instruction to students experiencing reading difficulties at all levels (pre-K through 12). Although some divide their time among other duties, IRA reports that many work solely with children and adolescents inside or outside of the classroom, primarily in small-group settings. Years ago, reading specialists were among the first to serve as Title I teachers. Today, however, they may also provide intensive literacy intervention to meet the needs of individual students (one-to-one in some cases) or they may support instruction that enables struggling readers to participate in and benefit from instruction in the classroom reading program. They are often key players at Tiers II and III in schools that have adopted a Response to Intervention (RtI) model.
- *Supporting teachers' learning as a literacy or reading coach.* The primary focus of reading specialists who serve as coaches is supporting teachers in professional development, helping them reflect on their own knowledge and implementation of evidence-based instructional practice in order to improve student learning. Coaches are an increasing presence at the middle and high school levels. More recently, their responsibilities include supporting early childhood literacy programs, thus expanding the influence they have throughout the system. They view staff development as a multilayered, long-term, ongoing process, encompassing a range of supportive endeavors that involve individual teachers or even entire schools.

- *Developing, leading, or evaluating the schoolwide or districtwide reading/literacy programs*. Although reading specialists often appear to have the same responsibilities as coaches—working with teachers—the difference is that the stance of the reading specialist is more systemic. They are often responsible for supporting school or district reform initiatives. With Response to Intervention (RtI) and new uniform core standards for students, they will be assuming an even greater role in the school assessment system as it is tied to school improvement initiatives. In order to coordinate and implement schoolwide or districtwide professional development, they must have a great deal of leadership expertise and experience. Historically, reading specialists have assumed administrative or quasi-administrative duties; overseeing, coordinating, and implementing all facets of a schoolwide or districtwide literacy program, including testing, collaborating with teams and literacy coaches, and possibly evaluating lessons (IRA, 2007; Moxley & Taylor, 2006).

Figure 2.4 on pages 38–39 is a sample matrix that features a composite of the roles, qualifications, responsibilities, professional development expectations, and evaluation methods for reading specialists and literacy coaches. It will provide an overview and a useful reference tool as we discuss these issues throughout the chapter.

### *The Reading Specialist: Qualifications*

The Literacy Coaching Clearinghouse (LCC) lists the following as qualifications for reading specialists:

- A valid teaching license,
- Previous teaching experience,
- Master's degree with concentration in reading education, and
- Substantial coursework in reading education that includes a supervised practicum experience working with struggling readers and supporting teachers, as a literacy coach.

We agree that reading specialists, especially those who work with struggling readers, should have the credentials suggested by IRA, NCTE, and LCC. However, there are a number of other aspects that are necessary to ensure success for reading specialists. An individual who is adept at working with struggling readers is not automatically as skilled at interacting with adults. We would make the case that given the increasingly collaborative roles reading specialists are assuming, more than ever, people skills are exceedingly important. We combined our ideas with some of the suggestions from IRA's 2006 *Standards for Middle and High School Literacy Coaches* and others (Dole, 2004; Echevarria, Vogt, & Short, 2010a, 2010b; Frost & Bean, 2006) who believe reading specialists must:

- Be highly knowledgeable, and continue to enhance their professional expertise at all levels from pre-K–12.
- Be affiliated with IRA, NCTE, or other national and international literacy-related organizations.
- Be excellent listeners, able to consider the perspectives of others.

| Sample Role Matrix for Reading Specialists, Coaches, Teachers, Paraprofessionals, Administrators | | | | |
|---|---|---|---|---|
| *Title* | *Qualifications* | *Responsibilities (include % of time spent on each of these)* | *Personal Professional Development Plan* | *Evaluation Plan* |
| **Reading Specialist** | • Minimum 3 years classroom teaching experience <br> • Master's in reading, language arts, or other literacy-related field <br> • Minimum 6 credits supervised practicum coaching experience | *Coordinate reading program (40%)* <br> • Assume a leadership position on the literacy team. <br> • Coordinate, interpret, and disseminate district testing results. <br> • Monitor progress on two-year plan. <br> • Evaluate literacy needs; consult with team and administrators. <br> • Lead teams in materials adoptions. <br> • Engage in school/ community initiatives. <br> • Monitor for adequate yearly progress. <br> • Problem solve as needed. <br> • Align program with state standards and evidence-based practice. <br><br> *Lead professional development (10%)* <br> • Support literacy professionals with research and staff updates. <br> • Help teachers develop professional development plans. <br> • Provide resources and training to teachers, paraprofessionals, and administrators. <br><br> *Teach reading intervention (15%)* <br> • Work with individual students. | • Attend state and IRA conference sessions related to school goals. <br> • Serve on state reading committee. <br> • Participate in reading professional network or IRA special interest groups. | Develop annual goals to be assessed using the following: <br> a) evidence of value-added student outcomes <br> b) a self-assessment report <br> c) principal observation and review of annual performance checklist <br> d) evidence of improved teacher-related outcomes |

**FIGURE 2.4  *Sample Role Matrix for Reading Specialists, Coaches, Teachers, Paraprofessionals, Administrators***

| Title | Qualifications | Responsibilities (include % of time spent on each of these) | Personal Professional Development Plan | Evaluation Plan |
|---|---|---|---|---|
| | | • Test students and serve on IP teams.<br>• Advise teachers in developing intervention plans for specific students.<br><br>*Serve as a school literacy coach (35%)*<br>(See description of coach's role below.)<br>• Many serve dual roles as reading specialists/literacy coaches. | | |
| ***Literacy Coach/ Reading Coach/ Instructional Coach*** | • Previous teaching experience<br>• Master's with emphasis in reading education or related field<br>• Minimum of 24 graduate hours of reading-related coursework<br>• Minimum 6 semester hours in supervised coaching practicum | *Provide teachers with direct support for literacy teaching, planning, instruction, and individual and school professional development goals (50%)*<br>• Assume an active role on the school literacy team.<br>• Consult with teachers about goals.<br>• Demonstrate, observe, and co-teach lessons; provide practical feedback.<br>• Provide information and research on literacy methodology.<br><br>*Work with Tier II and Tier III intervention initiatives (50%)*<br>• Consult, demonstrate, and help teachers implement the school's RtI programs in and out of classrooms.<br>• Assume a major role in ensuring the success of Level III intervention. | • Attend state and IRA conference sessions related to coaching and improving school literacy practices.<br>• Serve on state reading committee.<br>• Participate in reading professional coaching network; facilitate study groups.<br>• Incorporate resources from the Literacy Coaching Collaborative. | Develop annual goals to be assessed using the following:<br>a) evidence of value-added student outcomes<br>b) a self-assessment report<br>c) principal observation and review of annual performance checklist<br>d) evidence of improved teacher-related outcomes |

**FIGURE 2.4** (*continued*)

- Have the ability to work as part of a team.
- Honor confidentiality.
- Understand the demands of increasingly complex genres, particularly as they apply to the middle and secondary school cultures.
- Be knowledgeable about and able to implement the latest evidence-based practices needed to support English learners.

## The Importance of Creating a Job Description for the Reading Specialist

Does the reading specialist in your school have a written job description? Where is it filed? When was it written? Do teachers and administrators know what it says? How was it developed and by whom? We always find it interesting (and a bit troubling) that when we ask these questions as professors, few of our master's degree candidates have ever seen a formal job description, even some who are currently serving as reading specialists and literacy coaches.

When the first edition of our book was published in 2003, the concept of literacy coach was relatively new. To a large degree, coaches were reading specialists who spent a portion of their time demonstrating or co-teaching lessons with teachers—just another hat for the reading specialist to wear. By the second edition in 2007, we saw a definite trend toward coaching as a separate job designation with a separate title. The major distinction at the time was that literacy coaches assumed little program administration or systemic leadership. Times have changed. In many schools, literacy coaches and reading specialists are synonymous terms—the reading specialist IS the literacy coach. With so many of the same jobs being performed by reading specialists and literacy coaches, it is even more important for today's reading specialist to have a clearly defined, written job description that is disseminated to teachers and others involved in supporting reading in the school. Many of the misunderstandings about what reading specialists "do all day" can be resolved by completing this extremely important task. Later in this chapter, we give directions to the literacy coach on how to develop a job description in consultation with an administrator. If you are one of those reading specialists without a formal job description, you may wish to follow the suggestions we offer literacy coaches at the end of this chapter.

## The Literacy Coach

### What Is a Literacy Coach?

The term *literacy coach* is among the most widely used buzzwords in the field of reading instruction. Administrators whose schools have been identified as "in need of improvement" are hiring literacy coaches (sometimes referred to as *reading coaches*), often delegating that role to the reading specialist. This phenomenon is driven by the large amounts of money for professional development that have been allotted to schools under the Reading Excellence Act of 1998, No Child Left Behind Act of 2001, Reading Next, Race to the Top, and other government efforts to support school reform. We will be examining the various ways literacy coaches are defined and offering suggestions from our own professional organizations on the roles and qualifications of those who hold the title.

■ *Author Connection: Brenda*  The best coach I ever had was a nineteen-year-old academic advisee I met about four years after I began my college teaching career. Frank was a runner, and I would often see him out running early in the morning or late at night as I drove to and from the university, usually in the dark (after all, it's Wisconsin). One spring morning when he sauntered in for his semi-annual advising session, I said, "Frank, I see you running all the time. I've always wanted to run, but I'm almost fifty. I'm probably too old, and I don't want to get hurt." His eyes lit up.

"Dr. Shearer, I know you can do this. I'll help, and if you let me guide you, you won't get hurt."

First he asked what my goal was. I was puzzled. "I want to run. I want to lose weight. I want to get fit."

He said, "That's all fine, but you need a long-term and short-term target. When Oprah started running, her target was to run a half marathon within the year."

We collaborated and I decided that my long-term target was to run to Madison (about 250 miles) by plotting my daily distances on a map. We purchased huge county maps and every time I ran a mile, I'd mark the inch or two on the big map until I reached my goal. My short-term goal was to run the local 5K race three months later. Frank showed me how to stretch and how to warm up before and after I ran. He helped me plan a schedule of running and walking, gradually increasing the time rather than focusing on the distance. "Now," Frank said, "you have to think of yourself as a runner. When you want to eat something that's not healthy, don't pass it up because you don't want the calories, pass it up because *you are a runner, and runners don't eat that way.* I also don't want you to wait until you are in shape to buy a good running outfit. You need to do it now, because after all, *you are a runner!"*

At least once a week, Frank and his girlfriend would pop into my office to check my maps, ask how I thought I was doing, and see if I needed any support. Within two months, I surpassed my short-term goal of entering a 5K race; I entered and finished a five-*mile* race—dead last. A number of local runners who had finished long before came back out and ran the last half mile with me, cheering me on to finish. I called Frank at home, and even his mother was ecstatic.

Frank knew everything there was to know about human motivation. When I reflect on how much he understood about the importance of having me set my own attainable long- and short-term goals, about the importance of learning the process, and about intrinsic and extrinsic rewards, I am astounded. He also knew about change. His focus wasn't to change my behaviors, but to change who I thought I was. I often wonder what became of him. He's out there in the world somewhere teaching high school Social Studies. Perhaps some child you know will have him for a teacher. How fortunate.

### Roles and Responsibilities

Because of the expanding roles of literacy coaches, the Literacy Coaching Clearinghouse (LCC) now lists three classifications or titles for coaches:

1. *Literacy Coach,* broadly defined as one whose role it is to work with teachers to improve reading and writing instruction. IRA uses the term literacy coach and reading coach synonymously.

2. *Reading Coach,* a term associated with Reading First to describe coaches who work primarily in elementary schools and devote most of their efforts to improving teachers' reading instruction, with less emphasis on writing.

3. *Instructional Coach,* a title that is replacing "literacy coach" at the middle and secondary levels in some regions. This term is more acceptable to content area teachers because it focuses on the improvement of teaching and learning that is *supported* by literacy processes. This is a growing classification of the reading professional, fueled by the recent reforms and initiatives, particularly Time to Act. The premise is that teachers' first focus is on their content area and its particular demands related to specialized vocabulary, uses of language, and the written genres that comprise it. Two documents are essential to anyone assuming the role of instructional coach. The first relates to *Qualifications of the Instructional Coach,* developed through a collaborative effort among IRA, NCTE, and the professional organizations of many content areas. It can be found at http://www.literacycoachingonline.org/aboutus/instructional_coach.html. The second resource is the *Self-Assessment for Middle and High School Literacy Coaches,* developed by IRA and NCTE. It is designed to help instructional coaches determine where they need further professional development. It is available at http://www.literacycoachingonline.org/library/resources/self-assessmentformshsliteracycoaches.html.

### Roles and Responsibilities of a Literacy Coach, Reading Coach, or Instructional Coach.    A literacy coach or reading coach is a reading specialist who focuses on:

- *Providing professional development for teachers.* Simply put, literacy coaches support teachers in their daily work (Dole, 2004). This can be accomplished informally, through conversations and study groups, or more formally, in consultation, mentoring, modeling, planning, observing, and providing feedback (Lyons & Pinnell, 2001; Rosemary, Roskos, & Landreth, 2007). Coaches give teachers the additional support needed to implement evidence-based programs and practices. They support teachers in goal-setting, self-reflection, and self-assessment. Collaboration is at the heart of the literacy coach's job (Friend & Cook, 2007).

- *Assuming leadership of the school's entire literacy program.* Literacy coaches are often responsible for supervising long-term staff development by creating, supporting, and evaluating long-range program initiatives over extended periods of time (IRA, 2006). Although this may sound similar to the role of the reading specialist, there is an important distinction. Whereas the reading specialist is more concerned with the big picture, the literacy coach is on the front line, assuming a more hands-on approach, working in classrooms directly with teachers. The coach is the one who helps teachers implement the ideas from professional development initiatives in their day-to-day practice. Coaches are guided by evidence from the school or district's assessment processes, both formal and informal, and by their own observations and interactions with teachers.

- *Assuming a team perspective.* Coaches view literacy as essential to learning in all subject areas. This stance is grounded in the belief that all teachers are responsible for incorporating literacy in daily instruction; that content area teachers are best suited to meet the demands of specific text forms in their subject areas; that all are part of a systemic, schoolwide support team; and that fostering collaboration and team-building is vital to improving student outcomes (Cobb, 2005; Kahoun & Bjurlin, 2008).

This last item regarding a team approach is our own suggestion. Although the IRA/LLC definitions include collaboration, a growing body of evidence shows that a collaborative team approach to school reform is more powerful than anyone realized (Cobb, 2005; Fullan, Hill, & Crévola, 2006). The reading coach has a key role in the process. We believe current trends suggest this will be among the fastest growing components of the literacy coach's job in the next decade. We will explore this notion in subsequent chapters addressing the creation of the literacy team and the role of the coach in a number of collaborative efforts.

■ *Author Connection: MaryEllen*  We acknowledge that literacy coaches are sometimes called *reading coaches* or *instructional coaches,* particularly when working with middle and high school teachers. You will notice we sometimes use the term *coach* in this book as an all-encompassing title. Mostly, however, we continue to use the term literacy coach intentionally. We don't care what literacy coaches are called as long as they have the necessary training and expertise to do their jobs. However, we feel strongly that we need to advocate for the role of the *literacy coach* and not dilute the importance of *literacy* in content area instruction. We are literacy professionals first and foremost; and we believe content area teachers are best served when we use our knowledge and expertise as literacy professionals to help them improve their ability to use literacy in service of subject matter learning. We believe everyone benefits, teachers and students, when we focus on what it is we know and do best.

## Models of Literacy Coaching

### Exploring Six Literacy Coaching Models for Reading Professionals

As we explored the various ways in which different groups envisioned the role of literacy coach, we discovered they could almost all be grouped into six distinctive models: Informal Coaching, Mixed Model Coaching, Formal Literacy Coaching, Peer Coaching and Mentoring, Cognitive Coaching, and Clinical Supervision. However, you may find that your situation includes aspects of more than one model. If you are fortunate enough to be designated as a full-time literacy coach, your role may be relatively circumscribed, falling into a single category. However, many coaches are school or district reading specialists whose jobs are being recast. Often, they split their time between acting as a reading specialist and fulfilling their new role as literacy coach. Or they may be part-time Title I reading teachers and part-time literacy coaches. Some are even classroom teachers who have been relieved of a portion of their teaching responsibilities to act as coaches for their colleagues. We developed a matrix entitled Six Literacy Coaching Models for Reading Professionals (see Figure 2.5 on pages 44–45) to help you clarify various ways to define your role as literacy coach.

| Six Literacy Coaching Models for Reading Professionals—Roles and Responsibilities | | |
|---|---|---|
| *Model Description* | *Role* | *Tasks* |
| Informal Coaching Model | Support teachers outside of the classroom through conferences | • Confer with and assist teachers in planning, setting their own goals, developing lessons, and solving problems.<br>• Assist teachers in self-assessment.<br>• Help with materials and provide information.<br>• Participate in professional development with teachers.<br>• Consult on best ways to assess students.<br>• Participate as member of study groups.<br>• Help develop curriculum.<br>• Adopt attitude of co-learner. |
| Mixed Model/Elements of Informal and Formal Literacy Coaching | Support teachers, primarily outside the classroom, but includes some in-class observation | • Begin to look at areas of focus and need; assist in goal setting.<br>• Assist teachers in co-planning lessons, or working with students.<br>• Lead or join study groups.<br>• Lead professional development workshops.<br>• Assist teachers in using assessments to inform instruction.<br>• Confer with individual teachers on their focused goals and progress toward them.<br>• Adopt attitude of knowledgeable co-learner. |
| Formal Literacy Coaching Model | Support teachers primarily within the classroom | • Model lessons and confer with teachers.<br>• Co-teach lessons and strategies.<br>• Provide feedback on classroom events.<br>• Observe and help the teacher plan instruction for specific students or groups.<br>• Lead sustained professional development on teacher- or school-selected goals.<br>• Help teachers analyze video recorded lessons.<br>• Help individuals and groups assess progress toward common goals.<br>• Coordinate study groups.<br>• Assume nonjudgmental role, but assist in instructional improvement by providing focused feedback. |
| Peer Coaching and Mentoring Model | Support teachers in a mentoring role in classroom lesson format | • Model lessons in the classroom.<br>• Engage in co-teaching.<br>• Confer with teachers in pre-lesson planning.<br>• Mentor new teachers or assist with instructional improvement and problem solving. |

**FIGURE 2.5** *Six Literacy Coaching Models for Reading Professionals—Roles and Responsibilities*

| Model Description | Role | Tasks |
|---|---|---|
| Peer Coaching and Mentoring Model (continued) | Support teachers in a mentoring role in classroom lesson format (continued) | • Focus on assisting teachers in meeting administrative goals or schoolwide initiatives.<br>• Lead or coordinate study groups.<br>• Negotiate additional goals and a targeted focus with teachers.<br>• Observe lessons and provide focused feedback and suggestions.<br>• Maintain a nonjudgmental attitude.<br>• Focus on improving instruction.<br>• Assume a collaborative role, but act as experienced educator. |
| Cognitive Coaching Model | Observe teaching; provide focused feedback | • Engage in three-part process: a planning conference, observation, and reflecting.<br>• Jot notes for discussion and feedback.<br>• Focus on teacher's internal thought processes and overt teaching behaviors.<br>• Engage teachers in self-reflection to improve instruction.<br>• Provide suggestions.<br>• Assume a collaborative role, but engage in "guiding and providing suggestions."<br>• Lead or coordinate study groups. |
| Clinical Supervision Model | Evaluate lessons, provide formal feedback on teaching performance | • Primary responsibility is to engage in classroom observation.<br>• Act in a supervisory role.<br>• Assess teaching methods and evaluate performance.<br>• Provide formal written evaluative feedback.<br>• Plan and implement the school's professional development program.<br>• Coordinate schoolwide assessment.<br>• Engage in formal evaluation of teaching performance on which retention and tenure are dependent.<br>• Assume a traditional administrative role. |

**FIGURE 2.5**   (*continued*)

The Six Models organizer contains a wealth of information to enable you to define and compare the various roles involved at each level of coaching. The Six Models are arranged on a continuum from informal to formal. An in-depth description of each of these models can be found on our companion website.

## Revisiting the Vignette: Thinking Points

1. How might an understanding of the six models of literacy coaching help Caitlin and her principal begin a productive dialogue?
2. Which of these models do you think could prove the most useful for Caitlin?
3. Which model most closely resembles the way literacy coaches are used in your school?

### *The Literacy Coach: Qualifications*

Because the recommendations of IRA, NCTE, and LLC *include* literacy coaching as one of the roles of the reading specialist, no distinction is made between the qualifications for the two roles. There is an excellent reason for this. It is an attempt by IRA to ensure that those hired as literacy coaches are qualified individuals and to eliminate the widely varying criteria used by schools to fill literacy coaching positions, sometimes with unqualified people. Sharon Frost and Rita Bean (2006) explain that the scramble to fill literacy coaching positions happened so rapidly that standards for coaches were not yet in place. In 2004, IRA published *The Roles and Qualifications of the Reading Coach in the United States,* suggesting that coaches: (1) have experience and expertise at the grade level in which they will teach; (2) are knowledgeable in all aspects of reading processes, including assessment; (3) have experience working with teachers; (4) are excellent presenters and group leaders; and (5) have experience modeling in classrooms and providing feedback to teachers (Dole, 2004). Few of the first literacy coaches met those standards. The new directives added the expectation that a master's degree in reading include a supervised practicum in coaching.

IRA's *Standards for Middle and High School Literacy Coaches* (2006) and Betty Sturtevant's 2006 guide for middle and high school principals suggest that secondary coaches must also have fundamental knowledge and skills in the academic areas in which they will be coaching, such as science and mathematics. Therefore, we believe that not "just anyone" can be a literacy coach. Even an expert reading teacher with a high degree of knowledge about the research behind principled practice might not possess the content knowledge, the leadership qualities, the ability to give presentations, or the people skills necessary to fill this complex and challenging role. A Want Ad for the position might read something like this:

> **Wanted: Literacy Coach**   Seeking skilled literacy professional with master's degree in reading who requires little sleep. Must be good listener, diplomat, able to withstand resistance, keep a secret, multitask, and teach all ages from preschool to adult. Must have patience of Job, wisdom of Solomon, instant access to answers for all questions, and be able to provide materials on demand or develop them rapidly. Prefer someone with background in sales, cheerleading, counseling, public speaking, conflict resolution, and Olympic coaching—preferably in track and field.

One more thing: As Jan Dole (2004, p. 468) points out, it certainly helps to have a sense of humor. What this ad fails to convey is the deep satisfaction realized by reading specialists and literacy coaches when they see the changes that happen in themselves and others as they face the day-to-day challenges and rewards that come with the job.

Between 2000 and 2010, a number of researchers and authors expressed concern about the way schools were filling coaching positions (Toll, 2005; McKenna & Walpole,

2008; Wepner & Strickland, 2008). Research by Frost and Bean (2006) went on to confirm what many suspected:

- A number of highly qualified reading specialists had little education or experience in *coaching*.
- Some positions were filled with respected classroom teachers who lacked reading-related advanced degrees, but were known for their expertise in literacy instruction and their ability to collaborate with peers.
- On the other end of the spectrum, researchers discovered that some administrators were filling coaching positions with individuals who were performing poorly in the classroom, or those reassigned because their jobs were being eliminated.

By establishing standards that include literacy coaches and reading specialists, the International Reading Association is raising the bar. IRA is also setting the stage for universities to implement the newest level of professional development, *The Literacy Coaching Endorsement*. Educators see it as part of a career path for the literacy professional. A number of institutions are offering coursework leading to the Literacy Coach Endorsement and these programs include the supervised coaching practicum advocated by IRA. Concurrently, a number of states are beginning to establish their own licensure requirements, and those of us who champion the rights of children to receive quality literacy instruction are delighted (IRA, 2007). We are fairly certain that these initiatives will continue, although the rate of implementation will be affected by economic conditions.

## Dealing with Negative People and Learning from Your Mistakes

Who of us has not dealt with a negative colleague and come away knowing we handled it poorly? In many such situations we wish we were back on the playground and could yell, "Do Over!" as we did so long ago when there was a dispute about whether the ball was in or out. Unfortunately, we don't get to go back and erase our mistakes, but we do get to learn from them. The beauty of a mistake is that it causes us pain, embarrassment, guilt, or merely discomfort. In short, it motivates us to change. Nobody sitting in a recliner, wrapped in a warm blanket with a good book and a cup of hot cocoa was ever motivated to change.

When we deal with negative people, we sometimes say or do the wrong thing. In a weird way, the literacy coaching model, particularly Cathy Toll's (2005) informal model, can teach us a great deal about our style of interaction that we can carry over to ordinary encounters at home and at school. There are two important things you can do when dealing with negative people. The first is to listen, really listen, to what the person is saying and what the person is meaning. These can be two different things. The second thing is to ask rather than answer. Often, we misunderstand people's messages or their motives because we are thinking about our reply. A great way to counteract this is to pause whenever you are about to make a negative reply and say, "Could you tell me a little more about that?" or "I need to think about that. Can you explain more about your position?" The worst that can happen is that you *do* end up understanding more about just how misguided this person is!

More than likely, by showing the person that you are genuinely interested and respectful enough to want to find out more, the situation deescalates and you walk away with greater understanding and maybe even tolerance.

## New Directions: Issues and Perspectives for Literacy Professionals

A number of trends are evident in a review of resources and practices:

**1.** *Overlapping definitions of reading specialist and literacy coach.* It seems to us we have come full circle. In 2003, when we published the first edition of this book, the role of the literacy coach was just emerging as a function of the reading specialist's job. By the second edition, in 2007, most publications addressed reading specialists and literacy coaches as two separate job titles. Now, it seems that once again, as our previous discussion demonstrates, *literacy coach* is a subcategory of the *reading specialist* roles and responsibilities.

**2.** *The struggle to find successful literacy models for secondary and middle schools.* Particularly since the unveiling of the six Carnegie reports of the 2010 Time to Act adolescent literacy directives (see Chapter 9), schools are struggling to define the roles of reading professionals with regard to content area learning, assessment, and successful RtI structures.

**3.** *New literacies and literacy professionals.* We recognize the challenges in reconciling in- and out-of-school literacies and building an evidence base for incorporating new technologies and literacies in service of learning goals. This will be an area in which the literacy professional will need to remain current and find ways to support teachers in implementing strategies that research shows are effective.

**4.** *Professional development.* This is another area where practice is preceding research. The coach and specialist must continue to explore models of professional learning communities (PLC) that are increasing teacher effectiveness and enhancing student learning.

**5.** *Standards reform for literacy professionals.* Changing standards for literacy professionals and teachers are increasing the levels of education, accountability, and expertise expected of all who work with students and teachers. These require commitment of funds, time, and resources for materials, professional development, and administrative support.

**6.** *An increasingly diverse population.* New standards from a number of sources and organizations are addressing the need to improve outcomes for a student population characterized by diversity in culture and language. We see these challenges as opportunities. Every day we are gaining new insights on how to facilitate English acquisition and learning. We believe this focus will lead to new titles and classifications of reading professionals.

Revised standards for reading professionals and students help clarify what is expected of educators and literacy learners. They enhance the professional credibility of teachers by ensuring that the best practices, based on research, are being implemented by highly trained, knowledgeable, and efficacious individuals. However, we believe those who mandate high standards have a moral obligation to provide the additional resources necessary to meet the demands.

## BEYOND THE BOOK

### *Chapter 2 Focus Issue: Communication as Key to Effective Leadership*

One of the biggest changes in recent years for all of us is the ever increasing ease with which we can connect to others, share ideas, and disseminate information. We challenge you to think about the ways in which the reading professionals' jobs can be made more efficient through electronic forms of communication.

1. Within the next week, be aware of how information is handled in your school. Jot some notes for yourself or keep a list.
2. Be especially aware of how many paper copies could have been handled better electronically. Are any pieces of communication requiring feedback that would have been more effective in electronic form?
3. Also, ask yourself whether there are any items that you received electronically that were unnecessary? Were there some that would have been better left in paper form?

Throughout this book, especially in the chapters dealing with creating a literacy team, conducting a needs assessment, creating a two-year plan and implementing professional development, continue to ask yourself which of the resources lend themselves to electronic dissemination. Certainly most teacher surveys fall into this category.

Of course these newer ways to communicate are not without problems (challenges).

1. Ease of dissemination results in a great deal of junk in our email inboxes. Make sure each piece you are sending is important. If teachers are flooded with missives from you, they will look at your messages and say, "Oh, no, not him (or her) again!"
2. Create group or Facebook sites for teams and study groups to communicate efficiently. However, establish guidelines to prevent problems, such as one or two people "overcommunicating." After all, the group won't function efficiently if time is wasted reading trivia.

Our best advice is to model effective use of technology. As new vehicles are created, be the one to learn how to use them. In your quest to be a good leader, always look for ways to save time and facilitate communication by using all of the tools in your communication toolbox.

■ *Group Inquiry Activity*  This activity is designed for groups of four or more.

1. Half of the group will be assigned to reread the vignette about Caitlin and Ann. The others will be assigned to reread the Author Connection piece about Frank, the coach.
2. As you read your assigned piece, make a list of elements of effective coaching and provide an example, interaction, or phrase that illustrates each element.

3. As you compare notes, see how many elements of good coaching practice these pieces have in common.
4. With the members of both groups, list the three most important things literacy coaches can learn from sports coaches.

## Supervising Reading Specialists

If you are among the few reading professionals working as a district-level reading specialist and are assigned to supervise other reading specialists or literacy coaches, we suggest you adopt elements of the Formal Literacy Coaching Model and adapt them to your situation. This approach incorporates the best of the several models. One element involves guiding those you supervise to create their own goals. Your role is to support them as they engage in a process of growth and change. Another element of your job usually involves observation and feedback, hopefully in nonthreatening ways. Of course, if decisions about job retention are involved, you will have to proceed very honestly about your role and be genuine in your mission to help the person you are supervising to succeed. The hallmark of good leaders is the ability to evoke the best in those with whom they work. Your favorite administrator can provide the mentorship you may need to learn this often complex process.

## Study Groups

Within a single day, teachers must make hundreds, perhaps thousands, of decisions. Decision making requires three abilities according to Wasserman, as cited in Robb (2000a, p. 81):

1. the ability to observe students, then compare observations to similar and different situations and theoretical knowledge;
2. the ability to analyze the data collected from observations by selecting key points; and
3. the ability to interpret these points by forming hypotheses or hunches that lead to informed action.

An on-site study group can be organized to meet weekly or monthly to help teachers make decisions about issues related to teaching and learning. The purpose of the study groups is to read research articles, study theoretical perspectives, and work together as teacher researchers to observe student behaviors within the context of topics that are mutually explored. The study groups can meet as grade-level groups, small groups within a school's faculty, or groups that are comprised of teachers and specialists from throughout the district (Robb, 2000a). Reading specialists can play a key role in organizing and facilitating the study groups by soliciting interest in particular topics, providing access to journal articles and books, and working with the teachers to negotiate topics, the curriculum, and the roles of the participants.

Generally, study groups involve those who are willing to set aside the time and then follow through with the mutually agreed-on agenda. The group establishes a purpose, such as deciding how to group students effectively and flexibly for literacy instruction. A couple of volunteers research the books that are available on the topic, and study group members select one to begin their reading. They purchase multiple copies using a small grant from their school's PTO (Parent-Teacher Organization), determine discussion responsibilities, and set a time line for their meetings. They also establish a loose set of "ground rules" for their study group, such as committing to read the agreed-on chapters, promising to show up for scheduled discussion meetings, and deciding who brings the always-necessary refreshments. As with any group, study groups create their own culture, and when ground rules are established and agreed on early in the process, it is more likely that the study group will reach its goals.

While coaching several teachers in the same school (or reading specialists in the district), you might find some common issues tied to implementing your long-term literacy goals that would work well for study group topics. We recommend that you take a shared ownership approach to the study group process. The group belongs to everyone involved, and we recommend that your group rotate the role of facilitator, and that you share as a colleague (not an expert) in discussions. In some groups, a volunteer takes notes or keeps minutes of the group's activities; however, we have participated in groups where individuals kept journals and shared them during sessions. If you haven't participated in a study group at your school, we encourage you to do so. It can be an immensely rewarding experience.

## *Saving the Best for Last: Beginning the Job of Reading Specialist and/or Literacy Coach*

We purposely saved this topic until the end of the chapter because we liked the idea of ending with a new beginning. The more fundamental reason, however, was because now that you know all of the options for the role of the reading specialist or literacy coach, you are ready to carve your own path and negotiate your own role. Starting a new position is exciting and may fill your head with possibilities and hope. Some of you will begin careers as literacy coaches in new schools. More of you will begin your literacy coaching careers on home turf. The challenge inherent in assuming a new or additional role once you have been working in a school is that even if you understand your new position, others may not. In earlier chapters, we suggested that new reading specialists negotiate a job description. This is even more important for literacy coaches because of the wide variation in the way the role is defined and perceived. Particularly if you wear more than one hat, such as combination reading specialist and literacy coach, you need to let others know when you are acting as one or the other. This is tricky, even for the most seasoned professional. The first step is to meet with administrators and negotiate your role. As we mentioned, you may be in the enviable position of guiding your administrator in crafting your job description. Here are some steps you might take in the process.

**1.** *Meet with your administrator.* Ask your administrator what he or she hopes to achieve by adding a reading specialist or literacy coach to the school program. Listen carefully to the answer. This is a crucial conversation with potential for serious repercussions in your life and your career. It is imperative that you prepare for this discussion. Anticipate what your administrator might say, and think about how you will respond to a number of different ideas. Your motto here is, "No surprises!"

**2.** *Have a clear idea of your ideal role as a literacy professional.* Try to think like your administrator and figure out what she or he needs to hear. For example, focus on the administrator's goals. If it appears you are being asked to add to your responsibilities rather than reallocate your time, you might be tempted to recite all the things you already do and explain that you don't have time to add anything else to your schedule. This is honest, but not politically savvy. The focus is on *you*. Your administrator wants to hear that you have the goals of the *school* in mind. A better way to express this sentiment is to say, "This is a wonderful opportunity to achieve our goal of (fill in the blank) by expanding my job description to include literacy coaching. What portion of my time will we need to devote to this? Let's figure out how to reallocate some of my reading specialist responsibilities so we can accomplish our goal."

**3.** *Negotiate a job description.* The next thing you will have to do is to redefine your duties and responsibilities. Approach this task in the spirit of collaboration. Ask your administrator to help you figure out exactly what your job entails. You might want to use the IRA guidelines or the Six Model chart and your school's needs assessment and two-year plan to guide your deliberation. Again, this is a crucial discussion. Before you walk into that office, you should have a fairly clear idea of what you want your role as literacy coach or reading specialist to look like. Figure out each of your envisioned responsibilities and be prepared to explain how each component fits into the goals of the school. Since we are into mottos in this chapter, the one for this section is "Keep your eye on the prize." Your goal is to walk out of this meeting with an outline of your written job description.

**4.** *Disseminate the job description.* Despite reading specialists' best intentions and hard work, there will always be teachers and administrators who still do not understand how you fill your day. Reading specialists have been around for decades and there is still an aura of mystery out there. Literacy coaches' jobs are even more obscure to their teaching colleagues. We suggest asking your administrator how the two of you will make sure everyone is informed and on the same page about what you can and can't do as a literacy coach. It is especially important that teachers understand your nonevaluative and nonjudgmental role. Publishing your job description on the school website or newsletter, or distributing a written copy at the next faculty meeting is an excellent way to get the message out about your new role.

## Revisiting the Vignette

By now, you probably have realized that the literacy coach, Caitlin Howard, was put in a very difficult position by her principal, Ed Tagliano. Although he was looking to the literacy coach to work with Alex, the new teacher, Ed was unfamiliar with the role of the literacy coach. When Caitlin and Ed met and listened to one another, they decided that Caitlin will support Alex in reflecting about his lessons. She will guide him as he identifies his own goals and discovers how to accomplish them. Rather than telling him what to do, she will focus on what he wants to learn. Caitlin has learned a great deal from Ann. She feels confident that with her supportive assistance, Alex will continue to grow as a teacher while, at the same time, she will grow in her ability to serve him as his literacy coach.

## Points to Remember

Much has changed since the new millennium. Developments in how we envision the role of the reading specialist as coach, and the addition of coaches who are not credentialed reading specialists, have revolutionized the way we supervise and support teachers and their students. Government funds allocated for literacy improvement have resulted in powerful new models of professional development. Reading specialists and literacy coaches are attaining new levels of professionalism and responsibility. Literacy coaching models have largely transformed the notions of peer coaching and cognitive coaching, although these models are still found to be useful and effective in many schools. Teachers are making decisions about what they want to know and be able to do, and wise administrators and coaches are supporting these endeavors. Most surprising and gratifying is the fact that our colleagues in the middle and secondary schools are beginning to join us in our mission. All in all, there is new hope on the horizon for the future of literacy in the United States.

## Portfolio and Self-Assessment Projects

1. Review the Six Literacy Coaching Models. Choose elements from the various models to describe your ideal vision of what a literacy coach should be and do. For each component you select, explain your rationale. Create a web or other graphic organizer to illustrate your vision.

2. Synthesizing all of the examples in this chapter, describe the ways in which an effective informal literacy coach interacts with a teacher during a conference. Write a five-minute dialogue including what each might say in the meeting.

3. Write a job description for a newly hired districtwide reading specialist in charge of the reading program for a city of 50,000 people with fourteen elementary schools, three middle schools, and two high schools.

4. Select a professional development goal for yourself. Create a two-year plan, including a step-by-step implementation plan describing how you will work toward accomplishing your goal.

## Recommended Readings: Suggestions for Book Clubs, Study Groups, and Professional Development

Dole, J. A. (2004). The changing role of the reading specialist in school reform. *The Reading Teacher, 57,* 462–471. This article discusses the evolution of the reading specialist's role to that of literacy coach and research on how reading coaches meet an important need in teachers' professional development.

Moran, M. C. (2007). *Differentiated literacy coaching: Scaffolding for student and teacher success.* Alexandria, VA: ASCD. This is an excellent, practical guide, and a staple for the literacy coach's professional library. It contains a number of professional learning modules and especially interesting role-playing vignettes for literacy coaches.

Sturtevant, E. G. (2006). *The literacy coach: A key to improving teaching and learning in secondary schools.* Washington, DC: Alliance for Excellent Education. This is a comprehensive breakthrough document, supported by the Carnegie Foundation. If you are considering applying for one of the many available secondary literacy coaching positions, don't miss this guide.

## Online Resources

**http://www.literacycoachingonline.org**
The Literacy Coaching Clearinghouse is an essential resource. This comprehensive site is invaluable with its checklists, step-by-step guidance on professional development, team leadership, classroom planning, observation, evaluation, self-assessment, and more. It was the first to develop a special set of resources for the "instructional coach" at the middle and high school levels.

## Companion Website Resources

The following resources to support and extend your learning of this chapter can be found on our companion website (waveland.com/Extra_Material/32979/): key vocabulary, concepts, and other terms; extended examples; updated resources specifically tied to information in the chapter; related websites; and other support features. Also included on our companion website is a template for the Sample Role Matrix for Reading Specialists and Literacy Coaches (Figure 2.4) and a narrative discussion of each of the Six Literacy Coaching Models.

# 3

# *Forming a Literacy Team and Creating a Literacy Vision*

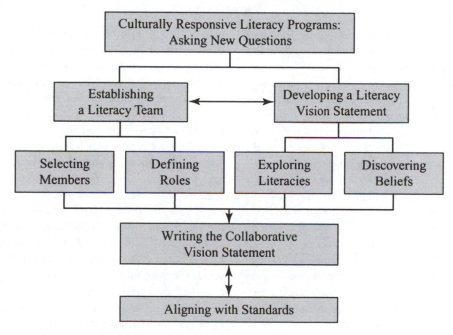

**FIGURE 3.1**   *Chapter Overview*

## *Learning Goals*

After reading, discussing, and engaging in activities related to this chapter, you will be able to:

1. Develop a context-driven written vision statement that is consistent with district, state, and IRA/NCTE Reading/Language Arts Standards.
2. Establish a collaborative literacy team and define the role of the team within the decision-making structures of the school and community.

3. *Personal Learning Goal:* In a three-minute brainstorming session, share what you know about developing a vision statement and establishing a literacy team. Write a goal or a question that reflects something you want to learn as we explore these topics. Share this with others in your group.

## Standards for Reading Professionals

This chapter provides focused support for current IRA Standards for Reading Professionals. See our companion website (waveland.com/Extra_Material/32979/) for a complete listing of the standards that align with this chapter.

### Vignette

Mark has been a fourth-grade teacher for seven years at a midsized (600 students), midwestern suburban elementary school. Recently, he completed a master's degree in reading, was hired as a reading specialist, and told by the principal that he was expected to "improve the reading program." Mark is a highly respected professional with excellent people skills. Teachers are relieved to let the responsibility for the reading program fall to him.

Although the neighborhood was formerly one of economic privilege, it is now almost entirely comprised of white middle-class English-speaking families. Fewer than twenty African American students attend the school. However, within the last five years, a small but growing number of Hmong families have moved into an area bordering the city and the suburb. Approximately fifteen students in the elementary school speak Hmong as the primary language of their home. The largest reformed synagogue in the metropolitan area is two blocks from the school and approximately one out of five students is from a home in which Judaism is practiced to varying degrees. Most of these students attend Hebrew classes and participate in activities at the Jewish Community Center. The school schedules in-service and professional development for teachers on the High Holy Days.

Of the forty-four teachers at Cedar Park Elementary, Mark is one of two African American males. The son of a bus driver and a third-grade teacher, Mark was raised in a predominantly African American middle-class urban neighborhood adjacent to this suburb, and experienced the undercurrents of distrust and prejudice between the adjoining Jewish and African American communities as he was growing up.

District test scores have stagnated in the last decade, hovering just above the state average for all schools, but slightly lower than schools with similar demographics. Officially, the school has always used a commercial reading series, but many teachers just close the door and "do their own thing." Recently the state has joined many other states in revising its model academic standards for reading/language arts to reflect the Uniform Academic Core Standards and evidence-based practice. The new standards have greatly increased the emphasis on content area reading at the elementary level. The state Department of Public Instruction is requiring every district to specify the classroom practices that align with each standard. Mark has been assigned the job of rewriting and aligning curriculum with standards. These must reflect what students should know and be able to do, how they will demonstrate this knowledge and ability, and how well they must perform. The standards will also shape the way teachers must teach.

## Thinking Point

Mark is at a loss as to where to begin to "improve the reading program." What are the first three things you suggest that Mark should do?

## Expanding the Vignette: Exploring the Issues

*There is a push for "transparency," making the district's vision, the scientifically-based practices, and the outcomes public. Mark distributes copies of the forty-page new standards for reading/language arts to all the teachers. The document lists content proficiencies students should acquire by the end of fourth, eighth, and twelfth grades. Rather than helping, the document has increased anxiety levels. The fourth-grade teachers are particularly anxious because they notice gaps in the knowledge of students depending on what was taught in previous grades and how it was taught.*

*Fortunately, these are faculty members who seem to value the ideas of others. Mark has always had a vision for the direction the reading program should take. Isn't a vision already implicit in the way things are done in the school? Mark knows that is not enough. Now it must be a written document with a follow-up plan. He wonders whether it's wise or ethical for any one person to develop a "shared vision" for the district. The district is changing; resources are more scarce; mandates and standards are changing; and Mark is convinced the reading program belongs to everyone.*

## Thinking Points

1. What additional issues can you identify?
2. What are some strengths that can be useful to Mark as his school begins to address the problems?
3. What are some short-term suggestions you would give Mark?
4. What long-term measures should Mark consider?

Keep your answers to these questions in mind as you read. We will revisit the vignette at the end of this chapter.

# Culturally Responsive Literacy Programs: Asking New Questions

Mark's position as reading specialist forces him to examine the literacy program in his school systemically. Until now, little attention has been focused on establishing a cohesive, systematic schoolwide literacy program. Indeed, few teachers know how reading is being taught in the classroom next door, nor do they know much about their colleagues' beliefs about reading/language arts instruction.

We believe in the power of the past to inform the future. Therefore, in the previous chapters, we provided an historical overview of reading instruction and a review of the evolution of the reading specialist. In this chapter, we guide the reading specialist in creating a literacy team whose mission is improving the school's literacy program. Included are possible roles and responsibilities of the team and its members, with emphasis on team building, collaborative problem solving, agency, and context. Two literacy cases are used to mediate understandings of the notions of "communities" and "literacies." The chapter concludes with a step-by-step, collaborative framework to identify core beliefs and develop a written vision statement.

■ *Author Connection: Brenda*  In my many years as an educator, I cannot count the number of times I heard a teacher say, "I close my door and I do my own thing." I probably said it myself, especially when I began my career as a first-grade teacher in an urban Milwaukee school at the height of the Civil Rights movement. Of course, I was searching for that one right way to teach reading and I was pretty certain I was zeroing in on it. Do I still believe teachers should possess a high degree of agency over the ways they conduct literacy activities in their classrooms? Of course, I do; MaryEllen and I both do. But we also believe there are some fundamental understandings that must support the decisions teachers make. Although the social and cultural context of Mark's school setting is very different from that in which I first taught, the fundamental questions necessary to develop dynamic, effective, and socially responsive literacy programs are the same. What is literacy? What do we know about evidence-based literacy instruction? What are the beliefs and cultural forces that shape the ways in which literacy is defined and used in and out of school within the various literacy "communities"? Who has agency in the decision-making processes?

It may seem to Mark that finding answers to these questions is a daunting task, and, indeed, it will require a substantial amount of work, especially if he reverts to traditional hierarchical leadership models. Mark will need to find new ways to think about these questions if he is to realize the hopes he has for building a strong program. He knows he can't do it alone. In this chapter, we will explore ways to define shared vision, the kind that supports the agency of teachers, parents, administrators, and students.

## Establishing the Literacy Team

### Teachers and Teamwork

Teamwork. It is evident in the heroic deeds of Red Cross volunteers working in teams to assist the victims of disasters. It is also evident in more humble feats, such as in the preparation of the fast-food cheeseburger, the result of a sophisticated ballet of teamwork. Yet, in 1993, Gene Maeroff, senior fellow at the Carnegie Institute for the Advancement of Teaching, pointed out that teamwork, for almost any purpose, was foreign to most teachers. Often the degree to which teachers were deemed successful was measured by how adept they were at working alone. It is probably safe to assume that most people recognize the power of teamwork to solve both long- and short-term problems and bring about change. Richard Wellins and his colleagues found that teamwork resulted in (1) increased knowledge and expertise, (2) ownership, and (3) empowerment for participants (Wellins, Byham, & Wilson, 1991). In Figure 3.2, we applied these assumptions to school literacy teams.

### A Strong Case for Creating a Literacy Team

What is the purpose of the literacy team? The literacy team is responsible for creating and implementing a collaborative vision with the goal of improving the school's literacy education program. Team members support a common vision, work to enhance the efficacy of all teachers through multiple professional development endeavors, support all levels of

---

### The Value of Literacy Teams

Literacy teams capitalize on the following strengths of teachers:

**Knowledge and Expertise**
Teachers are closest to their work. They are experts with a great deal of individual and collective knowledge and experience in the teaching of literacy. They know best how to enhance and improve their jobs.

**Ownership**
Most teachers want to feel that they "own" their jobs. They consider themselves professionals, capable of making meaningful contributions to the literacy goals of their school and community.

**Empowerment**
The Literacy Team provides possibilities for empowerment not available to individual teachers. Teams are given authority for important decisions about the fundamental nature and direction of the literacy program. Traditionally, such authority has been the sole province of administrators.

---

**FIGURE 3.2    *The Value of Literacy Teams: Underlying Assumptions***

programming and evidence-based practice, and make data-driven decisions. They create a long-term plan, unique to the needs and goals of the school, grounded in evidence based on multiple data resources, and embodied in their collaborative vision. Every endeavor of the team has one ultimate goal: *to ensure that all students receive the best possible literacy instruction.* With the growing presence of the literacy coach, collaboration and shared vision are much more a part of the school fabric. Today, we are able to combine what we learned from the educational leadership field (Deal & Peterson, 1999; Fullan, Hill, & Crévola, 2006) and the business community (Wellins, Byham, & Wilson, 1991) with a rapidly growing body of research from our own literacy colleagues related to forming teams and making them effective. We now have strong evidence that literacy teams have the capacity to improve teachers' classroom practice and students' learning (Cobb, 2005; Kahoun & Bjurlin, 2008; Fisher & Frey, 2007; Lambert, 2002). We need teams because we face challenges as educators that cannot be solved by any one person, for example:

- Improving literacy levels of all students.
- Reversing the growing inequities in achievement among subgroups within the school population.
- Creatively managing resources in times of economic constraints.
- Meeting the needs of an increasingly diverse population of students.
- Demonstrating the use of evidence-based instruction tied to "value-added" student outcomes.
- Gathering and analyzing complex sets of data used in decision making.
- Coordinating intervention systems and assessments.

Mostly, we need literacy teams because, when we structure them according to scientifically based principles of effectiveness, they work!

Teams are *communities* with a focus; they are affinity groups at their best. Kathy Hinchman and Patty Anders (2009) make a strong case for solving problems through "community." Among the points they make in support of using literacy teams (communities) to solve our problems are:

- Literacy is social; we construct meaning in networks with others.
- School is the place where literacy is at the center of all we do.
- We use reading and writing to solve problems, conduct business, communicate, exchange ideas, and construct knowledge.
- Perspectives anchored in individuals leave us blaming individuals when things go wrong, but grounding in community makes us all responsible for each of us.

Historically, the school's principal assumed autonomy over instructional leadership. And yet, with all the changes in the last twenty years, it seems obvious that no one person can have the knowledge, expertise, wisdom, time, or experience to do it all and do it well. Literacy teams make sense today more than ever.

### The Process of Forming a Literacy Team

Search any business section of the library and you will see a dazzling array of snappy titles about working in teams; these titles contain phrases like *unlimited team achievement* and *getting your team into high gear.* You get the idea. The point is that as much as we hear teachers decry the mentality of fostering the business model for running a school, we have gained much from "taking what we needed and leaving the rest." Many of the books written about supervision and administration of reading programs provide a wealth of information on the tasks that teams perform (Bean, 2009; McKenna & Walpole, 2008; Wepner & Strickland, 2008). In addition, a growing number of educational institutes, professional organizations, foundations, and U.S. Department of Education sites are developing excellent resources to guide team planning. We will provide you with a number of resources in this chapter.

### Possible Members of the Literacy Team

Although most resources supply lists of potential team members, little guidance is given about the considerations and challenges associated with the composition of teams. A school's literacy team is made up of a variety of stakeholders, often with seven to fifteen members (Patty, Maschoff, & Ransom, 1996). You want enough people to get the job done without having group size hinder efficiency. Usually, a team has representatives from several groups, including administrators; reading specialists; teachers; other support personnel such as psychologists, media specialists, and Title I teachers; and perhaps students, parents, and community members (Hinchman & Anders, 2009; Shearer & Vogt, 2004). There is some debate about whether parents and students should participate fully (or at all) in team processes or act in an advisory capacity. Many such decisions are site specific. The composition of the team will depend on the social context of your school and community as well as your specific goals and needs. Developing written job descriptions and team expectations is an important component of establishing the team.

## Issues Surrounding Effective Literacy Team Building

Building a literacy team appears to be a relatively straightforward process. Why then do we see so many team efforts fail to reach their goals? Gene Maeroff (1993) sees some elements present in effective teams that are missing in the usual school teams and committees. One is that an effective team understands how to *be* a team, a unit that sees itself as a force for change.

It's not enough to say, "OK, everybody! Get into groups. Now, cooperate." In 1997, Garmston warned that to form school improvement teams without teaching members the basics of working collaboratively is to invite disaster. We believe this notion may be even more important today as schools attempt to function more collaboratively. Garmston used this analogy to make his point. He asked how a baseball team could function if its players didn't know the difference between a bunt and a grand slam, or the roles and skills required to play first base as compared to center field. In sports we often hear that players need to learn "the fundamentals" of the game. So do educators.

It must be clear that each literacy team member is not acting with autonomy, but as a representative, willing to promote a group agenda. The first task for the team is to define the role of its members. For example:

> The responsibility of each member of the literacy team is to represent a specific group; to bring ideas, concerns, and suggestions from that group to the literacy team; and to disseminate the ideas, plans, and activities of the literacy team to the group.

Among the characteristics of effective teams are shared identity, clear focus, diversity of perspectives, role clarity, high levels of collaboration, administrative support, effective decision-making strategies, and continuous self-assessment (Gordon, 2004). This is a tall order, indeed! We suggest you make a checklist of these characteristics (remember, continuous self-assessment is one of them) and use it as a guide to team performance and progress.

## Asking the Right Questions

For the literacy team to begin its work, there are a number of important questions to be asked and discussed with school and/or district leaders and administrators.

1. What is the administrative support for the mission of the literacy team, such as adequate planning time and, most importantly, authority of the team to make decisions?
2. Are there provisions for training teachers in effective collaboration that is culturally responsive and consistent with discourse models of the school and of the various communities?
3. What measures will be taken to include all voices?
4. Is there a system to replace members in staggered two- or three-year terms to ensure continuity?

5. How will the group anticipate problems and adjust the process?
6. What are possible barriers related to people, resources, scheduling, attitudes, and training, and what proactive measures are in place for dealing with each of them?
7. How will the all-school literacy plan be assessed, adjusted, and modified using a formative model for short- and long-term goals?
8. How will the team disseminate information on programs, assessments, goals, and outcomes to the various communities in and out of the school?

Undoubtedly, as you start this process, you and your team members will think of additional issues. By dealing with some of these up front, the literacy team can avoid a number of roadblocks normally encountered in school literacy initiatives.

## Literacies and Communities: Asking New Questions

### What Are Literacy Communities?

Earlier in the chapter, we introduced the term *community* with regard to the literacy team. Because it is a grounding concept throughout the book, it deserves further explanation. In a complex social system such as a school or district, there are many subsystems, or communities. In her definition of *community*, Elizabeth Moje (2000) refers to circles of "position and power" to those of "kinship or friendship." Jim Gee (2004) refers to "affinity groups" or "affinity spaces." Individuals may belong to a number of these communities, many of which overlap.

We have purposely defined the term *community* as loosely as possible so educators can explore the concept in multiple and perhaps even novel ways. Within these communities, language and literacy may be used, valued, and defined in unique or highly specific ways. Some are more obvious than others, such as signs and billboards written in languages other than English. Some stretch our notions of traditional forms of literacy. These might include graffiti, online 'zines, artwork, blogs, music, fanfic, Facebook, Twitter, wikis, daytime dramas, cartoons, and logos on clothing. Others may involve values and the pragmatics of language, such as the way adults are addressed by children, the use of nonverbal signs and symbols to signify greeting, the way language is used in rites and ceremonies, or the emphasis on oral language over written language. Given the varied and complex ways in which humans construct meaning in social contexts, educators are moving beyond traditional text-based definitions of literacy to acknowledge multimodalities and multiliteracies (Knobel & Lankshear, 2009; Street, 2005). The challenge is to find ways to bring these multiliteracies and texts into the service of school and community goals.

## BEYOND THE BOOK

### Chapter 3 Focus Issue: Which Literacies Do We Privilege? Two Case Studies
To illustrate the concepts of communities and literacies, consider the two cases in Figure 3.3.

■ *Group Inquiry Activity* In groups of three or four:

1. List the literacies you can identify in Eric's home and community cultures.
2. List the literacies you can identify in Carmen's home and community cultures.

3. Put a checkmark next to those that would be honored and included in school literacy activities.
4. Analyze the experiences of both and decide how these events relate to current literacy perspectives.
5. How would your group define *communities?*
6. How would your group define *literacies?*
7. Make a list of some of the affinity groups (communities) to which members of your group belong. What are the unique literacies practiced in these groups?

---

**Case 1: Eric Torgerson**

Eric Torgerson was raised in a small midwestern community with a strong Protestant Scandinavian heritage. Although a few of the older residents spoke a bit of Swedish or Norwegian, English was almost exclusively the language of the home and community. After attending the nearby Lutheran college, Eric chose teaching as his life's work. He has taught fifth grade for twenty-two years and has a master's degree in elementary education. His wife, Jan, is a nurse and their twin sons attend the local high school. Eric identifies with the community of teachers who are politically conservative, and he is on the bargaining committee for the local teachers' union. It is safe to say that many would characterize him as serious and hardworking. Eric's father was a gifted and respected secondary mathematics and physics teacher. His parents were strict, even by the standards of the community, and the children were not allowed to venture far from home. Music was central to the culture of the Torgerson home. All of Eric's siblings received musical training from their mother, a talented pianist, and two of the seven children became professional musicians with symphony orchestras. Like his siblings, Eric can play a variety of instruments: violin, piano, tuba, and recorder. Holidays often featured performances by the family orchestra. Education was also highly valued in Eric's home. The children were surrounded by print, including newspapers, magazines, and shelves of nonfiction and fiction, many of them part of the traditional Western literary "canon." Lively family debates about politics, religion, and philosophy were standard at dinner-

time. Eric and his siblings were expected to know the issues of the day, and even the younger children were encouraged to voice reasoned opinions. Eric has continued to engage in the activities he loved as a child. He plays the organ at church and meets weekly to jam with three other local jazz musicians. He has a strong commitment to civic duty and has served on the boards of the town library and historical society. His interest in the history of the area, particularly that of the St. Croix River around 1900, is reflected in the research and writing he continues to do, made easier by all the online resources available today. Eric remains an avid reader, devouring books about philosophy and politics. Eric's wife and sons share his love of music. The Torgerson traditions live on as a new generation of visitors are treated to informal concerts by the family quartet.

**Case 2: Carmen Coballes-Vega**

When she was six, Carmen Coballes-Vega moved with her family from rural Arecibo, Puerto Rico, to the Lower East Side of Manhattan. Most of the adults there spoke Spanish or Italian, and their children were able to speak at least some English as well. Carmen's father worked as a courier for the New York Stock Exchange and her mother cared for children in their apartment. Carmen was the first member of her family to learn English. A neighbor showed her how to write her "full name" and helped her obtain a library card. Soon curiosity led her from the small nearby library to the medieval fortress on Fifty-Third Street. To get

*(continued)*

---

**FIGURE 3.3**  *Which Literacies Do We Privilege? Two Case Studies*

there, Carmen had to negotiate the subway system by herself. It was in this dusty old NYC library that Carmen Coballes-Vega became a lover of literacy, loading her arms with books and faithfully returning for more a week later. She describes a number of literacy experiences outside of those traditionally honored by the school: the beautiful ballads her father sang to her as he strummed his guitar, the stories of her Puerto Rican family heritage and culture shared around the kitchen table, and the rhythms of language echoing from the porches and balconies at night. Carmen often served as translator for several generations of her family, carefully writing *b-e-a-n-s* on the shopping list as her grandmother said, "habichuelas," translating recipes into Spanish as her mother cooked, or helping much older siblings learn to read English. She was often asked to accompany elderly neighbors to the doctor where she learned the discourse of medicine, translating information about aches, pains, diabetes, and heart problems. It was Carmen who completed all of the forms needed by the family and acted as a liaison between her parents and the school. Carmen received scholarships to attend college and earned a Ph.D. in education with a reading/linguistics emphasis. She is currently Dean of the College of Professional Studies at Metropolitan State University in Minneapolis. She remains a lover of language, and recognizes the power associated with the ability to negotiate literacy tasks in the dominant culture. Although she is current in many new literacies, her reading preferences lean strongly toward narrative and biography—books about people's lives. As an adult, she continues to share her own stories, not only with her children, but also with colleagues, community organizations, teachers, and professional groups, and, of course, with students in the College of Professional Studies.

**FIGURE 3.3**   (*continued*)

As you compare the rich cultural contexts of *both* Carmen's and Eric's childhoods, think about whose literacies and culture are more highly honored in today's schools. What are the implications for the students and for the school? In many ways, Eric's "communities" reflect the attitudes of the dominant midwestern culture with regard to the value and purposes of literacy. However, Kathy Au and Taffy Raphael (2000) would argue that many of Carmen's experiences are highly literate and accomplished, and that their applications may be even more advanced than some of those required in school. It is obvious that social and cultural factors within both families have had a profound effect on the identities of these individuals. Both share values with others in their various "communities." As a fifth-grade teacher, Eric's beliefs and values will be reflected in how he teaches and how he interacts with the culture of the school. Carmen's will be reflected in how she interacts with the culture of the university. Each parent, student, administrator, and teacher embodies the same sociocultural complexity. Literacy practices are imbedded in and defined by particular social contexts, and shaped by cultural values and local ideologies (Street, 2005). At the same time, these practices and beliefs define the culture of the school and the community. Thus, any of our initial questions about literacy can only be answered relative to the context of the communities in which they occur.

## Developing a Written Vision Statement

If you have ever been to a shopping mall, you can relate to standing in front of one of those mall maps, squinting at the little red and green and blue boxes (the various shops and stores) and emitting a sigh of relief when at last your eyes land on the "YOU ARE HERE" arrow. Just as a map shows you the way from where you are to where you want to be, so too, a vision statement illuminates a path or direction for a district or school to follow. Our first task in creating a vision statement is much like that of the disoriented mall shopper. We need to find out *where we are* relative to literacy and literacy instruction, so that we can figure out *where we want to go* and *how best to get there.* The vision statement embodies a mission or vision inspired by belief, theory, and research; it has practical implications for transforming the literacy curriculum; and it includes long-term commitment to collaborative planning and problem solving. From the social constructivist perspective, educators will not only want to determine *where* they are, but also *who* they are.

The vision statement has four important purposes:

1. It identifies beliefs and examines how they define literacy and literacy practice in various contexts.
2. It clarifies a general direction for change over time.
3. It motivates people to reorient their actions toward achieving the goal.
4. It coordinates the actions of different people in egalitarian ways.

Often, vision statements are created at the district level. However, there are many situations in which it is appropriate to develop a vision statement for a single school. In districts where schools are afforded a high degree of autonomy or where schools are managed on site, a school-level vision statement is more suitable. This is also the case for charter schools, private schools, and magnet schools in large districts.

Whether a vision statement is designed for a school or a district, the process is much the same. As you read the steps, you may substitute *school* for *district* or vice versa to fit your context. In either case, we suggest you collect the data and complete the group tasks at the school level using the framework below. If the vision statement is developed at the district level, the reading specialist and the literacy team can collect information, pool the data, and coordinate the tasks in individual schools.

## How Beliefs Shape Instructional Decisions

Why is it important for teachers to examine their individual and collective beliefs? Beliefs are powerful. Not only do individuals tend to hold onto beliefs, but there is evidence that they also embrace their misconceptions with the same tenacity. Research on misconceptions in science and physics demonstrates that, even when presented with powerful text evidence to the contrary, students cling to their misconceptions (Alvermann, Smith, & Readence, 1985).

It is precisely this powerful connection between beliefs and practices that impels us to identify beliefs at the beginning of any investigation of school programs. As teachers decide which beliefs to embrace, they also decide which to dismiss. Patricia Hinchey (2001) reminds educators that beliefs that are excluded have a powerful defining effect on literacy practice and on the culture of the school. She maintains that in addition to, "*What* is not there?" we should also ask, "*Who* is not there?" Whose voices and perspectives are missing? Shared vision requires agency of all teachers, even those who rarely share their opinions. Therefore, it is important to design collaborative inquiry in ways that not only honor, but also foster, multiple perspectives.

***The Role of Dissension in Shared Vision Models.***   We believe shared vision is not a coercive process. It does not mean everyone agrees on everything. Rather, in true collaboration, divergent perspectives are honored in that they inform, influence, and shape the thinking of the group. Dissension is necessary to the process of change and it goes beyond the concept of majority rule. It is a subtle process of socially negotiated decision making, and is more than simply giving lip service to the idea of listening to other voices. Groups committed to shared vision truly recognize how important and valuable divergent ideas are to moving the group's thinking forward, because dissenters often ask the questions the group should be asking.

## The Three Tasks in Developing a Literacy Vision Statement

The quintessential question in the process of developing a literacy vision for a school or district is to consider how various individuals will answer the question, "What is literacy?" Most educators are now comfortable with the idea expressed by Allen Luke and Peter Freebody (1999) that there is "no single, definitive, truthful, scientific, universally effective, or culturally appropriate way of teaching or even defining literacy" (p. 1). That said, there *are* ideas about literacy practices on which the vast majority of educators can agree. The task is to identify a set of shared beliefs about literacy and to transform school practice in the service of those beliefs within specific contexts.

***Task One: Search for an Existing Vision Statement.***   Of course you want to find out if a vision statement exists, but even if it does, it might warrant a makeover. You want to make this a true beginning for your school. Your vision statement has to have a F.A.C.E. It has to be Focused, Attainable, Clear, and Engaging. It has to inspire people and touch their hearts, so they are motivated to act. There are "cheerleader-types" among all school faculties. Get these people on board and immediately try to generate the kind of enthusiasm you want to sustain throughout the process of school improvement. Before you do anything else, give your school improvement project a name. For example, when the University of Wisconsin Oshkosh embarked on a restructuring of our teacher education program, we based it on a model we developed called "The Caring Intellectual." You could develop a theme or use an acronym, such as the "Lexington Excellence in Academics Program (LEAP)." Create a logo and put it on everything related to the project.

***Task Two: Survey Cohort Groups.*** Julie Meltzer and Susan Ziemba (2006) provide excellent guidance on working with teachers to create a schoolwide vision statement. They suggest using a Think-Pair-Share activity during a faculty meeting or workshop, so that teachers have a structured process for reaching consensus about a definition of reading. The literacy coach, reading specialist, or team members can visit department or grade-level meetings in which teachers are asked to consider and list:

1. The kinds of reading students are encountering in their classrooms,
2. The literacy skills that are most important to learning,
3. The demand of texts specific to particular content areas in which they teach, and

4. The kinds of agreements teachers are willing to make to ensure students have adequate reading and writing opportunities and instruction in every class. (Melzer & Ziemba, 2006)

We think it is also important to consider:

5. The kinds of literacy students are using outside of the classroom that might be important to incorporate within the classroom, and
6. Which literacies are most likely to grow in importance as these students become functional adults.

***Task Three: Disseminating the Vision Statement.***    The third task is celebratory. After the final statement is approved by administrators and presented at a formal meeting of the school board, you are ready to disseminate your work in any number of ways. Some suggestions are to put it on the school website, include it in the school newsletter, print it in the local newspaper, or make it into a poster to be displayed in the media center, the resource room, the district office, or the teachers' lounge. We hope your team will ensure that it does not disappear into the dark recesses of "the files," never to be seen again. Strive to keep your vision *visible*. The vision statement serves as the basis for the literacy program. All decisions about literacy curriculum, goal setting, methods, programs, and assessment are guided by this document. It is more than just a simple statement of beliefs. As with all visions, it looks beyond the present to what we see ourselves becoming.

# *Aligning with Standards: The Standards Reform Movement*

## *Changing Standards for Students and Professionals*

No discussion of school reform is complete without addressing standards. Our assumption is that you have a great deal of knowledge and experience working with standards and benchmarks (the indicators of progress toward the standards) in your state and your district. Because standards have such a profound effect on what gets taught, when, and by whom, it is appropriate to consider the standards for various educational stakeholders. However, our main concern in this chapter pertains to the Standards for the English Language Arts as they relate to *students*. Perhaps the biggest change in student-related standards is the push to develop a Common Core of State Standards in language arts and mathematics (and eventually other content areas) for grades K–12 across the United States. Another set of standards that has a powerful influence on what gets taught and what gets tested are the Standards for the Assessment of Reading and Writing (IRA/NCTE, 2009), reiterating the belief that the primary purpose of assessment must be to improve teaching and learning. As we discussed, there are changes occurring in the way professional associations, states, and schools are envisioning standards. We urge you to check periodically with your state department of education resources and the IRA website (www.reading.org) to check on any standards that are being revised or have been revised.

In order to provide you with current standards as they are updated, our companion website includes links to sites and organizations that support them as well as a discussion of the issues related to each. These include:

- Standards for Teacher Licensure (Interstate New Teacher Assessment and Support Consortium [INTASC] Standards)
- Standards for Institutions of Higher Education
- Standards for Reading Professionals
- Standards for the Assessment of Reading and Writing
- Student Standards
    IRA/NCTE Standards for the English Language Arts
    Common Core State Standards

## *Benchmarks: Progress Indicators toward Standards*

School districts are understandably concerned with ensuring that all students meet the state standards. Some state standards are broadly stated and cover a span of several years, while other state standards are specific for each grade level. How do we know that a sixth grader is making the kind of progress needed to meet a particular standard by the time he or she reaches eighth grade? That is where benchmarks come in. A benchmark is a focused, specific behavior or outcome related to the broader standard that can be used to gauge the learning trajectory toward that standard. The Common Core State Standards (National Governor's Association & Council of Chief State Officers, 2010) create a set of grade-by-grade benchmarks. Until schools across the country implement them and realign their curricula, we will rely on our current state and district benchmarks to keep us focused on our goals.

## *Writing and Aligning Standards, Benchmarks, and Curricula*

If you have the responsibility to write standards for your district, or if you serve on a standards committee, you may find the following five-step process helpful:

1. Write the standard or substandard.
2. List performance expectations for each semester.
3. Describe formal and informal assessments for the standard.
4. Identify sample activities used to teach the strategy or skill.
5. List the resources or tools used to mediate the learning activities.

As you examine your vision statement, the IRA/NCTE Standards, and your state standards, you will arrive at a list of standards for your school or district. A useful five-step organizing tool is a Standards-Based Curriculum Framework, such as the example in Appendix C, which is typical of one that aligns with state standards.

■ *Author Connection: Brenda and MaryEllen* We would like to conclude this chapter with a discussion of the frequently heard remark, "I close my door and do my own thing." As benign as that remark seemed to us thirty years ago, we would no longer be able to say it from a culturally and morally responsible perspective. This is why. We agree with Patrick Shannon (1999), that when we remove ourselves from a reform or program or mandate, we merely give silent support to that policy or program or mandate, as well as a default value to our schools. When we remain silent in our agreement or disagreement, we unknowingly support the status quo. Chomsky (1999) calls this "consent without consent." This is a wake-up call for teachers and reading specialists to lend explicit resistance to policies that contradict respected research findings and the values and beliefs forged by the sociocultural contexts in which they live and teach.

## Revisiting the Vignette

Now that you have completed the reading, discussion, and group activities in this chapter, think about the following questions. Compare your suggestions to those you made earlier. How do the dynamics of Mark's school and neighborhood influence how you answer these questions now?

1. What are the steps Mark should take to develop literacy standards?
2. What resources should he consult to assist him and his literacy team in developing the standards?
3. With whom should he and the literacy team share the school and district's vision statement?
4. Once the standards are developed, how should Mark use them to develop and implement curriculum and instruction that is congruent with the standards?

## Points to Remember

All systemic and lasting change begins with a culturally responsive vision statement. In order to be effective, the vision statement must be grounded in the beliefs of all the stakeholders. Therefore, the establishment of a literacy team, composed in ways that represent as many voices as possible, requires a great deal of planning. In addition, the team must be structured to allow input from individuals who are not team members. We have seen the powerful influence of beliefs on teacher practice. Changes in teaching require a great deal of time and support because they reflect fundamental changes in beliefs that are resistant to change. Among the most important insights for adopting a culturally responsive curriculum is to recognize the multiple literacies and multiple communities. Teachers can then find ways to honor the various print and nonprint literacies found in and out of school and use them in ways that serve instructional goals. Establishing a literacy team that includes a wide range of voices promotes the ownership necessary for sustaining long-term change. Finally, the school literacy goals and practices must align with state and IRA/NCTE Standards.

It is important to involve teachers in collaborative planning throughout the processes of identifying needs and beliefs, and structuring curricular changes over two years. Insights into the specific contexts of the school and knowledge about effective instruction guide the literacy team in conducting a comprehensive needs assessment. The information from the needs assessment is then used to plan curriculum, modify instruction, establish formative assessments, and determine staff development and support for change.

## *Portfolio and Self-Assessment Projects*

1. Imagine that you are asked to create a literacy team for your school or district. Describe how you will determine who will be included on the literacy team and provide your reasoning. Explain how the literacy team composition reflects context-specific needs.

2. Examine your district's and/or state's standards for the teaching of reading and language arts. Compare them to the IRA/NCTE Standards (available through IRA at www.reading.org) and the Common Core State Standards. In what ways are they congruent? In what ways are they different? Discuss the benchmarks that could be established at varied grade levels for your school/district standards. How might these benchmarks be assessed?

3. *Personal Goal:* Revisit the goal you set for yourself at the beginning of the chapter. Create a portfolio item that reflects what you have learned relative to your goal.

## *Recommended Readings: Suggestions for Book Clubs, Study Groups, and Professional Development*

Cobb, C. (2005). Literacy teams: Sharing leadership to improve student learning. *The Reading Teacher, 58*(5), 472–474. While there are a number of excellent articles on the work literacy teams do, this is one of the only ones in a literacy publication that deals solely with the idea of the literacy team, its composition and purpose. Charlene Cobb does an excellent job of examining the changing vision of leadership.

Fisher, D., & Frey, N. (2007). Implementing a schoolwide literacy framework: Improving achievement in an urban elementary school. *The Reading Teacher 61*(1), 32–43. This article is about much more than building a literacy team, and we will be referring to it when we discuss school improvement. It has two elements that make it germane to this chapter: (1) it contains a brief but important discussion of the structure of the literacy task force (team), and (2) it addresses some of the issues of culture, community, and diversity we discussed.

Gordon, S. P. (2004). *Professional development for school improvement: Empowering learning communities.* Boston: Allyn and Bacon. This is among a number of excellent books on professional development and leadership that might be suitable for a literacy team study group book.

Maeroff, G. I. (1993). Building teams to rebuild schools. *Phi Delta Kappan, 74*(7), 512–514. Maeroff provides the reader with step-by-step advice on team formation and long-term collaboration. The most helpful advice includes ways to overcome the pitfalls that lead to dysfunctional or ineffective teams.

Marzano, R. J., Waters, T., & McNulty, B. (2005). *School leadership that works: From research to results.* Alexandria, VA: ASCD. Marzano has been at the forefront of school leadership and school improvement for over a decade. He provides practical, research-based advice that has earned him the respect of teachers and administrators. This book is an excellent resource for all members of the school's improvement team, literacy team, or assessment team.

Meltzer, J., & Ziemba, S. (2006). Getting schoolwide literacy up and running. *Principal Leadership (Middle School Ed.), 7*(1), 21–26. This article would be an excellent grounding piece as you begin a school improvement project. It provides clear and practical guidance on crafting a vision statement as well as other helpful suggestions for the early stages of schoolwide literacy initiatives.

## Online Resources

**www.ed.gov**

This is the official website of the U.S. Department of Education (USDOE). The site has an extensive array of resources on a wide range of school-related issues. The site also provides support for teachers, with information on hundreds of content area topics and school reform initiatives, links to agencies such as National Institute for Literacy and other reading-related sites. You will also find links to free federal resources at www2.ed.gov/free/what.html.

## Companion Website Resources

The following resources to support and extend your learning of this chapter can be found on our companion website (waveland.com/Extra_Material/32979/): key vocabulary, concepts, and other terms; extended examples; updated resources specifically tied to information in the chapter; related websites; and other support features.

# 4

## *Determining a School's Literacy Needs and Developing a Plan*

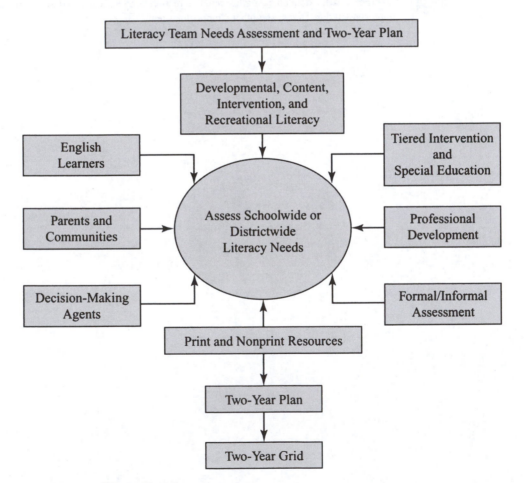

**FIGURE 4.1** *Chapter Overview*

## Learning Goals

After reading, discussing, and engaging in activities related to this chapter, you will be able to:

1. Design a systematic plan for assessing schoolwide and/or districtwide literacy needs, including a needs assessment survey.

2. Organize and analyze information related to the following elements of the literacy program: demographics, literacy curriculum and instruction, developmental and content literacy, intervention, recreational literacy, assessment, support for English learners, special education, parent involvement, community involvement, professional development, and resources.

3. Synthesize the information in a needs assessment summary.

4. Collaborate with the literacy team, administrators, teachers, and parents to create a school or district two-year literacy improvement plan based on the needs assessment.

5. *Personal Learning Goal:* In a three-minute brainstorming session, share what you know about this topic. Write a goal or a question that reflects something you want to learn about the topic. Share this with others in your group.

## Standards for Reading Professionals

This chapter provides focused support for current IRA Standards for Reading Professionals. See our companion website (waveland.com/Extra_Material/32979/) for a complete listing of the standards that align with this chapter.

### Vignette

*Janet Griffin has been hired as a school literacy coach and reading specialist in an urban K–6 elementary school in the Southwest with a student population of 1,100. Her principal, Mary Toby, is also new to the year-round school, but she has already proven she is a dynamic and forward-looking leader. One-third of the faculty are in their first two years of teaching. Janet is fluent in both English and Spanish. Approximately one-third of the 1,100 students in her school have been identified as Limited English Proficient (LEP). There is a comprehensive English Learner (EL) program to provide appropriate levels of in-class and pull-out support for the English learners, and the school is using a three-tiered model of intervention. Although almost half of the teachers speak at least some Spanish, all teachers struggle to find ways to deal with the language diversity within their classrooms. Teachers need help; the school reading program needs help; and Janet certainly could use some help herself. Janet and Mary have been moving fast. Their first accomplishment was to establish an enthusiastic, highly collaborative literacy team. The team is focused on one overarching goal: to improve literacy instruction for all children. This morning, Janet, Mary, and the team met for breakfast, and by the time they had to rush off, they had decided that they were eager to tackle developing a comprehensive needs assessment and long-term plan to improve instruction in reading. That's as far as they got. But they left with an agenda for their next week's meeting. Meanwhile, they were all assigned to think about it, and perhaps discuss it with peers. Next week's session will be spent addressing what they will need to know and do to make their vision happen.*

## Thinking Points

1. What specific things should Janet, Mary, and the team think about or do within the next week?
2. What are the core issues that they must confront?
3. What are some positive aspects that will serve them well in their process?
4. Do you have any cautions or suggestions for the team as they begin this task?

## Expanding the Vignette: Exploring the Tensions

*The team spent a busy week. Although they ran off quickly, Janet emailed everyone asking them to hold back, just for this week, on saying too much to teachers. This enabled them to get some data-driven evidence to support their belief that a needs assessment and two-year plan could make a difference. They also wanted to find out about the process.*

*Janet's thought was that they should spend the week compiling a list of questions they need to answer about the process, teacher involvement, data collection, research, and resources. At 7:30 A.M. the following week, team members arrived at the meeting, ready to share.*

## Thinking Points

1. What are some questions you might raise if you were on the team?
2. What are possible issues to address that are unique to the school?
3. Where could the team look to find information for crafting a plan?

# Assessing the School Literacy Program Needs

Because they are dedicated to creating a more effective literacy program, Janet and the team have just made a huge commitment. It will require an enormous amount of work. Even a literacy team cannot do it without help. We think this is actually a plus. This job, done correctly, will require a huge "buy in" from everyone. Janet and the team will need to make sure that every step of the process is made clear to all the teachers and other stakeholders. A huge flow chart or list of stages should be developed. Remember, you have to teach teams how to be teams. This project is about process AND product. Janet and Mary may not realize it, but because they have the team in place and they involved teachers in crafting the vision statement, they have already made an important move in the right direction.

## What Is a Needs Assessment?

A needs assessment is an evaluation in which information about the current status of the school literacy program is collected and examined. Its purpose is to document the probable needs for a program or service. The results of the needs assessment are used to determine priority goals, develop a long-term plan, and allocate funds and resources (Soriano, 1995). The needs assessment is one way to ensure that you are addressing *actual* rather than *perceived* needs.

# The Needs Assessment Process

## Creating a Demographic School Profile

The following *kinds* of data are typically found in school profiles. This data exists in every school, so you just need to locate it. See the example in Appendix E.

- *District demographics:* location, population, socioeconomic level, ethnicity, stability of population, and recent trends.
- *Student demographics:* number of students, ethnicity, percentage of English learners and their levels of English proficiency, socioeconomic levels, percentage of students receiving free or reduced cost lunch, stability of student population, attendance rates, graduation rates, jobs, special needs instruction, and participation in school and community activities and programs.
- *Professional demographics of teachers, administrators, and support personnel:* sociocultural characteristics, ethnicity, languages spoken, ratio of teachers to pupils, roles and levels of education, numbers of years of experience, degrees held, special training or expertise in methods or programs, such as bilingual education, RtI, ESL/EL, or Reading Recovery.
- *Parent, family, community members:* family composition, students living with biological parents, multigenerational families, foster families, homeless families, skills, talents, interests, relationships with and involvement in the school, involvement in social services and community, and the degree to which business and community persons are involved with the school.

A note of caution here: When writing demographic information, the reading specialist, literacy coach, and team members must be particularly sensitive to the kinds of language used. On occasion, we have seen demographic information that might be offensive to the district, the parents, or the community. When you are dealing with issues such as high poverty rates, a great deal of diversity, or sensitive political issues, it is helpful to keep in mind that you are creating a public document. We suggest that you do as we do—have others, in this case your team, read and edit this section very carefully.

## Planning and Collecting Descriptive, Quantitative, and Qualitative Data

Collaboration is essential. The good news is that almost everything you need already exists, with the exception of a survey or two. The job is almost like a scavenger hunt, so divide and conquer.

1.  Decide on and list the information you need to collect.
    - What are your questions? What do you want to know?
    - Is there one element of the school's literacy program that might need greater attention than others?
    - What will you do with the information? With whom will you share it?

2. Decide on the methods you will use to collect information.
   - How will the data be collected? Will you use a written survey? Interviews? Observations? Archival data (e.g., test scores, student records, district standards)? A combination of these?
   - Where or from whom are you likely to get the information you need, and who will collect it?
   - What assessment or survey instruments need to be developed? Who will develop them?

   See Figure 4.2 for questions to guide your data gathering.

3. Organize and analyze the information.
   - How will you consolidate, chart, or report information and determine what's missing?
   - How will you examine the various pieces of information in both macro and micro ways? That is, how will you determine what the big-picture ideas or themes are? These might include items such as books and resources or schoolwide assessment. Microanalysis is important because it can yield information such as how particular assessments are used in some grade levels but not others, or how parent volunteers are used very effectively in some classrooms but not at all in others.
   - How will you examine the connections among the pieces? For example, might low spelling scores be the result of teachers not using the spelling series?
   - How will you determine severity, special focus, or concentration (Center One, 1998)? That is, on a continuum, how serious are some of the identified problems, concerns, or needs, and how will you know if you spot them?

   What other things are important to examine? You want to make sure that your program is using evidence-based practices, so be certain to consider the following:

   - How is the school addressing the NCLB/ESEA mandate to teach the five identified areas for instruction: Reading Comprehension, Phonics, Phonemic Awareness, Fluency, and Vocabulary (plus writing, spelling, motivation, and other things YOU might think are important)?
   - How will you examine, analyze, and report the effectiveness of your three-tiered model (or other systems) of intervention?
   - What are some new opportunities and challenges you will face if and when your school implements the new standards and benchmarks?

Schools and other public institutions have been making strides toward "transparency." This means that they are making policies, practices, and outcomes available to everyone. The needs assessment can give you valuable data to use for accountability.

### Analyzing the Descriptive, Qualitative, and Quantitative Data

In the previous section, "Planning and Collecting Descriptive, Quantitative, and Qualitative Data," you collected a great deal of data. In step 3 of the process, you and the team

---

**Questions to Guide Data Gathering**

1. Demographics
   - What are the demographics of the school and community?

2. A Vision Statement
   - What is the district vision statement for reading/language arts?

3. The Literacy Team Members
   - Who are the members of the literacy team?

4. Description of School Literacy Programs
   - What do each of the components of the schoolwide literacy program (*developmental, content, intervention,* and *recreational*) look like?
   - What programs exist for *English learners*?
   - How are the needs of *special education* students currently met?
   - What programs are in place for *parents* and *communities*?

5. Resources
   - What are the print and nonprint resources in the media center and classrooms?
   - When, how, and where are technology resources used by students and teachers?
   - How are formal and informal assessments used to guide instruction?
   - Who are the agents in the leadership/decision-making processes?
   - Are financial resources and facilities adequate to meet instructional needs in literacy?
   - Are teachers included in decisions about systematic professional development?
   - How do teachers view their own professional development needs?
   - Who are all the stakeholders in this process (e.g., school psychologist, library/media, teachers, nurse, resource teachers, special education teachers)?
   - What is their involvement in the schoolwide literacy program?

6. Parent and Community Factors
   - How are parents and community members involved in literacy endeavors?

7. Analysis and Written Summary
   - How will the literacy team collect, organize, and synthesize information and list needs?
   - How will the needs be summarized and reported?

8. Using the Needs Assessment Summary
   - How will the needs assessment summary be used to create a two-year plan?

---

**FIGURE 4.2** *Questions to Guide Data Gathering*

developed your plan to analyze the data, looking for patterns and interconnections. As you analyze your data, when you find a piece of information that needs attention, try to identify other indicators that point to the same thing.

One exercise that many schools are finding extremely beneficial is the Data Retreat. The purpose of the data retreat is for all teachers, specialists and administrators to spend an extended period of time, usually a few days, examining all the kinds of information typically addressed in a needs assessment. The Wisconsin Department of Public Instruction (http://dpi.wi.gov/winss/templates/cesa.html) suggests analyzing data through three lenses that, when brought together, show clear patterns and provide focus for improvement plans and strategies. These lenses are:

- Achievement patterns (analyzing performance by grade and subject).
- Student patterns (using demographics to examine the performance of various subgroups).
- Program patterns (investigating whether school programs are improving achievement).

## Revisiting the Vignette: Thinking Points

1. Reread the questions at the end of the vignette. Reflect on how you answered them. How would you answer them now?
2. What are the challenges or important decisions facing the team?
3. What strengths of the team or the process can they take advantage of in their work?
4. What have they learned from the process thus far?

*Creating the Assessment Survey.* If you want to find out how teachers view various aspects of the literacy program, the quickest way is to create an anonymous survey using a Likert Scale. A Likert Scale is a five-point continuum with designations such as: 1 = Strongly Disagree; 2 = Disagree; 3 = Unsure; 4 = Agree; 5 = Strongly Agree. Participants are asked to circle a number on the continuum that best represents their feelings about each item. Some people like to use a one-to-six rather than a one-to-five rating scale because those who are surveyed tend to overuse a rating of 3. State each item in a positive way. You will want to allow some space for comments or explanations. Experience has taught us that the best results occur when the survey is no longer than one to three pages (see Figure 4.3). This definitely calls for some surgical precision because your goal is to get as much information in the smallest amount of space. Usually you have one shot to get it right. Again, that's where the team really counts. You might ask teachers to identify things that they do well in addition to areas in which they would like support through professional development. They could indicate if there are specific workshops or conferences they would like to attend.

*Before Distributing the Needs Assessment Survey.* After you have determined all the questions for the survey, it's time to format the survey. Here are some hints we have found helpful:

- Include, at the top of the first page, an introductory note from you and the literacy team. In a sentence or two, explain the purpose of the needs assessment, when and where it should be returned (give a date), and your names or just "Literacy Team."
- Include a few lines for demographic information about the respondents such as what grade level they teach; the years they've taught (group years for anonymity: 1–3, 4–6, etc.); additional literacy training they've had; and so on. This is important information when you begin examining responses.
- Use standard fonts and type sizes and an easy-to-follow format. Remember that you want as many surveys returned as possible, so make them easy to complete.
- Have your administrator review and approve the survey before you distribute it.

| *Instructional Practices: Developmental Reading (Grades K–6)* | | | | |
|---|---|---|---|---|
| **Strongly Disagree** | | **Unknown/ Unsure** | | **Strongly Agree** |
| **1** | **2** | **3** | **4** | **5** |
| In our school, there is adequate consistency *within* grade levels in our developmental reading program; that is, teachers in the same grade are covering mostly the same reading/ language arts content using similar approaches. | | | | |
| 1 | 2 | 3 | 4 | 5 |
| In our school, there is adequate consistency *across* grade levels in our developmental reading program; that is, teachers across the grades are using similar teaching methods and approaches. | | | | |
| 1 | 2 | 3 | 4 | 5 |
| In our school, our schoolwide developmental reading program is consistent with district standards for reading and language arts in the elementary grades. | | | | |
| 1 | 2 | 3 | 4 | 5 |
| The reading series we are currently using meets the literacy needs of most of the students in our school. | | | | |
| 1 | 2 | 3 | 4 | 5 |
| Most students are progressing satisfactorily in our school's developmental reading program. | | | | |
| 1 | 2 | 3 | 4 | 5 |
| I feel confident in my ability to provide the students in my classroom with an appropriate developmental reading program. | | | | |
| 1 | 2 | 3 | 4 | 5 |
| Comments about our developmental reading program: | | | | |

**FIGURE 4.3**    *Sample Items for a Needs Assessment Survey*

A needs assessment survey, created by one of our graduate students, is included in Appendix D. The teachers and administrators in her school completed it and it was included with all the other data collected for the needs assessment and two-year plan. It is essential to show the survey to your site administrator and get approval for distributing it to your teachers and other stakeholders.

*Analyzing the Survey Data.*    You have already analyzed the data from testing and programs; now you are ready to analyze the surveys. After you have collected all the data, calculate the percentages for each of the responses to the Likert Scale statements (see Figure 4.4). Note where there are strong or weak responses at either end of the continuum (see items 3, 4, 6, 7). You may also have items where responses are spread relatively evenly across the continuum, where some people may have strong feelings, but not all. What you're looking for are patterns across grade levels or within grade levels, or perhaps differences expressed by experienced versus beginning teachers, teachers versus other stakeholders, and so forth. In the example in Figure 4.4, which is an excerpt taken from an actual elementary school needs assessment survey, you readily see that the responding teachers, for the most part, are not satisfied with their present instructional materials and technology resources.

Next, read all written comments. Look for themes, areas of agreement or disagreement, and other ideas that can be clustered together. Are there contradictions between the Likert Scale responses and the written comments, or does there appear to be general agreement and support across both sets of data?

| *Instructional Resources* | | | | |
|---|---|---|---|---|
| Strongly Agree<br>1 | 2 | Unknown/ Unsure<br>3 | 4 | Strongly Disagree<br>5 |
| 1. There are sufficient books in my classroom library. | | | | |
| 1 = 0% | 2 = 12% | 3 = 19% | 4 = 25% | 5 = 44% |
| 2. There are sufficient books for SSR (Self-Selected Reading). | | | | |
| 1 = 0% | 2 = 1% | 3 = 31% | 4 = 25% | 5 = 43% |
| 3. Our schoolwide program supports SSR. | | | | |
| 1 = 0% | 2 = 0% | 3 = 12% | 4 = 19% | 5 = 69% |
| 4. Our Multimedia Center (MMC) is helpful for students. | | | | |
| 1 = 1% | 2 = 10% | 3 = 25% | 4 = 38% | 5 = 26% |
| 5. In the MMC and in our classrooms, students have access to appropriate technological resources (e.g., computers, listening centers, Internet access). | | | | |
| 1 = 0% | 2 = 0% | 3 = 31% | 4 = 31% | 5 = 38% |
| 6. I have the instructional materials I need for my developmental reading program (e.g., student anthologies, leveled readers, student practice books, transparencies, etc.). | | | | |
| 1 = 0% | 2 = 8% | 3 = 4% | 4 = 25% | 5 = 63% |
| 7. I have the instructional materials I need for providing in-class intervention for struggling readers and writers. | | | | |
| 1 = 0% | 2 = 1% | 3 = 12% | 4 = 31% | 5 = 56% |

**FIGURE 4.4**  *Analyzing Data on the Likert Scale*

As you read, tabulate, and summarize, be sure you identify strengths before focusing on the needs. Undoubtedly, there are many aspects of your school's literacy program that are strong and deserve to be recognized as such. Teachers, parents, students, and administrators need to hear what they are. Your report should list these strengths first. Only then should you move on to the next step and pinpoint your school's or district's literacy needs.

## Writing and Editing the Needs Assessment Report

Your data are gathered, you've analyzed the school's test scores, you have the survey results, and you've looked at each of the components of your school's literacy program (such as developmental reading, content area reading, technology, and others). You are now ready to create a public document relating your findings and highlighting the strengths, but most of all, your report will focus on the needs that will drive your short- and long-range planning.

Here is another juncture at which diplomacy is key. Let's say your teacher surveys reveal that teachers are complaining about the lack of support for professional development in content strategies. There are at least two ways to say this in your report. One is: "Teachers reported that they are unhappy about not getting enough professional development in the XYZ strategy." A much better way is to say, "Teachers indicated a need for increased opportunities for professional development in the XYZ strategy." We aren't advocating that you varnish the truth; however, it's best to state issues in the most professional manner that you can. A completed needs assessment summary, written by another of our graduate students, is included in Appendix E. This will assist you in both format and wording.

With the writing of the needs assessment summary, a challenging part of the literacy team's written work is complete. Next, the two-year grid is developed from the information collected in the needs assessment survey, and the literacy team is now ready to engage in systematic long-term planning to achieve the school's goals.

■ *Author Connection: Brenda*  Someone recently asked me why we should involve teachers in projects like the needs assessment and two-year literacy improvement plan. She suggested teachers need to know *what it is* about including them in the process that's important. Throughout the previous chapters, we cited numerous studies showing that collaborative efforts at school reform lead to enhanced outcomes (Bernhardt, 2009; Cobb, 2005; Deal & Peterson, 1999; Fisher & Frey, 2007; Fullan, Hill, & Crévola, 2006; Hinchman & Anders, 2009; Kahoun & Bjurlin, 2008; Lambert, 2002; Wellins, Byham, & Wilson, 1991). But the question I was asked made me curious as to *why that might be.* So I reexamined the pieces, looking for common threads. Here is what I discovered. By involving stakeholders (in this case, teachers) in shaping a vision (the vision statement) and articulating the goal (improving the effectiveness of the reading program), from the start, they have a sense of ownership—they are more likely to "buy in." Further into the process, when people have invested time and energy in sustained collaboration toward a common goal, if they sense that they truly share in making decisions, they feel efficacious (empowered). They are willing to work hard because they want to project to succeed, to meet its goal. To me, these are powerful reasons to believe teachers should be involved in every phase of the school improvement process.

In addition to all the positive outcomes we've just described, we've discovered one more. Many of our former graduate students reported that they were hired as reading specialists or literacy coaches based on the needs assessments and two-year plans they had developed as class assignments. Clearly, administrators are interested in hiring literacy professionals who can lead the school improvement process.

## Creating the Comprehensive Two-Year Plan/Grid

### What Is the Comprehensive Two-Year Literacy Improvement Plan/Grid?

A comprehensive two-year literacy improvement plan/grid is a written document. It incorporates the components previously developed, including school and district demographics, a list of literacy team members, a description of current practices, a summary of the findings from the needs assessment, and a proposal for professional development. The last task is to create your two-year plan/grid or schedule comprised of *a step-by-step layout of activities over a two-year period that will move from each identified need to the intended goals or targets.* The task is to pull the various pieces together into a comprehensive whole. Earlier work by the teachers and the literacy team has already determined that components of the two-year plan and the grid are aligned with the curriculum, the standards, and the vision statement. This plan is meant to be flexible; it is not an end in itself but, rather, the means for achieving improvement in the school literacy program.

Creating the two-year grid starts with the needs and identifies the people, resources, and professional development related to those needs. This information will guide you and the literacy team as you develop the two-year grid, spelling out the steps of the school improvement plan. The grid organizes the two-year plan into a visual format.

You'll find it helpful if you, the literacy team, and an administrator look at the list of identified needs together, and ask the following questions:

- Which items are high priorities?
- Which items require long-term commitments?
- How much and what type of professional development will be required for each?
- Which may involve in-class demonstrations by the reading specialist?
- Which require release time for teachers?
- Which can be accomplished more quickly than others?

By dividing the two-year period into four semesters, you can spread the tasks involved over time. Many schools even create a three-year grid, and, depending on your identified needs, you may wish to explore this option.

Here are some other suggestions to implement the process of addressing the needs through your two-year plan/grid.

- Begin working on the most ambitious need, the one requiring the greatest change, during the first semester.
- Approach these larger needs in four separate task blocks over the two years.

- Choose the second-biggest need and begin work on that one in the second semester.
- Find creative ways to have teachers act as mentors and coaches for each other.
- Troubleshoot with members of the literacy team about possible barriers to success and create proactive plans for overcoming them.
- Plan strategies you will use if you have to adjust the time line.
- Decide on staff development topics and schedule them over the two-year period (see Chapter 11 for information about professional development).
- Decide how you will evaluate and report incremental progress and successful goal achievement.

A comprehensive sample two-year plan/grid can be found in Appendix F. Notice that the teacher survey results are attached to the end of the document to show the percentages.

## Evaluating Progress toward Targets and Goals

An evaluation component on the two-year plan/grid suggests that the comprehensive two-year plan is a *formative* document. By this we mean that, at specifically designated points, progress toward the goal is evaluated and adjustments are made. These are designed to ask the questions, "How are we doing relative to our goal?" and "Do we need to adjust or add any elements to achieve our target by the end of two years?" For example, perhaps after the first semester you discover that content teachers are having a more difficult time than anticipated switching from a transmission model to one that is more integrated and interactive. The literacy team and a group of content area teachers might meet to brainstorm possible solutions, adjustments, and interventions that will support change. Maybe adjustment involves increasing the use of peer coaching or peer co-teaching. Perhaps the literacy coach could implement weekly mini-workshops on strategies. Whatever the adjustments, they are based on *recorded evidence* from informal surveys, observations, anecdotal records, and student project samples that reflect instruction and learning. There is no formal list or table of such evaluative procedures because they should reflect the unique contexts of the school and the instructional goals. In addition, evaluation should be heavily rooted in authenticity, using the daily events, activities, artifacts, and dialogues as bases for decisions (Valencia, 2004). Glickman, Gordon, and Ross-Gordon (1998, p. 272) offer a tongue-in-cheek classification of five ways by which we may make judgments about literacy programs and approaches:

- *Cosmetic method:* You examine the program, and if it looks good, it is good.
- *Cardiac method:* No matter what the data say, you know in your heart that the program is a success.
- *Colloquial method:* After a brief meeting, preferably at a local watering hole, a group of project staff members (the literacy team perhaps?) concludes that success has been achieved. No one can refute a group decision!
- *Curricular method:* A successful program is one that can be installed with the least disruption of the ongoing school program.
- *Computational method:* If you have data, analyze them to death. Whatever the nature of the statistics, use the most sophisticated multivariate regression discontinuity procedures known to humans.

Obviously, we don't subscribe to any of these methods of evaluation, as tempting as they may be. Instead, our recommendation is to encourage the literacy team to gather multidimensional evidence to see if what is being implemented is truly working. The U.S. Department of Education (as cited in Glickman et al., 1998, p. 277) describes the types of evidence that are effective in evaluating whether educational goals are being attained. As you read these generic recommendations, reflect on specific literacy-related artifacts you could collect for each type of evidence:

- Evidence demonstrating achievement/changes in knowledge and skills of students (performance assessments, test scores, structured observations of students' application of skills/strategies, content analyses of students' portfolios, projects, or products).
- Evidence demonstrating improvements in teachers' attitudes and behaviors (attitude assessments, surveys, interviews, structured observations, journals, logs, lesson plan books, self-reports, case studies).
- Evidence of improvements in students' attitudes and behaviors (review of school records; attitude assessments; case studies; structured interviews of students, parents, and teachers; journals; logs).

### Ongoing Questions about the Process of Change

One of the important concepts related to effective elementary and secondary literacy instruction is the notion of concurrent teaching of rich content and process (Zwiers, 2008). This is not only relevant to effective instruction, but it also has implications for needs assessments and two-year plans. Although it is necessary to evaluate progress toward identified targets and goals, it is also important for the team to evaluate the processes of change. Regularly, you should be asking questions such as:

- How are the stakeholders and the literacy team doing at acquiring collaborative skills?
- How are teachers doing with the change process?
- Who is taking ownership of the recommendations made in the two-year plan, including budget considerations?
- In addition to acting as a team, are we learning how to be a better team?

## Revisiting the Vignette

Reflect on how far Janet, the team, and the teachers have come. We know not all teachers have been enthusiastic about participating, but the success of a project like this has a huge impact on school climate.

1. What might Janet do to get the others involved?
2. What are the most effective components that contribute to the success of a project like this?

3. What are some of the most difficult issues or barriers you think Janet and the team faced?
4. How might they address these issues in the future?

## Points to Remember

In this chapter, we have examined the collaborative processes used in conducting an intensive examination of literacy programs, practices, resources, and stakeholders. This includes involving the literacy team in collecting, organizing, and analyzing data regarding the following: instructional practices (developmental, content, intervention, and recreational literacy), and resources, assessment, and services. Together, literacy team members collect data about each of the aspects of the school's or district's reading/language arts program, using surveys, interviews, and observations. This information is used to acknowledge the strengths and identify the needs of the literacy program. Together, the reading specialist and literacy team summarize the needs assessment information. Based on this information, they then create a focused, formative, comprehensive two-year plan with targets and goals and organize it into a grid. All aspects of the plan are then evaluated in an ongoing, authentic, multidimensional, and collaborative process.

## Portfolio and Self-Assessment Projects

1. Prepare an outline or narrative containing the specific arguments for engaging in a needs assessment and creating a comprehensive two-year plan. Write the two-page proposal for your principal or another administrator in your school or district.
2. Even though you may not have a literacy team in place yet at your school, create a needs assessment survey that you can pilot with either selected teachers or your entire faculty. Follow the procedures in this chapter for collecting and analyzing the data. Summarize your findings in a three- to five-page needs assessment summary. Remember to seek approval from your administrator prior to distributing any surveys to teachers.

3. Based on your needs assessment summary, create a two-year grid that reflects the needs you identified.
4. Incorporate the needs assessment summary and two-year grid into a comprehensive two-year plan suitable to submit to a principal, curriculum director, superintendent, or school board. Include a formative and summative plan for evaluating the school's progress in meeting the targeted goals.
5. *Personal Goal:* Revisit the goal you set for yourself at the beginning of the chapter. Create a portfolio item that reflects what you have learned relative to your goal.

## Recommended Readings: Suggestions for Book Clubs, Study Groups, and Professional Development

Bernhardt, V. L. (2001). *The school portfolio toolkit: A planning implementation and evaluation guide to continuous school improvement.* Larchmount, NY: Eye On Education. Although your school needs are highly idiosyncratic, a general guide to the evaluation and planning process can provide you with a structure for the task. Bernhardt has assembled a practical set of tools to assist your literacy improvement team.

Glickman, C. D., Gordon, S. P., & Ross-Gordon J. M. (2005). *Supervision of instruction: A developmental approach* (6th ed.). Boston: Allyn and Bacon. This is a general text written for any type of supervisor or administrator. Included is a helpful chapter on research and evaluation skills, with specific information on developing needs assessments and program evaluation tools.

Wepner, S., & Strickland, D. (Ed.). (2008). *Administration and supervision of reading programs* (4th ed.). New York: Teachers College Press. This is the latest edition of a classic. It remains a solid general reference book to guide program analysis and design.

## Online Resources

Your first step should be to check the resources available on your state department of education website. It is also informative to compare them to those listed on other states' sites. Below we list several excellent sites to get you started.

**www.dpi.state.nd.us/grants/needs.pdf**
This is a step-by-step guide to creating a needs assessment on the website of the State of North Dakota. It is well constructed, easy to follow, and an excellent resource for your team.

**http://dpi.wi.gov/winss/templates/cesa.html**
These are the guidelines on the state of Wisconsin Department of Public Instruction website. They were developed by CESA 7 (Cooperative Educational Services Agencies) and provide excellent guidance on implementing the data retreat.

**http://www.docstoc.com/docs/2622106/Tennessee-School-Improvement-Planning-Process-%28TSIPP%29-SIP-Templates**
This is the website of the Tennessee School Improvement Planning Process, a comprehensive resource on components of a needs assessment and plan for improvement. It contains samples of templates that might be especially helpful.

## Companion Website Resources

The following resources to support and extend your learning of this chapter can be found on our companion website (waveland.com/Extra_Material/32979/): key vocabulary, concepts, and other terms; extended examples; updated resources specifically tied to information in the chapter; related websites; and other support features. The companion website also includes templates for the Needs Assessment and the Two-Year Plan/Grid.

# Matching Context to Students: Assessment as Inquiry

## Learning Goals

After reading, discussing, and engaging in activities related to this chapter, you will be able to:

1. Describe a model of contextualized assessment.
2. Complete a Learner Assessment Profile (LAP).
3. Design, implement, and evaluate a school and/or district assessment plan based on a vision statement, needs assessment data, and a two-year plan.
4. *Personal Learning Goal:* In a three-minute brainstorming session, share what you know about assessment and instruction. Write a goal or a question that reflects something you want to learn as we explore this topic. Share this with others in your group.

## Standards for Reading Professionals

This chapter provides focused support for current IRA Standards for Reading Professionals. See our companion website (waveland.com/Extra_Material/32979/) for a complete listing of the standards that align with this chapter.

### Vignette

*Joan Forrester is the reading specialist at Crawford Middle School, and she has held this position for the past three years. The school is located in an urban district in a large western state. There are 1,200 students in the school, and Joan is the only reading specialist. She is responsible for the school assessment/testing program, for coordinating both the developmental and reading intervention programs for the school, providing demonstration lessons for teachers,* *and teaching reading half-day to students who have been identified as performing below grade level. There are three other reading teachers who are certified in English and they teach in the reading program. Students who are reading at or above grade level are enrolled in "language arts block" classes taught by the English teachers. Those below grade level are enrolled in Reading POWER classes, formerly known as remedial reading.*

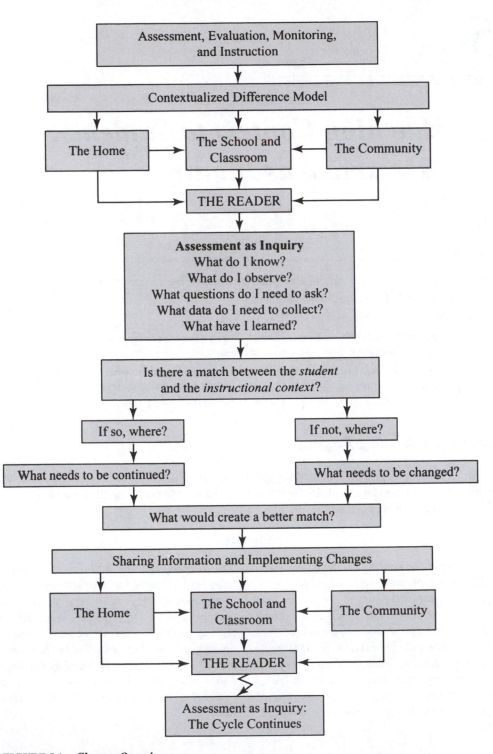

**FIGURE 5.1** *Chapter Overview*

*Joan's school district requires annual standardized testing for all students. In addition, the districtwide literacy team, of which Joan is a member, has discussed at monthly meetings the need for more uniform assessments of students' literacy development. However, the process has stalled because of disagreements about the choice of assessments, time, and accountability. Although the district literacy team agrees that standardized test scores provide little usable information for instructional planning, the team hasn't yet developed a more effective assessment system.*

*One of the newer reading teachers at Crawford Middle School is Elena Martinez. Elena is a conscientious teacher who is deeply concerned about her students' literacy development, but other than her secondary reading methods course she has had no additional preparation in reading/language arts. Elena is part of the school's literacy team, and was involved in writing a vision statement for Crawford's literacy program. She also helped Joan gather, tally, and analyze the survey data from the school needs assessment.*

*One Monday morning, Joan entered the teachers' lounge to pick up her mail. Before she made it to her box, Elena Martinez grabbed her and with some urgency whispered, "I just spoke with Jenny Stewart's dad and he's really worried that she's not progressing in reading as well as her twin sister, Emily. He brought in a copy of her standardized test scores and waved them in front of my face! He was almost yelling at me. 'Look at these scores! Jenny is a sixth-grader and this paper says she can only read at the fourth-grade level! Emily's scores say she's reading at the eighth-grade level. Why aren't you helping Jenny to read better?'"*

*Elena pleaded with Joan. "I really need your help to see if you think Jenny is having major problems with reading. I don't think she is because I often hear her read out loud. I just think her dad is overreacting to what I think are inaccurate test scores. I've done a few assessments with all my students, but I'm not sure what the results mean. I guess I need you to just tell me that I'm on the right track."*

## Thinking Points

1. What do you think the reading specialist, Joan Forrester, can do to help Elena?
2. What do you think her first steps should be?
3. What are some of the tensions that both Joan and Elena are faced with?

## Expanding the Vignette: Exploring the Issues

*Joan realized that any further conversation with Elena was going to have to wait until after school, so they agreed to meet then. Joan asked Elena to put together some of Jenny's materials, including writing samples, her work folder, test scores, and so forth. She then comforted Elena with, "We'll figure this out, Elena. I'll help you explain to Jenny's dad how she's doing in reading."*

*As Joan walked to her own classroom, she thought about how she was going to help Elena communicate to Jenny's dad about his daughter's reading progress. She also concluded that she, as the reading specialist, was going to have to do something about the lack of an effective, comprehensive, and consistent literacy assessment program in her school.*

## Thinking Points

1. What additional issues surfaced in the remainder of the vignette?
2. What are some short-term suggestions you would give Joan prior to her meeting in the afternoon with Elena?

3. What are some long-term measures that Joan should consider?
4. What are some proactive measures that a reading specialist could take to avoid confrontations with parents, such as the one Elena experienced with Jenny's father?

## Important Questions about Literacy Assessment

### How Do Literacy Assessment and Instruction Intersect?

In the world of the literacy professional, we don't have to go very far to hear heated discussion about assessment and instruction and which one should drive the other. We find it much more compelling and useful to adopt the perspective of Mokhtari, Rosemary, and Edwards (2007); that is, to focus on the *relationship* between assessment and literacy instruction. You will notice the close and at times interwoven ideas in this chapter and the one on intervention that follows. The separation of the two chapters is more one of format than philosophy. As you are aware by now, this book is grounded in the notion that all issues related to instruction are rooted in the unique cultural and social contexts of the community. According to Mokhtari and colleagues, the implication here is that "assessment and instruction issues are imbedded within broader power structures within a particular school and that both are influenced greatly by the decision model operating within the schools" (p. 354). Although assessment may have an influence on what gets taught, the sociocultural context in which we teach is the structure that influences our choices regarding assessment. If we believe that reading is the sum of a discrete set of skills, and if we emphasize skills in our teaching, we will choose assessments that test discrete skills.

## The Reading Specialist's Role in Assessment

In nearly every school and district, a major responsibility of reading specialists is communicating to teachers, administrators, and parents the reading strengths and needs of students. This includes interpreting and explaining standardized test scores, and making recommendations about necessary instructional changes based on the scores. Especially in an age of accountability, when standardized test scores are increasingly used as a barometer of students' and teachers' successes, reading specialists must also be able to balance mandated standardized testing information with more authentic assessment findings. This involves assessing and reporting findings from a variety of individual assessments such as those dealing with alphabet knowledge, concepts about print, phonemic awareness, phonics, spelling, writing, vocabulary, and comprehension. It also involves providing teachers with professional development related to assessment.

> *Authors' Note:* It is our expectation that you have completed at least one, if not more, undergraduate and/or graduate courses in the assessment and instruction process. Therefore, we are not discussing the assessment of particular reading problems, nor do we recommend specific assessment instruments. Rather, at the end of this chapter we've listed some titles of comprehensive texts on assessment that you may wish to review. If you have not had advanced preparation in assessment, we recommend you try to get the "big picture" in the sections that follow.

In this chapter, we discuss assessment as a process in which learners' backgrounds (such as their homes, families, and prior experiences), communities (such as neighborhoods, cultures, and ethnic groups), and current instructional contexts (such as their classrooms and schools) are valued and understood for the roles they play in literacy development. We will conduct an in-depth assessment of Jenny (called an LAP, or Learner Assessment Plan). Such an analysis is appropriate *only* for the few students requiring high levels of support, because it requires a substantial amount of time and effort.

## Contextualized Assessment

### Definitions of Assessment and Diagnosis

Over the years, reading specialists have used the words *assessment* and *diagnosis* to describe the processes for determining students' reading strengths and needs. Let's examine these words as defined in the *Literacy Dictionary* (Harris & Hodges, 1995):

- *Assessment:* The act or process of gathering data in order to better understand the strengths and weaknesses of student learning, as by observation, testing, interviews, etc. (p. 12)
- *Diagnosis:* The act, process, or result of identifying the nature of a *disorder* or *disability* [our emphasis] through observation and examination. Technically, diagnosis means only the identification and labeling of a disorder. As the term is used in education, however, it often includes the planning of instruction and an assessment of the strengths and weaknesses of the student. (p. 59)

We need to state up front that we have a difficult time with the term *diagnosis* when it is applied to reading. Why is this? Think about the last time you visited the doctor when you were ill. What process did you experience? Most likely it was something like this:

1. You checked into the medical facility.
2. You were led to an examination room where your *history* and vitals were taken.
3. The attending nurse and then the doctor questioned you about what your *problem* was.
4. The doctor *examined* you and gave you a *diagnosis*.
5. The doctor *prescribed* a medication for you and suggested that you *follow up* with a return visit in a particular amount of time.
6. You took the *prescription* to a pharmacy and it was filled.
7. You participated in a round of *treatment*.
8. You followed up (or didn't) with a visit back to your doctor.
9. Hopefully, eventually, you were *cured*.

Many of the italicized words or versions of them have been used in the field of reading for decades. As school and district reading specialists, we both took *histories;* we discussed students' reading *problems* or *disabilities;* we *examined;* we *diagnosed;* we *prescribed;* and we *treated.* In graduate school, we even did all this in a reading *clinic* during our *clinical* experience. Now, as you compare going to the doctor with teaching a child (or adolescent), where does this medical model break down? Can we prescribe medicines for our students? Are our students ill and should we be aiming to cure them? We believe there are better alternatives to what we view as this Deficit Model.

## What Is the Distinction between the Deficit Model and the Difference Model?

Those who embraced the notion that the job of the reading professional, particularly in compensatory programs such as Title I, was diagnosis of reading problems, operated out of a *Deficit Model*. More recent approaches to intervention reflect what has come to be known as a *Difference Model* (Ruddell, 2005), sometimes called a *Contextualized Difference Model*.

- *Deficit Model:* Something is missing (a deficit) that causes the problem. The teacher's role is to discover what's missing and teach it.
- *Contextualized Difference Model:* There is a mismatch between what a student needs and the instructional context (such as methods, materials, instruction, levels of support, differentiation, and other factors). The teacher's role is to locate the mismatch and adjust materials or instruction to achieve a closer match. Note that this is not a medical model in that it does not imply there is something wrong with the student. The onus is on the teacher to adjust instruction to meet the student's need.

### Factors to Consider in Contextualized Assessment

Contextualized assessment recognizes the complex social and cultural factors that affect learning. These factors are the home, the community, the student's identity, and the school and the classroom.

*Home factors* include elements such as family structure and stability; number of moves, locations, and changes of schools; economic and educational status; culture and language.

*Community factors* include the groups that make up the neighborhood and the students' surroundings. We use communities here in the broad sense, as we did in Chapter 3 with regard to Carmen and Eric (see Figure 3.3). These factors include religious and ethnic groups, and consider the ways language and literacy are used within communities. Values about literacy and language—and ways of interacting—are heavily influenced by these communities.

*Identity* is also influenced by communities, particularly those that make up our affinity groups (Gee, 2001a). There are fixed identity factors, such as ethnicity, and certain physical attributes, and there are identity factors that we choose. Affinity groups such as membership in scouting or gymnastics, or, in the case of adults, political groups or Harley Davidson clubs, shape how we see each other and how others see us. We amass a whole constellation of ideas about ourselves that constitute identity: a good singer, left-handed, a twin, tall, a fast runner, and so forth (Gee, 2001a, 2001b). Our work as teacher or barber, or our status as "baby of the family," contribute to our ideas of self-worth and efficacy. If a child has been self-labeled (or labeled by others) as "smart" or "stupid," that will certainly affect his or her learning.

*School factors* include the quality of the school, its resources and location, and the nature and support for learning provided in the student's classroom. The same class or school may be effective for one student and not for another. Another consideration is the continuity of the child's instruction, affected by the number of moves a family makes or the child's attendance patterns.

In the following chapter, as we discuss Response to Intervention (RtI), it is especially important to consider the factors associated with contextualized assessment, because contextualized assessment plays a major role in effective intervention. For further information about RtI, see Chapter 6.

## The Reader: Assessment as Inquiry

An experience that had a profound effect on MaryEllen's orientation toward assessment began a number of years ago with a young boy named Danny. We include this story for two reasons: (1) because there is such a mismatch between his experiences and the kinds of education most schools provide, and (2) to illustrate the importance of factors involved in contextual assessment—home, community, identity, and school—and how these factors challenge traditional ideas about assessment.

■ *Author Connection: MaryEllen*    I once had a student, Danny, who at age thirteen read and wrote at about the first-grade level. When I talked to him about his schooling experiences, I discovered that he had grown up as a "carny kid." With some further prodding, I learned that Danny's father worked for a traveling carnival, setting up and taking down the carnival rides, games, and booths that went to towns during the spring, summer, and fall months. His dad also "barked" for one of the carnival games; he was the "barker" who stood outside the booths and called people into them to play the various games. Danny was as worldly-wise as any child I knew. He'd traveled to small towns in nearly every state, and had met all types of "city people," as well as hobos and other transient carnival workers. He had never known his birth mother, but had dozens of surrogate mothers over the years. During his life, he had never lived in a house, only motels, and he had never attended the same school for more than four months (November to February). He had no school transcripts because they never caught up with him before he and his dad moved on.

## BEYOND THE BOOK _____

### Chapter 5 Focus Issue: What do we mean by literacy enriching experiences?

■ *Group Inquiry Activity*    What does it mean for children's experiences to be *enriching*? In education, we usually describe "enriching preschool experiences" as those that prepare children "to do school." Yet, it's hard to argue that Danny's experiences in the carnival had not been enriching. With a small group, brainstorm all the "literacy experiences" Danny undoubtedly had as a child growing up within the context of a traveling carnival.

Now, look at each item on your list in light of contextualized assessment.

1. For what, if any, school-related tasks would Danny's literacy experiences prepare him?
2. As teachers, reading specialists, and literacy coaches, how might we assess Danny in ways that give us a more accurate idea of what he knows and can do, so we can create a better match between this student and the educational context of his new school and classroom?
3. And while we're at it, (a) what types of "literacy" are we trying to promote in classroom contexts; (b) what are the benefits of these kinds of literacies in terms of successful participation in society; and (c) what are some limitations of these school-related literacies?

Because we believe the *interplay* of contextual factors (home, community, identity, and school) influences school performance, it is important to consider how such factors operate within a particular student. These factors are just as important to consider in a student like Jenny, about whom we are concerned, as they were with Danny. As we follow Jenny through a comprehensive assessment process, you will discover a number of aspects related to these contexts that yield valuable information. It will be helpful to refer to Jenny's completed Learner Assessment Plan (LAP) as we follow her assessment process (Figure 5.2).

---

## Revisiting the Vignette: Thinking Points

1. What questions might you have about the factors associated with Jenny's home, community, identity, or school?
2. Reflect on the issue of identity. How would you describe yourself (list three adjectives or phrases)? How would you describe others in your discussion group (list three adjectives or phrases for each)? Is your description of yourself the same as or different from those others hold? Why do you think this is so? What would you want others to know about you?
3. How would you describe an affinity group made up of reading specialists or literacy coaches? What descriptors would distinguish them from a group of classroom teachers?

## *Is There a Match between the Student and the Classroom Context?*

This step in the contextualized assessment process, adapted from Lipson and Wixson's (2003) diagnostic teaching model, requires that we begin answering the following questions:

1. If there is a match between the student's background, the instructional context, and the assessed strengths and needs, where is it? What needs to be continued?
2. If there is a mismatch between the student's background, the instructional context, and the assessed strengths and needs, where is it? What needs to be changed?

| Identifying Information | | |
|---|---|---|
| Name **Jenny Stewart** | Date of Birth **2/18/00** | Date of Report **3/7/11** |
| Parents **Edward and Maria Stewart** | | Phone **123-456-7890** |
| School **Crawford** | Grade **6** | Teacher **Elena Martinez** |

### Background: Home and Community

Jenny Stewart was referred by her teacher and parents because her academic performance is 2–3 years below grade level. Her parents are concerned about Jenny's reading and are considering hiring a tutor. Jenny has attended Crawford Elementary since first grade. During fourth grade, she received additional support in writing, three days a week. She lives with her mother, father, and fraternal twin sister, who achieves at or above grade level in all subject areas. Jenny's mother reports regular trips to the public library; Jenny also has a large library of books at home. Her favorite books are about ballerinas, ballet, and female athletes. She states she prefers having someone read aloud to her rather than reading to herself. Jenny's father reads to her at home and she reads to her mother. Jenny and her sister are involved in Girl Scouts, their church youth group, and ballet. Jenny states that she wants to play soccer with her friend, Allison, in the YMCA youth league but she hasn't joined yet. Her aspirations are to become a graphic artist like her mother. Jenny is of average height and weight for her age and is reported to have normal hearing and vision, no allergies, and she is currently not on any medication.

### The School and Classroom

Jenny is in a heterogeneous sixth-grade classroom with 28 other students. Her teacher, Mrs. Martinez, is in her third year of teaching sixth grade. The student population includes four special education students, seven English language learners, and two children who are receiving special services for the gifted. The four special education children attend Reading POWER classes; Jenny does not. For her core reading instruction, Mrs. Martinez uses the district-adopted reading series, *Literacy for All* (ABC Publishers). This integrated literature-based program includes spelling, grammar, and writing instruction; all literacy instruction is whole-class, and all students read the same core literature. Mrs. Martinez reads novels to her students, a chapter a day. All students have 20 minutes/day of DEAR (Drop Everything and Read). According to Mrs. Martinez, Jenny usually selects "very difficult books" for the DEAR time. Writing is taught in a workshop format once a week. A spelling list of 20 words from the reading series is provided to all students each week, with a Friday test. The teacher reports that her literacy assessment consists of end-of-theme skills tests that are a part of the reading series. During four classroom observations of the language arts block, Jenny participated very little or not at all, often looking out the windows or playing with objects in her desk. Only when Mrs. Martinez asked her direct questions did she say anything. She was observed to volunteer once during around-the-room oral reading. During DEAR, she paged through the difficult books, seldom or never appearing to read any extended text.

*(continued)*

**FIGURE 5.2** *Jenny's Learner Assessment Profile (LAP)*

*Note:* This Learner Assessment Profile is based on an actual LAP completed by a graduate student in reading at California State University, Long Beach. All identifying information for the student has been changed, and pseudonyms for the student, parents, and school are used here.

*Source:* Adapted from Lipson and Wixson (2008).

| Assessment Information | | |
| --- | --- | --- |
| *Assessment* | *Date* | *Findings* |
| Primary Spelling Inventory (Determines developmental spelling stage)[1] | 2/20/11 | Words correct: 8/25<br>Orthographic features: 44/60<br>Estimated stage: Within Word Pattern |
| Johns[2] Graded Word List (Leveled word recognition test) | 2/20/11 | Primer         19/20      Independent<br>Grade 2      18/20      Instructional<br>Grade 4      13/20      Frustration |
| Johns Basic Inventory (Child orally and silently reads leveled passages and answers comprehension questions) | 2/25/11 | Gr. 2   92 wpm  10/10 quest.   Independent<br>Gr. 3   70 wpm   7/10 quest.   Instructional<br>Gr. 4   50 wpm   8/10 quest.   Instructional<br>Gr. 5   42 wpm   6/10 quest.   Frustration<br>Silent reading of Gr. 4 (passage B): 7/10 quest. |
| Interest Inventory (Assesses interests and "favorites/least favorites") | 2/26/11 | Participates in ballet, soccer, and church activities; subscribes to *Teen People*; best friend: twin sister, Emily. Likes math, not reading; finds school "frustrating" but "fun" |
| Writing Sample | 2/25/11 | Completed approx. $\frac{1}{2}$ page on assigned topic of ballet; simple listing of reasons she likes ballet; multiple spelling errors; 2 sentence frags.; includes concluding sentence. |
| Standardized Test Scores: CST | 4/11 | Reading Vocabulary:      2 = Below Basic<br>Reading Comprehension:  2 = Below Basic<br>Total Reading:          2 = Below Basic<br>Spelling:               3 = Basic<br>Language Mechanics:     3 = Basic<br>All stanines are below average |

### *Analysis of Assessment*

*Interests:* Jenny's favorite activity and where she exudes the most confidence is ballet; she has taken lessons since age 4. Her twin sister, Emily, also attends ballet lessons. Jenny wants to learn to play soccer. Her intense dislike of reading is readily expressed: "I hate it. Emily loves it. My dad doesn't think I'm a good reader. I guess I'm not."

*Spelling:* Jenny demonstrates mastery in initial/final consonants; has difficulty with short vowel sounds of *a*, *e*, and *o*. Demonstrates accuracy with some digraphs/blends, except for *ck*, *sn*, *ch*, and *ght* spellings. Writing sample also confirms difficulty with these sounds/patterns (misspelled *has* and *pet*). Confuses diphthongs *ou/ow*. Most spelling errors in Within Word Pattern stage.

**FIGURE 5.2   (*continued*)**

[1]Primary Spelling Inventory: see Bear, Invernizzi, Templeton, and Johnston (2007).
[2]Johns graded word lists and leveled passages: see Johns, J. J. (2005).

*Reading:* Errors on graded word list include short vowels and vowel combinations (*ai, ea, a-e,* and *oa*). Word-by-word reading with finger pointing; long hesitations during oral reading of 3rd- and 4th-grade passages. When told pronunciation of unfamiliar words, quickly reads word in phrase with little attention to punctuation. Frequently looks to examiner for assistance and reinforcement; displays little confidence, especially in testing situation. Substitutes visually similar words (e.g., *frosty* for *forest*). Is hesitant to try any retellings (on 3rd-gr. passage provided few details, no overall main idea); requires prompted comprehension questions for all passages. Comprehends factual information well, despite frequent miscues and self-corrections. Fluency rates difficult to assess because Jenny stops and wants to discuss text—either with questions or connections she's making to her own experiences. Doesn't appear to use strategies while reading; focuses almost exclusively on word-by-word reading. Was observed during reading lesson often looking disengaged or confused by what Mrs. Martinez was teaching.

### Match or Mismatch with Present Instructional Context
*Matching Areas:*

Jenny wants to select her own magazines and books for DEAR. She enjoys listening to Mrs. Martinez read aloud. She likes to write when she can write about topics that are familiar to her, such as ballet. The writing workshop format lends itself to the type of writing Jenny does best.

*Areas of Mismatch:*

There is a mismatch in the type of reading instruction Jenny is receiving and what she needs. The areas of mismatch include the following:

1. *Texts:* Grade-level texts for Jenny's reading instruction are too difficult and frustrating for her.
2. *Nature of Instruction:* Whole-class teaching is not meeting Jenny's assessed needs. It is too easy for her to become disengaged and uninvolved during reading instruction and discussions.
3. *Spelling:* Whole-class spelling instruction with the same weekly lists for all students is inappropriate to Jenny's assessed needs. The words are too difficult and she is not learning word structure and patterns.
4. Although Jenny participates in daily DEAR, she is selecting books that are too difficult. Frustration-level reading materials will not improve her reading.

### What Might Achieve a Closer Instructional Match?[3]

We need to help Jenny develop confidence in and motivation to read. In order to accelerate her literacy development, we need to provide her with access to books that deal with topics she's interested in and wants to learn about (e.g., ballet and female athletes). We need to provide her with explicit and consistent instruction in reading in the following areas of assessed need: decoding strategies (including a review of orthographic patterns), comprehension skills, comprehension strategies, spelling, and writing instruction that focuses on varied genres. She will also benefit from fluency practice with instructional and independent level text. Most important, we need to continue to provide daily exposure to grade-level concepts, vocabulary, and text structures (such as she receives during work with the anthology and the teacher read-alouds), so that she can learn and practice reading skills and strategies in instructional level and independent level texts. We need to show her how to select appropriate and interesting texts for DEAR and at-home reading, and to monitor her text selection.

### Recommendations

It is recommended that Jenny work with the reading specialist for a period (30 min.) each day from now until the end of the semester. In consultation with Mrs. Martinez, the instruction will take place in the

*(continued)*

---

**FIGURE 5.2** *(continued)*

[3]Note how this section is written. Rather than saying, "Jenny needs . . . ," we're saying, "We need to . . ." See the difference? The collective *we* is also intentional, implying "We're all in this together for Jenny's benefit."

reading specialist's classroom for four days/week. One day a week the reading specialist will work in Mrs. Martinez's room with a small group of children who are experiencing similar reading difficulties. It is important that Jenny continue to have exposure to and involvement with the grade-level core literature/reading instruction during the regular language arts block. Based on Jenny's assessment, the reading specialist will work on the following:

*To Improve Spelling Knowledge:*
- Work with word sorts and word hunts each week to reinforce short vowels, vowel combinations, and diphthongs. The patterns and contrasts will be based on Jenny's assessed level (Within Word Pattern).
- *Use Words Their Way* (Bear et al., 2007) games and activities for vowel mastery; slowly introduce sorts and activities from the Syllables/Affixes stage.
- Implement a word study notebook for recording patterns and new words found during word hunts and VSS (Vocabulary Self-Collection Strategy).[4]

*To Improve Reading and Fluency:*
- Comprehension strategies[5] will be introduced, taught, and modeled daily with appropriately leveled text.
- Small-group instruction will facilitate literature discussion (guided reading) and comprehension development.
- Jenny will buddy-read familiar text with another child of like reading ability to build fluency; neurological impresse[6] may be used between teacher/student if buddy reading isn't successful.
- Graphic organizers will be used to help Jenny organize information during reading.
- Both narrative and informational/expository texts at around the 4th–5th-grade level will be used for the small-group instruction; gradually more difficult texts will be introduced as students, including Jenny, are able to read them.
- A variety of motivating and interesting narrative and informational texts at around the 3rd-grade level will be available for DEAR and at-home reading gradually more difficult texts will be introduced; topics initially will focus on ballet and women's sports.
- Dictated group stories will be used for writing instruction and for fluency building.
- Time each week will be spent in the reading specialist's classroom reviewing and reinforcing grade-level concepts and vocabulary from the adopted reading series.
- Mrs. Martinez will, on a regular basis, flexibly group students for discussion circles related to the anthology selections.

**Additional Comments**
At this point, it is not recommended that Jenny receive formal tutoring outside of school. We encourage Mr. and Mrs. Stewart to continue to support and monitor Jenny's at-home reading and writing, and to assist her in making appropriate choices for her reading practice. We will implement this plan until the end of the semester and will meet to review Jenny's progress at that time. Mr. and Mrs. Stewart, Jenny, Mrs. Martinez, and I will attend that meeting.

Profile Prepared By   *Joan Forrester*   Date: 3/07/11

Reading Specialist, Crawford Middle School

**FIGURE 5.2** (*continued*)

[4]Vocabulary Self-Collection Strategy (VSS): Ruddell (2005); Shearer, Ruddell, and Vogt (2001).
[5]Comprehension strategies: see Harvey and Goudvis (2000); McLaughlin and Allen (2009); Pearson, Harvey, and Goudvis (2005).
[6]Neurological impresse: see Flood, Lapp, and Fisher (2005).

---

*Observations and Insights*

3/25/11   After 2 weeks of small-group work (6 students) in Mrs. M.'s room, Jenny is still reluctant to participate. When called on, she responds but she won't volunteer information or engage in discussion. I think the group is too big; will halve it tomorrow and see what happens. J. F.

3/29/11   What a difference! I found several ballet books at the library and the 3 girls who are now in the reciprocal teaching group are avidly reading and talking about them. Jenny is gradually becoming more confident and involved . . . and because of her ballet background, she's even taking some leadership with the others. I think we're on to something here. . . . J. F.

4/3/11   Jenny's really enjoying VSS! I'm realizing that a key to her involvement is giving her some control over what she's doing. She likes to select her own vocabulary words to add to her Word Study book—and not surprisingly, most have to do with ballet. Today, she brought in the word "tutu" and asked if I knew where the word came from. When I told her I didn't, she giggled and said, "It's French—and it may have come from baby talk for a person's bottom." At this point, the whole group cracked up . . . nothing like 6th-grade humor! J.F.

---

**FIGURE 5.2**   (*continued*)

■ *Group Inquiry Activity*  For discussion purposes, take a look at Jenny's Learner Assessment Profile (LAP) in Figure 5.2. Review the background information that was gathered about her. What, if anything, is noteworthy in her background?

Notice that the assessment data suggest that Jenny is not a fluent reader of grade-level material. During her oral reading of the fourth-grade passage on the Johns Basic Reading Inventory, she read very slowly with many miscues. When Joan asked her to retell what she had just read, she was unable to do so, though she could answer comprehension questions when prompted. Also note that, although Jenny read the third-grade passage aloud, when asked to retell what she read, she was only able to recall a few details and missed the overall idea of the passage.

During Joan's observations in Elena Martinez's sixth-grade class, she noticed that the students were engaged in a whole-class reading of the novel, *Where the Red Fern Grows* (Rawls, 1961). Jenny occasionally volunteered to read aloud from the book, but she pulled back and participated very little during discussions, either with Elena or her peers. She appeared to follow and enjoy the story, but did not want to discuss it during class.

1. Based on the assessment information presented in Jenny's LAP, do you think there is a match or mismatch in the reading instruction that Elena is providing Jenny?
2. Why do you think so?
3. What are the areas of match?

4. What are the areas of mismatch?
5. What do you think might be interfering with Jenny's ability to read grade-level materials successfully?

Share your ideas with the others in your group.

### What Would Create a Better Match?

Within contextualized assessment, we may find we have a primary area or several areas of mismatch, and it might be necessary to prioritize by asking what is needed most.

For example, based on the assessment data, it appears there is a mismatch between Jenny's needs and some of the reading instruction she's receiving. Jenny cannot read independently or even instructionally at grade level in either the anthology selections or the novels. She also regularly selects books that are too difficult for the daily silent reading activity. There appears, then, to be a rather serious mismatch between the texts that are provided for Jenny and the texts that she needs for reading instruction and practice.

You might also suspect that the whole-class literature discussions that Elena engages her students in may not be meeting Jenny's need for the explicit teaching and modeling of decoding and comprehension skills and strategies. Thus, we can predict that a better match for Jenny would include intensive instruction in decoding and comprehension skills and strategies, using texts that she can read, *in addition to* (not in place of) continued exposure to the grade-level vocabulary, concepts, and texts taught in the reading series. It might also help her access the grade-level anthology and novels if she has scaffolded support, such as can be provided in small groups with teacher-led guided reading (Opitz & Ford, 2008).

At this point, it may be tempting to think, "Aha! We've got it!" But contextualized assessment involves more than a single solution or answer. Rather, there may be a number of ways to approach the mismatch found in Jenny's classroom literacy instruction. For example, Joan might offer to run a guided reading group in Elena's classroom so that students, including Jenny, can receive comprehension strategy instruction. Also, Joan might model the process for Elena so that Jenny's teacher can also work with a small group, using guided reading. Or, Joan might see if Jenny can come into the reading specialist's classroom for some intensive group work with several other students needing similar help with decoding and comprehension. Or, a combination of these ideas might be feasible. Since Jenny's school does not use an RtI structure, there may be other ways to support Jenny.

### Sharing Information and Implementing Changes

With all the information gathered, it's time to complete the Learning Assessment Profile and share the results.

■ *Group Inquiry Activity*  In a small group, discuss the following questions:

1. How do you think the completed Learner Assessment Profile should be shared with parents? What should the parents' role in the assessment–instruction process be?
2. How should it be shared with the classroom teacher?

3. Do you think that the completed LAP should be shared with the student? Why or why not? If your answer is yes, how might you do it in an individually responsive manner?
4. Do you think that the completed LAP should be shared with the literacy coach and principal, with other teachers (especially at the secondary level), or with other stakeholders, such as special education teachers?

How the LAP is written is important. Note that in the example of Jenny's LAP in Figure 5.2, information is provided in a factual way, without judgments or biases. The purpose is to achieve a closer match between Jenny's classroom context and her needs.

A sample LAP matrix is included on our companion website. You can follow the detailed process in this book to guide you in completing one for a student with whom you work.

## Implementing Changes

As you begin to implement changes, you may feel unsure as to whether they're effectively lessening the difference between a student's assessed needs and the instruction the student is receiving, and you might wonder if other changes are warranted. For example, let's say that the reading specialist, Joan, decides to organize a reciprocal teaching group in Elena's classroom. She teaches the four reciprocal teaching strategies (predicting, questioning, clarifying, summarizing) to the entire class and then, while Elena works with the rest of the students, Joan pulls together six others, including Jenny, for small-group work. However, she soon realizes that, despite the small-group environment, Jenny is still ill at ease and lacks confidence about participating. Joan, in consultation with Elena, decides that, in order to boost Jenny's confidence and participation, an even smaller group is needed. For the first two weeks of their work together, Joan works with Jenny and just two other children—and the book that they begin with is a high-interest, low-vocabulary informational book about ballet, Jenny's first love. Bingo! A match is established and Jenny becomes involved. Joan suspects that other students can be added gradually to the group, and that other books of interest to Jenny and the group can eventually be selected.

Contextualized assessment suggests that we need to try something different if our first idea isn't working. In other words, we need to search for a more appropriate context. In this case, changing the group size makes a difference in Jenny's participation. Joan also suggests that Elena incorporate more explicit instruction in comprehension strategies for all of her students, and she models how this can be done. Elena and Joan put up posters that list the comprehension strategies that good readers use, along with examples of students' think-alouds. Students make bookmarks with the comprehension strategies listed on them, and they are encouraged to talk about the kinds of personal connections they make while reading. All of these changes boost Jenny's confidence as she sees that all the students in her class need to learn comprehension strategies. Joan continues to work with Jenny on decoding and spelling in her own classroom, as well as in the small group with reciprocal teaching.

Gradually, Jenny begins to demonstrate that she's "getting it." She also begins to take a more active role in class discussions and, for the first time, she is able to summarize verbally what she reads, both from texts she reads at home (such as websites and magazine articles) and what she reads in school. When she writes her first research report, not surprisingly, the topic is ballet. During the oral presentation before her class, Jenny confidently shares what she has learned.

It's important to remember that contextualized assessment and instruction involve a flexible approach to planning, and they require that the reading specialist have a repertoire of assessments, instructional strategies, and materials available for students and teachers. You will notice on the Learner Assessment Profile that there is room for you to record the student's projected learning outcomes and recommended instructional approaches, both those attempted and those that were found to be successful. And don't forget to sign the LAP. As a professional, your signature demonstrates that you stand by your recommendations.

### What Happens Now?

It may be tempting to think, "Ahhh . . . all's better now." However, if you review the Contextualized Assessment cycle in Figure 5.1 at the beginning of this chapter, you'll see that the procedures are ongoing and continuous, rather than linear. Assessment and teaching are recursive processes, as we re-examine, rethink, replan, reassess, and reteach, continually striving for closer instructional matches for all students, just as we do in an RtI structure.

There's one last caveat about this assessment process. Remember our advice about LAPs. Few students require this type of comprehensive assessment and subsequent instructional change. But if you have students who are struggling, despite their intellectual, linguistic, or ability levels, they need (and deserve) appropriate literacy assessment and instruction. Contextualized assessment, situated in the Contextualized Difference Model, can assist you and the teachers with whom you work in differentiating instruction for these students.

## Assessment: Making Responsible Choices

Perhaps nowhere in the discussion of reading programs is there more confusion than in how to assess students. Because of the renewed emphasis on universal screening (that is, screening of all students), teachers need ways to assess many children efficiently and responsibly. They also need to show measurable gains, encouraging oversimplified means of assessing. What faster way is there than to engage in practices such as having students read from isolated word lists, measuring words per minute, or error rates, or numbers of sounds and letters known, and then charting and graphing these discrete skills? Such assessment practices have given rise to questions. Do they measure what we think is important about the reading process? Do they have a high predictive value? (Some do for certain age groups.) On the other end of the spectrum are standardized tests. We wonder about them as well. Are standardized tests and end-of-unit tests given more weight than they merit or used as they are intended? And what about observation and student engagement in authentic tasks? They are perhaps the least quantitative, but viewed by many as the most valuable tools in a teacher's arsenal. Are they valid and reliable ways to assess students? What about assessments such as story retellings, informal reading inventories, or instruments like the Developmental Reading Assessment or DRA, which assess students as they read from leveled texts and gives a more holistic and naturalistic view of the reader? They require specific training in administering and interpreting and fifteen minutes per student to administer. If Elena Martinez tests all twenty-eight students three times a year with DRA, she will need over four full days of instructional time. Such tests are dynamic sources of information, but are they more time-consuming than the information they yield warrants? The IRA (2002a) position statement on assessment available at www.reading.org addresses many of the issues reading professionals need to consider.

### Assessment Features

To think about the purposes of assessments, it is important to review a few basic concepts: summative and formative assessment, reliability, and validity. A brief, oversimplified explanation of the difference between formative and summative assessment follows.

*Formative* assessments are those we use to inform instructional decisions and to adjust specific aspects of instruction in order to meet our end goals. *Summative* assessments, on the other hand, are used at the end of instruction to determine a student's level of achievement or proficiency. Can an assessment be both? Yes. For example, a spelling test can be used midweek to help students and teachers know how a student is doing on progress toward the big test on Friday; that's formative. But the Friday test—same words, same test—is summative. In other words, use determines classification. If you have limited understanding of these terms, we urge you to go online or dust off your textbook from an assessment or statistics class.

*Reliability* refers to the consistency of a measurement. For example, not so long ago, IQ was thought to be a "constant" in that you *were* as smart as you *were,* period (not really true, but let's say it is). In other words, you are not a genius one day and below average the next, so if I give you an IQ test repeatedly, and it accurately measures your intelligence, that number should be the same next week as it is today or really close to it. Because generally, IQ tests administered repeatedly have a high rate of consistency, they are considered relatively *reliable,* at least statistically speaking. Reliability may not be an issue for something like an interest inventory or a test of your motivation. These measures will fluctuate to a greater degree than scores on an IQ test (all other things being equal, which of course they are not). Thus, repeated measures may not yield similar results. That's why your analysis of factors related to each assessment are closely tied to the purpose of the instrument.

*Validity* (and there are a number of kinds, but we won't get into that) answers the question, does this test or assessment REALLY measure what it sets out to measure? For example, if I want to test your golfing ability, and I give you a paper and pencil test on the rules of golf, that is probably not a valid test of your golfing ability. It *is* probably a *valid* way to test your memorization of the rules of the game, but watching you play golf is a much more *valid* way to assess your golfing.

### What Criteria Can We Use to Evaluate the Suitability of Various Assessments?

Peter Afflerbach (2007) developed the CURRV model as a means to analyze the suitability of assessments. First, Afflerbach believes *every test should be scrutinized for reliability and validity*. Then he offers three additional criteria in CURRV model:

1. *Consequences:* Appropriate assessments yield information helpful toward making students better readers. Inappropriate assessments can be less informative and have a negative impact on learning and motivation. In addition, we need always be mindful

of the high-stakes decisions or judgments that can be made about students, and we must be careful about who will have access to the scores and for what reasons.

2. *Usefulness:* Examines the *combination* of assessments—how each contributes to an appropriate mix. Are there any missing elements or ones we should consider adding or replacing?

3. *Roles and responsibilities:* This deals with the appropriate use of instruments. We need to examine whether we are using instruments to their full potential in order to realize the maximum benefits.

4. *Reliability:* We need to know the assessment yields consistent results; we count on these scores to be statistically accurate.

5. *Validity:* We need to make sure the instrument measures what it sets out to measure.

(pp. 17–22)

■ *Author Connection: Brenda*  Let's go back to an IQ test. When I taught first grade in an urban school in a Milwaukee neighborhood characterized by high poverty in the 1960s, we administered a paper and pencil IQ test. On it was a request to circle the "collie" and among the choices was, of course, a dog that looked just like Lassie. Almost none of my students had ever seen a collie. I wondered if my students would have fared better had they been asked to circle a more urban type of dog. What does this tell us about those who missed the question? Does that really tell us they are not as intelligent as other kids? This test item was *reliable* in that if you tested them next week, they still wouldn't know a collie, so their score would pass the consistency requirement. However, one could argue whether the question was valid, an accurate measure of their intelligence. Can a test be reliable, but not valid? Yes. Can a test be valid, but not reliable? Yes. Can a test be both reliable and valid? Yes. Can a test be neither valid nor reliable? Unfortunately, yes (but I hope you never use one).

## Assessment: Categories and Characteristics

### IRA and NCTE Revised Standards for the Assessment of Reading and Writing

In December 2009, IRA and NCTE released the newly Revised Standards for the Assessment of Reading and Writing. The eleven standards stress that instructional improvement is the primary purpose for assessment, and that all stakeholders, including teachers and families, must have equal voice in dimensions related to testing. Issues of fairness, consequences, and multiple perspectives are addressed as well. The standards reflect our current understandings about the complexity of literacy processes and the necessity for developing assessments that capture what it is we think is important about reading and writing. You can access the standards online in the Research and Policy area of the IRA website at www.reading.org.

### What Kinds of Literacy Assessment Are Used in Schools?

All kinds of assessments are used in schools. Not all of them are effective in meeting their purposes, and not all of them are used correctly. We have all heard the expression, "You can't make a pig fatter by weighing it more often." (We tried to find the origin of this statement but it seems many people are taking credit for coining the phrase.) Whoever first said it mirrored the concerns of many of us who worry that time spent screening and testing and monitoring is taking precious time away from instruction. We all know teachers who are so experienced, so knowledgeable, and so tuned in to their students' needs that they can diagnose problems with the precision of a surgeon. Still, we need not take offense when asked for evidence that students are learning. We expect our doctors, attorneys, therapists, and accountants to base their practice on scientific evidence. As professionals, we should not be intimidated by the suggestion that our instruction should be based on more than just our suspicions. We should welcome the opportunity to be held accountable for our instructional decisions.

McKenna and Walpole (2008) identify four classifications of assessment used in schools that align with each of these goals: screening measures, diagnostic measures, progress-monitoring measures, and outcome measures. Each represents different kinds of instruments matched to their purposes.

**1.** *Screening instruments,* administered to all students, should be targeted, brief, and aimed toward identifying students who are in need of support to progress in sync with their peers. They are designed to measure critical skills that are high predictors of future student performance. Jenkins and O'Connor (2002) found that multiple measures obtain better classification accuracy. Screenings can be used as baseline data to give us a snapshot of how well a student is progressing. However, they provide little specific instructional guidance.

**2.** *Diagnostic instruments* are often used as follow-up measures when a student performs poorly on a screening test. They are more time-consuming than screening. The diagnostic test, either norm-referenced or informal, is designed to identify where the difficulty lies. The RtI Action Network suggests that diagnostic assessments should be administered only if we can reasonably expect they will yield information that cannot be obtained through other more contextually situated measures.

**3.** *Progress monitoring* involves periodic assessment (usually informal measures, artifacts, or observational data). Once a student begins receiving differentiated support, progress monitoring helps determine whether the intervention methods are working or whether further instructional adjustments are needed. If the instruments used are closely tied to what is taught, they can help determine the kind of instruction needed as well.

**4.** *Outcome measurements* are the group-administered, norm-referenced, standardized assessments often administered toward the end of the year, and associated with high stakes. They are summative, used to determine whether a district or school, or a subgroup within a school, is making adequate yearly progress. They can help identify broad trends or global areas needing more emphasis, and are useful for district-to-district and state-to-state comparisons.

***Other Assessments.*** You will discover a number of novel ways individual teachers use assessments that are specific to their content areas or styles of instruction. Researchers, too, are seeking ways to modify and improve some of the things we already do, such as Cunningham and Smith's (2007) *Beyond Retelling.* Such specialized or single-purpose assessments may not fit neatly into any one category, or they may serve multiple purposes. Sometimes attempts to categorize assessments reduce them in ways that limit or diminish them, failing to capture their richness. For example, some huge projects include a literacy component, but synthesize various content understandings as well. These may not fit the categories listed above. Increasingly, methods implementing student **self-assessment** may be more difficult to categorize. A third issue involves finding ways to assess new literacies, ones that serve new purposes and adopt new forms. Remember, assessments develop *after* we discover a new "thing" to measure. For example, schools began to implement RtI as an intervention structure. *Then* we needed to develop ways to assess which elements of RtI were effective.

*New Dilemmas.* What do we know about the demands of reading informational texts in each of the content areas? Which strategies are specific to which kinds of texts? How can we measure these so we can help individuals in focused ways? Researchers are grappling with such questions right now. We need new understandings about knowledge and assessment and these will require new assessment paradigms.

■ *Group Inquiry Activity* Share within your group any assessment instruments you have found to be especially helpful in providing useful information for planning literacy instruction.

1. Which of the assessment instruments have you administered? Are there any that are new to you?
2. Have you analyzed assessment findings for each of them? If so, how did they change your teaching?
3. Would you be able to teach another person (such as a classroom teacher) how to use each of them?

If you feel unsure about how to administer assessment instruments and analyze their findings, consult the list of sources at the end of this chapter for assistance.

## *Comparing Assessments:* Measure for Measure

*Measure for Measure: A Critical Consumers' Guide to Reading Comprehension Assessments for Adolescents* (Morsy, Kieffer, & Snow, 2010), a Carnegie Foundation publication, is a comprehensive analysis and comparison of assessments designed to help administrators, reading professionals, and teachers become critical consumers and make intelligent selections of appropriate assessment instruments matched to specific goals.

*Measure for Measure* is based on the assumption that readers differ, texts differ, reading activities differ, and reading changes over time. A purpose-driven system should be able to implement screening that will identify children with poor comprehension. It should include diagnosis that can identify the subsets of individuals who need differentiation. It should be sensitive enough to pinpoint a student's instructional needs, and it should reflect authentic outcomes, ones teachers think are important. This will include standardized tests, but also assessments that capture both the complexity of the reading process and the student's critical thinking processes while reading. The authors describe an effective system as one designed to provide relevant and up-to-date information for teachers at strategically useful times (such as screening all incoming sixth graders entering middle school and ninth graders entering high school). Such a system requires coordination at the school and district levels to ensure that elements of screening, diagnosis, and progress monitoring are functioning as intended.

The research team sought to collect objective data on some of the most commonly used assessments and make comparative suggestions on how to characterize them relative to each other. In addition to the comparisons, *Measure for Measure* reported four trends among instruments:

1. Most of the assessments emphasized inferential questions.
2. None of the tests emphasized critical thinking.
3. Tests varied in the extent to which they included content area passages, and while some included separate scores for narrative and expository text, none targeted content-specific reading skills or knowledge.
4. Tests varied on a continuum, but confirm that there is a trade-off between efficiency and specificity of information about individual differences. (pp. 7–8)

What remains clear is that assessment of literacy is not a simple task; no one test can do it all. *Measure for Measure* illuminates some of the gaps in what we know about literacy and assessment. It provides a useful guide for further research.

You can download the report at http://www.carnegie.org/fileadmin/Media/Publications/PDF/tta_Morsy.pdf.

## *Implications for Developing Schoolwide Assessment Programs*

Before the team starts its process of assessment planning, it is important to review the vision statement and the overall district or school assessment plan. Your literacy assessment plan needs to be aligned philosophically with the bigger picture, not a stand-alone component. We suggest these steps to guide your process:

1. Analyze the contextual factors of community and identity as they apply to the culture of the school.
2. Using the data set from the needs assessment, take a snapshot of the school's current literacy programs, including materials, approaches, and interventions. Examine the strengths and weaknesses in developmental reading, intervention, media services, and technology.
3. Using the methods and resources suggested in this chapter, analyze all the assessments used as well as those available to you that have been field tested with a school population similar to yours. Keeping the school improvement vision in mind, prepare a plan that includes recommendations for appropriate literacy assessment and make sure administrators are on board.

4. Present your assessment plan at a faculty meeting, allowing time to introduce and explain the plan, as well as to seek feedback.

5. Provide teachers with a means to record assessment data that doesn't require an inordinate amount of time. Some districts require electronic formats which can be modified to fit individual needs. We have included a template for a Classroom Assessment Profile on our companion website that can serve as a starting point for capturing at-a-glance assessment information for a class. If your school has implemented an RtI format, visit the websites listed in Chapter 6 for additional recoding examples.

6. After teachers have had time to review the literacy assessment plan, rely on their input and feedback to make responsive modifications to the plan. It is important that teachers see assessment not as one more thing they have to do, but as a means to support them in instruction, using most of the things they already do.

## Implications for Developing Districtwide Assessment Programs

Recommendations for developing a districtwide assessment program are much the same as those for developing schoolwide programs. You will work closely with your team and administrators. Again, the vision statement, needs assessment, and two-year plan will guide you, as will district and state content standards. Districts are more focused on standardized assessments and Adequate Yearly Progress (AYP). Regardless of your personal feelings about standardized tests, we hope you have a long-term positive influence on the direction and philosophy of assessment in your district, shaping a program that is responsive to the needs of school and community as well as the students.

A chart that may be helpful to your work (see Figure 5.3) was created by Dr. Stephanie McAndrews (2008), Literacy Program Director at Southern Illinois University at Edwardsville, for her text *Diagnostic Literacy Assessments and Instructional Strategies*. Note that she clarifies differences between norm-referenced, criterion-referenced, and growth-referenced/authentic types of assessments. All three are necessary for a well-balanced assessment program, and each has a different purpose.

School psychologists are generally involved in administering norm-referenced tests, and of course, classroom teachers administer their yearly standardized tests and analyze the scores received for each student. Reading specialists and teachers both administer criterion-referenced tests or diagnostic instruments. However, all may be involved in growth-referenced/authentic assessments, often imbedded in RtI. What is important is that literacy specialists provide the support and professional development necessary in using the data and findings to inform instruction and to guide the development of appropriate literacy instruction for students.

## Revisiting the Vignette

Reflect on the next steps that Joan Forrester, Crawford Middle School's reading specialist, should take to establish a schoolwide assessment program that will foster more effective literacy instruction. In this vignette, Elena Martinez, Jenny's teacher, was very receptive to

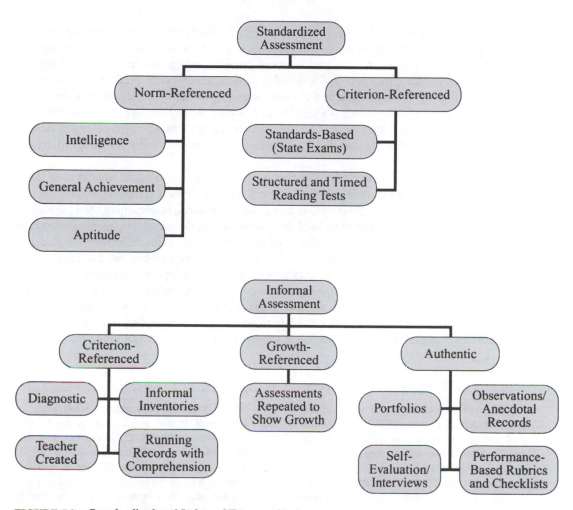

**FIGURE 5.3** *Standardized and Informal Frames of Reference*

*Source:* Figure from McAndrews, S. L. (2008). *Diagnostic Literacy Assessments and Instructional Strategies: A Literacy Specialist's Resource*. Reprinted with permission of the International Reading Association.

the reading specialist's suggestions and ideas. Consider a teacher you may know who would be less than receptive to a reading specialist's recommendations. How would you approach this person? What could you do to make this teacher more comfortable about having you in his or her classroom? What, if any, is the role of the literacy team in supporting teachers who are reluctant or resistant to change?

## Points to Remember

Integral to effective literacy instruction is an equally effective assessment process. Assessment and instruction should be inextricably linked in a recursive, ongoing, and dynamic way. All of the factors that shape a child's literacy development are considered: background experiences, home environment, communities in which the student resides, previous educational experiences, the current classroom context, and the student's assessed literacy skills and abilities. Instruction is designed around assessment data, predicated on the belief that multiple data sources can lead to varied instructional approaches, materials, and methods designed to meet a student's assessed needs. Establishing the right match between the student's needs and appropriate literacy instruction is the ultimate goal of contextualized assessment. Schoolwide and district assessment programs also can be designed around these basic principles.

As part of this process, it is important to think about who needs what kind of information. The superintendent and school board will want broad comparative data. Parents often want to know how their child is doing relative to peers, and teachers need the kind of information that will determine their daily instructional decisions. High-stakes testing, in the form of standardized, norm-referenced tests, may be the cause of anxiety for students, parents, teachers, and administrators. However, we believe that we can use standardized test scores to inform us about longitudinal trends and global performance of students within schools and districts. Likewise, we encourage more authentic means of assessment for making decisions related to reading/language arts instruction in the classroom. District reading specialists have the responsibility to inform, be informed, and work with all stakeholders in implementing and evaluating school and district assessment programs.

## *Portfolio and Self-Assessment Projects*

1. Select two of your students who are at different levels of literacy development. Use contextualized assessment to locate matches and mismatches in their instructional programs. For each student, complete a Learner Assessment Profile (LAP) or a format suitable for RtI. After eight weeks, reflect on your instruction. Which aspects were especially appropriate for the students' needs? What would you change? How did the LAP or RtI plan help you in focusing on what needed to be changed? What will you do next to assist these students in overcoming their assessed reading difficulties?

2. Consider the assessment instruments that teachers are currently using in your school. If these are effective, adapt the Classroom Assessment Profile on our companion website for your school's needs.

3. If your district does not have mandated literacy assessments, survey those instruments that are used. Is there consistency across the schools?

Should there be consistency? What kinds of assessment results are teachers using to plan their literacy instruction? Check with your district's curriculum coordinator, reading coordinator, or supervisor of testing. See if you can discover how decisions have been made regarding any required assessments for your district. Who made the decisions? What test/assessments are required? What type of in-service training do teachers receive about using these assessments to guide their instruction? What happens to all of the assessment findings? Are any students disadvantaged by the process? How do you know? As the reading coordinator, what would you do to either improve the process if it's not working effectively, or sustain and maintain it if it is?

4. *Personal Goal:* Revisit the objective you set for yourself at the beginning of the chapter. Create a portfolio item that reflects what you have learned relative to your objective.

## Recommended Readings: Suggestions for Book Clubs, Study Groups, and Professional Development

**Special Recommendation** McAndrews, S. (2008). *Diagnostic literacy assessments and instructional strategies: A literacy specialist's resource.* Newark, DE: International Reading Association. At last, a book on assessment written by a literacy expert for literacy specialists. Unlike many general assessment resources, this one is an up-to-date, focused reference just for us..This would be an excellent choice for study groups and professional development.

Afflerbach, P. (2007). *Understanding and using reading assessment, K–12.* Newark, DE: International Reading Association. Peter Afflerbach's book will help teachers apply what we know about testing and assessment to developing coherent, effective, and efficient assessment systems. This is a particularly helpful book for a school or district assessment team. However, coaches and specialists can use it to prepare for professional development.

## Online Resources

**Special Recommendation http://www.reading.org/General/Publications/ReadingToday/ RTY-0912_Assessment_Stds.aspx**
International Reading Association and National Council of Teachers of English. (2009/2010). *Revised Standards for the Assessment of Reading and Writing.* These standards reflect new understandings of literacy processes.

**http://www.carnegie.org/fileadmin/Media/Publications/PDF/tta_Morsy.pdf**
Morsy, L., Kieffer, M., & Snow, C. E. (2010). *Measure for measure: A critical consumers' guide to reading comprehension assessments for adolescents.* New York: Carnegie Corporation of New York. Part of the Carnegie Corporation's Time to Act reports, this guide to adolescent literacy assessment instruments is a valuable planning tool.

**http://www.ncrel.org/sdrs/areas/issues/students/earlycld/ea500.htm**
North Central Regional Educational Laboratory (NCREL). (1995–Present). *Assessment.* The NCREL website has a wealth of high-quality information on all aspects of assessment as well as links to important related sites. We recommend this as a "must use" resource for any literacy team. Resources are contributed by some of the most reputable literacy and school reform experts and all information is grounded in research and updated periodically. The site is perfect for teacher study groups.

## Companion Website Resources

The following resources to support and extend your learning of this chapter can be found on our companion website (waveland.com/Extra_Material/32979/): key vocabulary, concepts, and other terms; extended examples; updated resources specifically tied to information in the chapter; related websites; and other support features. The companion website for this chapter also includes templates for a Learner Assessment Profile (LAP) and a Classroom Assessment Profile to complete as you follow the step-by-step directions in the chapter.

# Differentiating Instruction to Meet Learners' Needs: Framing Literacy Intervention

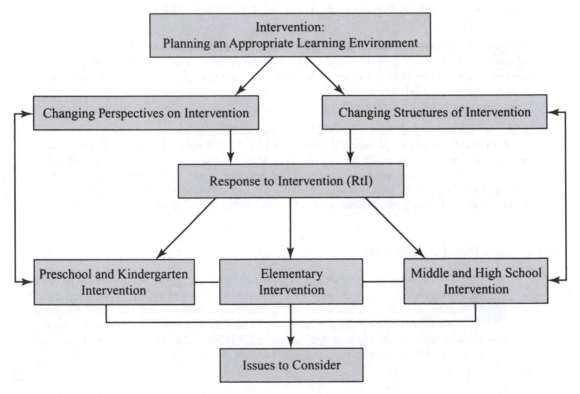

FIGURE 6.1 *Chapter Overview*

## Learning Goals

After reading, discussing, and engaging in activities related to this chapter, you will be able to:

1. Design school or district programs for readers and writers who need additional support with literacy acquisition.

2. Explain the roles of the reading specialist and literacy coach in literacy intervention programs, including Response to Intervention (RtI) models.

3. Describe how former deficit models of remediation and "warehousing" can be socially, psychologically, and emotionally damaging to students.

4. *Personal Learning Goal:* In a three-minute brainstorming session, share what you know about effective literacy intervention. Write an objective or question that reflects something you want to learn as we explore these topics. Share this with others in your group.

## Standards for Reading Professionals

This chapter provides focused support for current IRA Standards for Reading Professionals. See our companion website (waveland.com/Extra_Material/32979/) for a complete listing of the standards that align with this chapter.

### Vignette

The sixth-hour bell rings and 2,200 students at Chicago's Boniface Middle School shuffle between classes. It's a hot September afternoon and students can hardly believe they've only been back in school for three weeks—it seems they never left. Several minutes later, as the bell rings to signal the start of the last period, Julio, a popular seventh-grader who reads about two years below grade level, bursts into Liana Casal's Title I reading classroom, obviously upset and on the verge of tears. Usually, Liana is standing near the door, greeting Julio and the other five students, two girls and three boys, in this literacy intervention class. Today, however, she is at her desk. Her district is just beginning to engage in planning for the process of school reform, and she is going over her notes from today's meeting. As Julio slams his books on the desk and puts his head down on his arms, silence drops like a guillotine on his classmates and their teacher. Julio has always struggled with reading. With a mixture of anger, hurt, and embarrassment, he recounts that on his way to class three friends made fun of him because he had to go to the room where the "stupid kids go to read baby books." Liana notices the look on the faces of the other five students. They seem to share Julio's hurt and embarrassment, almost as if the words had been aimed at them.

Liana has been a Title I Reading Teacher for twelve years at Boniface. Approximately 40 percent of Boniface students are African American, another 20 percent are Hispanic English learners, exhibiting various degrees of proficiency in both languages, and the remaining 40 percent are predominantly native English speakers. Although a smaller percentage of white children are in the Title I program, the ethnic mix of Liana's students reflects the diversity of the school and neighborhood. The area is one of poverty, and many students struggle with reading and writing. Fortunately, Liana is knowledgeable about school-related literacy and various programs of effective intervention, although her Title I program is a pull-out model. The goal is to provide intensive intervention, creating proficient readers and writers, and obviating the need for continued intervention. Liana has high standards, and she is well liked and trusted by her students, who receive one hour of small-group (six students) daily literacy instruction in place of the regular developmental reading class.

*Both Liana and Julio's grandparents came from Mexico, and although both have been raised in a dominant English-speaking culture, Spanish is significant in the cultures of home and the immediate community. Liana and Julio consider* *themselves proficient bilingual speakers. Julio appears to have a sizeable English vocabulary and above-average intelligence; all of his education has been in English.*

### Thinking Points

1. How might Liana react to Julio?
2. What would you suggest that she should do or say in response to his frustrations and concerns?

### Expanding the Vignette: Exploring the Issues

*Liana has the next hour free and finds Tony, the literacy coach, in the copy room. She is upset by Julio's experience and confesses to Tony that she did not know what to say. Indeed, she has struggled with the issues of stigma and damage to self-esteem inherent in providing extra literacy help to struggling students ever since her first Title I assignment. Even though she speaks fluent Spanish, it has been two generations since her family left Mexico, and she feels out of touch with the lives of Spanish-speaking students who have recently moved to Chicago. Liana also admits that* *she knows little about the home cultures of her African American students or her white students. She recounts to Tony that she did her best to reassure Julio he was definitely not "stupid" and he was fortunate to be getting extra help in reading in a supportive environment. However, Liana acknowledged that, even as she spoke, it was clear to her and to Julio that her words were of little help, no matter how noble her intentions. She wondered what she could do to help her students overcome the stigma of being singled out and separated from instruction with their peers.*

### Thinking Points

1. What issues and questions have you identified in the vignette?
2. How might Tony, the literacy coach, respond to Liana, the Title I teacher?
3. What long-term or periodic measures would you suggest to Tony or to Liana to deal with the issues you raised?
4. Is there anything proactive that could have been done to avoid this problem? Do you know of any fundamental systems or plans in your district that involve reading specialists, literacy coaches, and teachers that could alleviate or diminish the problem of students being singled out and labeled?

Keep your answers to these questions in mind as you read. We will revisit them at the end of the chapter.

## *Providing an Appropriate Learning Environment*

Liana's dilemma as described in the opening vignette is familiar to Title I, RtI, and special education teachers, and to all who work with readers for whom literacy acquisition does not come easily. Caring professionals recognize the tension between providing the kind of support that is characteristic of intensive intervention and contributing to the diminished self-esteem that such differential treatment often evokes. We recognize that being fully literate may not ensure access to a high-paying job and a happy life, but we understand the high levels of literacy required for the average individual to get through a single day, and we want more for students than just survival. We want them to have full access to the job world, to the political process, to social inclusion, and to our institutions of higher education. We want individuals to be able to read, locate the information they need, receive pleasure from reading, and make personal connections. We also want to help them figure out how to use literacy in moral, legal, and ethical ways. We want it all for them.

The core beliefs that drive our vision for this chapter and determine its composition are:

1. Everyone involved in the school community is responsible for creating literate students.
2. Differences in literacy acquisition, use of language, and ethnicity can and do position students outside of the school culture, often leading to overidentification in special education programs.
3. We can help all students increase literacy proficiency by differentiating what we do for individuals within groups and providing support before they fail.
4. Students need *connection*. They need their teachers to show them how to bring their differing lived experiences and prior knowledge into the classroom, and how to use these to enhance learning.

This chapter provides an overview of research-based intervention practices in elementary schools. It also examines the rapidly growing intervention initiatives for adolescents and preschool students. We will discuss the framework for Response to Intervention (RtI) and other intervention structures. The methods for differentiating instruction we provide are grounded in a long tradition of solid evidence. Although often framed within an RtI structure, the elements of high-quality classroom instruction—(1) opportunities to engage in rich discussion and critical thinking, (2) focused and imbedded skill and strategy instruction, (3) self-regulating practices, and (4) incorporation of writing, representing, listening, and speaking—are still integral to effective evidence-based practice no matter how your school structures intervention. As you read the chapter, we hope you will reflect on the following statement, which is at the core of our belief system: *The components of evidence-based practice and what works for struggling readers have not changed.*

These new formats for intervention have huge implications for the roles reading specialists and literacy coaches must play. You will find a wealth of information and we will guide you to additional resources to support your work with struggling readers and their teachers. In addressing the topics in this chapter, we will be discussing a number of challenges. Challenges are inherent in any process of growth and change. Whenever you see the word *challenge,* a word so many researchers use when they don't have all the answers, we suggest you replace it with the word *opportunity*. We believe that's what challenges really are.

## Changing Perspectives on Intervention

### The Origins of Response to Intervention (RtI)

With the passing of the Individuals with Disabilities Education Improvement Act (IDEA), signed into law by President George W. Bush in 2004, Response to Intervention (RtI)

...he a model designed to identify and provide early, preventive support (intervention)
...idents experiencing reading difficulties. According to The National Association of
...Directors of Special Education (NASDSE), the two overarching goals of RtI are to
deliver evidence-based interventions and to use students' responses to those interventions
for determining instructional needs and intervention. In particular, educators and legislators were concerned about the rapidly growing numbers of students placed in special
education programs, particularly the disproportionate numbers whose culture, language,
economic status, or ethnicity differed from that of the dominant culture (IRA, 2004).
Instead of the previous "wait-to-fail" models based on the discrepancy between a student's
IQ and achievement, RtI sought to support all students through high-quality instruction,
continuous review of student progress, collaboration, and parent involvement. IDEA 2004
allowed districts to use up to 15 percent of their special education budget to fund RtI's intervention initiatives. It is important to note that *there is no mandated program* as such that *is*
RtI: rather, it is more of a structure. We agree with the Wisconsin Department of Public
Instruction core belief that:

> Response to Intervention is a process for achieving higher levels of academic achievement
> and behavioral success for all students. Because RtI is a systems change process, an RtI sys-
> tem may align to other school improvement processes your school or district is currently
> using. (http://dpi.wi.gov/rti/index.html)

Until recently, intervention in literacy focused on elementary school, especially grades one
through three. Within the last decade, intervention has rapidly expanded. Because we
recognize the developmental nature of literacy, researchers are exploring programs for
preschool and kindergarten associated with goals of RtI: providing high-quality instruction, monitoring progress, and removing barriers that prevent very young children from
experiencing success in early literacy (Kirp, 2007; NICHD, 2004). In addition, *Reading
Next—A Vision for Action and Research in Middle and High School Literacy* (Biancarosa &
Snow, 2004, 2006) raised awareness about the plight of the millions of high school students
(one in four) likely to leave school without a diploma and without the necessary skills to
ensure a productive future. We have tried retaining many of them to no avail. Beginning in
1932, dozens of studies have shown that retention doesn't work (McGill-Franzen & Allington,
1993). It is costly, damaging, and has little educational value. Academic achievement and
self-concept are negatively affected and those children are far more likely to drop out of
school than students who were never retained (Shepard & Smith, 1990). Under the U.S.
Department of Education Striving Readers initiative, funds became available for the development of effective adolescent literacy programs, particularly in districts with high numbers of Title I students. In spite of the fact that adolescent literacy has been a hot topic for
researchers for over twenty years, intervention for these students remains the exception
rather than the rule. Recently, however, administrators, literacy leaders, and teachers began
to question whether the principles associated with RtI could also hold promise for these
adolescents.

An added challenge for those developing adolescent literacy intervention programs
is reversing the damage to self-esteem caused in part by the years these students spent
comparing themselves to their peers (Colvin & Schlosser, 1997/1998).

Such a student is Eliza Nawman, the central character in Myla Goldberg's wonderful novel *Bee Season.* In this book, Eliza is the daughter of Rabbi Heimel Nawman, and the sister of brilliant Aaron Nawman. She is also a student in Ms. Bergermeyer's combination fourth/fifth-grade class. Eliza, along with everyone else in the school, is aware that this is the room to which all the "unimpressive fifth graders" have been assigned. In the last three years, Eliza has come to realize she is among those "from whom great things are not expected." By this time she has grown accustomed to those posters of puppies and kittens clinging precariously to the ropes and ladders they are struggling to climb. Usually such posters include supposedly motivating captions, such as *Hang in there!* and *If at first you don't succeed. . . .* Because she is a C student, Eliza is among those who never win school contests, get chased by boys, or become Student of the Week. As a result, when the annual school spelling bee is announced, Eliza hopes the pain and humiliation will be mercifully terminated by swift defeat. "She has no reason to expect that this, her first spelling bee, will differ from the outcome of any other school event seemingly designed to confirm, display, or amplify her mediocrity" (p. 2).

■ *Author Connection: Brenda*  As I read the passage in *Bee Season,* I thought about all the Elizas, both male and female, I came to know in my many years of working with readers "from whom great things were not expected." Most of these students did become competent and confident readers and writers, or at least adequate ones. In fact, many have completed degrees at universities and technical colleges. But I still worry about those whose literacy skills are marginal, the ones who "got away." How are they doing?

Some students need a great deal of support with literacy activities, and I am saddened about students like Eliza because their teachers didn't understand that literacy is socially situated, that students deserve to experience rich discourse models and a variety of challenging materials within the same settings as their peers, that they have a right to read books that reflect their own experiences, that by choosing different approaches and materials, we can alter internal and external literacy events, and, especially, that these students are perfectly capable of making decisions about their instruction.

## Response to Intervention (RtI) in the Elementary School

Perhaps the most effective way to explore the past and present research base for effective intervention in elementary schools is to show how principled intervention can be supported within the structure of RtI. Imbedding sound practice within the RtI model will provide you with a richer understanding of the interplay between a program's *structure* (the RtI framework) and its *content* (high-quality instruction).

### What Do We Know about Struggling Early Elementary Readers?

In the last decades of the twentieth century, increased focus on early intervention resulted in a number of effective models aimed at helping beginning readers. Among them are

Reading Recovery (Pinnell, Fried, & Estes, 1990); Early Intervention in Reading (EIR) (Taylor, Short, Shearer, & Frye, 1995); and Success for All (Slavin, Madden, Dole, & Wasik, 1996). These programs and others like them are effective in increasing the literacy proficiency of young children. In addition, they continue to inform us about characteristics of successful intervention. We know that in effective models:

- Reading for meaning is the primary consideration and fluency is among the major goals.
- Intervention is frequent, regular, and of sufficient duration.
- Instruction is fast-paced, using a variety of sequenced and selected texts and leveled books.
- Familiarity with print is gained through reading and writing.
- Intervention is coupled with sound first instruction. (Pikulski, 1995)

The proliferation of these programs, designed primarily for first-graders, became the basis for exploration of ways to help both younger and older students.

### RtI: The Three-Tiered Model in the Elementary School

Mention RtI to many educators and you will hear that it is a three-tiered model of intervention. You may be surprised to know that there is no legal requirement to use a three-tiered model (Allington & Walmsley, 2007). Since there is no official RtI "program," there are many ways for schools to enact RtI. U.S. Department of Education (USDE) regulations support many different models in use today (Zirkel, 2006). Some schools are adding a fourth tier corresponding to special education services. A variety of commercially prepared RtI programs and materials are available for schools to adopt. As with all instructional products, some are excellent and some are not. Allington and Walmsley (2007) warn that no packaged program can differentiate instruction and meet the needs of all students. They argue that packaged programs are among the elements that got us here in the first place, and that whether or not schools choose to conceptualize RtI in the three-tiered model, "what's most important is that struggling readers are offered targeted, expert, and intensive reading instruction *before* they are labeled as students with learning disabilities" (p. ix).

At all three tiers, guiding principles for RtI include high-quality instruction, continuous review of student progress, and collaboration among professionals. Universal screening, that is, screening of all students, is conducted at set intervals, such as three times a year, or quarterly for younger students, to identify struggling readers as early as possible. However, assessment occurs more frequently at Tiers II and III. Because time and again evidence shows us that the teacher's expertise is among the most powerful predictors of student achievement (Pressley, Allington, Wharton-McDonald, Block, & Morrow, 2001; Ruddell, 2004), professional development to support evidence-based practice is essential. This requires time for teachers to plan and implement new practices and to evaluate the impact of professional development on their teaching and on student learning (Desimone, 2009; Fullan, 2005; Joyce & Showers, 2002; Marzano, Waters, & McNulty, 2005).

Parent involvement is a strong component in RtI. Any decisions, particularly those that involve moving a student between tiers, include parents. Parents should also be informed of their right to request a formal evaluation of their child for special education services at any time (Noell, 2008). The evaluation must be completed within a specified time, often 60 to 90 days, depending on state statutes.

Figure 6.2 on pages 120–121 provides an overview of the components of tiered intervention in one elementary RtI program. You can refer to it as we describe the elements in each tier. See our companion website to obtain a template for developing an overview of your own Three-Tiered Intervention Matrix.

***Tier I—Core Instruction Interventions.*** Tier I can best be characterized as a preventive and proactive model. In response to scores on universal screening and the teacher's informal observations and assessment, the teacher adjusts or modifies teaching (intervention).

**High-Quality Core Instruction:** Before RtI came along, researchers had already confirmed that a high-quality curriculum, based on expert teaching, is effective (Allington & Johnston, 2002; Pressley, Allington, Wharton-McDonald, Block, & Morrow, 2001). High-quality instruction is that offered by teachers who have a high degree of knowledge related to literacy development and understand the factors that inhibit literacy acquisition and who are skilled in implementing methods that enhance literacy development. The challenge for RtI is to incorporate all we know about successful intervention and apply it in a three-tier model.

**Screening and Monitoring:** In the previous chapter, we examined the instruments and practices commonly used in screening and monitoring progress. The National Center on Response to Intervention (www.rti4success.org) defines screening as follows: *Screening* involves brief assessments that are valid, reliable, and evidence-based. They are conducted with all students or targeted groups of students to identify students who are at risk of academic failure and, therefore, likely to need additional or alternative forms of instruction to supplement the conventional general education approach. By documenting before and after intervention progress, the effectiveness of the instruction can be ascertained (Jenkins, Graff, & Miglioretti, 2009). *Monitoring* involves examining data from all sources, including student responses to questions, daily work artifacts, and observational information, and using that to make decisions. Performance can be recorded as consistent ongoing evidence of progress, identifying students who need additional support and adjusting instruction as necessary. Periodic "quick screenings" using one-minute word recognition lists, one-minute freewrites, and running records on current guided reading books are ways to accomplish this goal.

**Differentiated Instruction:** Differentiated instruction is based on evidence from assessments and observations. There are many ways the classroom teacher might respond to individual needs. These include adapting materials, implementing targeted literacy centers, engaging in further explanation, reteaching, and allowing for additional practice. Differentiated literacy centers are unlike the stations so commonly used in the 1970s and 1980s. In differentiated literacy centers, instruction is based on student assessment data. Centers employ multilevel resources, include levels of support based on needs, enable varied responses for each skill or strategy, and use a simple coding system to select activities within the student's zone of proximal development (Southall, 2007; Vygotsky, 1978).

| Sample Three-Tiered RtI Intervention Matrix (K–6) | | | |
|---|---|---|---|
| *Tiers of Intervention* | *S = Setting, P = Population Served, I = Instructional Agent, M = Materials, PRT = Parent, C/RS = Coach/Reading Specialist's Role* | *Intervention* | *Assessment and Monitoring* |
| **Tier I** Universal Education: 75–85% receiving some level of support for a time during the year | S = Regular education classroom <br> P = 75–85% <br> I = Classroom teacher with collaboration, support, and professional development <br> M = High-success leveled texts <br> PRT = Informed on progress and interventions; in on decisions <br> C/RS = Serve as mentor; facilitate/oversee RtI; provide professional development, consult | • High-quality initial instruction <br> • Increased differentiated instruction (targeted to immediate needs) <br> • Some use of instructional stations/literacy centers <br> • Specific interventions <br> • High levels of authentically engaged time (minutes of writing and reading connected text) <br> • Flexible grouping | • Summative: universal screening 3 times a year; standardized tests <br> • Formative: teacher monitoring of daily events, anecdotal records, student work samples, running records, retellings, rubrics <br> • Student self-evaluation |
| **Tier II** 10–20% receiving increased support | S = Classroom, but may include limited pull-out, similar in and out of class instructional cycle <br> P = 10–20% <br> I = Classroom teacher with support personnel (reading teacher or reading specialist) <br> M = High-quality leveled texts, *most* materials similar both in and out of classroom <br> PRT = Informed on progress and interventions; in on decisions <br> C/RS = Work with student for 30 minutes 3–5 times per week (pull-out) Increase support, coaching, collaboration, and professional development | • Extends (not supplants) Tier I classroom instruction <br> • Pull-out 30 minutes 3–5 times per week in addition to Tier I time <br> • More differentiation, more intensity, more reteaching <br> • Groups of 3–5 students <br> • Regular education texts and materials but some supplementary materials at times <br> • Instruction stresses guided comprehension, cognition, modeling, questioning, feedback, repetition, imbedded skill practice | • Monitoring/review of formal and informal data every 2 to 4 weeks <br> • Standardized tests, possible individual testing <br> • Formative data same as Tier I, but more detailed/focused <br> • Assessment planned collaboratively by teacher and coach/reading teacher or specialist <br> • Evaluate outcomes |

**FIGURE 6.2   *Sample Three-Tiered RtI Intervention Matrix (K–6)***

| Tiers of Intervention | S = Setting, P = Population Served, I = Instructional Agent, M = Materials, PRT = Parent, C/RS = Coach/Reading Specialist's Role | Intervention | Assessment and Monitoring |
|---|---|---|---|
| **Tier III** 5–10% receiving intensive support | S = Pull-out instruction <br> P = 5–10% <br> I = Reading professional/ learning specialist <br> M = increased use of specialized materials when necessary <br> PRT = Informed on progress and interventions; in on decisions <br> C/RS = Coach coordinates intervention with team approach, provides professional development, assists with assessment Reading Specialist may be the intervention teacher | • High-intensity pull-out instruction <br> • Two 30-minute sessions daily <br> • Group of 3, but 1 to 1 preferred <br> • Intense modeling, cognitive coaching, targeted skill and strategy instruction, and practice in authentic tasks; highly individualized support <br> • Use of regular education reading materials and texts or special materials <br> • Fidelity to common goals | • Close monitoring with summative/formative assessment by reading specialist and classroom teacher <br> • Data collected and reviewed weekly in consultation <br> • Collaborate on inclusion or referral for possible special education services |

**FIGURE 6.2** *(continued)*

***Grouping of Students:*** Classroom teachers use whole-class instruction, flexible groups, single purpose skill or strategy group sessions, and individualized instruction. In Tier II, instruction is provided in small groups of no more than five, but ideally three. In Tier III, students receive instruction in groups of three or less, and often, one-to-one as needed (Howard, 2009; Opitz & Ford, 2008).

***Collaborative Support and Problem-Solving:*** Although the coach or reading specialist may guide the overall Tier I processes, whenever possible, teachers' collaboration with colleagues is preferable to direct coach involvement for at least two reasons. First, ownership and responsibility are key if RtI is going to work. For too long, students who struggled were *given away* instead of being instructed with their peers. Second, the effectiveness of co-planning among colleagues is supported by a substantial research base (Deal & Peterson, 1999; Friend & Cook, 2007; Lambert, 2002; Marzano, 2007). Grade-level colleagues are the day-to-day experts and are in the best position to support each other in problem-solving. Peer initiatives may include teachers working in grade-level groups, forming study groups, sharing materials, creating a "bank" of literacy centers or other materials for differentiation, co-teaching or observing lessons, and meeting regularly to exchange ideas. They might also consult members of the school's literacy commit-tee or intervention committee for help (Cole, 2007).

***Parent Involvement:***  Parent involvement at Tier I (and other tiers as well) involves frequent communication and progress reporting. Parents can provide a great deal of helpful information about a child's interests, background, home culture, and needs. To the level that is appropriate, support for parents may include providing them with materials, activities, and training to facilitate the child's literacy growth. However, these decisions are carefully considered on an individual basis. Parents are regarded as important consultants and allies. The RtI website (www.rtinetwork.com) has many suggestions for schools and many resources for parents.

**Tier II—Targeted Group Interventions.**  Typically, in Tier II, struggling students continue to receive reading instruction with their peers as well as additional support. However, the levels of instruction and intervention are more intense, with the goal of providing support for the shortest amount of time until the student no longer needs the intervention in that tier.

***Instructional Intensity:***  Additional support is provided to struggling students in a more focused and individualized manner, perhaps by extending the classroom instruction for that day, reteaching a lesson, providing additional time in an after-school or summer school reading program, or preteaching to enable a student to benefit from an upcoming lesson in the regular education classroom.

***Guidance and Support for Students and Teachers:***  At the Tier II level, the literacy coach may offer guidance and support to the classroom teacher as she or he works with students, or a reading specialist or other professional might provide additional intervention in a daily pull-out program.

***Alignment with Classroom Instruction:***  The materials and methods used in the pull-out sessions are as closely aligned with those in the classroom as possible. Support is *additive* (in addition to), not *supplantive* (in place of) instruction in the regular classroom, enabling smooth transitions.

***Frequent Monitoring:***  Increased attention to student progress is a major part of Tier II planning. Students may be evaluated more frequently to ensure that they are benefiting from intervention.

***Parent Involvement:***  Parents remain allies, providing key insights into what they are seeing at home with regard to reading. They are informed and involved in any decisions about moving their child from one tier to another (in both directions).

**Tier III—Intensive Individualized Interventions.**  The U.S. Department of Education is clear that RtI is a general education intervention initiative. The *intensive instruction* typically associated with Tier III of RtI is reserved for readers who have received additional help in Tiers I and II, but continue to struggle with learning to read. It is data-driven, focused, and highly individualized.

***Involvement of Reading Experts:***  Usually, intensive intervention for these students involves a highly qualified reading expert, such as the reading specialist or other professional, working with the child. Reading is a complex cognitive process and students who struggle require instruction that accommodates the complex array of problems that can occur.

***Pull-Out Instruction, Small-Group or One-to-One:*** Intervention is provided outside of the classroom, most often in a one-to-one or very small group setting, sometimes twice a day. The methods may employ specialized materials as supplements to those in the classroom. However, it is important to ensure that, as much as possible, *the reading instruction is philosophically in line with the literacy practices within the regular classroom* and that the classroom teacher is part of a collaborative, coordinated instructional effort.

***Parent Involvement:*** Parent involvement is sustained. Because parents have been involved in decision-making and instructional support from the beginning, they remain critical partners, who support school efforts and who receive any support they need to contribute to their child's literacy learning.

After students have received the intensive intervention provided in Tier III, those who continue to experience significant difficulties may be referred for evaluation for special education services. Some schools identify Tier IV to distinguish their special education program.

### Revisiting the Vignette: Thinking Points

1. What might be included in the discussion between the literacy coach and Liana?
2. List three (or more) questions they might ask themselves.
3. Where could they look for resources to answer these questions?
4. Who should be involved in future meetings regarding Julio and others like him?

## Intervention at the Preschool and Kindergarten Levels

### What Do We Know about Intervention at the Preschool and Kindergarten Levels?

Intervention for our youngest learners focuses on *prevention* of future delays in literacy and language growth. Such programs devote a great deal of attention to the development of literacy and language by providing a range of early individualized services aimed at helping preschoolers and kindergarteners acquire literacy and language skills.

Elfrieda Hiebert and Barbara Taylor (2000) shared their findings from a study of effective kindergarten intervention. They suggest that a solid foundation for reading can be established by:

- Restructuring literacy activities for the whole class;
- Defining the role of the teacher as supporting *individuals* through informal conversation in planned and skillful ways, rather than through one-to-one or pull-out programs; and
- Providing activities and experiences that involve foundational processes of reading and writing, overall literacy and book concepts, and phonemic awareness (Ayres, 1998; Durkin, 1974–1975; Hansen & Farrell, 1995; Phillips, Norris, & Mason, 1996).

Instruction resides in the focused engagement and structured discussions during book reading, poetry chanting, and other typical kindergarten activities. However, sustaining momentum in these language-rich kindergartens requires a reading specialist, teachers, and other school personnel who are committed to ongoing professional development (see Chapter 11).

Less formal measures aimed at helping kindergartners who lack exposure to story reading attempt to recreate the lap-reading experience (Klesius & Griffith, 1996), the mutually rewarding, highly social, interactive, book-sharing scenario between child and parent. In this language-rich dyadic model, both parent and child interrupt the reading frequently to comment, point out features, ask questions, or make experiential connections (Dickinson & Smith, 1996; Teale & Martinez, 1996). These discussions become increasingly complex as the adult skillfully reduces the amount of scaffolding (Bruner, 1983) to reflect the child's growing knowledge of character, story elements, cause and effect, and other elements of comprehension (Vogt & Nagano, 2003). Margo Wood and Elizabeth Prata Salvetti (2001) found that carefully trained university volunteers in the America Reads Challenge and community volunteers were able to conduct high-quality, focused, read-aloud discussions.

Isabel Beck and Margaret McKeown (2001) noticed that children often ignored text information and responded to questions about story content by focusing on pictures and background knowledge. They developed an approach to read-alouds called Text Talk, in which the teacher intersperses reading with open questions and discussion and follows each story with explicit vocabulary instruction. Continued investigations such as these provide teachers, tutors, and caregivers with information about how best to support literacy awareness and development for these children.

A strong problem-solving approach undergirds RtI efforts at this level and parental involvement in assessment and planning is crucial. A review of comprehensive research from a number of sources reveals overwhelming agreement on the elements of effective early literacy programs: a language-rich environment, a focus on vocabulary, phonological awareness, letter/sound knowledge, and print awareness (Kirp, 2007; Maeroff, 2006; NICHD Early Childhood Network, 2004). At the University of Kansas Center for Response to Intervention in Early Childhood (CRTIEC), Tier I RtI is described as *early care and intervention*; that is, evidence-based services and supports implemented in generic settings.

***Universal Screening at Preschool and Kindergarten.*** Juli Pool and Evelyn Johnson provide in-depth analysis and comparison of a wide variety of assessment instruments. Their work, *Universal Screening for Reading Problems: Why and How Should We Do This?* (2009) can be found on the RtI Action Network at www.rtinetwork.org/Essential/Assessment/Universal/ar/ReadingProblems.

Invernizzi, Justice, Landrum, and Booker (2004/2005) suggest considering the following essential criteria in choosing an appropriate screening tool for preschool and kindergarten-age children:

1. It must examine children's early literacy skills across the four core skills.
2. It must effectively and accurately differentiate between those children who are at risk and those who are not.

3. It must be efficient and easily administered.
4. It must meet minimum standards of technical adequacy for validity and reliability. The goal of the measure is to minimize the number of misclassified cases. (Johnson, Pool, & Carter, 2009)

As students move through Tier II and require more intensive intervention, teachers require more support as well. Tier III requires expanding curriculum, instructional practice, and professional development resources. In the CRTIEC model, Tier III intervention is consistent with special education encompassing early care and intervention as well as more specialized settings, planning, and implementation.

***Parent Involvement in Early Childhood RtI.*** In a research synthesis of effective school–family partnerships (Carlson & Christenson, 2005), certain intervention components stood out as being more effective. The most successful practices stressed:

- Collaboration and dialogue between families and schools;
- Joint monitoring of student progress;
- Parent interventions that focused on specific measurable outcomes;
- Interventions emphasizing the role of parents as tutors in a defined subject area; and
- School–family consultation.

Research demonstrates that parent involvement in intervention for preschool-aged children results in significant gains and greatly enhances the outcomes for these children (Carlson & Christenson, 2005; Huebner & Meltzoff, 2005). For example, when parents were supported in using dialogic reading (rich discussions about the story, pointing to different features of print, playing with sounds and words during reading, discussing characters' feelings, chanting, and other literate behaviors), their children made sizable gains in language development, including number of words and mean length of utterance (Huebner & Meltzoff, 2005). Dialogic reading is a structured, evidence-based book-sharing intervention shown to promote language skills of two- to three-year-olds, in which a caregiver learns to engage a child in one-to-one reading using open-ended questions to tell a story jointly (Whitehurst et al., 1988).

McConnell, Carta, and Greenwood (2008) provide an excellent overview of the challenges of translating the tiered model to preschool. Many of them are similar to those encountered in intervention programs for older students, such as lack of resources, few models of long-term efficacy, limited availability of qualified personnel to support Tiers II and III, and limited time and space to carry out additional instruction. Like their system-wide counterparts, early childhood intervention programs grapple with the paucity of research-based models that show what works for which students under which conditions (McConnell, Carta, & Greenwood, 2008).

There are some unique challenges at the preschool level. Lack of stringent professional certification requirements for childcare professionals, early childhood teachers, and instructional assistants is a problem that is currently being addressed. These educators need to be respected and held to the same high standards and afforded the same access to professional development opportunities as their elementary and secondary colleagues.

# Intervention at the Middle and High School Levels

We know how hard it continues to be for many middle and secondary teachers to embrace the notion that they are responsible for helping students use reading and writing to enhance subject area learning. Recent school reform initiatives, core standards, and sanctions have made changes in that direction necessary. Most schools we know started to address this idea by requiring all teachers to attend professional development on content area reading and writing, and by increasing the presence of specialists and coaches in middle and secondary classrooms. Now, there appears to be even more pressure to adopt models of intervention, such as RtI, that require even greater responsibility, coordination, and collaboration for concurrent literacy and content instruction (Echevarria & Vogt, 2011). We realize not all middle and secondary teachers are not on board with us yet. We are, however, committed to providing you with examples of how pioneering schools and districts are restructuring intervention. We hope that no matter where you are on the continuum of progress in this area, you will use the information as a catalyst for reflection and discussion. We realize the information available at the time of this writing is limited. Our companion website will be valuable in informing you of new research findings and program examples. We will continue to update the site and encourage you to check what's new on a regular basis.

## What Do We Know about Struggling Adolescent Readers?

In a study of adolescent struggling adolescent readers, Vogt (1997) confirmed the findings of earlier investigators (Kos, 1991; Meek, 1983) that a long history of failure had resulted in poor grades, low self-esteem, avoidance of reading-related tasks, and behavioral difficulties. More unsettling is that many struggling adolescent readers had given up all hope of ever improving their reading ability.

Keith Stanovich (1986) and MaryEllen Vogt (1989) also uncovered a number of disturbing incongruities between both preservice and in-service teachers' attitudes and practices relative to high and low achievers. When compared to opportunities given to lower-achieving peers, higher-performing students were given more time to read, asked higher-level questions followed by more wait time, provided with richer materials, and given more opportunities to lead. Such discrepant opportunities led Keith Stanovich to describe a phenomenon he called the "Matthew Effect," borrowed from the Book of Matthew. When it comes to literacy development, "The rich get richer, and the poor get poorer."

■ **Group Inquiry Activity**  With others in your group, explore the following issues:

1. Using a brainstorming technique called the Whip, take turns as each person provides a response to the question, What are some reasons not all students achieve literacy proficiency in our schools?
2. When all group members have contributed three ideas, discuss the responses and add to the list.
3. Develop a group reply to the following question: Given unlimited resources and the necessary commitment, could we help all students, especially those like Julio, reach their literacy potential? Provide reasons for your answer.

4. Place an R before ideas expressed by your group that involve readjustment of instruction. Place an IE in front of ideas that would require increased expenditures.
5. Which of these ideas might be helpful to Liana?

Share your responses with others in the class.

### Establishing an External RtI Framework for Adolescents

***Organizing and Coordinating Services and Programs.*** In middle schools and high schools across the United States, forward-looking school reformers are embracing the challenge of developing stronger programs for struggling adolescent readers. Although few RtI models are available to guide these endeavors, shared information on successes is finding its way into professional journals and onto reputable Internet sources. Because of the complicated infrastructures of middle and high schools, it is no surprise that some are turning to commercial programs such as READ 180 (Scholastic, 2002), a comprehensive software program that has been around awhile, but is now adapted to meet RtI specifications. In an *Education Weekly* article by Christina Samuels (2009), a quote by Darryl Mellard, director of the University of Kansas Center for Research in Lawrence, Kansas, sums up the dilemma: "Without scientific literature outlining an overall method of applying RtI to secondary schools, educators have only their 'best guesses' for what components a program should have to be successful." Samuels describes a program at Palmer High School in Colorado Springs:

> ***Structuring Service:*** The school organized the resources and programs already in place into tiers of increasingly intense intervention, exploring and adding other types of intervention for students. This included establishing a tutoring center, available to students and staffed at all times during the school day. One of the features we found especially compelling was that the center was available to any student who needed more reinforcement or help in a particular subject. Even high-achieving students who were enrolled in the school's International Baccalaureate Program began to use the center's services. This is particularly appealing to counteract the stigma associated with pull-out programs.

> ***Screening and Monitoring:*** Screening involved the use of a computerized assessment instrument that provided lexile levels and reported areas of strength and difficulty. It was aligned with the state standards and administered to all middle school students. Additional data were obtained from Colorado's state standardized tests, and teacher and parent recommendations.

***Issues Surrounding Instructional Practice.*** Although we owe much to the educators who are addressing the challenges of forging new territory, until details become available from a number of successful RtI-structured programs for adolescents, attempts at duplicating them are inherently limited. If there is one thing we want you to remember about RtI, it is this:

> There is nothing magic about a three-tiered structure. RtI is a delivery system, not an internal instructional system. Instruction is what takes place within the classroom—the research-based literacy processes and procedures, taught by committed, skillful professionals—that constitutes principled intervention.

### Research-Based Adolescent Intervention Practices

***Striving Readers.***  There are a number of middle and secondary schools applying what we know about adolescent literacy intervention to models, other than RtI, that meet the goals of Striving Readers. The U.S. Department of Education Striving Readers initiative is designed to accomplish two goals:

- To raise middle and high school students' literacy levels in Title I-eligible schools with significant numbers of students reading below grade level, and
- To build a strong, scientific research base for strategies that improve adolescent literacy instruction.

Government funding is available to schools for developing projects meeting the Striving Readers goals and criteria, which must include:

- A *supplemental* literacy intervention targeted to students reading significantly below grade level;
- A *schoolwide* literacy program for improving student literacy *in all disciplines;* and
- A strong *experimental evaluation* component.

Schools must be willing to design programs with rigorous attention to what Yeaton and Sechrest (1981) refer to as "strength of treatment." Strength of treatment is defined as the likelihood that the treatment could have its intended outcome. Programs that receive funding must clearly outline the scientifically-based elements they plan to implement before they can be approved for funding. Strong treatments contain large amounts of practices in pure form leading to change. Assessments of strength are made independently of knowledge of outcome of treatment in any given case. For more information, greater detail, and examples of successful intervention programs created by schools under the Striving Readers initiative, see www2.ed.gov/programs/strivingreaders.

The pioneering San Diego Striving Readers' Project, *Building Academic Success for Adolescent Readers* (McDonald, Thornley, Staley, & Moore, 2009), is one of the strongest and most descriptive examples of a successful Striving Reader project. It incorporates five curriculum sets and shows great promise for helping struggling adolescent readers.

***Five Curriculum Sets:***  Building on a research base from a study done in New Zealand, McDonald, Thornley, Staley, and Moore (2009) developed five sets that form the basis of their Student Literacy Instruction in the Content Areas (SLIC) curriculum:

1. Previewing text and applying knowledge about text forms to prepare for the reading and writing tasks ahead.
2. Using the language and surface features of the text to build prior knowledge before reading.
3. Enhancing comprehension by using complex processing skills, such as inference and synthesis, while continually cross-checking new understandings using the reading with the previewing.

4. Solving vocabulary problems as they arise during the reading.
5. Writing for a range of purposes and audiences.

Because the researchers found that students were able to use these strategies across content areas, it was imperative to support teachers in using stable routines for helping students as they encountered new texts and tasks. Teachers were supported in facilitating orientation to text, a focus on task analysis, note-making, questioning and discussion, and adjusting writing to the intended task.

Our best advice is to use the resources from established, reputable educational organizations such as the International Reading Association (www.reading.org), the RtI Network (www.rtinetwork.org), National Middle School Association (www.nmsa.org), National Council of Teachers of English (NCTE; www.ncte.org), Association for Supervision and Curriculum Development (ASCD; www.ascd.org), and many more wonderful professional affiliates. These sites will keep you connected to the latest information on RtI in adolescent literacy intervention programs. They are wonderful starting points, featuring overviews of topics and multiple links to sources. More important, they contain lists of research and practitioner publications, books, podcasts, discussion groups, reports on effective programs, and other valuable current resources.

Companion
Website

We will continue to update you on new resources as we find them. Please check our *Reading Specialists and Literacy Coaches in the Real World* companion website.

### Historical Overview of Adolescent Literacy Intervention

Much of what we know about struggling adolescent readers came from research in the 1990s and early 2000s. We invite you to share in some of the insights we gained during our intervention research in collaboration with our colleague, Martha Rapp Ruddell. Our findings and those of others confirmed the following:

1. *Adolescents (and even beginning readers) benefit when strategic reading (and writing) are modeled by the teacher, and supported during reading through peer discussion and peer mediation (problem-solving). Socially situated language processes invite awareness of the rules of discourse.* (Anderson, Chan, & Henne, 1995; Cooper & Pikulski, 2002; Gee, 2004; Ketch, 2005; Palinscar & Brown, 1984; Shearer, Ruddell, & Vogt, 2001; Vogt & Nagano, 2003)

2. *With carefully planned scaffolding, students benefit from the challenge of reading literature and informational texts that include a wide range in level of difficulty.* (Fournier & Graves, 2002; Rothenberg & Watts, 1997; Shearer, Ruddell, & Vogt, 2001; Van den Broek & Kremer, 2000; Vaughn, Klingner, & Bryant, 2001)

3. *Students are motivated to remain engaged longer through difficult texts when (1) they are able to select from a range of materials and topics that connect to their lived experiences and interests, and (2) they are able to choose the vocabulary to study from the words they encounter in context.* (Fisher & Frey 2007; Guthrie, Van Meter, Hancock, Alao, Anderson, & McCann, 1998; Shearer & Ruddell, 2006)

4. *Students benefit from, and are capable of participating in, goal-setting and evaluating their proficiency in learning to be critical and strategic readers.* (Bong, 2004;

Ehren, 2008; Guthrie & Wigfield, 2000; Shearer & Ruddell, 2006; Shearer, Ruddell, & Vogt, 2001; Watson Pearson & Santa, 1995; Zimmerman, Bandura, & Martinez-Pons, 1992)

5. *Students benefit when they are able to use online literacies that capitalize on social networking skills to expand and enhance traditional comprehension models.* (Street, 2005; Leu & Castek, 2006; Lewis & Fabos, 2005; Shearer & Ruddell, 2006)

6. *Students benefit from socially situated language processes that invite awareness of the rules of discourse.* (Rosenblatt, 1994; Vygotsky, 1978; Gee, 1990)

7. *Students benefit when selecting words they wish to study that are imbedded in contexts encountered in and out of school.* (Ruddell, 2005; Ruddell & Shearer, 2002)

Motivating students who have struggled with reading for years is crucial if RtI efforts are to succeed. This is particularly true with middle school and secondary students. Although many educators believe that the damage is irreversible for such students, a significant amount of research confirms just the opposite. Dr. Barbara Ehren's (2008) article, "Response to Intervention in Secondary Schools: Is It on Your Radar Screen?," available on the RtI Action Network (http://www.rtinetwork.org/Learn/Why/ar/RadarScreen) addresses this and other myths related to RtI and older students. She echoes findings that when provided with the instructional support to succeed, given opportunities to plan their instruction, and empowered to engage in goal-setting and self-evaluation, adolescents exhibit high levels of motivation and engagement (Guthrie, 2002; Guthrie & Wigfield, 2000; Hock, Deshler, & Schumaker, 2005; Moje, 2006; Shearer & Ruddell, 2006). Glenda Beamon Crawford's (2008) breakthrough book on adolescent motivation spells out methods for differentiating instruction that provide new hope for reaching disenchanted adolescent readers.

## The Role of the Reading Professional in RtI

### Organizing an Instructional Support System

We believe that every aspect of a successful and egalitarian literacy program is based on a single core belief:

All staff members are responsible for the education of all students.

Unless this idea is imbedded in our hearts and minds as well as in our written vision statements, it is pointless to pretend that we can reach the children who are not experiencing academic success. Overwhelming evidence supports the efficacy of educational teamwork and collaboration (Cobb, 2005; Friend & Cook, 2007; Marzano, Waters, & McNulty, 2005). Today's teachers are better educated than those of any generation that came before them. Our job as reading professionals is to continue to support their ability to provide high-quality literacy instruction for all students.

According to IRA (2007), reading specialists and literacy coaches will need to be:

• Open to change in how students are identified, how progress will be monitored and measured, how data are used to make instructional decisions, and how interventions are selected and implemented.

- Involved in team efforts of observation, support, and problem-solving.
- Engaged in providing direct and indirect service to implement the RtI process.
- Able to act as facilitators and information conduits, suggesting interventions that are closely aligned with the core literacy program used in the classroom.
- Willing to adapt to a more systemic approach to serving schools. This will involve adopting a less traditional service role in favor of increased consultation and collaboration in regular education classrooms.

### Criteria for Selecting Appropriate Screening Instruments

The reading specialist or literacy coach can help in selecting screening approaches that are: (1) not too costly, (2) not too time-consuming, and (3) not too cumbersome to administer. However, the number one characteristic of a good screening device is accuracy. Our first question should be: "Does this assessment instrument accurately identify students at risk or not at risk for reading failure?" (Jenkins, 2003). Another factor to consider is what Messick (1989) calls *consequence validity*—this means that the overall effect for the student must be positive. Messick's point is that in order to achieve consequence validity, all students identified in screening must receive *timely* and *effective* intervention. We share the underlying concern that appropriate placement for readers with severe problems may be delayed in schools in which RtI processes are cumbersome or overly complicated.

### RtI and the Literacy Professional: Serving Individual Students

The implementation of RtI will require fundamental changes in the instructional roles of reading professionals. The International Reading Association (IRA) lists the possible roles for the reading specialist/coach in supporting individual students in RtI structures. They include:

1. Providing reading instruction for struggling readers in classrooms or pull-out programs.
2. Consulting with a student's teacher on specific intervention strategies and activities to be implemented in school and at home.
3. Assisting, modeling, and training teachers to use informal targeted assessment and data interpretation to inform decision making and guide instructional planning.
4. Observing the student in instructional settings to identify progress, needs, and possible barriers to intervention.
5. Leading professional development that is aligned with school improvement initiatives, consistent with practices that are evidence-based, supportive of teachers' individual needs and goals, designed to include self-reflection and self-assessment, and targeted to specific outcomes. (See www.reading.org/Resources/ResourcesByTopic/ResponseToIntervention/Overview.aspx.)

## RtI Issues to Consider

There are many positive aspects associated with RtI.

***Shared Responsibility and Ownership.*** Allington and Walmsley (2007) attribute some of the abrogation of responsibility in the past to the belief on the part of teachers that "it can't be done" and "it's not my job." They suggest that RtI offers a chance to shift the attitude of a school's staff to "it can be done" and "it's my job." Such an attitude honors the professionalism, knowledge, and abilities of our teachers. Administrators and those in power are responsible for the process, too. An RtI process can enhance greater collaboration and consultation between general education and special education teachers as both serve as intervention providers, thus leading to a more unified educational program (Collins, 2008). The expectation is that there will be a commitment of the resources, time, materials, and professional development necessary and that these will be monitored as well. Because parents are informed about their child's progress and involved in decision making at all levels, they also assume a greater degree of ownership and responsibility.

***Reduction of Special Education Placements.*** One of the more important aims of RtI shared by almost all educators is reducing the overidentification of students for special education—specifically, the overidentification of children of poverty and those from homes whose language or culture differ from that of the dominant culture (Echevarria & Vogt, 2011; Echevarria, Vogt, & Short, 2010a, 2010b; Fisher & Frey, 2007; Klingner & Edwards, 2006; McGill-Franzen & Allington, 1993). Educators also expect RtI to decrease inappropriate referrals to special education for students who do not have disabilities so that special education can focus on students who do. Because educators must document measures taken to support a student who is struggling before more intense levels of intervention are implemented, the student is more likely to receive help in a less restrictive setting before being sent for help outside of the classroom. We would love to tell you that RtI has achieved this goal; and there *are* indications that this may well be the case, but such a claim would be premature. In spite of promising early reports that specific schools or districts are experiencing success in reducing special education placements with RtI, it will take time to establish the long-term evidence to justify or generalize such claims.

***Ongoing Assessment and Monitoring.*** In contrast to the wait-to-fail deficit models of the past, progress monitoring informs educators about the rate and size of gains made by individuals. According to McKenna and Walpole (2008), where "gains are moderate to negligible, RtI calls the approach into question and causes teachers to think and plan differently" (p. 67). Monitoring over time can reveal progress toward benchmarks as well as change over time. By plotting the learning trajectory, teachers can decide whether a particular intervention is accomplishing its goal. Systematic record-keeping and monitoring help teachers make adjustments daily as they key into problems within natural contexts.

***Multilayered Professional Development.*** In her 2008 IRA Conference presentation, *Making RtI Work for Children, Teachers, and Schools*, researcher Mary K. Lose made the case that the child who struggles the most requires the teacher with the most expertise. We join Dr. Lose and the many educators who have long championed this idea (Allington, 2006; Frost & Bean, 2006; Shearer, Ruddell, & Vogt, 2001). U.S. Department of Education guidelines include the directive that RtI provide teachers with the support they need to meet the needs of their students. When qualified reading professionals support teacher efforts to expand and share their expertise, teachers will be more capable and feel more confident in teaching reading. We wonder how many students were referred for special education in past decades because their teachers lacked the collaborative support of their peers or because there were no literacy coaches or highly trained reading professionals to help them.

***Coherence with the School Vision and Comprehensive Plan.*** RtI can be an integral part of a district's school improvement plan and can allow for a great deal of flexibility in the way it is implemented. When intervention programs succeed, we all succeed.

There are also some issues related to RtI that cause concern for many educators.

***All Intervention Is Not Created Equal.*** Spending *extra time* supporting a student is effective only if what happens during the time is educationally sound (Allington & Johnston, 2002; Allington & Walmsley, 2007; Yeaton & Sechrest, 1981).

***Assessment Issues.*** It's not that teachers disagree about the importance of monitoring students closely or adjusting teaching according to students' progress. Standards and benchmarks can help us determine the goals we want to reach, but we need to determine if we are on track to meet them. The question is: What constitutes responsible, meaningful, helpful assessment? The previous chapter addressed many of these issues. Teachers need support to understand the implications of choosing one assessment tool over another. *Measure for Measure* (2009), discussed in Chapter 5, can help educators compare features of the many instruments available for middle and high school assessment.

***Time Constraints.*** Assessment and monitoring take precious time. Even the quick one-minute readings and brief checklists associated with CBM take time and organizational effort. To some extent, we can try to collect a great deal of data within our everyday classroom events. However, this isn't always the case, particularly at Tiers II and III. We need to be mindful of the impact assessment has on allocation of time for instruction.

***Culture and Language Considerations in RtI Implementation.*** Janette Klingner and Patricia Edwards (2006) raise important questions with regard to culture and language in RtI models. One of their concerns involves assessment and monitoring. The question remains: What works with whom, by whom, and in what contexts (Cunningham & Fitzgerald, 2002)? Klingner and Edwards (2006) ask: What should first- and second-tier intervention look like for culturally diverse students? For English learners? For students living in high-poverty areas? Should it be the same? If not, how should it look, and how can we make sure it is responsive to children's needs? In Chapter 7, we will address the issue in greater depth, specifically as it applies to English learners. For a discussion of RtI and English learners, see Echevarria and Vogt (2011), or refer to our companion website for updated information.

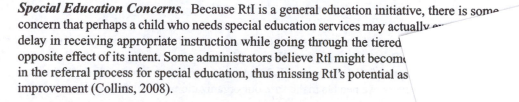

***Special Education Concerns.*** Because RtI is a general education initiative, there is some concern that perhaps a child who needs special education services may actually delay in receiving appropriate instruction while going through the tiered opposite effect of its intent. Some administrators believe RtI might become in the referral process for special education, thus missing RtI's potential as improvement (Collins, 2008).

***State Support and Leadership.***  In a 2009 article in *Reading Today,* the IRA Commission on Response to Intervention examined results from three surveys related to the prevalence of RtI. The first was a 2007 nationwide survey of *state* special education personnel who reported that *all* fifty U.S. states had RtI training under way (http://ies.ed.gov/ncee/edlabs/regions/west/pdf/REL_2009077.pdf). However, a 2009 survey of *district-level* special educators indicated that fewer than half of the states are providing leadership and support for RtI (www.spectrumk12.com/rti_survey_results). Not only did 28 percent indicate their states were not providing leadership and support for RtI, 26 percent reported they did not know what was happening at the state level. In 2008, 37 percent of *state council liaisons* to IRA's Commission on RtI reported that their states were *not* implementing RtI. The commission report raised the question, *"Would a survey of classroom teachers and literacy professionals agree with the findings of the special educators that 50% of district level RtI efforts are 'unified' efforts between special education and general education?"* (*Reading Today,* October/November 2009, p. 3).

You may think of additional challenges (opportunities) associated with RtI that you have discussed with other reading professionals or encountered in your school. While RtI may not be the answer to all of our problems, it appears to hold promise as a *structure* in which to address issues affecting many students and teachers. The harsh reality is that mandates without money, personnel, and resources to back them may have limited benefit. It will take time to ascertain the extent to which particular aspects of RtI help us educate struggling learners with their peers.

## RtI: Making It Work

To implement RtI, schools need to have a plan to address the collaboration that the RtI process demands and to facilitate the development of professional community and collective accountability for student success. The IRA Commission on Response to Intervention (RtI) has adopted six key principles to guide members' thinking and professional work in the area of RtI (Senge, Cambron-McCabe, Lucas, Smith, Dutton, & Kleiner, 2000):

1. Scheduling time and space for teachers to meet and talk.
2. Interdependent teaching structures (team-teaching, teaching teams).
3. Physical proximity (those who work together have classrooms that are close together).
4. Communication structures (identify how information and knowledge will be exchanged throughout the school).
5. Teacher empowerment and school autonomy (teachers need to be given the opportunity to make decisions about their work).
6. Rotating roles (rotating membership on committees helps to allow for the diversity of the professionals in the school and gives all professionals opportunities to make positive contributions).

IRA is part of six professional organizations collaborating to share ideas with the RtI Network. This is encouraging. We are pleased to see such genuine collaboration. If we, as members of IRA, believe collaboration and group problem-solving are key to successful endeavors, we need to make sure our organizations model that process.

## Points to Remember

This chapter deals with one of the most difficult questions you face as a literacy professional: what to do with your students who, despite all your efforts, knowledge, and experience, continue to struggle to acquire literacy skills. Supporting struggling readers is such a complex process. Like snowflakes, each student is one-of-a-kind, and so are their reading difficulties. Since the turn of the century, many elementary schools have adopted Response to Intervention as the structure for their intervention programs. Early care and preschool programs are rapidly embracing this model, too. It is encouraging to find that middle schools and high schools are beginning to explore incorporating RtI. The multiple-tiered RtI model supports quality initial instruction, universal screening and assessment, parent involvement, differentiated instruction, and levels of intervention that increase in intensity for students who continue to struggle.

In our quest to help students we must consider their unique social and cultural contexts, the ways in which they use language, and the purposes language serves. Factors such as motivation and self-esteem can compromise progress, particularly for older students. However, RtI offers promise for identifying students who need help and responding to their needs. By using differentiated instructional techniques, the teacher can provide targeted short-term intervention with the aim of improving student achievement. As wonderful as this may sound, it will take incredible cooperation and effort from everyone in the literacy community. It will also require schools to devote considerable time and resources to professional development. New perspectives about intervention might offer promise for Liana as she seeks better ways to help students like Julio in the years to come.

## Revisiting the Vignette: Thinking Points

1. How are Julio's needs the same as those of an elementary struggling reader?
2. How are his needs different?
3. Which aspects of the educational structures in most middle and high schools might facilitate adopting an RtI orientation to intervention?
4. Which aspects might hinder adopting an RtI orientation to intervention?
5. How might Liana and her school/district address facilitating aspects and hindering aspects?

## Portfolio and Self-Assessment Projects

1. Make a map, matrix, or chart that synthesizes the structure of intervention in your school (or district). It should contain the kinds of components present in Figure 6.2 *Sample Three-Tiered RtI Intervention Matrix (K–6),* but you may include other categories or eliminate some. Your final product may or may not look similar to the matrix in this book.
2. In consultation with your literacy team, prepare a PowerPoint or Whiteboard presentation for your colleagues, the principal, or the school board on ways to improve or restructure intervention. It should include: (1) an overview of data on the existing program; (2) an evidence-based list of options for improvement or restructuring; (3) specific goals you and the team envision; (4) an action plan, including roles of teachers, administrators, and parents, a timeline, and an estimate of the cost of implementation; and (5) a description of the ways you will assess outcomes of your plan.

3. Design a professional development plan for yourself to improve your knowledge of assessment issues.

4. Create a portfolio item that reflects your learning relative to the goal you set for yourself at the beginning of this chapter.

## Recommended Readings: Suggestions for Book Clubs, Study Groups, and Professional Development

Crawford, G. B. (2008). *Differentiation for the adolescent learner: Accommodating brain development language and literacy.* Thousand Oaks, CA: Crawford Press. In this truly groundbreaking book, Crawford doesn't just examine the lack of motivation characteristic of so many disenchanted adolescent learners, she shows educators what to do about it. Particularly timely to schools implementing RtI, Crawford explores practical methods for differentiating instruction and engaging students. Chapter 5, outlining specific teaching differentiation strategies, is a must read.

Klingner, J. K., & Edwards, P. A. (2006). Cultural considerations with Response to Intervention models. *Reading Research Quarterly 41*(1), 117. This RRQ article would be excellent for a study group session. It is important for all teachers, but it is essential for those who teach in *high diversity* contexts. Klingner and Edwards examine a number of factors that do not show up in aggregate data but have a significant impact on the success of intervention programs in schools with diverse populations.

Howard, M. (2009). *RtI from all sides: What every teacher ought to know.* Portsmouth, NH: Heinemann. Mary Howard writes from a classroom teacher's perspective, but manages to provide suggestions for creating an RtI program in reading. Her passion makes this an interesting read.

Opitz, M. F., & Ford, M. P. (2008). *Do-able differentiation: Varying groups, texts, and supports to reach readers.* Portsmouth, NH: Heinemann. This is another great book from the two Michaels (Opitz and Ford). It is one of those practitioner books that teachers want to keep handy and revisit again and again. If you are concentrating on differentiation, this is the book for you. It combines common theory, common sense, and an array of practical ideas.

## Online Resources

**http://www.reading.org** and **http://www.rtinetwork.com**

The International Reading Association has established a Commission on Response to Intervention to synthesize the latest information for reading professionals. Our organization is working with other professional groups to share resources on the RtI Action Network. The RtI network publishes a monthly online newsletter that contains a wealth of useful information. Check on these sites regularly to explore the latest research and practical ideas. They contain active links to many other RtI-related sites and resources.

**http://www.readingrockets.org**

The Reading Rockets project is composed of PBS television programs, available on videotape and DVD; online services, including the websites ReadingRockets.org and ColorinColorado.org; and professional development opportunities. Reading Rockets is an educational initiative of WETA, the flagship public television and radio station in the nation's capital, and is funded by a major grant from the U.S. Department of Education, Office of Special Education Programs.

## Companion Website Resources

The following resources to support and extend your learning of this chapter can be found on our companion website (waveland.com/Extra_Material/32979/): key vocabulary, concepts, and other terms; extended examples; updated resources specifically tied to information in the chapter; related websites; and other support features. The companion website for this chapter includes a template of a Three-Tiered Intervention Matrix.

# 7

# *Language and Literacy Development for English Learners*

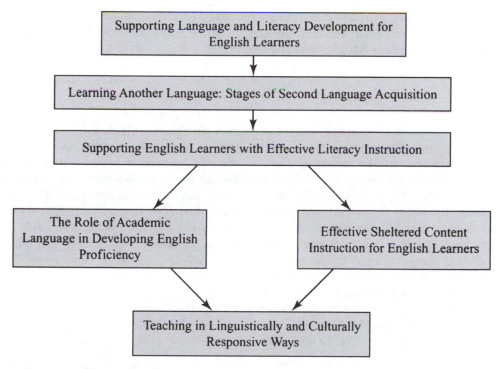

FIGURE 7.1    *Chapter Overview*

## Learning Goals

After reading, discussing, and engaging in activities related to this chapter, you will be able to:

1. Explain how primary language (L1) literacy impacts second language (L2) literacy development.
2. Analyze the appropriateness of language and literacy programs for English learners.
3. Explain the role of the reading specialist and literacy coach in supporting students who are English learners.
4. *Personal Learning Goal:* In a three-minute brainstorming session, share what you know about effective literacy instruction for English learners. Write an objective or question that reflects something you want to learn as we explore these topics. Share this with others in your group.

## Standards for Reading Professionals

This chapter provides focused support for current IRA Standards for Reading Professionals. See our companion website (waveland.com/Extra_Material/32979/) for a complete listing of the standards that align with this chapter.

## Vignette

Susan Weiss, the reading specialist at Thomas Jefferson Elementary School, straightened up her desk in preparation for the arrival of Felipe Rodriguez, the district bilingual coordinator. Susan asked Felipe for help in providing more appropriate instruction for the growing number of English learners at Jefferson after she observed a recent reading lesson in a third-grade classroom. During that whole-class lesson, one boy, Jose, who had recently arrived in the United States from Mexico and who had very little English proficiency, sat in the corner of the room with crayons and a coloring book. For the entire lesson, he sat and colored while the other children participated in a shared reading experience with the teacher. When asked why Jose was coloring while the others were involved in the story, the teacher responded with some exasperation, "Jose can't speak any English! How do you expect him to participate in a grade-level reading lesson? Besides, I thought he could be successful. He didn't seem to mind, and anyway, it wasn't all that long that he was coloring."

### Thinking Points

1. What are the issues Susan and Felipe should discuss?
2. How might Susan approach Felipe about appropriate assessment and instruction for Jose?

### Expanding the Vignette: Exploring the Issues

*The rapid growth in the number of English learners (ELs) had taken Susan's school district by surprise, primarily because until recently, the rural Indiana community had very few students whose home languages were other than English.*

*Susan glanced over the list of questions she was prepared to ask Felipe. These included the following:*

1. *What does research say about effective ways to teach reading to students acquiring English?*
2. *What can teachers do to help ELs learn content when they cannot read the textbook?*
3. *How can we tell whether an EL student has a reading problem or is having trouble with English?*

### Thinking Points

1. Do you know the percentage of English learners in your school? In your district?
2. Do you know how many and what languages are spoken by the students in your school? Your district?
3. Do you know the extent to which the literacy development needs of your ELs are being met?

## Supporting Language and Literacy Development for English Learners

Across the United States, thousands of immigrant students with little or no English proficiency enter elementary, middle, and high school classrooms. Some of these students arrive with very little or no formal education or literacy development. Other English learners in our schools are native-born, but they also lack proficiency in academic language, resulting in serious achievement gaps when compared to their language-proficient peers. In fact, nearly four out of five English learners in the elementary grades, and approximately 60 percent of secondary ELs were born in the United States and have been educated entirely in U.S. schools (NCELA, 2009).

In contrast to these students, other ELs may arrive in the United States literate in their first language with a history of continuous and successful educational experiences in their native countries. Because these students have developed academic language and knowledge, they will most likely be able to make a smooth transition into U.S. classrooms as they learn English.

The academic gap between non- or limited-English speaking students and their English-proficient peers has continued to grow, in large part because of the lack of literacy skills and academic language many bring to U.S. schools (Vogt, 2005). Students may acquire conversational English in less than two years, but academic language proficiency may require from five to seven years (Cummins, 2006). Just learning "new words" isn't enough; there are content concepts, procedural steps, specific content vocabulary, and English structure that must be taught to ELs, along with the specific academic content (Cummins, 2003).

# Language and Literacy Development for English Learners

While the number of English learners has increased substantially in the United States, the number of teachers who are prepared to teach them effectively has not kept pace. At the time of this writing, only a few states require all preservice teachers to take coursework in ESL (English as a Second Language) teaching methods. Clearly, teachers require targeted preparation and professional development in working with second language learners if these students are to be successful academically. The number of certified ESL teachers does not meet the demand of the increasing numbers of language minority students in the public schools, so the responsibility for educating these youngsters increasingly falls to elementary and secondary content teachers, and the specialists and coaches with whom they work.

■ *Author Connection: MaryEllen*  Frequently, I have been asked how I (as a reading specialist) became involved in codeveloping the SIOP® Model, a framework for planning lessons that concurrently teach content and language to English learners. My interest was kindled many years ago when I noticed the growing number of youngsters whose home language differed from the language of instruction (English). In the mid to late 1970s, thousands of immigrant children from Vietnam and Cambodia entered California schools. Few, if any, of these children had any formal schooling. A few had been taught in Thai refugee camps by caring adults, some of whom had been teachers prior to the Vietnam War. I well remember one little Cambodian girl who entered my seventh-grade classroom one morning, speaking no English whatsoever. It was mid-semester and she appeared terrified by everything that was so new to her. We had no "newcomers' program," nor any other provisions to help her and others like her make it through the day. I had no idea how to help her, other than smiling and being gentle with her. About fifteen minutes after she came into my classroom, we had an unannounced fire drill. I will never forget the look of utter terror on her face as the alarm blasted throughout the school. As everyone hurriedly stood up and filed out of the classroom, I grabbed her hand and had her walk with me. We all walked out to the ball field behind the school, lined up, and waited patiently until the "all clear" bell was rung. The look on my new student's face turned from fear to total confusion when we all marched back into the classroom and resumed the lesson that I had barely begun. This child changed forever how I thought about the immigrant children in my classes (as well as others whose first language isn't English). I pledged to figure out the best way to teach the content information they need in order to be successful, productive adults. I also knew at that moment that these children had to learn English—we could not afford to wait to teach content until the students' English was established. We, as teachers, had to learn how to teach both simultaneously. And that's how it all began for me. It wasn't until 1995 that we began working on the SIOP® Model, and when we did, I had the picture of this scared little girl still imprinted on my mind.

## Learning Another Language

Not surprisingly, students who can already read and write well in their primary language have an easier time adjusting to school in which a new language is spoken because most of what they have learned about how language "works" can be transferred to the new language system (August & Shanahan, 2008). While learning English, much of what ELs need instructionally depends on their stages of English proficiency. These have been described as a series of stages numbering from 3 to 7, depending on the source. Your state EL standards may have different labels and designations, but most fall within the following broad classifications (Echevarria, Vogt, & Short, 2010a, pp. 246–247):

- **Preproduction:** Students at this stage are not ready to produce much language, so they primarily communicate with gestures and actions. They are absorbing the new language and developing receptive vocabulary. Still, students can be expected to respond verbally as well as by pointing, gesturing, and imitating sounds and actions. Students can follow shared readings and will use illustrations and graphic clues to attach meaning to printed materials. They may choose to illustrate characters, objects, and actions to convey meaning, and will benefit from sentence frames that assist in formulating English sentences that require only one word produced independently, for example, "I like the poem because it is _____ (funny, silly, sad)."
- **Early Production:** Students at this level speak using one or two words or short phrases. Their receptive vocabulary is developing, and they understand approximately one thousand words. Students can answer "who, what, and where" questions with limited expression, and can recite and repeat poems, songs, and chants. Again, students at this level benefit from and can use sentence frames, which they complete with words and short phrases, for example, "The poem was funny because _____."
- **Speech Emergence:** Students speak in longer phrases and complete sentences. However, they may experience frustration at not being able to express completely what they know. Although the number of errors they make may increase, they can communicate ideas and the quantity of speech they produce also increases. Students can retell simple stories using pictures and objects, and can engage in dialogues, interviews, or role plays. They comprehend simple passages and can follow text during group reading. They can also use simple sentences and details in their writing, write from dictation, and write using a variety of genres.
- **Intermediate Fluency:** Students may appear to be fluent, and they engage in conversation and produce connected narrative. Errors are usually of style or usage. Literacy and content lessons continue to expand receptive vocabulary, and activities develop higher levels of language use in content areas. Students at this level are able to communicate conversationally and in group discussion, but still may have difficulty with academic language. They may engage in independent reading according to their level of oral fluency and prior experiences with print. They are able to write with detail in a variety of genres. *Note:* Many English learners appear to get "stuck" at this level, and it's important that their teacher(s) recognize that intermediate speakers still need English instruction, especially in academic language and vocabulary.
- **Advanced Fluency:** Students communicate very effectively, orally and in writing, in social and academic settings. They are able to write in greater detail in a wide variety of genres, and for a wide variety of purposes, including creative and analytical writing.

**BEYOND THE BOOK** _____

*Chapter 7 Focus Issue: Understanding Language Learners*

■ *Group Inquiry Activity*    Reflect on when you learned a second or additional language, whether in childhood, in high school, or in college. In a group, discuss your responses to the following questions:

1. In the early stages of learning the language, how did you feel?
2. When you were required to respond orally in the new language to the teacher's questions, how did you feel? What did you do?
3. At what point in the language acquisition process did you begin to gain confidence in speaking?
4. After two years of formal study, how well prepared were you to learn content material (such as math or chemistry) in your new language?
5. What are the implications of your group's responses for teaching English learners?

## Supporting English Learners with Effective Literacy Instruction

Several research syntheses have provided an overview of the language, literacy, and academic needs of language minority students and suggested how schools should plan instruction accordingly (August & Shanahan, 2008; Genesee, Lindholm-Leary, Saunders, & Christian, 2005; Gersten, Baker, Shanahan, Linan-Thompson, Collins, & Scarcella, 2007). Based on these syntheses and other existing research studies, Goldenberg (2008) suggests that teachers can support language minority students with the following:

- High-quality literacy instruction for English learners that is similar to high-quality literacy instruction for other native English speaking students, but provides accommodations and support to develop high levels of English proficiency.
- Intensive small-group intervention based on reading assessment data with focused explicit instruction on the five core reading elements (phonological awareness, phonics, reading fluency, vocabulary, and comprehension).
- High-quality vocabulary instruction throughout the day with essential content words taught in depth, and instructional time that addresses the meanings of common words, phrases, and expressions that have not been learned.
- At least ninety minutes a week of instructional activities in which pairs of students at different ability levels or language proficiencies work together on structured academic tasks.
- Predictable and consistent classroom management routines (diagrams, lists, easy-to-read schedules, and so on).
- Graphic organizers that assist students in comprehending content information.
- Additional time and opportunities for practice of key content concepts.
- Redundant key information (e.g., visual cues, pictures, physical gestures).
- Instruction that identifies, highlights, and clarifies difficult words and passages within texts to facilitate comprehension.

- Consolidating text knowledge by having the teacher, other students, and ELs themselves summarize and paraphrase.
- Extra practice in reading words, sentences, and stories in order to build automaticity and fluency.
- Opportunities for extended interactions with teachers and peers, adjusting instruction according to students' oral English proficiency.
- Targeting both content and English language objectives in every lesson.
- Beginning in the primary grades, development of academic language.

## The Role of Academic Language in Developing English Proficiency

Have you been on yard or cafeteria duty recently when you overheard a group of English learners chatting in English? You may have marveled at their seeming ease with their new language. However, as you observe this group of students, you recognize several that you have in class who are having a difficult time reading and writing in the content areas. How can they sound so fluent in English on the playground or during passing periods, and still have such difficulty with English in the classroom?

Jim Cummins (1979; 2000) suggests a demarcation between the conversational or social language spoken in informal settings and the more formal, academic language used in school settings. Second language learners can learn to communicate conversationally in a relatively short amount of time due to substantial contextual supports, such as facial expressions, gestures, and body language (Echevarria & Graves, 2011). In contrast, learning academic language in English is considerably more challenging because it lacks contextual support and is more abstract than concrete. Note the following definitions of academic language (also called academic English):

- "Academic English is the language of the classroom, of academic disciplines (science, history, literary analysis), of texts and literature, and of extended, reasoned discourse. It is more abstract and decontextualized than conversational English" (Gersten, Baker, Shanahan, Linan-Thompson, Collins, & Scarcella, 2007, p. 16).
- "Academic language is the set of words, grammar, and organizational strategies used to describe complex ideas, higher-order thinking processes, and abstract concepts" (Zwiers, 2008, p. 20).

For English learners (and struggling readers and writers), academic language plays a critical role in school success. As a reading specialist and/or literacy coach, it is important to understand the essential differences between conversational English and the academic language of mathematics, history/social studies, science, and the language arts, so that in your role as coach, you may assist teachers in recognizing and teaching the academic language of the varied content areas.

Academic language includes many aspects, such as content vocabulary, the language of reading and writing, grammar, prosody, language used for self-talk, and academic discourse, and it can be both generic and content-specific (Vogt, Echevarria, & Short, 2010). For example, many academic words and processes are used across all content areas (such as *demonstrate, estimate, analyze, summarize, categorize*), while others pertain to specific subject areas (*idioms, characterization, symbolism* for Language Arts; *angle, ratio, dispersion* for Math). It is important to remember that academic language represents the entire range of language used in academic settings, including elementary and secondary schools.

In addition, for English learners, there is frequently disparity between their word-level and text-level skills and this may be due to their oral English proficiency (Lesaux & Geva, 2008). Well-developed oral proficiency in English, which includes English vocabulary and syntactic knowledge plus listening comprehension skills, is associated with English reading and writing proficiency. Therefore, reading and language arts teachers and specialists must teach not only the components of reading (phonemic awareness, phonics, vocabulary, fluency, comprehension), but also the features of different text genres, especially those found in subject area classes, such as textbook chapters, online articles, laboratory directions, math word problems, and primary source materials (Short, Vogt, & Echevarria, 2010, 2011).

Academic writing is also an area that is affected significantly by limited oral English proficiency, and the writing process must be taught to ELs explicitly, with teacher modeling, posting of writing samples, use of sentence frames, and even having students occasionally copy words or text until they gain more independence (Vogt, Echevarria, & Short, 2010). English learners should be encouraged to write in English early in the second language acquisition process, especially if they have literacy skills in their native language. Errors in writing are to be expected and should be viewed as part of the natural process of language acquisition. Remember to provide scaffolding with language practice, such as partially completed graphic organizers for prewriting and sentence frames for organizing key points and supporting details.

As a reading specialist and/or coach, you have the opportunity to help teachers learn how to teach academic language effectively. As you work with teachers, remind them of the following:

- Since proficiency in English is the best predictor of academic success, teachers should spend a significant amount of time teaching the academic vocabulary required to understand a lesson's topic.
- In order to acquire academic language, lessons need to be meaningful and engaging for students and provide ample opportunity for them to practice using language orally.
- Successful group work requires intentional planning, including teaching students how to work effectively with others. Grouping students in teams for discussion, engaging partners for specific tasks, and other planned configurations increase student engagement and oral language development.
- Jeff Zwiers notes that "academic language doesn't grow on trees" (2008, p. 41). It must be carefully taught.
- For students who speak a Latin-based language such as Spanish, cognates may help in teaching some words. For example, *predict* in English is *predecir* in Spanish; *justify* in English is *justificar* in Spanish; *communication* in English is *communicacion* in Spanish.

What is important to remember is that teaching academic language can enable English learners and struggling readers to be successful throughout the school day so that they can read, write, and speak as knowledgeable and informed readers. Obviously, the context of the literacy and subject area classroom has much to do with English learners' language and content acquisition, as the description that follows suggests.

### Effective Sheltered Content Instruction for English Learners

For many years, the term *sheltered instruction* has been used in the ESL and bilingual education fields to describe the type of focused instruction for language minority students that Goldenberg (2008) and others advocate (Echevarria, Vogt, & Short, 2008, 2010a, 2010b). Consistent, systematic implementation of effective sheltered techniques in each and every lesson has resulted in academic gains and improvement in English proficiency for language minority students (Echevarria & Short, 2009; Echevarria, Short, & Powers, 2006). This approach uses English as the medium for providing content area instruction while emphasizing the development of English proficiency. This integration of language acquisition and subject matter learning honors the notion that language is acquired in meaningful contexts (Krashen, 1985). It provides comprehensible input about content concepts and fosters connections with students' experiences and prior knowledge (Cummins, 1984; Echevarria & Graves, 2011; Echevarria, Vogt, & Short, 2008). Sheltered instruction stresses the development of students' English proficiency, content knowledge, cognitive and academic skill development, and reasoning—all required for learning in content areas.

The Sheltered Instruction Observation Protocol (SIOP)® Model (Echevarria, Vogt, & Short, 2008) was designed to assist teachers, supervisors, peer coaches, and others in creating and evaluating sheltered content lessons. Among the SIOP® features for the effective instruction of English learners are the following (Echevarria, Vogt, & Short, 2008, pp. 222–227):

- Clearly defined, posted, and orally reviewed content and language objectives reflected in lesson planning, lesson delivery, and assessment of student knowledge and application.
- Appropriate age and grade-level content reflected in lesson planning and delivery.
- Supplementary materials (e.g., photos, illustrations, graphs, models, demonstrations) used to a high degree.
- Adaptation of content (e.g., texts, assignments) for levels of students' English proficiency (note that this does not mean changing content standards—rather, this may involve adapting texts and providing alternate means for ELs to access the content).
- Meaningful activities (e.g., authentic reading/writing and hands-on application opportunities) integrated throughout the lesson.
- Concepts explicitly linked to students' backgrounds, prior experiences, and past learning.
- Key vocabulary emphasized (e.g., purposefully selected, introduced, written, highlighted), reviewed, and assessed.
- Speech appropriate for students' English proficiency levels (e.g., slower rate, clear enunciation; simple sentence structure for beginners; varied response expectations).

- Clear explanations of academic tasks (e.g., what it means to "share with your partner," "discuss, " "list," "summarize," etc.).
- A variety of techniques used to make content clear (modeling, visuals, hands-on activities, gestures, pantomime, demonstrations, etc.).
- Ample opportunities for students to use cognitive and metacognitive learning strategies.
- Consistent use of scaffolding techniques.
- A variety of question types, including higher order, with sufficient wait-time after questioning, and multiple ways of responding to questions, such as group response.
- Frequent opportunities for teacher–student and student–student interactions.
- Grouping configurations that support language and content objectives (not just whole class).
- Ample opportunities for students to clarify concepts in the LI (primary language), if possible with other students, an aide, or the teacher.
- Appropriate pacing of content delivery depending on students' language proficiency.
- Regular feedback provided to students on their output (e.g., language, content, work).
- Assessment conducted on students' comprehension and learning throughout the lesson and at its conclusion (e.g., spot-checking, group activity, oral and written responses).

These features have been summarized from a list of eight components and thirty features that are part of the Sheltered Instruction Observation Protocol (SIOP®) Model. By teaching language arts, math, science, social studies, and other content subjects using these techniques, ELs are afforded a much greater opportunity to function in the mainstream (Ramos-Ocasio, 1985). Also, when the techniques are implemented systematically, consistently, and to a high degree, English learners outperform their EL peers in sheltered classes where the teachers do not implement the SIOP® Model (Echevarria, Short, & Powers, 2006).

In addition to sheltering content for ELs, it's important to remember that:

- Participation in some programs designed for English learners may result not in bilingualism, but in subtractive bilingualism, or loss of the child's primary language (Wong-Fillmore, 1991).
- Children who are forced to give up their primary language and adjust to an English-only environment may not only lose their primary language, but may also not learn the second language well (Wong-Fillmore, 1991).
- When children lose their primary language relationships with parents, grandparents, and others in the culture, they may also have difficulties with identity issues; there may be additional emotional, social, and cognitive developmental consequences for these children (Cummins, 1981).
- When children are able to use the complex and rich understanding of their primary language in their instruction, they are able to transfer these skills to a new language.

## The Issue of Dialect

Although the needs of English learners has been an area of study and focus for several decades, there has been less discussion about teaching students with dialect differences. Most everyone has a dialect, a variety of language, usually regional or social, that is distinguishable from others in pronunciation, vocabulary, and grammar. Teachers often feel it's their job to reinforce conventional English and discourage nonstandard dialects. It's undeniable that some people *do* privilege certain dialects, such as a Boston accent over, perhaps, a Mississippi accent, and there may be some children who suffer because of a teacher's lack of understanding of dialects. For these teachers, there may be misunderstandings about the differences between dialect, and "bad" or "poor" grammar, "inappropriate" language, "ignorant" speech, or "improper" ways of communicating. In fact, Wolfram (1991) points out there is no evidence that language variation, such as pronouncing *with* as "wif" or saying, "She didn't pay no attention" instead of "She didn't pay any attention," interferes in any way with understanding or learning. The National Council of Teachers of English (NCTE) took a strong position in 1974 affirming students' rights to the patterns and variations of their nurture, and championing their rights to their own identity, voice, and style (pp. 2–3). You might remember the Ebonics controversy in Oakland, California, in the late 1990s, in which there were heated discussions about whether students had the right to use Ebonics (an African American dialect) in schools, whether Ebonics should be taught, or whether the schools had the right to actively discourage students' use of the dialect. Because of these ongoing arguments, we urge that such issues remain a source of thoughtful and enlightened conversation among literacy educators.

## The Role of the Reading Specialist and Literacy Coach in Supporting Programs for English Learners

In larger school districts, it is unlikely that literacy specialists and coaches will be required to develop ESL/ELD or bilingual programs, although they may be expected to assist in creating and implementing effective sheltered content classes. Further, since English learners can have difficulty learning to read in either or both L1 and L2, it is essential that reading specialists have understandings of first and second language and literacy acquisition. In smaller districts, when a single non-English speaking family relocates to the community, it is often the reading specialist who is assigned to work with the children. Because of the wide variety of students' home languages, teachers, reading specialists, and coaches may lack knowledge of the language and culture of these students. Therefore, an understanding of sheltered content instruction is extremely important for these teac

It is also necessary for reading specialists to work with teache cial educators, and bilingual specialists to assess the language p acquisition of English learners properly. Too often ELs are referred education programs because of reading and language difficulties needs to be able to ascertain whether a student has a true reading difficulty he or she is experiencing in the classroom is related to h language proficiency.

For example, it is important to recognize that your usual battery of reading assessments, such as phonemic awareness and phonics tests, IRIs, and vocabulary measures, may be unreliable for some of your English learners. The phonology of a student's native language may differ substantially from that of English, and thus some of your ELs may not be able to distinguish or reproduce the sounds (phonemes) of English because these sounds may not exist in their home languages. The consonant sounds may vary considerably and English vowel sounds may be nonexistent.

Additionally, the orthography (spelling system) may cause difficulty if it is quite different from English. Some studies that compare orthographic knowledge have found that bilingual learners can satisfactorily negotiate the differences in the orthographies; others suggest there may be problems. The following questions may be helpful as you are trying to ascertain whether an English learner's reading and learning difficulties warrant a special education intervention (Echevarria, Vogt, & Short, 2008, p. 193):

1. What evidence do you have that a particular student is having difficulty with reading and learning?
2. Do you have any evidence that this student has difficulty reading and learning in his or her home language? If not, how might you gather some? If you are not fluent in the student's language, is there another student who is? Is there a community liaison or family member who could provide information about the student's first language (LI) literacy development?
3. If your evidence points to a reading and/or learning problem, what have you and other teachers done to accommodate the student's needs?
   a. Are the student's teachers incorporating cognitive and metacognitive strategy instruction in the language arts and content subjects?
   b. Are the student's teachers adapting content and texts to provide greater accessibility?
   c. Are the student's teachers scaffolding instruction through flexible grouping?
   d. Are the student's teachers providing multiple opportunities for practice and application of key content and language concepts?

If teachers are providing appropriate sheltered instruction and the student is still struggling academically, and if your intervention in reading isn't accomplishing your goals, then a referral for special education services may be warranted. For further information about the overreferral of English learners to special education, see the IRA position paper titled, "The Role of Reading Instruction in Addressing the Overrepresentation of Minority Children in Special Education in the United States," available on the IRA website (www.reading.org).

## Helping Children Use Language to Communicate, Interpret, and Organize Their World

What follows are some additional ideas about how to provide a learning environment in our schools that honors and values the linguistic and cultural diversity we all share.

- Educators can create an environment that values the language and culture of the child's home. They can encourage children to use their first languages for clarification, while supporting their acquisition of English, and they can help students explore and value their rich literacy autobiographies.
- If qualified minority-language speakers are not available, collaboration with parents and linguistically diverse members of the communities can provide opportunities for children to use their language and to validate its importance.
- Because strong family/school partnerships provide cultural continuity, parents can be encouraged to talk to their children and share oral and written stories in the home language. They can be encouraged to share these stories and cultural artifacts with the child's class.
- Gestures, actions, pictures, manipulatives, and other mediating tools are all ways for the teacher to enhance communication (Okagaki & Sternberg, 1993). Classroom signs and directions on the wall can incorporate students' languages. English-only teachers and classmates can value and support an English learner's language and culture by learning common phrases and expressions in the student's home language.
- Teachers and students can be encouraged to view different styles of discourse and regional dialect as additions to the richness and diversity of the classroom.
- Just as Carmen (see Chapter 3, Figure 3.3) translated within her Puerto Rican community, students can use translation in the classroom to enhance literacy.
- Drawing specific attention to the rich metaphorical, poetic, and often lyrical languages, styles, and dialects of other cultures might do much to enhance the linguistic repertoire of all Americans.
- Provide students of various ethnic and cultural backgrounds with multiple opportunities to see their lives, beliefs, experiences, and appearances represented in school settings and instructional materials.
- Multicultural literature can help all students (and their teachers) understand and appreciate multiple perspectives including non-Western views of the world (Bean, 2001).

As much as we educators want to provide for all students' language and literacy needs, this is not an easy task for many teachers, primarily because most represent the majority culture, both linguistically and culturally. As Patty Schmidt points out in Other Voices, students in undergraduate and graduate education programs and teachers in all parts of the United States are from predominantly white, middle-class cultures. She provides a model for helping prepare educators to support learning in culturally diverse classrooms. As a literacy specialist or coach, you might find the following process a powerful way to engage in conversation with your fellow teachers and administrators.

## OTHER VOICES: Patricia Ruggiano Schmidt

*Dr. Patty Schmidt, a professor in the Education Department of LeMoyne College in Syracuse, New York, has written and published a number of books and articles on facilitating culturally responsive connections among teachers, parents, communities, and learners. Preliminary studies implementing her* ABCs of Cultural Understanding and Communication *demonstrate its promise for changing teacher education in substantive ways.*

*ABCs of Cultural Understanding and Communication* Research and practice demonstrate that strong home, school, and community connections not only help students make sense of the school curriculum but they also promote literacy development (Au, 1993; Heath, 1983; Schmidt, 2000, 2005; Xu, 2000). However, in recent years home, school, and community connections have become a significant challenge.

There are various reasons for this challenging situation. First, as our school population has become increasingly diverse, both culturally and ethnically, our teaching population has consistently originated from European American, suburban experiences. Typically, educators describe themselves as white and middle class; often they add during discussions about diversity, "I'm an American; I don't have a culture." Second, most present and future teachers have not had sustained relationships with people from different ethnic, cultural, and lower socioeconomic backgrounds. As a result, much of their knowledge about diversity has been influenced by media stereotypes. Third, school curriculum, methods, and materials usually reflect only European American or white culture and ignore the backgrounds and experiences of students and families from lower socioeconomic levels and differing ethnic and cultural backgrounds (Delpit, 1995; Walker-Dalhouse & Dalhouse, 2001). Fourth, many teacher education programs do not adequately prepare educators for "culturally relevant pedagogy" (Ladson-Billings, 1995), a term that directly relates to making strong home, school, and community connections. Fifth, when cultural differences are ignored in classrooms, student fears and alienation increase. Consequently, this disconnect has become a national problem whose influence has been linked to poor literacy development and extremely high dropout rates among students from urban and rural poverty areas (Schmidt, 1999).

As a teacher educator, I searched for ways to prepare present and future teachers for the diversity in their classrooms. I discovered that the most successful programs are those that incorporate authentic encounters with people from different backgrounds and experiences while learning content related to racism, sexism, and classicism (Cochran-Smith, 1995; Tatum, 1997). Furthermore, these programs claimed that teacher self-knowledge may be the first consideration when attempting to help teachers understand diverse groups of students.

With all of the above in mind, I designed and developed the model known as the ABCs of Cultural Understanding and Communication. It is a process founded on the premise that knowing oneself is basic to the understanding of others. Present and future K–12 teachers who experience the model often begin to successfully connect home, school, and community for literacy learning (Xu, 2000; Leftwich, 2001; Schmidt, 2005). The model's five steps are supported by previous research and are briefly explained in the following paragraphs.

*Step 1: Autobiography—Know thyself.* First, each teacher writes an autobiography that includes key life events related to education, family, religious tradition, recreation, victories, defeats, and so on. This helps to build awareness of personal beliefs and attitudes that form the traditions and values of cultural autobiographies (Banks, 1994). Because it is well documented that writing is linked to knowledge of self within a social context (Yinger, 1985), writing one's life story seems to construct connections with universal human tenets and serves to lessen negative notions about different groups of people (Progoff, 1975). The autobiography experience sets the stage for the second step, learning about the lives of culturally different people.

*Step 2: Biography.*   After several in-depth, audiotaped, unstructured, or semistructured interviews of a person who is culturally different, each teacher constructs a biography from key events in that person's life. This helps teachers begin to develop the cultural sensitivity necessary to analyze similarities and differences in the two life stories (Schmidt, 1998a, 1998b, 2000; Spindler & Spindler, 1987).

*Step 3: Cross-cultural analysis and appreciation of differences.*   For the third step in the process, each teacher studies the autobiography and biography and charts a list of similarities and differences, which leads to the fourth step.

*Step 4: Self-analysis of differences.*   Self-analysis of differences is a key component of the process. The teacher carefully examines the chart that lists similarities and differences and writes an in-depth self-analysis of cultural differences, explaining the reasons for any personal discomforts and/or positive affects. Through this process, teachers begin to acquire insights about others and sense their own ethnocentricity (Spindler & Spindler, 1987).

*Step 5: Home–School–Community Connection Plan for Literacy Development.*   After experiencing the previous steps in the process, K–12 teachers design year-long plans for connecting home, school, and community for students' reading, writing, listening, speaking, and viewing development based on numerous modifications of the ABCs Model made for their own classrooms and schools. They see ways to develop collaborative relationships with families in an atmosphere of mutual respect, so students will gain the most from their education (Schmidt, 2005). The ABCs of Cultural Understanding and Communication helps teachers learn about family and community values and shows them how to value what communities and families know.

After teachers have experienced the ABCs model, they design lesson plans for culturally responsive instruction. They make connections with students' backgrounds, interests, and experiences to teach the standards-based curriculum. Learning becomes more meaningful and relevant as teachers draw on students' prior knowledge. Recent studies of these teachers' lessons have demonstrated seven characteristics of culturally responsive literacy instruction (Schmidt, 2005). They include:

1. *High Expectations:* Teachers support students as they develop literacy appropriate to their ages and abilities.
2. *Positive Relationships with Families and Community:* Clear connections with student families and communities are demonstrated in terms of curriculum content and relationships.
3. *Cultural Sensitivity:* The curriculum is reshaped and mediated for culturally valued knowledge, connecting with the standards-based curriculum as well as each individual student's cultural background.

4. *Active Teaching Methods:* Students are involved in a variety of reading, writing, listening, speaking, and viewing behaviors throughout the lesson plan.
5. *Teacher as Facilitator:* The teacher presents information briefly, giving directions, summarizing responses, and working with small groups, pairs, and individuals.
6. *Student Control of Portions of the Lesson:* A "healthy hum" is present in the classroom, with students speaking at conversational levels about the topic studied, while they work in small groups and pairs.
7. *Instruction with Groups and Pairs:* There is lower anxiety when students complete assignments individually, but usually they work in small groups or pairs, with time to share ideas and think critically about their work.

When implementing successful culturally responsive instruction, teachers became aware of these specific characteristics. As they created lesson plans and observed videos of their classrooms, it became apparent that these seven characteristics were elements that provided a structure for assessing their own lesson plans.

Additionally, when teachers were asked to define culturally responsive teaching during professional development sessions, they provided the following list:

- Participating in self-awareness and cross-cultural analyses exercises.
- Talking frequently with family members.
- Sharing experiences from our family lives.
- Asking for help in obtaining community resources related to the curriculum.
- Learning about community resources.
- Sharing information for the child's education on a neutral or equal playing field.
- Encouraging family involvement in the creation and implementation of in-service programs.
- Creating lessons that include reading, writing, listening, speaking, and viewing, and that connect home, school, and community.

One teacher said it best when explaining culturally responsive instruction: "Everybody benefits when there is culturally responsive teaching . . . children, families, teachers, and community."

■ *Group Inquiry Activity*   Because so many teachers come from white middle-class backgrounds (even those who teach in culturally diverse settings), many have never been challenged to consider the implications of their own ethnicity. Whether or not your childhood included culturally diverse experiences, we ask that you consider the following questions:

1. In what ways is it disadvantageous to grow up in a majority culture?
2. Are there advantages?
3. What are the implications for *teachers* who were raised in such a context?
4. What are the implications for students of these teachers, and how does the degree of diversity in the school affect your answer to this question?

In a fascinating article, Althier Lazar (2001) describes her research on preparing white preservice teachers for urban classrooms. Her conclusions are cautious ones. Lazar found that, for the most part, her students worked hard to become aware of their own "whiteness" and cultural privilege. They did in fact increase their recognition of biases in the structure and classroom events within urban schools. The study contradicts the conclusion drawn by Haberman (1996) that European Americans may not be the best choice as teachers for culturally and linguistically diverse students. However, in spite of the intense focus on understanding these cultural dynamics, a small number of preservice teachers persisted in their biased assumptions about children's abilities and a few remained insecure about teaching in urban schools. Lazar concludes we have a long way to go in understanding the complexities involved in the processes of preparing such teachers to work in urban settings. Clearly this interesting line of inquiry and the questions that Patty Schmidt poses have great potential to inform all of us.

### Linguistically and Culturally Responsive Instruction

We would like to add a few caveats about culturally responsive instruction. First, as Au (2000) suggests, no matter how much the idea (culturally responsive instruction) seems to make sense pedagogically, we have yet to see a body of research to support its efficacy. Second, we want to caution educators to beware of superficial attempts to respond to language and culture, such as celebrating "heroes and holidays" or other single events where foods, crafts, clothing, or aspects of language and culture are placed in the forefront briefly. We suggest that these measures must be coupled with rich classroom experience; that teachers and reading specialists find ways to incorporate values, literature, beliefs, and images in their instruction; and that activities allow connections that defy the common stereotypes. We urge you to consider using the suggestions of Ann Watts-Pailliotet (2000) and David O' Brien (2001) by providing avenues for expression that allow *all* students, not only those with limited English language proficiency, to express their knowledge through art, music, or intermediality.

The role of the reading specialist/literacy coach is to provide teachers with support, guidance, ideas, and models of instructional practice that respond to language and culture in a variety of ways. Culturally responsive instruction does not imply abandoning or lowering our goals, expectations, or standards, for such a stance is inherently discriminatory. Rather, like all good instruction, it makes full use of all the resources available to meet the existing goals. We would argue that a student's background knowledge and experience and culture and values are important resources on which connections to new content knowledge can be based. If we are to use the "cultural capital" (values, behaviors, experiences, tastes, perspectives) children bring to school as Au (2000) and Nieto (1999) suggest, we will have to find ways to help students make personal connections between the worlds of their school and community.

## Revisiting the Vignette

Although Susan Weiss, Jefferson Elementary School's reading specialist, is not particularly knowledgeable about the instructional needs of English learners in her school, she is wise to collaborate with her district's bilingual coordinator as a start. If she is expected to serve as a resource and coach in her school, she will need to do some reading about current, accepted, and proven approaches for teaching ELs. She also should teach a small group of English learners while implementing sheltered instruction techniques and approaches, so that she'll be credible when she works with other teachers. She might want to form a study group with colleagues in order to learn more about how to plan appropriately for English learners. Asking for help, and not feeling inadequate when her school experiences a rapid increase in the number of English learners, is an important step for Susan to take. These students deserve the best she and her fellow teachers can offer them, and her willingness to learn, practice, and adapt her teaching are all important to their eventual mastery of English and academic content.

## Points to Remember

While English learners need explicit reading instruction in the same five components (phonemic awareness, phonics, vocabulary, fluency, comprehension) as their native-speaking peers, they need additional instruction and practice to develop oral fluency. Teachers need to carefully assess ELs' literacy development and language proficiency, if possible in both the L1 (home language) and English, especially before determining that a student has a reading disability. English learners develop conversational English before academic language, and often find the latter to be very challenging when reading and writing. Therefore, reading specialists and literacy coaches need to help classroom teachers identify and explicitly teach the academic language of the content areas. This can be accomplished through effective and appropriate sheltered instruction with the SIOP® (Sheltered Instruction Observation Protocol) Model, which was designed to simultaneously develop English proficiency, academic language, and content knowledge. Finally, teachers' sensitivity and awareness of their own and their students' cultural and linguistic backgrounds will enhance their teaching of diverse students.

## Portfolio and Self-Assessment Projects

1. Create a linguistic family tree, going back as far as you can to explore and define your linguistic heritage and culture. How many languages can you identify that have been spoken by your near and distant relatives? How have these languages and cultural groups defined who you are today?

2. Design, teach, and evaluate a sheltered instruction content lesson. Videotape yourself as you are teaching and determine the degree to which you provided your students with access to grade-level concepts, texts, content, and vocabulary. Reflect on your teaching and what you can do to provide a linguistically and culturally responsive environment for all your students.

3. Review the literacy support materials that are included in your district-adopted reading program (K–6). These may include assessment instruments, extra-support handbooks for struggling readers and English learners, classroom management materials or handbooks, workbooks, and more. Analyze these materials according to the following criteria:

   a. Appropriateness for the literacy development of students acquiring English as a second or multiple language.

   b. Appropriateness for students with physical limitations such as hearing or vision problems.

   c. Whether these materials are considered to be supplementary or integral to the core program—that is, does this handbook (or other material) provide students with access to the core curriculum? Based on your analysis, make recommendations about the use of the support materials for students in and out of the "mainstream."

4. Engage in Dr. Schmidt's ABCs of Cultural Understanding process. Share your completed project with your group, class, or colleagues.
5. *Personal Goal:* Create a portfolio item that reflects your learning relative to the goal you set for yourself.

## Recommended Readings: Suggestions for Book Clubs, Study Groups, and Professional Development

August, D., & Shanahan, T. (Eds.). (2008). *Developing reading and writing in second-language learners: Lessons from the report of the National Literacy Panel on language-minority children and youth.* New York: Routledge (copublished with the Center for Applied Linguistics and the International Reading Association). This comprehensive volume represents what was known at the time of the writing about all aspects of literacy development in language-minority students, including relationships between L1 and L2 literacy, the impact of sociocultural contexts, instruction, professional development, assessment, and recommendations for future research.

Bear, D. R., Helman, L., Templeton, S., Invernizzi, M., & Johnston, F. (2007). *Words their way with English learners: Word study for phonics, vocabulary, and spelling instruction.* Upper Saddle River, NJ: Pearson Merrill Prentice Hall. Based on the original *Words Their Way* books, this special EL edition includes spelling inventories in English, Spanish, Chinese, and Korean, and accompanying pictures for sorts and games, word lists for sorting, and translations of pictures for naming and sorting. Activities and instructional recommendations are based on English learners' language proficiencies and stages of spelling development.

Echevarria, J., & Graves, A. (2011). *Sheltered content instruction: Teaching English language learners with diverse abilities* (4th ed.). Boston: Allyn and Bacon. This text explains in detail the needs of English learners and builds a strong rationale for providing appropriate instruction based on individual students' needs, particularly for those receiving special education services. Sheltered content instruction is described and a variety of effective instructional techniques are explained.

Echevarria, J., Vogt, M. E., & Short, D. (2008). *Making content comprehensible for English learners: The SIOP® Model* (3rd ed.). Boston: Allyn and Bacon.

Echevarria, J., Vogt, M. E., & Short, D. (2010a). *Making content comprehensible for elementary English learners: The SIOP® Model.* Boston: Allyn and Bacon.

Echevarria, J., Vogt, M. E., & Short, D. (2010b). *Making content comprehensible for secondary English learners: The SIOP® Model.* Boston: Allyn and Bacon. These books describe in detail how to plan, teach, and evaluate sheltered content lessons. They focus on the Sheltered Instruction Observation Protocol (SIOP®), an instrument that guides lesson planning, lesson delivery, and lesson evaluation. The SIOP® Model, when implemented consistently, systematically, and to a high degree, has been found to significantly and positively impact English learners' language acquisition and content knowledge.

Reiss, J. (2008). *102 content strategies for English language learners: Teaching for academic success in grades 3–12.* Upper Saddle River, NJ: Pearson Merrill Prentice Hall. This book includes descriptions of a variety of instructional techniques and activities especially appropriate for English learners as well as theoretical foundations for providing instruction to ELs, rationales for each activity, and reflective discussion questions for each chapter.

## Companion Website Resources

The following resources to support and extend your learning of this chapter can be found on our companion website (waveland.com/Extra_Material/32979/): key vocabulary, concepts, and other terms; extended examples; updated resources specifically tied to information in the chapter; related websites; and other support features.

# 8

# *Implementing a Comprehensive Literacy Program in the Elementary School*

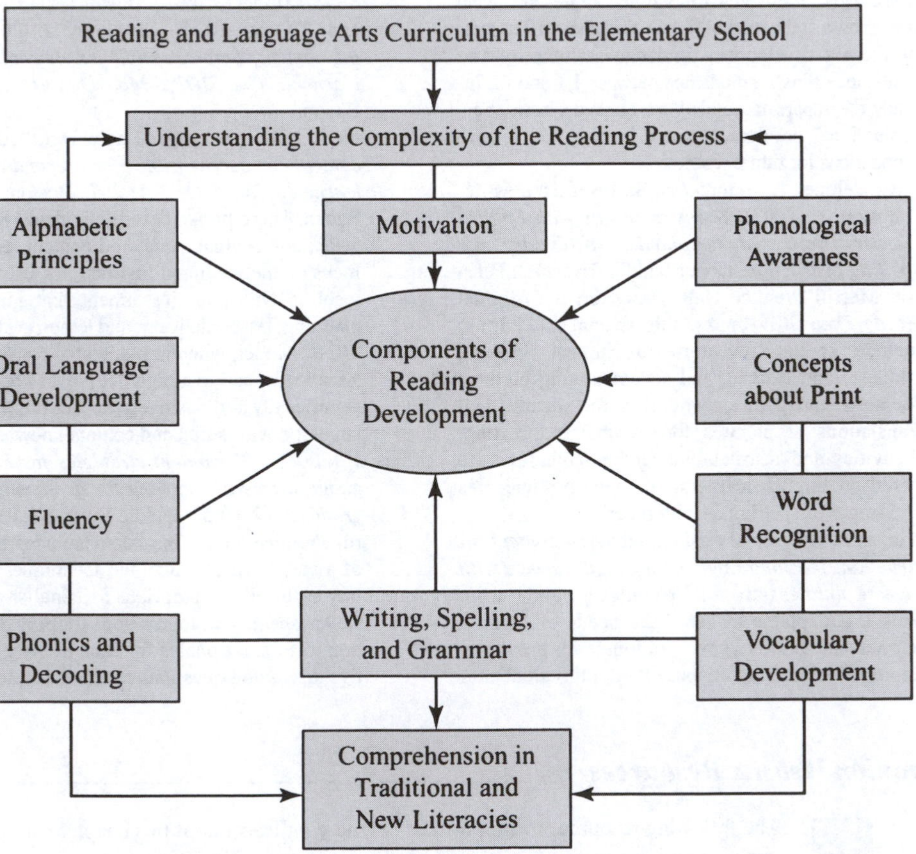
Reading and Language Arts Curriculum in the Elementary School
Understanding the Complexity of the Reading Process
Alphabetic Principles
Motivation
Phonological Awareness
Oral Language Development
Components of Reading Development
Concepts about Print
Fluency
Word Recognition
Phonics and Decoding
Writing, Spelling, and Grammar
Vocabulary Development
Comprehension in Traditional and New Literacies

**FIGURE 8.1** ***Chapter Overview***

## *Learning Goals*

After reading, discussing, and engaging in activities related to this chapter, you will be able to:

1. Provide an overview of the reading process.
2. Describe a standards-based elementary school curriculum in reading and language arts.
3. Work with students, parents, teachers, and administrators in implementing and sustaining an effective elementary literacy program.
4. *Personal Learning Goal:* In a three-minute brainstorming session, share what you know about effective elementary literacy programs. Write a goal or a question that reflects something you want to learn as we explore this topic. Share it with the members of your group.

## *Standards for Reading Professionals*

This chapter provides focused support for current IRA Standards for Reading Professionals. See our companion website (waveland.com/Extra_Material/32979/) for a complete listing of the standards that align with this chapter.

### Vignette

*It is the beginning of a new school year and Claudio Martelli has just been hired in his first position as a reading specialist at Lincoln Elementary School in the southern United States. The school is characterized by a high level of diversity, with 40 percent Caucasian students, 32 percent Hispanic students, 17 percent African American students, and 9 percent Southeast Asian students. The school operates year-round with four different tracks; one of the tracks (approximately 120 students and four to five teachers) is on vacation at any given time.*

*New to the district, Claudio has been hired on a ten-month contract, and will be working with all four tracks in grades kindergarten through fifth. There are a variety of reading programs in place at Lincoln, including bilingual, transitional bilingual, sheltered instruction (SI), special edu-*cation, *and English mainstream instruction. This school also has a large number of first-year teachers in the primary grades.*

*The principal has several specific jobs in mind for the reading specialist. First, the school has been identified as "needing improvement" because of low test scores in reading. The principal feels it is part of the reading specialist's responsibility to work to improve them. Also, Claudio is expected to focus his efforts on assisting the first-year teachers with their language arts programs, as well as developing strategies to improve reading across the grade levels, particularly with the English learners. Although Claudio will oblige his principal by assisting the new teachers, he is also eager to help struggling readers in all grades.*

### Thinking Points

1. What are some of the issues that Claudio faces as he begins his new job?
2. What are the first three things you think he should address?

## Expanding the Vignette: Exploring the Issues

*One of the first steps Claudio took was to distribute an introductory newsletter to all teachers on the staff. He also invited the first-year teachers to join him each week for a one-hour meeting related to reading/language arts, and stated that these meetings would focus on the following topics: assessment, management, instructional strategies, and guided reading. Most of the new teachers, although feeling overwhelmed by the onset of the school year, appeared to welcome the new reading specialist's offer of assistance.*

*Marcia Wilson, one of the first-year teachers, recently entered teaching as a second career. She was assigned to a third-grade mixed class of twenty-four students, a number of whom are intermediate speakers of English, with a few transitional English speakers.*

*Within the first few weeks of school, Marcia noticed that one of her students, Visal, was having difficulty with reading and writing—he seemed to be significantly behind his peers. Eight years old and the middle child of five in his family, Visal speaks only Cambodian at home. He speaks English only during school time. He has attended Lincoln since kindergarten and has always been in bilingual and transitional classes. Because of her concerns about Visal's literacy development, Marcia asked Claudio to stop by her classroom to*

*see if he had any suggestions for how she might better meet the child's needs.*

*Responding to Marcia's request for help with Visal, Claudio reviewed the boy's cumulative file, noting his previous standardized test scores, as well as former teachers' written comments. He then scheduled an observation in Marcia's third-grade classroom during the reading/language arts block. He noted that she taught reading as a whole-class endeavor, with the same literature anthology used for all students. Similarly, skill and strategy lessons were taught whole-class, and from the daily schedule posted on the board, it appeared there was no scheduled time for a teacher read-aloud or self-selected reading by students. Perhaps most important, Claudio observed that Visal and others were unengaged during the reading lesson, and at times, appeared confused.*

*Claudio decided that he needed to visit some other classrooms, particularly those of the first-year teachers. He discovered that a variety of materials and approaches were in use, and found inconsistencies in the amount and quality of available reading materials. As Claudio ventured into the classrooms of the more experienced teachers, he realized that there, too, were an assortment of methods and materials that the teachers were using for their individual reading programs.*

### Thinking Points

1. Identify what you think are the three possible reasons Visal is experiencing difficulty with reading. Of the three, which should be the primary focus of Claudio's work with Marcia?
2. What information about the school's and district's reading program(s) does Claudio need? Where will he likely find this information?

## *The Reading and Language Arts Curriculum in the Elementary School*

Before we can make recommendations to Claudio about how to implement a balanced, comprehensive reading program in his school, let's examine the reading process, especially for beginning and developing readers. In doing so, we can begin to identify the critical literacy elements that must be present in pre-K, primary (K–2) and intermediate (3–5) classrooms.

## The Reading Process

Over the past thirty years, researchers have investigated the interrelatedness and reciprocity of the language processes (Heath, 1983, 1994; Moll, 1994). We know with certainty that language and literacy develop through multiple and varied interactions with other human beings (Harrison, 2004). According to Louise Wilkinson and Elaine Silliman (2000), literacy learning is a social activity, integrated with oral and written language, requiring active student engagement.

One aspect of oral communication is especially required for success in school: "[Students] must know with whom, when and where they can speak and act, and they must provide speech and behavior that are appropriate for given classroom situations" (Mehan, 1979, p. 133). If you have taught kindergarten, you noticed that children with pre-K schooling experiences know how to "do school," and they have decided advantages when they enter kindergarten (Morrow & Gambrell, 2004).

Effective literacy instruction is situated in relevant, meaningful experiences that help children transfer new learning to other settings, such as their homes and communities (Barone & Xu, 2008). In the sections that follow, we provide a brief overview of how readers develop proficiency. For many of you, this overview will serve as a review. It is beyond the scope of this book to go into great detail about complex literacy processes and development; therefore, if you desire more information, we refer you to the recommended readings at the end of this chapter and others throughout the book.

***Reading and Writing Development.*** In order to understand how beginning readers learn to read and write and why some children have difficulty, researchers have investigated what it is that successful beginning, developing, and proficient readers do. They have examined the relationship between oral language development and beginning reading; how children acquire understandings about the alphabet, concepts of print, sound–symbol relationships; and how comprehension is fostered. Some researchers have described reading acquisition through developmental continua for oral language, reading, and writing (Chall, 1983; Ehri, 1994). Others maintain that the unique perspectives, experiences, oral language competencies, and backgrounds of each individual child are more likely to provide information about how literacy is acquired (see Dyson, 1993, 1994; Sulzby, 1994; Yaden, Rowe, & MacGillivray, 2000). The way readers approach and understand texts is largely influenced by their experiences, purposes for reading, familiarity with a topic, and motivation. This holds true for all readers, beginning, developing, or fluent.

***Foundations for Learning to Read.*** Recent research has informed us about the importance of providing foundations that enable students to make sufficient progress in learning to read and write. As we briefly discuss each of these, reflect on the implications for pre-K and elementary schools' reading programs. As you read, think about the reading materials, methods, approaches, and supplemental resources that need to be in place in order for teachers to achieve success in teaching children to read and write.

***Oral Language Development.*** As young children begin to explore and develop language, they hear words and sentences, realize how language is used, and develop understandings about the phonological structure of English (or their home language, if other than English), long before they come to school. They also develop understandings about how the world works through interactions with a wide variety of texts, including images, words, forms, shapes, and whatever they use to textualize their world (Wade & Moje, 2000). We need to examine what these texts are in order to use the multiple literacies of the home and the community to enhance school literacy acquisition.

For example, perhaps you have heard a young child say something like, "My mom *goed* home" or "My mom *told* me that story already!" These oral language patterns tell us about young children's (and some English language learners') developing understandings of English morphology, syntax, and text structure (Barone & Xu, 2008). If students are frequently corrected (or perhaps chastised) for these types of oral language "errors," this may have a negative impact on their subsequent language production. We encourage children to experiment with language so they may begin to internalize and adopt flexibly the uses of conventional English as they learn the various contexts for particular speech acts (such as the classroom, church, or the supper table).

Thus, the notion of "correct" English has given way to the appropriateness of a particular discourse form as a reflection of its context. Certainly, we want children to know conventional English forms of the dominant culture in which they live, primarily because this makes it easier to participate as a citizen with full rights. However, we also recognize that using conventional English (or any other discourse model) has implications about what the accepted form of speaking implies, including the speaker's stance, voice, and perspective.

Frequent read-alouds from children's literature (Fisher, Flood, Lapp, & Frey, 2004), nursery rhymes, and songs all help develop oral language fluency, and they assist children in understanding how the language works in a variety of contexts (Morrow & Gambrell, 2004). Research clearly reveals that children's oral language facility serves as an important building block for later reading and writing development (Hiebert, Pearson, Taylor, Richardson, & Paris, 1998).

***Knowledge of Letter Names and Concepts about Print.*** A strong correlation exists between children's knowledge of letter names and their success as beginning and developing readers (Snow, Burns, & Griffin, 1998). However, just knowing letter names does not guarantee later reading proficiency; the relationship between letter-name knowledge and reading achievement is more complex than simple causality (Adams, 1990).

The names of most letters offer clues to the sounds they represent and children who can accurately name them begin to develop understandings of letter–sound associations. The understanding that letters represent the sounds of spoken and written English is often referred to as the *alphabetic principle*.

As young children listen to, play with, and look at many stories and books, they begin to develop an understanding about print concepts (Clay, 1985, 1991), which include:

1. *Directionality:* In English, print runs left-to-right and top-to-bottom. We read from the front of the book to the back.

2. *Meaning:* Print carries the meaning in books, not the illustrations.
3. *Speech-to-print match:* One spoken word matches one written word.
4. *Spacing:* Printed words have spaces before and after them.
5. *Book concepts:* Books have authors, illustrators, titles, beginnings, and endings.
6. *Sentences:* Sentences begin with capitalization and end with punctuation.

***Phonological and Phonemic Awareness.*** "Phonological awareness, simply stated, is an awareness of the phonological segments in speech—the segments that are more or less represented by an alphabetic orthography. This awareness develops gradually over time and has a causal reciprocal relationship to reading" (Blachman, 2000, p. 483). Phonological awareness includes the ability to perform tasks such as rhyming and alliteration, and it is considered to be at a more rudimentary level than phonemic awareness.

"Phonemic awareness, which involves awareness and manipulation of individual sounds [phonemes] in spoken words (e.g., being able to segment a spoken word such as *fish* into three separate sounds, /f/, /i/, /sh/), greatly facilitates learning to decode printed words" (Spear-Swerling, 2004, p. 517; Yopp, 1992).

As children develop phonemic awareness, they recognize that a word has a sequence of sounds that can be blended, segmented, and rhymed. Phonemic awareness has been found to be a very strong predictor of later reading achievement, and children who demonstrate phonemic awareness in the beginning stages of learning to read are less likely to develop later reading problems (Goswami, 2000; Wilkinson & Silliman, 2000). Children who have not been exposed to word play, nursery rhymes, and hundreds of stories may need explicit instruction in identifying, counting, rhyming, blending, and segmenting the sounds in words. While phonemic awareness enhances the process of learning to read, learning to read also strengthens phonemic awareness.

***Phonics.*** Phonics is the relationship between the letters in written words and the sounds in spoken words. The letter–sound relationships of phonics are a set of visual directions that tell readers how to pronounce words they have never seen before (Fox, 2003). That phonics knowledge is a precursor and strong predictor of reading proficiency is a fact no longer argued in the research literature (National Reading Panel, 2000; Wilkinson & Silliman, 2000).

Benita Blachman (2000) states that, despite evidence that children can develop phonological awareness and phonics knowledge outside the context of literacy instruction, "There is considerable evidence that this instruction is enhanced when the connections to print are made explicit" (p. 487). We are teaching phonics when we demonstrate that the letter *m* represents the first sounds heard in the words *monkey, milk,* and *Mike.* We are also teaching phonics when we help children compare and contrast the sounds represented by words such as *mad/made* and *fin/fine* (Bear, Invernizzi, Templeton, & Johnston, 2007; Fox, 2003).

Michael Pressley (2000) suggests that the ability to recognize chunks, such as *ight, ing,* and *ake,* can be used by analogy to read new words. Although some teachers think that teaching children to decode through analogy is a new concept, it is not. In Figure 8.2 on page 162, you see a lesson and illustration taken from a phonics book titled *A Peep into Fairyland,* published in 1927! Notice the blackboard example of the onset rime/phonogram (Moore & Wilson, 1927, p. 113).

**FIGURE 8.2**   *Onsets and Rimes from* **A Peep into Fairyland: 1927**

*Source:* M. Moore & H. B. Wilson. (1927). *A Peep into Fairyland: A Child's Book of Phonic Games, First Grade.* D. C. Heath.

One last point needs to be made about phonics. A valid criticism leveled at the whole language movement was that children were being taught to rely too much on context and picture cues, and too little on phonics when decoding unknown words. What is clear in the research is that struggling readers appear to rely more on context clues than proficient readers do (Snow, Burns, & Griffin, 1998), in part because they have ill-developed decoding skills. Therefore, we advocate focusing children's attention on phonics in the beginning stages of learning to read, while helping them to use context and other clues such as pictures, to support and confirm. At the same time, we strongly urge the reading of good literature to assist children in understanding *why* they are learning all about sound–symbol relationships.

■ *Group Inquiry Activity*   In groups, discuss the following questions:

1. Why do you think teaching phonics is such a political and emotional issue for so many people?
2. Because it is viewed with such controversy, what specifically can reading specialists do to clarify issues surrounding phonics instruction?

3. How can you inform the public and policymakers, including boards of education, about appropriate and effective phonics instruction?

4. What *specifically* can you do to impress on parents, administrators, and policymakers that reading is a complex process, not just a matter of teaching students to "bark at print"? This question is so important because it has to do with methods, approaches, reading resources (such as workbooks versus good literature), teacher preparation, and professional development.

Discuss your answers to these questions with others in your school or graduate class.

***Instant Word Recognition.*** Even though about 84 percent of English words are phonetically regular (Blevins, 1998), there are a large number of words that students must read that cannot be "sounded out" by using phonics. Therefore, beginning readers must also develop a large repertoire of words they can read instantly. The sight words that children must learn to read rapidly and accurately include words such as *the, of, who, you,* and *was.* High-frequency words are those that are most often used in texts written for children. Adams (1990) reports that approximately 90 percent of words found in children's and adults' reading books consist of 5,000 common words (p. 184). Cooper and Pikulski (2000) state that approximately 300 words represent about 65 percent of words in texts, and only 500 words account for 90 percent of the running words in children's texts (p. 18). Instant recognition of these high-frequency words is a characteristic of skillful beginning and developing readers.

***Fluency.*** *Fluency* is defined as the "freedom from word identification problems that might hinder comprehension in silent reading, or in the expression of ideas in oral reading, or automaticity" (Harris & Hodges, 1995, p. 16). Fluency is closely related to *automaticity,* described as accurate and quick word identification, a reading skill discussed in the research literature for decades (LaBerge & Samuels, 1974). Fluent readers not only automatically read words but they can also *control* their reading; that is, they read with purpose and accuracy, and can devote attention to constructing meaning rather than figuring out words (Blachowicz & Ogle, 2008; Harrison, 2004; Rasinski, 2004). Unfortunately, in many schools, fluency instruction and practice are misconstrued as a "race to the finish." We discourage the practice of timed readings, except for an occasional fluency assessment by the teacher, out of the view of classmates. Students should *never* time each other's oral readings with a stopwatch, which we both observed recently in upper-grade classrooms. In reality, fluency appears to develop best through guided repeated reading, which involves students orally reading familiar passages with explicit feedback from the teacher. Independent silent reading also appears to be related to fluency (National Reading Panel, 2000). Thus, teachers are urged to assess, encourage, and model independent, self-selected reading by children.

***Vocabulary Development.*** Research evidence suggests that there are strong relationships among the following factors (Snow, Burns, & Griffin, 1998):

- A reader's background knowledge and vocabulary development.
- Vocabulary knowledge and reading comprehension.
- The amount of reading one does and vocabulary development.

That is, children develop vocabulary through reading; reading enhances children's vocabulary development and background knowledge; and vocabulary knowledge contributes to reading comprehension. For beginning readers, each new day brings opportunities to expand their conceptual understanding and vocabulary development. Listening to stories, discussing and sharing, writing, playing with words, listening to and creating poems, singing, and observing life all provide opportunities for vocabulary growth (Dickinson & Smith, 1994). Bill Nagy (1988) suggests that this type of vocabulary development occurs incidentally, and that literally thousands of new vocabulary words are learned this way. Cooper and Pikulski (2000) state that "although the research on the powerful influence of wide reading on vocabulary development is compelling, some students under some circumstances may profit from the direct teaching of vocabulary . . . [even though] direct teaching is not as powerful in achieving overall growth in vocabulary and comprehension as is wide reading" (p. 229).

It is important to recognize that vocabulary instruction has two goals. The first is acquisition of new meanings; for example, a teacher may preteach vocabulary to facilitate learning in a science lesson. However, many teachers forget the second aim of vocabulary instruction, which is to teach students strategies for independent vocabulary acquisition. Camille Blachowicz and Peter Fisher (2002) concur and add that research studies suggest four main principles to guide vocabulary instruction:

1. Students should be active in developing their understanding of words and ways to learn them.
2. Students should personalize word learning.
3. Students should be immersed in words.
4. Students should build on multiple sources of information to learn words through repeated exposures. (p. 504)

In keeping with these principles, many teachers have adopted the Vocabulary Self-Collection Strategy (VSS) (Haggard, 1982; Ruddell, 2005; Shearer, Ruddell, & Vogt, 2001). This approach encourages students to select words from anywhere that is important to them (such as reading, TV, music, interests, or school), and to incorporate these words in class spelling and vocabulary lists. VSS has been shown to be highly effective in increasing motivation, awareness, and independent vocabulary acquisition (Ruddell & Shearer, 2002).

For English learners, vocabulary development is obviously crucial. It appears that reading skills transfer from the first (LI) to the second language (L2) only after a level of proficiency in the L2 oral language has been achieved. Additionally, it's been estimated that, in order for English learners to understand about 85 percent of most texts, they need to know about 2,000 high-frequency words (Blachowitz & Fisher, 2002, p. 514). For these students, there exists a paradox: Less frequent words that need to be learned are usually encountered only in reading, but the English learners don't know enough words to be able to read well. As with phonics teaching, there is some disagreement among researchers as to how much direct versus indirect teaching is most effective for English learners. From our experience and research, contextualizing vocabulary and encouraging English learners to learn words through VSS are both effective approaches.

It has been estimated that students need to learn approximately 3,000 words per year if they are to complete high school with an adequate vocabulary (Beck & McKeown, 2001), and evidence clearly suggests that teachers must use both incidental and direct methods for reaching this goal. We also know there is a strong correlation between vocabulary knowledge and comprehension, but we have little understanding of the exact nature of the interaction. Any number of variables impinge on our understandings of the links between vocabulary and comprehension, and serve both to obscure that understanding and emphasize the complexity of the relationship itself (Ruddell, 2005).

***Comprehension.*** In the last few decades we have made great progress in our understandings about how human beings construct meaning as they read, write, and speak (Vygotsky, 1978). We also know that other forms of visual representation can be used to facilitate comprehension (Horn & Giacobbe, 2007), and that technology offers us new opportunities and challenges (Hendron, 2008; Richardson, 2009). For example, Mark Condon and Colin Harrison (2009) demonstrated that even the youngest students can use technology tools to create, share, and read "RealeBooks" in digital, online, and print formats (http://www.realewriter.com). A free version of RealeWriter allows anyone (teachers, parents, or students) to include images, photos, or scanned art into a book that can be printed or shared electronically. Higher-end versions allow young authors to include voices, music, and sound effects.

One of the most promising discoveries is that young readers are capable of benefiting from instruction in the use of highly sophisticated cognitive processes, such as critical literacy, once reserved for much older students (Van Sluys, Lewison, & Seely-Flint, 2006). We also know that individuals can help one another make sense of text through social negotiation, that is, discussing, questioning, thinking out loud, problem-solving, speculating, and cross-checking with others about meanings of words or ideas (Daniels, 2002; Kucan & Beck, 1997). Many of the strategies employed in today's classrooms focus on teacher modeling of the explicit comprehension and critical literacy processes they use while reading (Buehl, 2009; Costa & Garmston, 2002; Palinscar & Brown, 1984), including the connections they make to themselves, to other texts, and to the world (Rosenblatt, 1994). Classrooms have become hands-on workshops (living laboratories) for learning strategic reading (Dorn & Soffos, 2005; Serafini, 2006).

Several comprehension strategies have been reported as especially important to teach. These include prediction, generating questions, determining importance, drawing inferences, and self-monitoring (Allington & Johnston, 2002; McLaughlin & Allen, 2009; Wilhelm, 2001). Other researchers have suggested that imagery, story grammars, question answering, and prior knowledge activation are also critical (Block & Pressley, 2002). When strategies are taught, modeled, reinforced, and practiced with sufficient scaffolded support, it appears that students' comprehension is considerably improved (Pardo, 2004; Pressley, 2000).

Michael Pressley (2000) suggests that teachers should focus attention on two other aspects of comprehension instruction, in addition to the metacognitive strategies. These are developing word-level competencies (defined as decoding) and building background knowledge, so that children can make personal connections with what they're reading. Duffy (2002) would add that just "teaching" is not enough. Strategy instruction must be explicit when helping students learn to use a repertoire of strategies in combination.

## BEYOND THE BOOK

### *Chapter 8 Focus Issue: Comprehension Difficulties*

Using your knowledge and experience about comprehension, discuss the following with your group:

1. Why do you think comprehension has been perceived as so difficult to teach?
2. Why do you think many children develop reading problems when they move into grades 4, 5, and 6?
3. Claude Goldenberg (1993) found that when students participate in instructional conversations (a scaffolded instructional model in which teachers use techniques to elicit students' responses and engage them in discussion), comprehension improves. Why do you think this occurs? What is the role of discussion (not interrogation) and conversation in a balanced literacy program?
4. What can a reading specialist and/or literacy coach do to help teachers become more effective in teaching comprehension?

---

***Spelling and Grammar in Reading and Writing.*** Whereas there may be a lack of agreement among researchers about whether reading development can be characterized through stages or phases, there is little disagreement about characterizing spelling as a developmental process (Bear, Invernizzi, Templeton, & Johnston, 2007; Templeton & Morris, 2000). For beginning readers, there appear to be very close relationships among reading, writing, and spelling, and young children should be encouraged to use their knowledge and understandings of phoneme–grapheme relationships (sound–symbol) when they write. This is often referred to as *invented* or *temporary spelling.*

For older and developing readers, spelling instruction that emphasizes an inductive or an exploratory approach is most effective, especially when students are working at their own appropriate developmental level. This type of approach encourages word learning through analogy (see Bear et al., 2007). For struggling spellers, however, it appears that a deductive, systematic, and direct approach is more beneficial. The focus for older students should be on the interrelatedness of spelling, phonics, morphology (word structure), and vocabulary (Templeton & Morris, 2000).

Research strongly discourages teaching grammar as isolated skill exercises or as a subject separate from the other language arts. Instead, we encourage teachers and reading specialists to teach grammar through writing—using pieces of text, both narrative and expository, as models. Practices such as writers' workshop, explicit modeling of writing strategies, guided writing, 6 + 1 Trait Writing, self-assessment, Readers' and Writers' Notebook, differentiation, and new literacies associated with technology have renewed the focus on writing instruction (Allington & Shanahan, 2006).

## *Recent Insights into Effective Practice*

There are thousands of resources for elementary school reading educators, and volumes have been written on just about every aspect of reading instruction. We can't possibly include them all. However, we decided to forge ahead and attempt to give you a brief and decidedly limited overview of some of the evidence-based practices currently seen in schools. We understand the dangers of providing such a list: We may have missed common practices near and dear to the hearts of some teachers or failed to include your work or that of your favorite researcher, presenter, author, or speaker. However, the list of resources in Figure 8.3 reflects recommendations from teachers in the field, and is meant to be a starting

| Aligning Research with Principled Classroom Practices | |
| --- | --- |
| *Research-Based Assumptions* | *Elementary Classroom Practices* |
| Provide direct instruction in decoding and comprehension strategies that promote independent reading; balance direct instruction, guided reading, and independent reading, writing and word study—even at the pre-K level (Fountas & Pinnell, 1996; Gambrell, Morrow, Neuman, & Pressley, 1999; Opitz & Ford, 2001; Snow, 2005). | *Balanced Literacy* (Blachowicz & Ogle, 2008; Cunningham & Fitzgerald, 2002; Moore, 1997; Morrow & Asbury, 1999)<br>*Readers' Workshop* (Dorn & Soffos, 2005; Serafini, 2006)<br>*Guided Reading* (Fountas & Pinnell, 1996; Opitz & Ford, 2008)<br>*4 Block Model* (Cunningham, Hall, & Defee, 1998) |
| Building fluency in reading is important (LaBerge & Samuels, 1974). However, the acquisition of reading skills and the disposition to be a reader should be mutually inclusive goals (Allington, 2006; Katz, 1992). | *Imbedded Phonics/Balanced Literacy* (Block & Pressley, 2002; Calkins, 2006; Fountas & Pinnell, 1998)<br>*Reading Recovery* (Clay, 1991)<br>*Fluency* (Allington, 2008) |
| Elementary readers benefit when strategic reading (and writing) is modeled by the teacher and supported during reading through a variety of modes, including peer discussion and problem-solving (mediation) (Dorn & Soffos, 2005; Pressley, 2000; Routman, 2001; Taylor, Graves, and van den Broek, 2000). Students benefit when they are taught methods for self-assessment of their reading and writing processes (Tierney, 1991). | *Apprenticeship; Peer Mediation; Thinking Out Loud; Problem-Solving; Scaffolding Comprehension Instruction and Imbedded Strategies* (Allington & Johnston, 2002; McLaughlin & Allen, 2009; Routman, 2003)<br>*Cooperative Learning* (Marzano, 2007)<br>*Literature Circles* (Daniels, 2002; Harvey & Daniels, 2009)<br>*Cognitive Coaching* (Costa & Garmston, 2002)<br>*Think-Alouds* (Kucan & Beck, 1997; Wilhelm, 2001)<br>*Reader's Notebook* (Buckner, 2005)<br>*Arts &Literacy/Talking, Drawing, Writing* (Horn & Giacobbe, 2007; Zemelman, Daniels, & Hyde, 2005)<br>*Guided Student Self-Assessment* (Richardson, 2009) |
| Young writers benefit when given extended opportunities for strategic writing that is modeled by the teacher and supported during writing through peer discussion and problem-solving (mediation) (Calkins, 2006; Routman, 2001). | *Guided Writing* (Oczkus, 2007)<br>*Writers' Workshop* (Fletcher & Portalupi, 2001; Ray, 2006)<br>*6 + 1 Trait Writing* (Culham, 2003)<br>*Writers' Notebook* (Buckner, 2005)<br>*Strategic Writing/ Writing and Studying* (Calkins, 2006; Ray, 2006; Routman, 2005) |
| Readers and writers benefit from purposeful inclusion of Web 2.0, Read/Write, and collaborative literacies to enhance critical thinking, collaboration, and project-based learning (Leu, 2005). | *Wikis, Podcasts, Blogs, and Web2.0 Tools* (Condon & Harrison, 2009; Hendron, 2008; Richardson, 2009)<br><br>*(continued)* |

**FIGURE 8.3**   *Resources for Aligning Research with Principled Practice in Kindergarten and Elementary School*

| *Research-Based Assumptions* | *Elementary Classroom Practices* |
|---|---|
| Comprehension includes generating and testing hypotheses, questioning, summarizing, and critical reading across genres and content areas (Palinscar & Brown, 1984; Pearson, Harvey, & Goudvis, 2005). | *Strategic Reading/Reciprocal Teaching* (Buehl, 2009; Fountas & Pinnell, 2001; Keene, 2008; Palinscar & Brown, 1984)<br>*Question–Answer Relationships (QAR)* (Raphael, Highfield, & Au, 2006)<br>*Critical Literacy* (McLaughlin & DeVoogd, 2004a; Simpson, 1996; VanSluys, Lewison, & Seely-Flint, 2006) |
| Growth in vocabulary, spelling, and orthographic conventions are supported through rich contexts of reading and writing and reflect inside and outside of school language and literacies (Bear, Templeton, Helman, & Baren, 2003; Blachowicz & Fisher, 2002; Shearer & Ruddell, 2006). | *Words Their Way* (Bear, Invernizzi, Templeton, & Johnston, 2007)<br>*Word Walls* (Maeroff, 2006; Wagstaff, 1999)<br>*Robust Vocabulary Instruction* (Beck, McKeown, & Kucan, 2002; Flanigan & Greenwood, 2007; Ganske, 2000; Stahl & Nagy, 2005)<br>*Vocabulary Self-Collection Strategy (VSS)* (Ruddell, 2005; Shearer & Ruddell, 2006) |
| Students benefit from differentiated instruction and intensity of support based on varying individual needs and implemented in appropriate grouping configurations from whole-class to small-group to individual (Fuchs, Fuchs, Mathes, & Simmons, 1997). | *Tiered Instruction and Intervention/Response to Intervention (RtI)* (Ehren, 2008; Fuchs, Fuchs, Mathes, & Simmons, 1997, Howard, 2009)<br>*Flexible Grouping* (Caldwell & Ford, 2002; Cunningham, Hall, & Defee, 1998; Ford, 2005)<br>*Differentiation* (Opitz & Ford, 2008)<br>*Literacy Centers* (Southall, 2007) |
| Learners need connections to their lived experience and culture, including outside of school literacies and media forms (Knobel & Lankshear, 2009; Street, 2005). They need sheltered imbedded support for English language learning in reading, writing, listening, and speaking (Gersten, Baker, Shanahan, Linan-Thompson, Collins, & Scarcella, 2007; Heath, 1983; Moje, 2006). | *Sheltered Instruction (SIOP® Model)* (Echevarria & Graves, 2011; Echevarria, Vogt, & Short, 2008, 2010a, 2010b)<br>*ELL Instruction/Dual language Instruction* (Barone & Xu, 2008; Freeman, Freeman, & Mercuri, 2005)<br>*New Literacies* (Hendron, 2008; Leu & Castek, 2006; Lewis & Fabos, 2005; Richardson, 2009) |

**FIGURE 8.3    (*continued*)**

point for your explorations. Exploring any one of them will lead you to a rich array of related resources. Full citations for all of the items are included in the references at the back of the book. Many are suitable for book clubs, study groups, or professional development.

## *Revisiting the Vignette*

You may recall from the opening vignette that the reading specialist, Claudio, observed several teachers to see how they were implementing literacy instruction. He also distributed a needs assessment and compiled the results, which he shared with his staff and administrators. From this assessment, he learned that many of the teachers, new and experienced alike, had only surface understandings of the reading process. He therefore asked his principal for fifteen minutes at the beginning of each monthly staff meeting to review and talk about the various elements of a comprehensive reading program. He was able to purchase several copies of professional texts that were made available to his teachers on a check-out basis. He also shared the monthly journal, *The Reading Teacher* (an IRA publication). Together, the teachers reviewed these materials and established a list of programmatic areas that needed strengthening.

A concern that surfaced was the teachers' feelings of inadequacy in teaching reading to English learners. Claudio requested the assistance of his district's ELD (English Language Development) specialist who agreed to conduct workshops related to sheltered instruction and English language development. Claudio followed up throughout the year with additional support and assistance, observations, and conferences, especially with the beginning teachers. Marcia Wilson, the third-grade teacher in the vignette, began to explore how to differentiate her literacy instruction and to provide more appropriate support for her English learners. Assessment began to serve as the springboard for her instructional decisions, and as the year concluded, Marcia expressed her gratitude to Claudio for his assistance, support, and patience.

## Points to Remember

Reading involves complex processes that require a purposeful reader to integrate a variety of skills and strategies, flexibly and critically, to construct meaning in specific contexts with a variety of texts, print and nonprint. Beginning readers and writers develop understandings about the alphabetic principle, phonological awareness, and concepts about print. Fluency, rapid and accurate decoding, is gained through reading manageable texts and through exposure to rich literature. Children benefit from experimenting and approximating while they write and spell (invented spelling). Although there is some disagreement in the field about precise stages or even the notion of developmental phases of reading, it can be helpful to assess and be attentive to how children gain proficiency. Vocabulary development and spelling are enhanced through both direct and indirect approaches to teaching. Grammar can be taught through teacher and peer discussions about students' writing, as well as more explicit means. Comprehension instruction involves explicit and implicit instruction in decoding skills, background building, and metacognitive strategies. Influential teachers are more likely to provide students with the motivation to become high-achieving, competent strategic readers. An overview of research-based practice reflects our new understandings about literacy and learning.

An important responsibility of the reading specialist and literacy coach is to assist teachers in developing deep understandings about the reading process, assessment, approaches to teaching reading, appropriate grouping configurations, and the special needs of English learners. Information about what teachers know about reading can be gained through needs assessments and observation.

## Portfolio and Self-Assessment Projects

1. As a school reading specialist or literacy coach, how could you communicate to your principal those elements of your school's reading program that need improvement? What might you say if the needs have been identified through your observations of new and experienced teachers? What is your responsibility to the teachers related to confidentiality? How can you communicate what you perceive as the school's literacy needs without jeopardizing your relationship with the teachers in your school? For your portfolio, create a plan for observing teachers, discussing findings with them, and then reporting the results to your principal, while maintaining a nonevaluative stance.

2. *Personal Goal:* Revisit the goal you set for yourself at the beginning of the chapter. Create a portfolio item that reflects what you have learned relative to your goal.

## Recommended Readings: Suggestions for Book Clubs, Study Groups, and Professional Development

Barone, D., & Xu, S. H. (2008). *Literacy instruction for English language learners Pre-K–2.* New York: Guilford Press. Diane Barone and Shelley Xu's book is one of the few that addresses very young English learners. It is a valuable addition to the discussion of language and culture in Chapter 7.

Blachowicz, C., & Ogle, D. (2008). *Reading comprehension: Strategies for independent learning.* New York: Guilford Press. It is evident in this book why Camille Blachowicz, long known for her excellent work in vocabulary, and Donna Ogle, who originated K-W-L, have led the field of literacy for so long. This book is practical and wise, with ideas that can be incorporated immediately into research-based practice.

Harrison, C. (2004). *Understanding reading development.* Thousand Oaks, CA: Sage. This is no ordinary book about reading. Rather, it is a fascinating one-of-a-kind exploration of why and how children read. We highly recommend this as part of your personal library as well as a staple for study groups and professional learning communities.

Harvey, S., & Daniels, H. (2009). *Comprehension and collaboration: Literacy circles in action.* Portsmouth, NH: Heinemann. As you read this book by these brilliant authors, you will be caught up in the wisdom and enthusiasm that make Stephanie Harvey and "Smokey" Daniels such powerful educators of teachers and students.

Zemelman, S., Daniels, H., & Hyde, A. (2005). *Best practice: Today's standards for teaching and learning in America's schools* (3rd. ed.). Portsmouth, NH: Heinemann. This is one of the few books geared toward elementary literacy that features research-based practices in all subject areas including art, dance, music, and drama.

In addition to the resources above, please refer to any of the resources cited in Figure 8.3. Full citations are provided in the References in the back of this book. We included some that are particularly suited to book clubs or study groups. We could have listed many more.

## Companion Website Resources

The following resources to support and extend your learning of this chapter can be found on our companion website (waveland.com/Extra_Material/32979/): key vocabulary, concepts, and other terms; extended examples; updated resources specifically tied to information in the chapter; related websites; and other support features.

# 9

# *Implementing a Comprehensive Literacy Program in Middle and Secondary Schools*

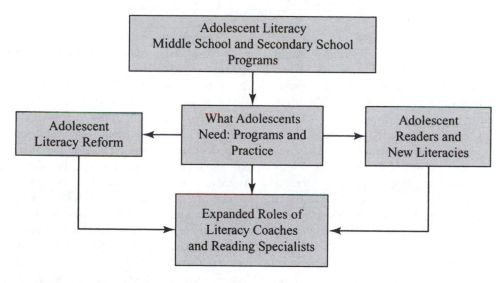

**FIGURE 9.1** *Chapter Overview*

## *Learning Goals*

After reading, discussing, and engaging in activities related to this chapter, you will be able to:

1. Identify and explain the issues and perspectives shaping literacy instruction in middle and secondary schools.

2. Describe ways to incorporate integrated strategies and innovative instructional activities that meet the needs of today's adolescents.

3. Identify and evaluate aspects of effective middle and secondary literacy programs.

4. Understand the roles of literacy coaches and reading specialists in adolescent literacy programs.

5. *Personal Learning Goal:* In a three-minute brainstorming session, share what you know about literacy programs in middle and secondary schools. Write an objective or question that reflects something you want to learn as we explore this topic. Share this with others in your group.

## *Standards for Reading Professionals*

This chapter provides focused support for current IRA Standards for Reading Professionals. See our companion website (waveland.com/Extra_Material/32979/) for a complete listing of the standards that align with this chapter.

### Vignette

*Judy and the literacy team have just completed their needs assessment for the Timber Valley School District in rural West Virginia. As the new secondary literacy coach in this small community, Judy is anxious to begin on the right foot and project an image that she is here to serve teachers. The superintendent and principals of the three schools (elementary, middle, and secondary) agree that Judy's job will be to coach content area teachers as they implement the new literacy-imbedded curriculum and to serve as a resource for teachers rather than working directly with students. The teachers have an afternoon teachers' workshop every month, a two-and-one-half-hour block of time devoted to professional development. At the first meeting, Judy introduced herself, shared her job description, and emphasized some of the services she could provide. Generally, the reception Judy has received from teachers has been favorable. She recognizes how fortunate she is to be in a district that is willing to employ a full-time secondary literacy coach in a resource role.*

*As Judy and the literacy team examine the newly completed needs assessment, they discover that students at the secondary level are receiving little or no strategic literacy instruction in the content areas. They also note that scores on the mandated tests in all areas show a general decline from those at the elementary and middle school levels. Teachers know they need to improve literacy levels in the content areas, but their high degree of anxiety is evident. As Judy walks down the hall at Timber Valley High School and peers into classrooms, she observes one teacher after another at the front of the room lecturing students in the traditional transmission model. She is convinced that students aren't being provided with the opportunities for thinking and problem-solving that are necessary to succeed in life, much less improve their test scores. From her limited contact with these teachers, she is convinced that if they only knew a better way to approach their teaching, they would be willing and eager to change. Judy is excited because she has a wealth of materials to share. This is one problem she can fix.*

### Thinking Points

1. What is your first reaction to Judy's situation?
2. What would you recommend to Judy as a place to start?

## Expanding the Vignette: Exploring the Issues

*Judy meets with the secondary principal and explains her plan to create a set of resources for all content areas. She spends many hours preparing a binder of dozens of interactive teaching strategies such as K-W-L, Semantic Feature Analysis, I-Charts, Text Frames, and Analogy Graphic Organizers. She creates instructions for each strategy and includes content area examples. The binders are comprehensive, attractive, and user-friendly. Judy puts one in every teacher's mailbox in the high school. She includes a letter explaining*

*how teachers can adapt their lessons to include these strategies and that she is available and eager to assume her role as literacy coach. Several weeks pass. A few teachers mention the binders and thank Judy, but she sees no evidence that even a single teacher is using the resource she has created or invited her to act as coach. Whenever she tries to engage teachers in conversations about the binders or literacy coaching, they say they intend to invite her in, but haven't gotten around to it yet. Judy is confused and a bit hurt.*

### Thinking Points

1. What additional issues have you identified in the vignette?
2. Why might the teachers be resisting Judy's offers?
3. What are some short-term and long-term measures Judy could take?
4. What might Judy have done differently to bring about the changes she and the team see as necessary?

## *Adolescent Literacy: Issues and Perspectives*

■ *Author Connection: Brenda* This vignette is adapted from one developed by Kristin Anklam and Deb Rupnow, two graduate students in my Administration and Supervision class. It is particularly powerful in that it illustrates one of the most common and frustrating problems a literacy coach encounters. What do you do when you are convinced you have the solution to a problem? How do you cope when you know that if you could just get (fill-in-the-name) to do (fill-in-the-teaching-practice), a big problem would be solved? This vignette generated a great deal of emotionally charged discussion in our class because it tapped into the very heart of the change process. In order for people to change behavior, they must change internally. They must change what they believe. In effect, they must change who they are. The binder was a wonderful resource, but it was presented in such a way that it was doomed to fail in its goal of changing classroom practice. In fact, our class began to characterize all such ideas, ones that were ambitious and well meaning, but doomed to failure as "bad binders." The metaphor of a bad binder has come to mean more than just a folder. The gesture Judy made failed to bind individuals together in a common goal, it failed to bind the teachers into a community of learners, and it failed to bind the literacy coach in one-to-one relationships with teachers. As we think about the challenges of transforming literacy programs in middle and secondary schools, the bad binder metaphor will be useful. Keep it in mind as you read this chapter. Perhaps you will find a number of ideas to help Judy and her reading specialist and literacy coach colleagues when we revisit the vignette.

### Beliefs and Practices of Content Area Teachers

When students emerge from our universities, ready to begin careers as content area teachers, their beliefs reflect a strong commitment to interactive teaching and hands-on, activity-based literacy and content instruction. Why, then, when we visit their classrooms a year or two later, do we find some of them using highly traditional teaching models? How can they possibly revert to the transmission model of teaching that is the antithesis of their stated beliefs? After all, haven't we been focused on content area literacy since the 1970s, when the movement to incorporate reading instruction into content teaching started to gain momentum? Perhaps one of the problems was and is that the momentum never came from content teachers but from university professors, administrators, and reading specialists. Marty Ruddell describes those early days when the remedy was to bring in a professor for a day of professional development to convince middle and secondary teachers of their responsibilities and to model the strategies that would incorporate reading into their content teaching. She states, "I have faced many a tight-lipped, arms-crossed faculty under those circumstances, and I'm not alone in that experience. The success of these efforts varied widely (just as it does today)" (Ruddell, 2005, p. 10). Indeed, when we teach undergraduate content area literacy courses, we see many future subject area teachers enter our classes with the same enthusiasm they take to the dentist's office. Our course in reading is required or there is no way they would be there because, "Hey, I'm not a reading teacher, I'm a science (or P.E. or music, or whatever) teacher." As literacy professors, we assure them of the primacy of their subject areas and by the end of the semester, many recognize that literacy can support and enhance content learning.

We suggest there may be some compelling reasons why new teachers are not incorporating content literacy strategies into their teaching. David O'Brien and Roger Stewart (1992) offer insights into resistance to content area reading that are tied to the culture of the school. Like Judy in the vignette, most reading specialists and professors believe these teachers misunderstand the ways content area reading can "improve their teaching." Thus, these well-meaning educators have been trying to "fix" the attitudes of content teachers. When we examine the culture of the schools, we find that there are responsible and effective teachers who choose not to incorporate more reading into their teaching. Some cite the poor quality of materials available in traditional texts (O'Brien & Stewart, 1992). Additionally, in some content areas, reading may be seen as a second-rate approach to hands-on learning (Schallert & Roser, 1989). Despite years of content area literacy courses in teacher education programs and increased pressure on content area teachers to imbed literacy strategies in their instruction, it sometimes appears that O'Brien and Stewart's 1992 conclusions might still be the case.

### Revisiting the Vignette: Thinking Points

1. How does the information about resistance align with your perceptions about content area teachers' beliefs and practices in your school or district?
2. In what ways are they similar or different from those Judy encountered?
3. What might you explain to Judy or suggest to her based on what you read about resistance?

In this chapter, we explore the world of adolescent readers, the educators who work with them, and the roles of literacy professionals working in middle and secondary schools. You will find that we offer the latest recommendations on components of effective programs and research-based practice. Groundbreaking research from the Carnegie Foundation and professional organizations have had a powerful influence on literacy education in middle and high schools. Educators are recognizing that different content areas (domains) require different kinds of thinking and unique academic vocabulary and language use. For example, mathematics is a domain that requires students to "think and speak like a mathematician," whereas sociology requires a student to "think and speak like a social scientist." Each domain has a way of structuring text, and each requires strategies unique to that domain. Understanding texts in disparate subject areas requires students to be aware of the specific literacy structures and reasoning within these domains. Because they are the experts in their subjects, content area teachers must be involved in teaching their students how to think and communicate in the various fields of knowledge. We also expand our discussion of technology because so much of what counts as literacy for these students occurs in out-of-school settings using nontraditional forms. These literacies are rapidly redefining responsive school practice.

## The Call for Reform in Adolescent Literacy

A strong case can be made that the area of greatest reform in recent decades is that of adolescent literacy. As the first decade of the new century ended, there could be no doubt that adolescent literacy was the subject of great interest. Adolescent literacy remains the focus of intensive research with considerable funding from government and private agencies and organizations. All of these efforts are aimed at shedding new light on what adolescent literacy learners need, the components of effective practice, and the educational reforms required in order to respond to the research findings. Although the publications come from different sources, with each providing a list of directives for adolescent literacy instruction, their suggestions are remarkably similar. We have included a brief overview of a number of them. However, we encourage you to obtain the original documents and inform yourself of the important information they include.

### Time to Act

The launching of the Time to Act reports in 2009, arguably the largest research endeavor related to adolescent literacy, was a major event in the history of adolescent reading. Funded by the Carnegie Corporation, Time to Act was designed to set an agenda for advancing adolescent literacy for college and employment. The culmination of six years of work by top researchers in various aspects of adolescent literacy, it was actually a set of six separate breakthrough publications under one umbrella. The first report was Time to Act; the other five covered (1) adolescent literacy in and out of school, (2) reading in the disciplines, (3) an annotated bibliography of adolescent literacy textbooks, (4) adolescent literacy programs, and (5) a guide to reading comprehensive assessments for adolescents. A full bibliographic citation and the location of the website for you to access each report is included in the Recommended Readings section at the end of this chapter.

## IRA and NCTE: Positions and Policies

IRA's 1999 Adolescent Literacy Position Statement (Moore, Bean, Birdyshaw, & Rycik) laid the groundwork for much of the reform that followed. In 2006, NCTE published its policy research brief *Principles of Adolescent Literacy Reform,* bringing valuable insights and resources to the crucial issue of improving instruction for adolescents. Its orientation raises concern about our "growing under-literate class" and the fact that ". . . simply being able to read and write is not enough" (p. 4). This position statement suggests that if we are to continue to participate in a global economy, workers need to be competent and confident practitioners of complex and varied forms of literacy. The document categorizes research and recommendations in three sections: (1) Overview of Adolescent Literacy, (2) Professional Development: The Route to Reform, and (3) Professional Development to Improve Adolescent Literacy. NCTE suggests that "reforming adolescent programs demands attention" to the following: motivation, comprehension, critical thinking, and assessment.

## National Association of Secondary School Principals: Creating a Culture of Literacy

Among the most exciting documents, guidelines, and opinion pieces resulting from adolescent literacy reform efforts is the National Association of Secondary Principals' *Creating a Culture of Literacy: A Guide for Middle and High School Principals* (NASSP, 2007). Support from the Carnegie Foundation and the Bill and Melinda Gates Foundation enabled NASSP to distribute a free copy of the guide to every middle school and high school principal in the United States. The document is arguably among the boldest and most powerful statements in support of literacy to come from an educational organization not directly related to reading. It suggests that literacy practices—specifically, reading, writing, and speaking—are fundamental to promoting learning and advancing ideas among diverse individuals. At the heart of its intent is this excerpt from its preface:

> As important as food and shelter are to human survival, education is to human development. Education makes it possible to think, dream, act, and build further knowledge. And there can be no education without literacy. (NASSP, 2007, p. v)

*Creating a Culture of Literacy* states that if secondary schools are to meet the academic instructional needs of the adolescent, there are **several key elements** that must be in place to implement a comprehensive adolescent literacy program. These essentials include: (a) committed and supportive school leaders; (b) balanced formal and informal assessments that guide the learning of students and teachers; (c) ongoing, job-embedded, research-based professional development; (d) highly effective teachers in every content area who model and provide explicit instruction to improve comprehension; and (e) strategic and accelerated intervention. The report is available at http://www.principals.org/portals/0/context/52924.pdf.

***Race to the Top.***   One of the most ambitious of the literacy reform initiatives is Race to the Top (see Chapter 1). It is part of the stimulus funding *specifically* aimed at preparing students for college or careers. To obtain more information on the components of Race to the Top and the grant criteria, see www.ed.gov/programs/racetothetop.

| *Reading Next:*<br>*A Vision for Action in Middle and High School Literacy* | |
| --- | --- |
| ***Elements Supporting***<br>***Instructional Improvement*** | ***Elements Supporting***<br>***Infrastructure Improvement*** |
| • Direct explicit instruction<br>• Effective instructional principles imbedded in content<br>• Motivation and self-directed learning<br>• Text-based collaborative learning<br>• Strategic tutoring<br>• Diverse texts<br>• Intensive writing<br>• A technology component<br>• Ongoing formative assessment of students | • Extended time for literacy<br>• Professional development<br>• Ongoing summative assessment of students and programs<br>• Teacher teams<br>• Leadership<br>• A comprehensive and coordinated literacy program |

**FIGURE 9.2**    *Reading Next: Elements Supporting Instructional and Infrastructure Improvements*

### Assessing the School's Literacy Program and Engaging in Self-Assessment

*Reading Next: A Vision for Action in Middle and High School Literacy* (Biancarosa & Snow, 2004) includes fifteen elements proven to support instructional and infrastructure improvement. As you engage in planning your middle and secondary school improvement initiatives, you can use the overview in Figure 9.2 to analyze whether these research-based elements are present in your school's adolescent literacy program.

Literacy coaches and reading specialists are also beginning to recognize the importance of self-assessment to their professional growth. IRA and NCTE together created a valuable tool to assist in the process: *Self-Assessment for Middle and High School Literacy Coaches,* available on the Literacy Coaching Clearinghouse website (http://www.literacycoachingonline.org/library/resources/self-assessmentformshsliteracycoaches.html).

## What Adolescent Readers Need

The following list synthesizes the recommendations from IRA, Reading Next, NCTE, and the six 2010 reports from the Carnegie Foundation and other research publications for principled adolescent literacy programs and practices. Figure 9.3 on pages 178–180 includes the research that grounds each of the ten elements and the related practices that reflect the application of these constructs to classroom instruction.

### The Ten Essential Elements of Principled Classroom Practices for Adolescent Literacy Instruction

Adolescent learners need:

1. An assessment-based and evidence-based literacy program with explicit, mediated, and socially situated comprehension instruction.

2. Instruction in domain-specific strategies and critical thinking that prepares them for college and employment.
3. Opportunities to consume and produce a wide variety of text forms.
4. Curriculum that honors sociocultural contexts and language foundations.
5. Rich engagement, appropriate challenge, self-directed learning, and motivating instruction.
6. Meaningful, explicit, imbedded, and independent strategies for vocabulary acquisition.
7. Instruction in technologies that incorporate in- and out-of-school literacies to facilitate content learning.
8. Differentiated instruction, based on principled assessment, that includes appropriate levels of support.
9. Instruction that values and incorporates opportunities to make connections to lived experience.
10. Opportunities for in-depth, student-directed, and teacher-supported inquiry to extend content learning.

| *Ten Essential Elements of Principled Classroom Practices for Adolescent Literacy Instruction* | |
|---|---|
| ***Research-Based Assumptions*** | ***Middle and Secondary Classroom Practices*** |
| 1. Adolescents need an assessment-based literacy program of comprehension instruction imbedded in rich content that values peer mediation for *comprehension,* teacher discussion, collaboration, and social learning (Moje, 2007; Shearer, Ruddell, & Vogt, 2001). | *Strategic Reading* (Duffy, 2002; Fisher & Frey, 2004) *Strategy Collections: Strategic Literacy Practices* (Buehl, 2009; Wood & Harmon, 2001; Zwiers, 2008) *Reciprocal Teaching* (Palinscar & Brown, 1982) *Social Construction of Literacy/Social Justice* (Cook-Gumperz, 2006; Luke, 1999; Moje, 2007) |
| 2. Adolescents need explicit instruction in domain-specific literacy practices and *critical literacy* provided in their content area classrooms to prepare them for college and employment (Biancarosa & Snow, 2004; Moore, Bean, Birdyshaw, & Rycik, 1999). | *Readers'/Writers' Workshop* (Frey & Fisher, 2006; Stevens, 1995) *Comprehension/Cognitive Strategies* (Conley, 2008; Tovani, 2000) *Critical Literacy* (Comber, 2001; Harrison, 2007; Simpson, 1996) |
| 3. Adolescents need to *consume and produce* a wide variety of rich text materials across genres and literacies. This includes domain-specific *writing and representing.* They need classroom instruction that recognizes the benefits of using reading and writing as a means to enhance learning in content areas. (Saddler & Graham, 2005; Smagorinsky, 2006) | *Collaborative Writing* (Saddler & Graham, 2005; Yarrow & Topping, 2001) *Inquiry Writing/Writing to Learn* (Boscolo & Mason, 2001; Shanahan, 2004; Wilhelm, 2007) *Explicit Strategy Instruction in Writing* (De La Paz & Graham, 2002) *Writing Workshop* (Atwell, 2007; Fletcher & Portalupi, 2001; Gallagher, 2006) *Talking, Drawing, Writing* (Horn & Giacobbe, 2007) |

**FIGURE 9.3**   *The Ten Essential Elements of Principled Classroom Practices for Adolescent Literacy Instruction*

| Research-Based Assumptions | Middle and Secondary Classroom Practices |
|---|---|
| 4. Adolescents need a curriculum that honors students' sociocultural contexts and language foundations, capitalizes on individuals' diverse funds of knowledge, and provides literacy support for successful learning (Au, 1993; Barton, Hamilton, & Ivanec, 2000; Dillon, 2000; Genesee, Lindholm-Leary, Saunders, & Christian, 2005). | *Scaffolding* (Fournier & Graves, 2002; Keene, 2008)<br>*Literacies and Identity Formation* (Gee, 2001a; Hock, Deshler, & Schumaker, 2005; Lewis, 2001; Medina, 2005; Schmidt & Finkbeiner, 2006)<br>*Bidirectional Instruction /Second Language Acquisition* (Cummins, 2003; Garcia & Baker, 2007)<br>*Situated Language* (Gee, 2004; Moje, 2007) |
| 5. Adolescents need rich, engaging, motivating instruction that promotes *flow*. They need opportunities for self-directed learning and the ability to set achievable goals that promote efficacy. (Bandura, 1993; Csikszentmihalyi, 1997; Eccles, Wigfield, & Schiefele, 1998; Seligman, 1972; Smith & Wilhelm, 2006) | *Self-Efficacy* (Bong, 2004; Guthrie, 2002)<br>*Webquests and Movies, Pop Culture, Project Learning* (McClelland, 1987; Ryan & Deci, 2000)<br>*Book Clubs/Adolescent Boys and Girls as Readers* (Brozo & Gaskins, 2009; Daniels, 2002; Knobel & Lankshear, 2005; Smith & Wilhelm, 2003; Tatum, 2008)<br>*Motivating, Podcasts, Blogs, and Web2.0 Tools* (Hendron, 2008; Richardson, 2009)<br>*Motivation and Engagement* (Guthrie, 2002; Shearer & Ruddell, 2006) |
| 6. Adolescents need vocabulary instruction that combines (a) explicit vocabulary instruction, (b) in-context vocabulary instruction, and (c) strategies that promote independent vocabulary acquisition (Harrison, 2007; Nagy, 1988). | *Vocabulary Instruction/Word Study* (Blachowicz & Fisher, 2002; Cunningham, 2009; Shearer & Ruddell, 2006)<br>*Vocabulary and Critical Thinking* (Carnicelli, 2001) |
| 7. Adolescents need instruction in technologies that facilitate their ability to use new forms of in-school and out-of-school literacy practices (Leu, 2010). | *Incorporating Outside of School Literacies* (Fisher & Frey, 2004; Hull, 2003; Kist & Ryan, 2009)<br>*New Literacies/Web 2.0* (Hendron, 2008; Leu, 2010; Parker & Chao, 2007; Richardson, 2009) |
| 8. Students benefit from differentiated instruction and intensity of support based on individual needs that are linked to *responsive assessment,* and implemented in appropriate grouping configurations from whole-class to small-group to individuals. (Fuchs, Fuchs, Mathes, & Simmons, 1997) | *Assessment as Learning* (Costa & Garmston, 2002)<br>*Tiered Instruction and Intervention/Response to Intervention (RtI)* (Ehren, 2008; Fuchs, Fuchs, Mathes, & Simmons, 1997; Howard, 2009)<br>*Differentiation/RtI* (Crawford, 2008; Cunningham, Hall, & Defee, 1998; Ford, 2005; George, 2005)<br>*Assessment and Differentiation* (Moon, 2005)<br>*Literacy Centers* (Southall, 2007) |
| 9. Learners need connections to their lived experience and culture, including out-of-school language and literacy forms (Lankshear & Knobel, 2003; Street 2005). They need sheltered, imbedded support for English language | *Culturally Responsive Instruction* (Moje & Hinchman, 2004)<br>*Sheltered Instruction (SIOP®Model)* (Echevarria, Vogt, & Short, 2010b)<br><br>*(continued)* |

**FIGURE 9.3** *(continued)*

| Research-Based Assumptions | Middle and Secondary Classroom Practices |
|---|---|
| learning in reading, writing, listening, and speaking (Gersten, Baker, Shanahan, Linan-Thompson, Collins, & Scarcella, 2007; Heath, 1983; Moje, 2006). | *ELL/Dual Language Instruction* (Freeman, Freeman, & Mercuri, 2005; Garcia & Baker, 2007) |
| 10. Adolescents need opportunities for in-depth, student-directed and teacher-supported inquiry to extend content learning. They need opportunities to engage in project learning and to explore ideas individually as well as collaboratively. (Johnson & Johnson, 1986; Olson, 2006) | *Choice of Role-Audience-Format-Topic (RAFT)* (Buehl, 2009; Santa, 1988) <br> *Internet Collaborative Inquiry: Wikis, Newsfeeds, Podcasts, Blogs* (Parker & Chao, 2007) <br> *Multimediating: Synchronistic Use of Multiple Forms of Media in Consumption and Production* (Lankshear & Knobel, 2003; O'Brien & Dubbels, 2009) |

**FIGURE 9.3**   *(continued)*

## New Literacies and the Reading Professional

### What Are the "New Literacies"?

We are all familiar with basic literacy, that is, facile reading and writing in conventional ways. The Internet and new developments in technology continue to give rise to complex forms of reading and writing that challenge our assumptions of what constitutes text and the processes that define literate activity. We refer to these as "new literacies," and they include the use of information literacy, technology literacy, critical literacy, and media literacy. The Internet provides access to unprecedented amounts of information, yet brings with it new challenges in efficiently locating and manipulating that information. Students need to sift, scan, sort, and locate information from a wide variety of genres (information literacy). They must learn how to use new technology tools, understand what each can and can't do, and select the proper tool to accomplish their goals (technology literacy). They need to be able to give weight to the importance of the information, decide on its value and credibility, authority, accuracy, bias or perspective, and thoroughness, and *then,* use their judgments to make decisions about whether and how to use the information (critical literacy). They also need to use overlapping information across and among media sources. For example, a home page, such as that of AOL, may include print text, music or sound, dozens of links, video clips, audio clips, photographs, artwork, advertisements, and changing headlines—all competing for the "reader's" attention. Many home pages are best characterized by their multimodal nature. Navigating through the collective and competing sources requires an important skill set (media literacy).

Still, there are a number of print-related literacy skills that are also important in technology-based literacy, including locating information, asking and answering questions, thinking critically and evaluating information, synthesizing, and communicating ideas.

## BEYOND THE BOOK

### *Chapter 9 Focus Issue: Technology Self-Test*

Test yourself on your knowledge of the following terms. Rate yourself from 1–5.
1 = Unknown term   2 = Little knowledge   3 = Somewhat familiar   4 = Know how to use it
5 = Skillful user

| | | | | | |
|---|---|---|---|---|---|
| Web 2.0 | 1 | 2 | 3 | 4 | 5 |
| Blogs | 1 | 2 | 3 | 4 | 5 |
| Wikis | 1 | 2 | 3 | 4 | 5 |
| RSS | 1 | 2 | 3 | 4 | 5 |
| Aggregators | 1 | 2 | 3 | 4 | 5 |
| Social bookmarking | 1 | 2 | 3 | 4 | 5 |
| Flickr | 1 | 2 | 3 | 4 | 5 |
| Microblogging | 1 | 2 | 3 | 4 | 5 |

(Definitions are provided at the end of this chapter.)

In your group:

1. Share your understandings of the technology-related terms and their applications.
2. Are there any applications or technologies that you use to enhance your teaching?
3. What are some of the things that hold teachers back in terms of incorporating technology?
4. How might they be addressed?
5. If you could choose one technology-related goal for yourself as an educator, what might that be?

### *Using Technology in Adolescent Classroom Activities and Projects*

What does all this mean to educators? How do we deal with what Knobel and Lankshear (2005) call "post typographical" forms of text production, distribution, and reception using electronic media? Teachers are still figuring out the answers to these questions. However, some are forging the way with new ideas about what constitutes sound classroom practice. Don Leu (2010) and the New Literacies Research Team at the University of Connecticut (www.newliteracies.uconn.edu) are leading the way in discovering effective ways to incorporate the new literacies of online reading comprehension into the classroom. Because of limited space, we will highlight just a few ways teachers can incorporate the use of technology to enhance student learning. We hope these will pique your curiosity and impel you to explore the wonderful things teachers are doing with instructional technology.

Many teachers are discovering how valuable wikis or controlled, closed Facebook sites can be for student engagement and learning. At the top of almost every wiki page is an "Edit Page" icon, sometimes requiring a pass code. Once teachers get in, they can add, delete, or update information. They can help students use a class wiki to create group papers or projects, write their own textbooks, construct tutorials, or share and update study notes or outlines. Teachers who are reading this textbook as part of a college literacy course could respond to the vignettes through their own class wiki. One of the great features of wikis is that they can be rolled back, like peeling an onion, so that teachers can observe the evolution of the information from earlier versions. The lack of control related to open posting poses unique problems for teachers. However, there are many ways for teachers to establish policies about public uses of technology and ensure that contributors identify themselves. Educators can work with the school technology coordinator and the media specialist who are familiar with these issues and who have access to related resources.

Sites such as *blogger.com* allow teachers to create blogs with controlled access features, limiting a blog site only to students in their classrooms. Blogs can be a great source for posing questions, adding thoughts or comments about an assigned reading, or continuing a class discussion. Blogging is an excellent tool for allowing students to comment on a controversial issue. Although teachers can use blogs to post student work, Hendron (2008) reminds us that we need to get students' and parents' permission before doing so.

Digital storytelling allows students to use text, graphics, photos, animation, and sound to create their own stories. Perhaps digital storytelling will soon be incorporated into the hundreds of Young Authors celebrations and contests throughout the country. Digital storytelling can be a way to teach content area subject matter as well.

Assessment can incorporate new literacies. Students have been using PowerPoint to create electronic portfolios for quite a while. At the time of this writing, Web 2.0 capabilities can take portfolio assessment to a whole new level. We urge you to try applying some of the standard text-based strategies to materials encountered on the Internet.

## Motivation and the Adolescent Learner

■ *Author Connection: Brenda*  When it comes to motivating students, I'm convinced that the folks who develop those ubiquitous video games are beating us at our own game. When it comes to motivating kids, nobody does it better. When I was in college in the 1960s, I learned about B. F. Skinner's behaviorist principles and all about shaping human behavior through extrinsic rewards and punishments. That first year of teaching, I actually handed out M & Ms to my first-graders for lining up quietly or finishing their work. I am pleased to inform you that I progressed to more enlightened practices over the next thirty-five years. However, I am still fascinated by the puzzle of understanding human motivation, particularly when I watch the things that captivate our kids.

If you want to see the embodiment of the flow experience, watch one of your students using an electronic game system. A kid can play for hours in a trancelike state. Why? Because the creators of those games have one goal in mind—to keep you playing the game. Partly driven by what he observed while watching his young son, linguistic theorist Jim Gee (2004) has done some fascinating work related to this phenomenon. Games are designed with levels of goals. Each goal is difficult but attainable with sustained skill building. One example of the genius of the system, and there are many, is that there are little rewards built in as you play, so that you don't have to win or lose like you do in a football game. The rewards are just random enough to keep you "hungry" for the next one. When you finally master a level, the game-maker raises the bar. Each level of difficulty is just a bit above "what you can do today." If only Vygotsky (1978) were alive to see what they've done with his zone of proximal development theory! I bet he'd love it.

## Assessment Issues in Adolescent Literacy

*Measure for Measure: A Critical Consumers' Guide to Reading Comprehension Assessments for Adolescents* (Morsy, Kieffer, & Snow, 2010), a Carnegie Foundation publication, is a comprehensive analysis and comparison of assessments designed to help administrators, reading professionals, and teachers become critical consumers and make intelligent selections of appropriate assessment instruments matched to specific goals. You can download the report at http://www.carnegie.org/fileadmin/Media/Publications/PDF/tta_Morsy.pdf.

In addition to the comparisons, *Measure for Measure* reported four trends among instruments:

1. Most of the assessments emphasized inferential questions.
2. None of the tests emphasized critical thinking.
3. Tests varied in the extent to which they included content area passages, and while some included separate scores for narrative and expository text, none targeted content-specific reading skills or knowledge.
4. Tests varied on a continuum, but confirmed that there is a trade-off between efficiency and specificity of information about individual differences. (pp. 7–8)

## Role of the Reading Professional in Adolescent Literacy Programs

In Chapter 2, we discussed the roles and responsibilities of reading specialists and literacy coaches. However, we believe there are unique aspects of these jobs with regard to adolescent programs that warrant additional exploration. Although reading professionals acting as literacy coaches in middle and secondary schools have many of the same responsibilities as those in elementary schools, there are some differences. In *The Literacy Coach: A Key to Improving Teaching and Learning in Secondary Schools,* a Carnegie-funded project published by the Alliance for Excellent Education, Elizabeth Sturtevant (2006) addresses some of the special challenges facing adolescent literacy professionals, such as the large numbers of struggling readers in secondary schools, the lack of resources and qualified professionals, and the difficulty enacting change in content area classrooms. This document supports the idea that highly qualified reading specialists in sufficient numbers retain their traditional role in working with struggling readers. However, Sturtevant makes a distinction with regard to the job responsibilities of those serving as coaches, those whose primary duties support teachers. She describes a coach's responsibilities as follows:

1. Collaborate with teachers to develop curriculum and effective instructional approaches in literacy and literacy in the content areas.
2. Provide professional development for teachers, particularly within the areas of literacy across the curriculum.
3. Model literacy strategies in content classrooms.
4. Help middle and high school faculty create individual and school-based professional development plans.
5. Support school administrators and teachers to develop and use a schoolwide literacy plan. (p. 12)

You can download the full report on the Alliance for Excellent Education website (http://www.all4ed.org/files/LiteracyCoach.pdf).

We are pleased to see the rapid changes in the roles of reading professionals in middle and secondary schools. All over the country, schools are hiring literacy coaches or are expanding the role of reading specialists to include coaching teachers. No longer do administrators perceive the role of the literacy professional as limited to working with readers who need additional support. Of course, helping such students and others who work with them will always remain extremely important, but there are new and exciting possibilities that come with new roles. Because the roles are changing so rapidly, many reading specialists and coaches are struggling to define all the duties and responsibilities expected of them. One of the suggestions we have is to start with two grounding items: your job description and your school's long-term goals (two-year plan). You can then create a Middle or Secondary Teacher Resource Request, such as the one in Figure 9.4, and distribute it in the first few weeks of the semester. Visit our companion website for a Sample Teacher Request Form to adapt for your professional needs.

Of course, your Teacher Request Form will be unique to your school context, but it is an effective way to inform teachers of possible services you can provide. As a reading professional, you have the opportunity to be a powerful force for change. However, our experiences with content area teachers have given us insights on how to proceed. There are a number of reasons that the enthusiastic and sincere efforts of reading professionals are often meet with so much resistance. Among the most common is the mistake made by Judy (with her bad binder) in the opening vignette. Now imagine another scenario:

*Judy, the new literacy coach, surveys the content classroom teachers in her high school about their classroom literacy practices and their needs, and discovers that their need to meet content standards has opened them to suggestions. Judy looks at the curriculum and the unit plans of the teach-* *ers. One by one, she finds an appropriate strategy. If she recognizes a small number of receptive teachers with a common interest, she might meet with them, demonstrate the technique, and offer to serve as a literacy coach. She approaches more reticent teachers one by one, saying, "I have a*

Teacher's Name _____ Grade _____ Room # _____

Planning Times: _____ Ext. #___

Dear Faculty,

I am trying to determine how I can better serve the school as your Reading Specialist/Literacy Coach. Below is a list of services that I can offer you. Please check those that interest you and place the sheet in my mailbox when complete. I can provide articles or information on any of these topics. If I know your areas of interest, whenever I read something about that topic, I will share it with you. Some of these involve *very* new concepts and techniques. *Undoubtedly some will be unfamiliar. Please circle any unfamiliar terms* and I will provide a brief overview in your mailbox or talk to you.

_____ Model specific learning strategies, such as vocabulary, test-taking, questioning techniques, etc. Specify: _____

_____ Make presentations to your class on specific strategies. Specify: _____

_____ Co-teach lessons. Specify: _____

_____ Evaluate textual materials with you/find and adapt material for a specific student.

_____ Assist in incorporating intertextuality into content instruction.

_____ Help with/demonstrate culturally responsive teaching and materials.

_____ Determine the reading ability of students.

_____ Demonstrate or help with collaborative grouping.

_____ Assist in implementing group discussion strategies.

_____ Co-teach/demonstrate integrated content/process literacy strategies.

_____ Demonstrate current Reader Response strategies.

_____ Assist with a variety of appropriate strategies for English learners.

_____ Help incorporate a wide variety of nontraditional literacies.

_____ Help with critical, effective Internet use and current technology.

_____ Help with activity-mediated teaching.

_____ Locate information/journal articles on a specific topic.
        Specify: _____

_____ Demonstrate/help implement Vocabulary Self-Collection Strategies (VSS).

_____ Provide assistance for incorporating adolescent literature in content instruction.

_____ Help locate culturally diverse literature for content areas.

_____ Facilitate critical literacy instruction.

_____ Arrange for visits from people outside the school.

_____ Read aloud to your content area class. (I love to do this.)

_____ Facilitate inquiry writing/project-based learning.

_____ Help with instructional planning for specific lessons or help locate books.

_____ Provide staff development to assist you in recertification or research.

_____ Other: _____

Thank you. I look forward to hearing from you. My extension is # 7777.

Sincerely,

Reading Specialist/Literacy Coach

**FIGURE 9.4   *Middle School/Secondary School Teacher Resource Request Form***

*strategy that I think you'd really like. I'd like to try it with your students; perhaps we could try it together or I could demonstrate it for you. It fits perfectly with your lesson on (fill-in-the-blank)."*

*Judy spends her first semester making these connections. Meanwhile, she becomes an astute observer of the beliefs, practices, and culture of the school and of the teachers. She makes sure everyone understands her role and that she is visible as she works side by side with teachers. During this semester, she works with the literacy team, surveys teachers, explores the literacy communities in and out of school, and aligns her goals with the needs assessment. Only then does she begin the process of putting together a systematic plan for gradual change that is responsive to the needs of both the school and the teachers. She is careful to begin with only one major strategy. Judy's first project is carefully chosen. Although she is interested in several large reforms, such as assisting content teachers in the use of interactive strategies and incorporating more writing into content area instruction, she thinks about which goal is the least threatening and implements that one first. She also considers who the strategies are appropriate for and tries to determine if there are teachers for whom they are not.*

*In this case, she devotes most of her energies to coaching those who are most receptive and focusing on team "leaders." Her approach pleases many of the teachers who have no idea how to help struggling students. By the end of the first semester, she has established herself as hardworking and supportive. Now she is ready to begin the kinds of changes that require teachers to "buy in." She is ready to begin working with those who are more reluctant. However, she will introduce strategies gradually, one at a time. Of course, she'd like the reform to happen more quickly, but that is not the nature of true transformation.*

This process takes a great deal of time, and it can be frustrating, but we assure you that your efforts will result in the kind of trust-building necessary for lasting and substantive change. If you establish your credibility by working alongside teachers, you will avoid the "Do as I say" reputation so often associated with the old notion of the reading specialist. In our enthusiasm to help teachers and children, it is easy to forget to ask teachers what they might want from us as reading specialists. We developed the Middle/Secondary Teacher Resource Request Form to achieve several goals for the reading specialist, but it is easily modified to meet the needs of the literacy coach. It establishes an attitude that you are responsive to teachers and willing to listen before you set an agenda. It helps teachers understand your job description, and the things you are able to do for them. It will help you understand the teachers' needs and their approaches to classroom instruction.

## Revisiting the Vignette

Now that we've investigated some possible roles of the reading specialist/literacy coach and examined a number of difficulties they encounter in secondary and middle schools, you probably have a number of ideas for Judy.

1. What advice do you have for Judy that might be more effective?
2. What was it about the binder, a wonderful resource, that produced such disappointing results for Judy and the teachers?

## *Points to Remember*

Over the past decade, the emphasis of literacy learning in the secondary schools has moved away from "reading in the content areas" and notions of "every teacher is a reading teacher" to viewing content learning through a much broader lens. Although teachers are still encouraged to use a variety of approaches and activities, and to move away from the "sage on the stage" transmission model, the focus isn't so much on the activities as it is on investigating novel ways to meet new challenges. When secondary teachers adopt new perspectives, they may focus as much on the "why" as they do on the "what." Why is this (whatever we're studying) important and relevant? Who decided this? Even if we deem it's important, why should we think it's important for all learners? Someone made the decision to include this topic in our textbook—who was it? And why did that person include it in this form? Who would disagree and why would they do so?

If today's adolescents are going to be able to participate in the society of the future, they need to be taught to ask these questions—and then seek answers to them in unconventional ways. They have already shown us they are capable of this. They are showing us the new face of literacy in the secondary school.

## *Portfolio and Self-Assessment Projects*

1. Role-play in your small group. One of you will be Judy and the others will be content area teachers. Explore the tensions from the vignette. First approach the teachers as Judy did initially. Then replay the scene incorporating a strategy you think might be more effective. Share your insights or reproduce your role-playing with the whole class. If you choose this as a portfolio item, you may videotape the session and critique the interactions.

2. Interview a secondary-level reading literacy coach. How does the person's job description address the new literacies and align with core standards? Map this information in any way that you choose.

3. Take a traditional lesson in a subject area and transform it to incorporate one of the new forms of technology used by students in their out-of-school literacies.

4. Collaborate with your group to use one of the Web 2.0 tools to enhance learning in this chapter. Perhaps you can set up a wiki or discussion site. Be sure to engage in self-assessment of your processing.

5. *Personal Goal:* Revisit the goal you set for yourself at the beginning of the chapter. Create a portfolio item that reflects what you have learned relative to your objectives.

## *Recommended Readings: Suggestions for Book Clubs, Study Groups, and Professional Development*

The following are excellent comprehensive textbooks on adolescent literacy instruction.

Hinchman, K. A., & Sheridan-Thomas, H. K. (2008). *Best practices in adolescent literacy instruction.* New York: Guilford Press.

Lewis, J. (Ed.). (2009). *Essential questions in adolescent literacy: Teachers and researchers describe what works in classrooms.* New York: Guilford Press.

Wood, K. D., & Blanton, W. E. (2009). *Literacy instruction for adolescents: Research-based practice.* New York: Guilford Press.

The following resource includes excellent ideas on incorporating new literacies in the classroom.

Leu, D. (March, 2010). *My top ten ideas on how to integrate the new literacies of online reading comprehension into your classroom.* Keynote address at the Virginia State Reading Association Conference, Virginia Beach, VA.

The following resources are excellent collections of practical, motivating, evidence-based strategies.

Buehl, D. (2009). *Classroom strategies for interactive learning* (3rd ed.). Newark, DE: International Reading Association.

Wood, K. D., & Harmon, J. M. (2001). *Strategies for integrating reading and writing in middle and high*

*school classes.* Westerfield, OH: National Middle School Association.

Zwiers, J. (2008). *Building academic language: Essential practices for content classrooms.* San Francisco: Jossey-Bass.

## Online Resources

### Essential Reports on Adolescent Literacy: Six Comprehensive Carnegie Foundation Research Reports

Carnegie Foundation on Advancing Adolescent Literacy. (2010). *Time to act: An agenda for advancing adolescent literacy for college and career success.* New York: Carnegie Corporation of New York. http://www.carnegie.org/fileadmin/Media/Publications/tta_Main.pdf

Kamil, M. L. (2010). *Adolescent literacy and textbooks: An annotated bibliography.* New York: Carnegie Corporation of New York. http://www.carnegie.org/fileadmin/Media/Publications/PDF/tta_Kamil.pdf

Lee, C. D., & Spratley, A. (2010). *Reading in the disciplines: The challenges of adolescent literacy.* New York: Carnegie Corporation of New York. http://www.carnegie.org/fileadmin/Media/Publications/PDF/tta_Lee.pdf

Levin, H. M., Catlin, D., & Elson, A. (2010). *Adolescent literacy programs: Costs of implementation.* New York: Carnegie Corporation of New York. http://www.carnegie.org/fileadmin/Media/Publications/PDF/tta_Levin.pdf

Moje, E. B., & Tysvaer, N. (2010). *Adolescent literacy development in out-of-school time: A practitioner's guide.* New York: Carnegie Corporation of New York. http://www.carnegie.org/fileadmin/Media/Publications/PDF/tta_Moje.pdf

Morsy, L., Kieffer, M., & Snow, C. E. (2010). *Measure for measure: A critical consumers' guide to reading comprehension assessments for adolescents.* New York: Carnegie Corporation of New York. http://www.carnegie.org/fileadmin/Media/Publications/PDF/tta_Morsy.pdf

## Companion Website Resources

The following resources to support and extend your learning with this chapter can be found on our companion website (waveland.com/Extra_Material/32979/): key vocabulary, concepts, and other terms; extended examples; updated resources specifically tied to information in the chapter; related websites; and other support features. The companion website also includes a template for the Teacher Request Form found in this chapter.

## Definitions of Technology Terms

*Web 2.0*   This is sometimes known as the Read/Write Web, because it enables users to create as well as consumer information. Sites such as Facebook, Wikipedia, blogs, and Twitter are examples of Web 2.0. All of the terms below are examples of Web 2.0 technologies. They do a better job of illustrating what is possible through Web 2.0 than any definition can.

*Blogs*   Short for weblogs, *blogger.com* defines a blog as follows: *A blog is a personal diary. A daily pulpit. A collaborative space. A political soapbox. A breaking-news outlet. A collection of links. Your own private thoughts. Memos to the world.* See http://www.blogger.com.

*Wikis*   Wikis are collaborative information sites on which contributors can update and alter information that others have posted. The most popular example by far is Wikipedia, a remarkably reliable site considering its open entry structure.

*RSS*    These letters stand for Really Simple Syndication, in which you can "subscribe" to specific information that is updated directly to your computer as soon as it is posted. With RSS, lecture notes can become newsfeeds, and students who have installed a newsreader application (one that checks periodically to deliver postings) no longer have to check for posts. They receive them instantly, automatically, because they are in effect subscribers. This is but one small example of RSS, an application that will revolutionize the future. Most of us use only a small percentage of the features associated with the programs installed on our computers. RSS has the potential to allow us to subscribe only to the components we need, much the way we do with phone or cable services.

*Aggregators*    These vehicles are the "postal workers" of RSS. They continually look for new postings and deliver them to the RSS subscribers (in the case above, students). Hendron (2008) likens them to the "You've Got Mail" notifications that update your email.

*Social bookmarking*    This is a way of "tagging" or bookmarking information we need by assigning keywords, much like the keywords used in library searches or journal searches. Networks of individuals can use these tags to access related sites that are often personal.

*Flickr*    This is a photo and video hosting website that allows users to post, share, and tag images, photos, and videos.

*Microblogging*    People are eager to connect with other people and microblogging makes it very simple. The best known example is Twitter. Posts are limited in length to 140 characters and can be sent via mobile texting, instant message, or the web.

# 10

# *Selecting and Evaluating Instructional Materials and Technology Resources*

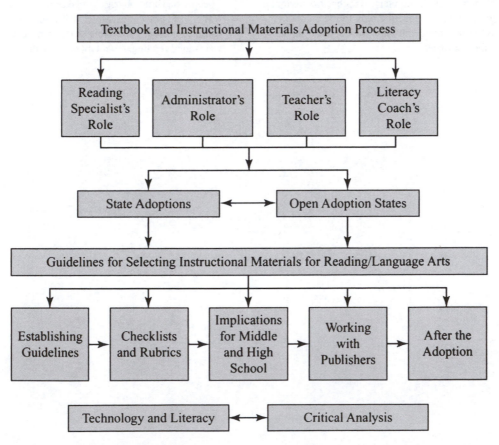

**FIGURE 10.1** *Chapter Overview*

## Learning Goals

After reading, discussing, and engaging in activities related to this chapter, you will be able to:

1. Describe the role of instructional materials in teaching reading/language arts.

2. Position trade books, literature-based series, basals, informational texts, and supplemental resources within an effective reading/language arts instructional program.

3. Prepare guidelines for the selection of instructional materials for a reading/language arts program, using research and district, state, and national reading/language arts standards.

4. Serve as a member or chair of a school's or district's reading/language arts adoption committee.

5. Work with teachers on how to use instructional materials, including technology, appropriately and effectively for teaching reading/language arts.

6. *Personal Learning Goal:* In a three-minute brainstorming session, share what you know about selecting and evaluating instructional materials. Write a goal or a question that reflects something you want to learn as we explore these topics. Share this with others in your group.

## Standards for Reading Professionals

This chapter provides focused support for current IRA Standards for Reading Professionals. See our companion website (waveland.com/Extra_Material/32979/) for a complete listing of the standards that align with this chapter.

### Vignette

*Huong Nguyen, the district reading specialist in Butterfield School District, is heading out the door of her office when the phone rings. "Hi Mrs. Nguyen. This is Sam Dowell, the sales representative for ABC Publishing Company. I'm in the area and wondered if I could drop by your office for a few minutes to show you some new reading materials." Because the ABC resources generally comply with her district's standards, Huong makes an appointment for the next day and rushes off to a meeting with a group of teachers, reading specialists, and literacy coaches from the sixteen elementary schools in the district.*

*The purpose of the meeting is to begin the process of adopting a new reading series for grades K–8. As chair of the committee, Huong realizes she's embarking on a very important activity, perhaps one of the most critical that she oversees. The current reading series that has been in place for the past six years has not been very well received by some teachers and administra-*

*tors, and reading scores have stagnated in some schools while they've dropped in others. At the time of the last adoption, however, there was great enthusiasm about the prospective new program. Teachers embraced its beautiful books, the many supplemental resources, the stories and other reading texts, and the apparent ease with which they could follow the teacher's guide. However, implementing the program was a nightmare; materials were late to arrive, incomplete orders were received, promises of professional development were ignored, the sales representative left the company soon after the adoption, and the string of replacement sales reps who had been in and out of the schools had not been helpful. To top things off, it quickly became apparent that despite spending hundreds of thousands of dollars, teachers found the many components confusing and unmanageable. As Huong contemplated the forthcoming meeting about the next adoption, her anxiety grew.*

## Thinking Points

It's important as a reading specialist or literacy coach that you know how your own school and district adopt instructional materials, and that you recognize what to value when you select instructional materials. How many of these questions can you answer?

1. What is the textbook adoption process in your school district?
2. Is your state on a cyclical adoption or do the school districts in the state have the option of adopting materials whenever they wish?
3. Does your entire district adopt one set of reading materials or can each school's staff choose any materials they like?
4. In the past, how have you made decisions about the instructional materials you have used to teach reading and language arts?

## Expanding the Vignette: Exploring the Issues

*As Huong enters the meeting room at the district office, she overhears the following comments from the teachers who are awaiting her arrival:*

> *"I don't see why we need a new series. I like the one we have now! The stories are still good and kids like them."*
>
> *"I can't wait to get the new series! I really don't like the stories in the one we have, and I'm tired of the activities in the teacher's guide."*
>
> *"Did you hear that XYZ School District got a whole bunch of free paperback books when they adopted the Reading for Life series? We need to look at it and see if we can also get those books!"*
>
> *"I don't even use a reading series, so I don't care so much about it. It's the new teachers who need a series, not experienced ones like us."*

*Huong fully realizes that the teachers, reading specialists, and literacy coaches in the room have strong feelings about the adoption of reading instruction materials. She also knows that for this to be a successful process, she's going to need to tread softly and bring the divergent views of the committee members together so that, whatever decision they make, teachers and administrators will be satisfied with it. Administrators, particularly the Superintendent, will be scrutinizing the process, as will parents and, of course, the school board. Huong distributes the agenda to the reading adoption committee and calls the meeting to order.*

## Thinking Points

1. What are some tensions that Huong is facing as she begins the textbook adoption process?
2. Why does the textbook adoption process become so emotional? If you were Huong, what might you do to diffuse the emotions and reduce the tension at the beginning of the process?
3. As a district reading specialist/supervisor, what should Huong's relationship with the various publishers' sales representatives be?

# The Textbook and Instructional Materials Adoption Process

As a reading specialist, you will (or should) have a major responsibility for assisting teachers in your school and district in selecting the best instructional materials available. As a literacy coach, you will most likely be responsible for helping teachers effectively implement the district reading program and the adopted instructional materials. At some point in your career, you might serve as your district's reading supervisor or coordinator. As such, one of your major responsibilities will be the oversight of the periodic adoption and purchase of your district's reading programs.

The level of your involvement in the adoption of instructional materials may vary greatly from school to school, from district to district, and from state to state. In some schools and districts, the reading specialist serves as the chair of the adoption committee and coordinates the entire process. In others, committees are chaired by curriculum coordinators or other administrators, such as principals. In still others, a chair may be elected from an eclectic group made up of parents, teachers, administrators, and support personnel, and the school site reading specialists share an equal role with other teachers. In a few districts, all decisions regarding instructional materials for reading are made at the district level, without any teacher input.

Whatever your situation, we believe that reading specialists *must* take a leadership role during the adoption of reading series or programs *as well as other instructional materials.* Reading specialists and literacy coaches are the ones in the school and district who have a thorough understanding of the reading process, who know the district reading/language arts standards, who should be able to sort through the "sparkle and glamour" of packaging and promotional pieces and ultimately get to the heart of what's there: the philosophy, scope and sequence, content, and instructional approach recommended for using the materials. Therefore, our purpose in writing this chapter is to assist you in this process by increasing your awareness of what to look for as you review instructional resources. Further, we discuss how to work with publishers' sales representatives, the textbook adoption committee, and the administrators who have to pay the bills and report the test scores. Because Huong is the person in charge of her district's textbook adoption, her anxiety as described in the vignette is understandable—this is one of the most difficult, emotional, and important responsibilities of reading specialists, district reading supervisors, and literacy coaches.

A note before we begin: What follows is a description of the textbook adoption process, and the reading specialists' and literacy coaches' roles in coordinating and implementing it. Some of you may be in districts where no commercial reading program is used, and/or your personal belief system is such that you do not support the use of commercial reading instructional materials. We personally endorse the use of great literature in every classroom, but we also acknowledge that commercial reading programs serve the purpose of assisting teachers with planning, offering a wealth of instructional activities and strategies, and providing consistency and support for district standards and frameworks. Also, those of you teaching in Reading First schools and districts most likely adopted a commercial program as part of your grant writing process.

Therefore, in this chapter we're not focusing on how to select award-winning literature, including trade books, for the purpose of instruction or classroom libraries. We encourage you to contact the International Reading Association for their annual Children's Choices selections of excellent literature (www.reading.org), as well as other award-winning collections such as the Newbury and Caldecott winners. At the same time, we're not suggesting that basal or literature-based reading series constitute a school's or district's instructional *program*. Rather, basal and literature-based reading series are instructional resources and, as such, reading specialists and literacy coaches must be knowledgeable about them and take leadership in their evaluation, selection, and implementation.

### State Adoptions

Sixteen states currently engage in what has come to be known as "state adoptions." These states include Alabama, Arkansas, California, Florida, Georgia, Indiana, Kentucky, Louisiana, Mississippi, New Mexico, North Carolina, Oklahoma, South Carolina, Tennessee, Texas, and West Virginia. State adoptions generally occur for a particular subject area on a regular cycle, such as every seven years. The process differs somewhat from state to state, but typically the state legislature allocates funding for instructional materials based on the adoption cycle. School district committees then review, pilot, and purchase materials for the respective subject area during the allocated period of time.

Not surprisingly, textbook purchases represent millions of dollars and most major publishers create special reading programs specifically for states according to their particular content standards. Because of the amount of money involved, states have very stringent rules and regulations that govern the adoption process. It is very important if you are the chair of an adoption process or committee, or simply a committee member, that you are fully aware of the regulations that govern your state and district adoption process.

### Open Adoption States

The other states not listed as adoption states are considered open territories. That means that individual districts within these states may adopt reading/language arts (or other subject area) materials on cycles that they determine, based on state funding allocations. Most school districts and states still have some sort of adoption cycle (generally six to ten years) for subject areas, but there is little uniformity in the process across each state and from district to district. When instructional funds are released, districts and schools make decisions about purchases. Typically, there are committees that make these decisions, and piloting of the materials occurs widely. In some districts, instead of a committee decision, materials are selected through an all-teacher vote. As with state adoptions, there are differences in how much access to teachers and reading committees the publishers have—this again is in reaction to past practices that many deemed unethical or inappropriate.

In the next section, Dr. Deb Carr, a reading supervisor and curriculum coordinator from Pennsylvania, an open territory, shares her thoughts on the adoption process and budgeting for instructional materials.

### OTHER VOICES: Dr. Deb Carr

*Dr. Deb Carr is the Reading Supervisor and Curriculum Coordinator for the Hazleton Area School District, Hazleton, Pennsylvania. She is a former secondary reading teacher and reading specialist. In addition to her full-time position in the school district, she also teaches part time in the reading specialist/MA program at King's College, Wilkes-Barre, Pennsylvania. She is a district-level educator who advocates for literacy in everything she does.*

In our district, a reading adoption is serious business. This is a decision that is at the heart of the elementary education program. It is a decision our district lives with for at least eight years. Everyone wants to be on the adoption committee. The volunteer committee reviews all of the existing programs and then decides which will be piloted. That decision becomes increasingly difficult, with every program claiming to be "research-based" and every program "aligned to the state standards." Sorting it all out is a challenge. The discussions about which books to pilot must be based on the needs of the students and the teachers, and the piloting can take from three to six months.

In the past, all pilot materials were provided to the district at no cost; today, that varies from publisher to publisher. It is best to focus on only two pilots with a pilot for each grade level and each school building. Of course, during the piloting period, the teachers divide themselves between the two pilots and settle into their own camps. I believe it is the supervisor's responsibility to focus the analysis of each program through pointed questioning. Developing Venn diagrams for comparing and contrasting program components provides a powerful visual. Discussions about the different reading programs happen throughout the adoption process. In actuality, these are ongoing in the sense that I am facilitating information so that the people on the adoption committee and in the classrooms have the background knowledge to make the decision—a decision based on sound research practices rather than the color of the pages in the Teacher's Edition. I see too many supervisors trying to step back from that process, but I think you must coach the adoption committee through the process.

As school districts scramble to do more with less, this process of selecting reading materials becomes even more critical. Each new government report or research review reveals the need for new (or even old) materials to meet students' needs. The adopted program must stand the test of time with enough flexibility that all learners are addressed with a variety of activities and materials. Too many new programs are written to standards that can and will change. Is the program's standards' crosswalk written on each page in the teacher's edition or is it an insert that can easily be adjusted when the standards change?

Regardless of the currently embraced reading philosophy, there are realistic costs involved in providing reading teachers with what they need. Understanding the budget process is integral to planning the implementation of these new initiatives. This planning needs to take place anywhere from two to six years ahead of the purchase of new reading materials. In an adoption year—the year the business office sets aside immediate and residual funds for a program—it is important to identify materials for the immediate adoption year, but also materials that students and staff will need in the future, in perhaps six years. For example, a basic core anthology purchase with a few theme books may not lend itself easily to today's focus on intervention. What about guided reading instruction? Are leveled texts built into the program? What other supplemental materials, including assessments, are warranted? Which materials are essential? How can you seek additional funding through grant or community donations? Just deciding on the program components requires planning for securing funds in appropriate budget categories (supplemental texts, workbooks, and professional resources). If funds are not placed in appropriate categories at the initial preparation stage of a district budget, that step can take weeks to adjust, depending on your business office's procedures. Securing grant funds to cover interventions or other materials can take months. Even these funds must be placed in appropriate budget categories. Saving book club bonus points to purchase leveled reading collections could take years. So, you can see that coordinating the purchase of materials can be a complicated, multifaceted, and ongoing process.

The results of the adoption process really represent what your district believes about reading instruction. I don't mean that you have to select a camp, but you ought to be reviewing the available programs as much as the teachers and asking the direct questions to get them to look beyond the glitz. Your questions should lead teachers to what they should be looking for. I find that walking through an entire lesson in the program—start to finish—gives me a flavor. Does it take fourteen worksheet pages before you get to the meat of the lesson? Is writing instruction an "add-on" or an integral part of a lesson? Is comprehension really developed or are strategy tags just listed on the teacher pages? Are students reading the same theme books written at different levels or different theme books on related topics?

I find it ridiculous when I hear some supervisors say they have had a "blind adoption." This means that the teachers don't know what publishing company they are reviewing. These days, you are adopting a publishing house as well as a text. The staff development they provide and the reputation of that firm is now associated with your district. Does the publisher stand behind its work and its authors, or is it just trying to kick out an old program for another state adoption? Is this a publisher that sets the pace in the field or does it play catch up?

Too often, teachers spend their own money for materials for their classrooms. This happens when funds are not available, when teachers are looking for creative extensions to themes or test preparation activities, or even when the teachers have not embraced the district's philosophy, so they purchase materials to match their own beliefs or biases. It also happens when teachers do not realize the wealth of materials within the adopted core programs. There are serious instructional issues when the adopted core materials are ignored, and when teachers plan theme extension projects that last for months. On the other hand, the race for demonstration of "Annual Yearly Progress" has put teachers on the verge of worksheet-and-computer-program mania in search of the quick fix to demonstrate the mastering of standards. There are worksheets and computer programs to track every skill and strategy under the sun. Regardless of the promise of tracking standards' benchmarks, the quality of materials needs to be maintained. District leadership needs to establish a balance and to develop guidelines for the implementation of materials with a keen sense of where our students need to be and what they need in order to get there.

## Revisiting the Vignette

■ *Group Inquiry Activity*  Now that you've read the discussion about textbook use and adoption processes, do a Think-Pair-Share (think alone, share with a partner, and then the class) with the following questions:

1. What are the issues in adopting instructional materials that Huong will need to address?
2. What do you see as the primary responsibilities of the school site reading specialist during a reading series adoption?

3. Why is it important that school and district literacy teams work collaboratively during a reading series adoption?

## Guidelines for Selecting Instructional Materials for Reading and Language Arts

### The Adoption Process: Step by Step

The selection process starts about two years before the adoption, especially if you plan to set up pilot classrooms. Recall that Huong Nguyen has created an adoption committee, being careful to include reading professionals, teachers, media specialists, technology coordinators, resource teachers, university professors, students, parents, and principals. Not all members have to be at all meetings. Decide which tasks can be accomplished by subgroups and presented to the committee.

Here are possible steps in the process:

*Step 1:* Provide background research on best practice.

*Step 2:* Examine district standards and the school's philosophy.

*Step 3:* If your district is under a state adoption system, examine the policies and secure a list of approved series or content area texts. If you are in an open adoption state, obtain a copy of the state guidelines. States often have specific criteria that a series must include. Some of these will surprise you (and teachers), so it is important to inform yourself and others. Also check to see if your district has its own set of guidelines. People tend to forget these things exist as time passes and administrators and educators come and go.

*Step 4:* Develop a list of tasks and dates for completion. Also create a timeline and distribute it widely.

*Step 5:* Arrange for delivery of materials to be displayed in a designated area for thoughtful examination and comparison. Schedule committee meetings with the publishers and keep a calendar indicating dates for their presentations. It is important to give each of them equal time and opportunity.

*Step 6:* Now you are ready to engage in comparison and evaluation of the materials.

Our companion website includes *Establishing Guidelines: Twenty Questions for Examining Textbook Reading Series Materials.* These questions will help your committee in the early stages of establishing guidelines and making the initial screening of materials. Some teams skip this and proceed directly to creating the Textbook Adoption Survey included later in this chapter, but we find it helpful to spend at least some time reflecting on the Twenty Questions.

## BEYOND THE BOOK _____

### Chapter 10 Focus Issue: Examining Instructional Materials
The following excerpt is the eighth question in the guide referred to above.

After you read the questions, follow the steps in the Group Inquiry Activity as part of this Beyond the Book exercise.

What are the expectations of the materials regarding what children and adolescents know and can do?

- Are these appropriate to your school community?
- What are the social skills (e.g., discussion, cooperative learning) and values being taught, modeled, and reinforced through the instructional plan and the literature?
- Are they appropriate for your school, district, and community contexts?
- Are the stories and other literature pieces representative of the students who will be reading them? That is, will the students "see themselves" in the various texts they're reading and can they identify with the contexts?
- Does the literature represent a variety of perspectives and views so that children/adolescents will have the opportunity to expand their own thinking? Keep in mind that in some conservative communities, there are those who believe that schools should not be involved in discussions about values, ethics, and social contexts—they believe these discussions should be left to the family. What we're advocating here is that during your review and evaluation of reading resources and programs, you pay careful attention to the literature selections and instructional recommendations in terms of the values, perspectives, biases, and contexts that are included. Then you'll be ready when the questions about them come your way.

Follow these steps in the Group Inquiry Activity.

■ *Group Inquiry Activity* Bring to class a student anthology and a teacher's guide from the series or program you are currently using in your school. If you teach in a middle or high school, bring the current literature textbook that is being used. If you don't have access to a reading series or literature textbook, select a content area textbook appropriate for a particular grade level. In other words, bring something students are expected to read!

1. Divide into groups with like materials and focus on the questions above.
2. Take a critical literacy stance as you carefully examine the various texts. Begin by selecting an informational or expository text. From what and perhaps whose perspective is the text written? Does the author appear to have an "agenda"? If so, what is it?
3. What words does the author use to persuade or cajole readers to buy into a perspective or agenda? Look carefully at particular words and phrases, such as *we* (who is the "we"?); *you* (who is the collective or individual "you"?); *our* (whose "our"?); "It will be beneficial . . ." (for whom? according to whom?).
4. Divide a piece of paper into three columns and enter your analyses:
   - Perspective (whose?)
   - Agenda (what?)
   - Proof (words or phrases that the author uses)
5. Discuss how these elements align with your program goals.

As an example, critical literacy theorist Alan Luke once demonstrated this point at an IRA conference with an Australian social science textbook. The selection Luke chose was a discussion about land in Australia that some people wanted to keep undeveloped, whereas others (the developers) wanted it to be used for commercial purposes. Even though the chapter was supposed to be an objective account, on careful examination it was clear that the author shared the developer's perspective. For example, an author could use phrases such as "a left-wing group," "environmentalists," "radical," or "anti-development" to describe those opposing development. Those promoting development could be described as "pro-community," "pro-family," or "community-oriented." While these examples may seem obvious, others may be much more subtle. Look through your materials and see what you can discover! Share your findings with others in the class.

### Creating a Textbook Adoption Survey

After you have completed the six-step process above and addressed some of the questions on our companion website, you are ready to synthesize all the elements that are important to your selection process. The sample shown in Figure 10.2 on pages 200–202 moves through a series of elements for ranking and weighting and culminates in a recommendation from each participant.

### Implications of Adoptions for Middle and High School Literacy Programs

Basically, all of our previous suggestions regarding the evaluation and selection of reading materials apply equally to elementary and secondary schools. The twenty guidelines (see the companion website) and their questions should also be asked when reviewing literature anthologies, intervention materials, and books for independent reading in grades 6 to 12.

However, there are some additional guidelines that need to be considered when selecting reading instructional materials for adolescents. The central issue concerns readability—the ease or difficulty of the texts that are selected. As students get older and gain in reading ability, the span in their reading levels also increases. In 2000, Laura Robb called for the use of a variety of books at students' instructional levels. She stated that, for adolescents, "friendly, readable texts can lead to a pleasurable reading experience because the learner comprehends and becomes involved . . . involvement in and comprehension of nonfiction texts increase when these books contain many stories and vignettes" (Robb, 2000b). Since then, a great deal of research has demonstrated the benefits of matching students to the right books at the right time (Wilburn, 2009).

Chris Tovani (2000) adds that older secondary students need to be exposed to and have access to books that are "important" to them, books that have personal meaning and value. She describes what she calls "fake reading," so commonly seen in secondary classrooms. This phenomenon manifests itself in book reports given on books never read, use of *Sparks Notes* from the Internet, and a general avoidance of all or nearly all reading. What's most troubling about "fake reading" is that many students successfully engage in this practice throughout high school. Once at the university, however, they usually discover that "fake reading" no longer works for them.

*Textbook Adoption Survey*

For: Subject Area _____      Grade Level/Course _____

Publisher Rep.: _____  ph/email _____  Literacy Specialist/Chair _____

### Baseline Textbook Information

Title: _____      Author: _____

Publisher: _____      Copyright: _____

Lexile Level #: _____

Go to: www.lexile.com → Educators → Lexile → Book Database: Insert <u>Title</u> or <u>Author</u>

I rank this text: 1  2  3  4      My recommendation: Adopt this text?  Yes  No  Maybe

### Cost Projection

**# of Units (Books)** _____ **X  Cost per Unit** _____   =   **Baseline Expense** _____

**Supplemental Materials** _____ **+ Misc. Expenses** _____ = **Additional Expenses** _____

**Shipping Charges** _____

**Total Adoption Expenses** _____

**Are free materials promised?** _____   **Support for implementation?** _____

**Directions:** Please rank the following text attributes. *Note:* The last column (marked IMP) includes an X on items the committee believes should be given more weight. You may also put an X after any additional ones you think deserve greater weight or cross off any we indicated.

3 = Excellent   2 = Acceptable   1 = Poor   0 = Not Acceptable   N/A = Not Applicable
NF = Not Found   IMP = Important

| I. Structural Features of the Text | 3 | 2 | 1 | 0 | N/A | NF | IMP |
|---|---|---|---|---|---|---|---|
| 1. Text includes table of contents, glossary, index, appendix, and other appropriate structural aids. | | | | | | | |
| 2. Text format is appealing, print size is appropriate. Text/material is durable, size is appropriate (# of pages). | | | | | | | |
| 3. Organization emphasizes core concepts of the course and reflects unified core standards and state curriculum. | | | | | | | X |
| 4. Text reflects sheltered instruction for ELs. | | | | | | | |
| 5. Sequence follows a logical pattern. | | | | | | | |
| 6. Text sequence is appropriate in scope (# of concepts) and concept progression. | | | | | | | |
| 7. Teacher editions are clear, usable, and provide instructional activities and *suggestions for differentiation*. | | | | | | | X |
| 8. Supplemental materials are available and stress the concepts presented in the text. | | | | | | | |
| 9. Arrangement of text boxes, charts, side matter, and visuals are appropriate: closely linked to text, not too numerous; do not detract from the flow of main ideas. | | | | | | | |
| 10. Authors use format devices to signal the introduction of new concepts/key terms (bold, italics). | | | | | | | |

**FIGURE 10.2  *Textbook Adoption Survey***

| II. Content and Instructional Features | 3 | 2 | 1 | 0 | N/A | NF | IMP |
|---|---|---|---|---|---|---|---|
| 1. Objectives are *clearly stated* and in line with our goals for our students in the subject area and our two-year plan. | | | | | | | X |
| 2. Text explicitly reflects domain-specific reasoning and problem-solving strategies. | | | | | | | X |
| 3. Instructions are clear and explicit. | | | | | | | |
| 4. Text and materials contain the right amount of scaffolding *for the particular group* of students. | | | | | | | |
| 5. Materials are sensitive to sociocultural issues and stereotypes. | | | | | | | |
| 6. Format accommodates different styles of learners; presents information in a variety of ways (not just one way). | | | | | | | |
| 7. Instruction and activities help students use their prior knowledge to make text-to-text, text-to-world, and text-to-self connections. | | | | | | | X |
| 8. Instruction and activities show students clear connections between information, application, and real life. | | | | | | | |
| 9. Text balances information and critical thinking. | | | | | | | |
| 10. Instruction guides students from concrete to representational to abstract OR from abstract/general to specific. | | | | | | | |
| 11. Students have opportunities for independent practice. | | | | | | | |
| 12. The text indicates key words and phrases. | | | | | | | |
| 13. The main ideas, concepts, and important information are clearly stated and explained. | | | | | | | |
| 14. The book identifies and reinforces the most important vocabulary words and concepts through *repetition, integration, and meaningful use.* | | | | | | | X |
| 15. New concepts are explicitly linked to students' prior knowledge and experience—linked to real-world examples. | | | | | | | |
| 16. Vocabulary pacing (concept density) is within the ability of the students to gain meaning from the text. | | | | | | | |
| 17. Some links, references, and activities involve seeking information outside of the text (encourage bringing in real-world information, web searches to encourage inquiry). | | | | | | | |
| 18. The lesson progression guides students through the learning with aids that support them through the text. Some of these include prereading supports (objectives, key word lists, chapter overviews, margin notes, glossing, guided reading, questions before, during and after summaries, extension activities). | | | | | | | X |
| 19. Education for employment skills are represented. | | | | | | | |
| 20. Illustrations, graphs, maps, charts, and so on make key concepts concrete, add clarity, and feature the most important concepts. | | | | | | | |

| III. Assessment Features | 3 | 2 | 1 | 0 | N/A | NF | IMP |
|---|---|---|---|---|---|---|---|
| 1. Assessment focuses on main ideas, concepts, and skills. | | | | | | | X |
| 2. Text employs a number of ways to assess learning and understanding, including knowledge of information, application, and production. | | | | | | | X |
| 3. Assessments are aligned with the core concepts and are appropriate in amounts of attention given to more important and less important content. | | | | | | | |
| 4. Questions and activities draw attention to the organizational patterns of the text and other learning strategies. | | | | | | | |

(*continued*)

| | 3 | 2 | 1 | 0 | N/A | NF | IMP |
|---|---|---|---|---|---|---|---|
| 5. Assessment centers on the students' understanding of the process as well as the product. | | | | | | | X |

| *IV. Relevance and Motivation* | *3* | *2* | *1* | *0* | *N/A* | *NF* | *IMP* |
|---|---|---|---|---|---|---|---|
| 1. Content, format, and presentation of information are interesting, engaging, and relevant. | | | | | | | X |
| 2. Activities are meaningful, motivating, and challenging to students at varying levels of learning and ability. | | | | | | | X |
| 3. Materials allow students to think critically and creatively. | | | | | | | X |
| 4. Materials engage students in socially appropriate group learning and collaborative problem-solving. | | | | | | | |
| 5. Text includes response modes and choices that honor students' out-of-school literacies and/or provide vehicles for connecting home literacies with those in school. | | | | | | | |

**COMMENTS:** For each category, please list (a) the features that appealed to you most; (b) those that appealed to you least; (c) anything not included in the survey that you noticed; and (d) any other comments you wish to share. You may continue your comments on the back of this form if more space is needed.

### Section I: Structural Features

a) Most helpful features

b) Least helpful features

c) Other elements

d) Additional comments

### Section II: Content and Instructional Features

a) Most helpful features

b) Least helpful features

c) Other elements

d) Additional comments

### Section III: Assessment Features

a) Most helpful features

b) Least helpful features

c) Other elements

d) Additional comments

### Section IV: Relevance and Motivation

a) Most helpful features

b) Least helpful features

c) Other elements

d) Additional comments

**On a 1–10 scale (1 = unacceptable and 10 = highly recommend), I would rate this text: _____**

We strongly recommend that students be involved in the selection of the materials they'll be reading. Invite one or two middle and secondary students to serve on the reading committee that will be reviewing the instructional materials. Give them a voice in the process.

## Working with Publishers and Sales Representatives

### During the Selection and Adoption Process

1. Maintain a strictly professional relationship with publishers' representatives (who, by the way, do not like to be called vendors). Many of them were teachers and administrators with master's degrees in education before they assumed their current positions.

2. Be cautious about accepting gifts or dinners. Many districts have policies about this. If you are given anything or taken to lunch, keep a list, and be sure to write a thank you note.

3. Provide publishers' representatives with the contact information (email and/or phone) of the committee chair and any other appropriate individuals. Indicate the best times to call or contact.

4. Beware of promises for "freebies." *Nothing* is free. Most costs are absorbed into the basic components. Remember, textbook publishing is big business and many representatives have sales quotas.

5. Keep notes and records of all phone calls, meetings, presentations, and other correspondence. Write down dates materials were ordered, delivery dates promised, free materials, actual delivery dates, and anything else promised, such as professional development. Get all promises in writing. This goes for supplementary materials and *especially for follow-up professional development* during implementation. Ask for a written professional development proposal.

6. Remember that conferences, especially those of your state association and IRA, are excellent places to preview reading series and other materials from a variety of publishers.

7. Pay close attention to the level of support you are given during the adoption process. If a representative is slow to return calls or to support teachers during the decision-making period, you can be fairly certain you will see even less of that person after the sale is made!

### After the Adoption: Implementation

All too often, we hear stories about districts that spend tens of thousands of dollars on new series, only to have them delivered to the school's doorstep without any follow-up support to help teachers in their transition to using the new materials. In the first year or semester after the adoption, publishers are the ones who should provide professional development. Of course, you will already have gotten this commitment in writing. During that first year, the reading specialist's or literacy coach's primary role is to support teachers in their classrooms. Later, the reading specialist or coach provides group workshops focused on common issues or helps address individual concerns. That is why it is essential to your credibility that you get to know the program thoroughly.

You may be asked to monitor teachers to make sure everybody is implementing the new program. Your job is to support, not to coerce, so be certain everyone (administrators) understands this. If you are to have duties with regard to implementing the series, be sure to get these expectations in writing from your administrators. If you encounter teachers who resist changing to the new program, approach them individually, offer support, demonstrate lessons, and encourage them until they reach a higher level of comfort. Resisters are the folks with whom you most need to develop trust, so try not to involve administrators until it is absolutely necessary. Remember, we don't all change or learn at the same rate.

## Leveled Reading Materials: Matching Them to Students

One of the ways assessment and instruction intersect is matching readers to books at the "just right" level of difficulty, known as the *instructional level*. This is commonly considered the level at which the student misses no more than one word in twenty, or can answer at least seven out of ten comprehension questions. There are three common systems of leveling books. Guided Reading Level (GRL) rates books in difficulty from A to Z for grades 1–6, with the student's level determined by the teacher administering a reading record and the student retelling or answering questions. Another system is Scholastic's Lexile System, in which books are leveled from 200 to 1700+ and a student's reading level is determined through either a standardized test, at least once a year, or a one-to-one reading inventory, which can be administered more often. It is geared toward comprehension. The third system is the Developmental Reading Assessment (DRA). It begins with level A, but switches to a 1–44 rating system. It is typically administered three times a year and rates comprehension, accuracy, and fluency. An excellent explanation of leveled reading can be found in Deborah Wilburn's (2009) article "What Is Leveled Reading?: Helping Kids Become Better Readers by Matching Them to the Right Books at the Right Time," on the Scholastic website at http://www2.scholastic.com/browse/article.jsp?id=10216. This site includes an excellent chart comparing the three systems, which can be downloaded by teachers.

RtI, implementation of guided reading, and other initiatives have rekindled attempts to develop weighted mathematical formulas that gauge the readability levels of texts. Although today's formulas incorporate numerous factors, after more than fifty years of tinkering, they still rely heavily on the same two factors they always did: sentence length and word difficulty (often measured by the length of the word or its number of syllables). We share the concerns of David O'Brien, Roger Stewart, and Richard Beach (2009) that teachers routinely assign numerical indicators to texts and administer Degrees of Reading Power (DRP) or Lexile tests to match students to "level-appropriate" materials without considering the positive and negative consequences of doing so. The same shortcoming of previous formulas persist. They can only measure factors outside of the reader. Surely, any of us would agree that a reader's interest (or lack of interest) in a topic, motivation, maturity level, ability to connect to the piece, and other factors have a considerable effect on its readability for any particular student. Also, we have to remember that Shakespeare's line, "To be or not to be; that is the question," would probably place it at about a first-grade level of difficulty, in spite of the fact that understanding what the author means reflects a considerable concept load. O'Brien and colleagues also remind us of all the highly motivated Harry Potter devotees who devour J. K. Rawlings books in spite of the fact that their Lexile measures would preclude them from being matched with these books. We are not suggesting that you abandon all attempts to match students with appropriately difficult materials. Rather, we advocate that you do so thoughtfully, book by book and student by student, employing the same forethought reserved for all of your other instructional decisions. It is probably wise to consider the measured difficulty level of a book as only one factor.

## Technology: In- and Out-of-School Literacies

The first point we need to make about technology and its uses by students and teachers is that these tools are to be used *in conjunction with* the traditional sound practices we use with print text. Our students will most likely still spend the majority of their time navigating through traditional print sources of information. Both of us remember discussions we had in the early 1990s with other professors who predicted we would soon have a paperless society. Here we are over a couple decades later and although our email inboxes are constantly full, so are our regular mailboxes (alas, mostly with junk mail).

Yes, yes, we all know our students are tech savvy. We get that. We have all seen the TV shows warning us about predators, cyberbullying, and sexting. Many schools have installed multiple filters and policies that prevent students from engaging in any literacy activities that are not prescribed and protected (Olsen, 2006). Of course, as fast as these measures are put in place, students are even faster at finding ways around them. Olsen described how a student set up what is called a web proxy from his home computer, so when he was at school, he could direct requests for banned sites like *MySpace* through a web address at home, thereby tricking the school's filter. Some of us are challenged to keep up, but remember, we don't have to be at the forefront. Our younger colleagues and our students will probably be the ones to help forge the way for us in knowledge related to technology.

Our focus in this section will be devoted to addressing the ways teachers and students use technology. A number of ideas for using technology in elementary and secondary school classes were suggested in the two previous chapters. How did you do on the technology quiz in Chapter 9? If you did not take it, you might want to do so before you proceed to the discussion that follows here.

### In- and Out-of-School Uses of Technology

Bill Kist and Jim Ryan (2009) describe the contradictory aims that influence the use of technology in today's schools. On one hand, we want to make school relevant to the lives of our students and bring the outside world into our classrooms. On the other hand, to our students, the outside world *is* constant social networking, texting, tweeting, blogging, RSS, and sharing digital images—the very things we block from the literacy repertoire of school. Stand at any school door in the morning and you will see students clicking off their handheld devices at the very last moment when they enter the school. At the day's end, as they stream out the door, you'll find them reaching into their pockets to retrieve their lifelines to the world and with a click, they are once again linked to social networks.

Our goal is not to teach you all the new forms of technology in use today, partly because technology is always changing and our information will be old before the ink is dry on these pages. Another reason is that you need to experience these forms of communication to understand them—the printed page falls short. The third reason is that, although we consider ourselves relatively facile in the new technologies, we do not have the expertise that those on the cusp of emerging forms possess. Our purpose here is to address the issues and raise the questions that confront schools seeking to situate new literacies within traditional ones.

## *Uses of Educational Technology: Past and Present*

One of the most important breakthroughs in technology has been called Web 2.0, sometimes called the Read/Write Web. It is important that you understand what it is. Since 2004, we have been able to co-create information as authors and consumers, subscribe to sites that update information automatically as soon as it is posted, and manipulate content easily without having to know HTML or any other programming. Although new technologies will foster new classifications, three categories are typical of the ways educators use technology. For example, not long ago, businesses and individuals paid large amounts of money to web page designers who knew how to work with complex programs and specialized computer languages. The new generation of programs enable anyone with basic computer skills to set up an interactive Facebook page with wonderful images, instant updates, a high degree of interaction, and vehicles for others to post and, in effect, alter the site. Web 2.0 computing is highly malleable.

1. *One of the oldest uses of technology involves computer-based learning or tutorials.* These are learning packages, applications that are basically self-contained. You might hear them described as discrete educational software, or integrated learning systems. This category includes software applications such as PowerPoint, Microsoft Word, Read 180 or other stand-alone applications we use as vehicles to deliver content (Murphy, Penuel, Means, Korbak, & Whaley, 2001). Some of these claim to be "interactive" because they include leveled stories, allow readers to move at their own pace, and ask comprehension questions to which the student responds. However engaging they might be, students read the stories alone, answer questions alone, and earn points alone. This may be fine on an occasional basis, but it is important to understand that these programs are not a substitute for literacy instruction (Lefever-Davis & Pearman, 2005).

2. *Web-based inquiry systems, such as Webquests, are inquiry-oriented activities that link to outside resources, but within controlled parameters.* Teachers can structure their use of technology to engage students in substantive projects requiring collaboration, synthesis, inquiry, and problem-solving related to content area learning.

Webquests usually consist of a set of tasks or questions, then provide students with the links they need to complete the inquiry. Therefore, they limit the search to relevant sites. Traditional searches on *Ask.com*, *Bing.com*, or *Google* fall into this category.

3. *The third use of technology involves high levels of creativity. In this kind of learning, students use nontraditional vehicles (such as blogs, podcasts, electronic posters, or original websites) to explore and demonstrate their knowledge of traditional content.* Students can be authors and consumers at the same time. These are the Web 2.0 uses of technology that hold promise (and challenge) for bringing out-of-school literacies into the classroom. See Chapters 8 and 9 for more information and references to resources for using new technology with elementary and secondary students.

## The Literacy Teacher and Effective Technology Use

If we believe that the quality of the teacher is the most important factor in student learning (Darling-Hammond & Berry, 1998), it follows logically that teachers need to be capable and knowledgeable about technology if they are to help their students. That is why *a strong, well-conceived, systematic, sustained Technology Plan, supported by professional development, should be an integral part of the School Improvement Plan.* It should be backed by sufficient funds and the allocation of the requisite time and support. One of the first steps is determining where your school stands in its use of technology. The NCREL website (www.ncrel.org/sdrs/areas/issues/methods/technlgy/te1000.htm) includes a variety of resources and links to assessment tools. Remember, the goal in learning about technology is not just to learn about technology. It is to enhance your personal and professional life. Teachers always strive to enhance student learning, facilitate access to information, and foster higher-level thinking. There are ways to use technology to accomplish these ends (Hendron, 2008; Richardson, 2009), and the teacher's goal is to find out what they are. Literacy professionals can help.

The New Literacies Research Lab at the University of Connecticut (www.newliteracies.uconn.edu) is at the forefront of research related to understanding comprehension processes associated with emerging technologies and the most effective ways to teach students to use information technology. The New Literacies Research Team is focused on identifying the new skills, strategies, and dispositions required for learning on the Internet.

### What Do Teachers Need to Know to Remain Current?

In order to be fully literate, there are things teachers need to know and be able to do with regard to technology. If you skipped the last chapter on adolescent literacy, we included a technology section and a self-test covering a number of key terms related to current technology. That section builds the background knowledge necessary for getting the most out of this chapter, so again, we recommend you refer back to it.

1. *Teachers need to be able to incorporate the most commonly used basic methods of technology to enhance teaching, such as PowerPoint, whiteboard, and Web 2.0.* They should also know basic ways to incorporate the use of active websites as they teach, modeling their own critical thinking and their steps in searching for information and choosing which links to open. Just as we model our cognitive processes with regard to comprehension of traditional print media, we should also model our comprehension processes with regard to other media. This includes critical questioning of the motives, information, bias, content selection, presentation methods, and qualifications of the producer (Harrison, 2007; Pailliotet, 1998). For example, we should know who is behind the materials; who produced the site, why they chose the images, devices, colors, music, or media combinations they did. We also need to think about what is missing—in other words, whose voice, perspective, or information did the author omit.

    Some of the processes we use to gather or create information are domain-specific, meaning they require different kinds of thinking in different *domains* (content areas). No longer must a student sit in his or her bedroom doing traditional homework assignments in isolation. Electronic notebooks, emailing, instant messaging, and other social uses of the Internet allow for collaboration among teachers and students. Today, these are considered low levels of technology use. It is helpful for teachers to know how other educators are using educational technology, particularly within their content areas. For example, in the past, WebQuests were particularly popular in science and social science. However, new techniques for collaborative production of online projects by students have become extremely popular. Although high-quality WebQuests are still *extremely* useful, they are no longer novelties. New applications (apps) for handheld devices make phones into research and production tools.

2. *Teachers need to know how to adapt evidence-based strategies used with print text and enact them in an electronic world.* Jim McGlinn (2009b) demonstrated how to adapt a comprehension strategy first developed in 1946 and use it to enhance Internet literacy. In other words, we can use many of the same research-based comprehension strategies, but enact them in an electronic world. We believe this will be a growing area of interest and we will continue to inform you of new information about such instructional innovations on our companion website.

3. *Teachers need support to select quality technology materials that are consistent with their beliefs about principled instruction.* We all know how difficult it is to select the best materials and programs when it comes to traditional *print* material. It is even more difficult for most teachers to recognize quality materials that employ technology. Unfortunately, many uses of technology warrant caution. Particularly with NCLB/ESEA and RtI, we are seeing software programs that "diagnose," create lesson plans, organize assessment data, and "teach" phonics. We find it particularly disturbing that so many of these programs are developed for special education students, those with the greatest need for support from highly skilled teachers. There are, however, some wonderful commercial as well as free products that contain frameworks for strategies, systems for recording student observations and managing records, and checklists for various decision-making processes. Many of them are practical, efficient,

and highly useful, particularly the ones found on federal and state government websites and those of professional organizations. Throughout this book, we direct you to a number of them. The literacy professional can help teachers sort all of this out. In addition, reading professionals, those who know evidence-based literacy practice, must collaborate with technology specialists to review available software and establish quality and usefulness.

4. *Teachers should be familiar with the International Society for Technology in Education (ISTE) Standards and how they affect classroom teachers.* The literacy specialist can meet periodically with those responsible for supporting technology use (usually the technology coordinator and media specialist) to keep current with new information and to understand how these professionals will be working with teachers in the next quarter of the school year.

5. *Teachers need to understand the ways their students are using technology outside of school and the purposes that drive such use.* Teachers need to attempt to stay current with some of the things not often associated with school activities and not often taught to them by technology coordinators. For example, we believe teachers should push themselves to do things that technologically facile adults do. By 2010, technologically capable adults knew how to set up a Facebook page, engage in social interaction, use programs such as Skype to interact in sound and picture across distances, download and share music and artwork with computers and handheld devices, and use wireless means to communicate and send images from anywhere, contribute to wikis, set up blogs, or tweet their responses to news items.

We have questions about students' literacy development in and out of school that research will need to address. Are students' proficient (and rapid) writing skills *demonstrated* as they use their phones, computers, and other handheld devices? Do these transfer to the kinds of *school writing* required by high schools and universities, and do schools recognize them as *literate behaviors*? Is there a difference between students' comprehension, skill, and strategy use with print and electronic materials (such as textbooks and Internet searches)? Don Leu and colleagues at the University of Connecticut New Literacies Research Team have found that some students with serious reading deficiencies with print materials are capable (albeit slow) readers of online text (Leu, 2010). What are the implications for assessing these youngsters?

## Integrating Literacy and Technology into the Curriculum

To become fully literate in today's world, students must become proficient in the new literacies of *information and communication technology* (ICT). Therefore, literacy educators have a responsibility to integrate these technologies into the literacy curriculum in order to prepare students for the literacy future they deserve.

The International Reading Association (2001) believes that much can be done to support students in developing the new literacies that will be required in the future. We believe that students have the right to:

- Teachers who are skilled in the effective use of ICT for teaching and learning.
- A literacy curriculum that integrates the new literacies of ICT into instructional programs.
- Instruction that develops the critical literacies essential to effective information use.
- Assessment practices in literacy that include reading on the Internet and writing using word-processing software.
- Opportunities to learn safe and responsible use of information and communication technologies.
- Equal access to ICT.

### *Ethics, Authorship, and Attribution*

New difficulties arise when we use sophisticated tools. They are worth discussing with teachers and students. For example, if a student downloads a number of images from different websites and puts them together in novel ways, but does not actually create any of the images, is the student plagiarizing? Is he an author or just a user? What about using downloaded music or DVD clips in a student project, or incorporating a newspaper or magazine photo? What about a report in which a student uses many cut-and-paste excerpts?

Fair Use Laws are ambiguous, but generally consider four factors that determine whether or not something constitutes fair use:

1. The nature of the copyrighted piece.
2. The purpose of the user, especially whether he or she plans to use it in commercial ways.
3. The amount of the piece used in relationship to its size as a whole.
4. The effect it will have on the market value of something that is for sale, such as commercial DVDs, music CDs, or books.

Of course, this is a gross oversimplification of the issue. It is helpful to visit the U.S. Copyright Office Fair Use website at http://www.copyright.gov/fls/fl102.html.

We believe most teachers and students do not intentionally violate Fair Use Laws. Rather, in their day-to-day work, they sometimes forget to consider this issue. In our graduate classes, we have often seen well-meaning students who bring materials for the class or turn in projects that include copyrighted material. As reading professionals, we have an obligation to help raise awareness about Fair Use Laws and, of course, lead by example.

### Thinking Points

These questions are for your self-reflection. You need not discuss them with your group.

1. What do you know about copyright laws?
2. Do you ever make multiple copies of a page from a textbook or commercially prepared activity to use with students that is meant to be purchased?
3. In your day-to-day preparation of materials for teaching, do you think about Fair Use copyright issues?

4. What are the issues for reading specialists and literacy coaches to consider with regard to Fair Use Laws, and should they be addressed in professional development? If so, in what way?

## The Role of the Literacy Professional and Technology

### Technology and the Literacy Professional: Roles and Responsibilities

When you are in an airplane, the flight attendant always announces that if there is a loss in cabin pressure, you are to put on your own oxygen mask first and then help others. This holds true for instructional technology as well. One of the newer tasks for reading specialists and coaches is to keep current on the latest developments in educational technology and some of the ways successful teachers are using these tools to improve instruction. Then they will be ready to work with teachers and students.

*Professional development* is the key to supporting teachers in the three separate areas regarding technology that merit our attention:

1. Teachers' knowledge and effective use of technology in their out-of-school lives.
2. Support for keeping current in uses of educational technology.
3. Figuring out evidence-based ways for students to use new literacies in the classroom.

Research shows that isolated workshops will not suffice (Sparks & Hirsch, 1997). Instead, professional development for using technology needs to be geared to the needs of individual teachers. To that end, it is important that teachers have access to hands-on learning, ongoing support in using the technology in their teaching, and follow-up discussion, reflection, and self-assessment.

Because we believe that instructional technology is not a separate "subject," but rather a natural part of a person's reading and writing repertoire, it seems appropriate that the literacy coach will assume a key role in supporting teachers' use of technology in the natural progression of classroom events. This may include:

1. Supporting a teacher's implementation of instructional technology in the same way the coach would address methods and materials in any print-related endeavor.
2. Showing educators how to teach their students to apply the principles of critical literacy to the online material they encounter.
3. Showing teachers how to assist their students in scanning websites, highlighting key ideas electronically, judging the usefulness of a site, locating needed information, and viewing side-by-side items simultaneously (efficiently) on their screens rather than opening and closing sites.
4. Providing demonstrations and consultation outside of the classroom and supplementing that support with in-classroom observation.
5. Collaborating with the technology specialists to align with and enact the initiatives outlined in the school's long-term improvement goals (two-year plan).

6. Providing sustained professional development through workshops and facilitating peer group collaboration to support the implementation of new technology and innovative methods.

7. Disseminating information and conducting workshops aimed at helping teachers adapt the print-based content strategies common to their content areas for use with online resources.

## Revisiting the Vignette

At the end of the first year of her work with the district reading committee, Huong Nguyen felt satisfied that a great deal had been accomplished. Together, they had reviewed reading/ language arts research, internalized the state and district content standards, and generated a textbook adoption survey, such as the one in Figure 10.2, that they would all use the following year when it was time to review various publishers' instructional materials. They had drafted a timeline, scheduled publishers to present their materials, and organized subcommittees to review different components of the programs. Further, they had agreed that, by the beginning of the spring semester, piloting of the top three reading programs would be in place in six schools. The pilot teachers and procedures for piloting would be finalized in the fall. The final decision about the adoption would be made by April 15 of the following year. As Huong reviewed the plans and reflected on the year's work, she remembered her earlier concerns and fears. There was still a great deal to do, but the foundations for the adoption had been established thoughtfully and carefully. They were on their way.

## Points to Remember

School-site reading specialists, literacy coaches, and district reading supervisors must be directly involved in decisions related to the adoption of reading/language arts instructional materials. They should facilitate the formation of a district-level reading committee made up of representatives from the literacy teams of all of the district's schools. Based on district and state guidelines, policies, and recommendations relative to the adoption of reading series/programs, they should work with the reading committee to develop evaluation guidelines based on standards and school/community needs. The next step is to create a textbook adoption survey (see Figure 10.2) to be used during the review of the instructional materials. Throughout the adoption, it is important to foster and create professional relationships with publishers' sales representatives and consultants. Following the adoption, it is important to assist teachers in implementing the new program. This is facilitated through demonstration lessons, professional development, and ongoing monitoring and review of the school-site and district reading programs.

It appears that technology will continue to transform notions of what literacy is, and what it means to be literate. Because technology changes at such a rapid rate, reading specialists and literacy coaches are encouraged to work with school and district technology resource people to select and evaluate resources for classroom use. District guidelines and policies for providing a safe environment for children must be developed and followed. Media analysis is a powerful way to help children and adults understand events that unfold around them and affect their lives.

## *Portfolio and Self-Assessment Projects*

1. Investigate your district's textbook adoption process. Who currently makes decisions about the literacy-related instructional materials? What, if any, is the role of teachers, administrators, students, reading specialists, media specialists, and other stakeholders in the selection and evaluation process? Write a proposal for your school or district on how to improve the adoption process.

2. Examine either an elementary reading program or a secondary English or literature program. Using the recommendations for balanced elementary reading programs (Chapter 8) or secondary literacy programs (Chapter 9), determine the extent to which the program you're reviewing is research-based and instructionally sound. What are the strengths of the program? Its weaknesses?

How well would the teachers in your school and/or district be able to implement the program? What types of assistance and professional support might they need?

3. Evaluate your personal and professional technology skills. List three technology-related things you would like to learn. They can be school- or home-related. Create a one-year personal technology improvement plan. Include how you plan to learn these things, the resources you will need, a timeline, and how you will assess yourself.

4. *Personal Goal:* Revisit the objective you set for yourself at the beginning of the chapter. Create a portfolio item that reflects what you have learned relative to your objective.

## *Recommended Readings: Suggestions for Book Clubs, Study Groups, and Professional Development*

Hendron, J. G. (2008) *RSS for educators: Blogs, newsfeeds, podcasts, and wikis in the classroom.* Eugene, OR: International Society for Technology in Education (ISTE). This is the most accessible technology resource for teachers we have seen. Hendron is obviously a good teacher who knows how to explain complicated technology concepts clearly to adults who are not particularly facile in their use. If you are perplexed by Web 2.0, ways to keep current, and uses of instructional technology, start here.

Knobel, M., & Lankshear, C. (2009). Wikis, digital literacies, and professional growth. *Journal of Adolescent & Adult Literacy, 52*(7), 631–634. Knobel and Lankshear have earned their reputation as pioneers in the field of technology and instruction. Their newest article draws on and extends their previous work and incorporates both research and practice.

Leu, D. (March 2010). *My top ten ideas on how to integrate the new literacies of online reading comprehension into your classroom.* Keynote address at the Virginia State Reading Association Conference, Virginia Beach, VA. Don Leu, Director of the New Literacies Research Lab, is a continued source of practical, cutting-edge information about sound pedagogy related to technology.

## *Online Resources*

**http://www.newliteracies.uconn.edu**
The New Literacies Research Lab at the University of Connecticut, directed by Dr. Donald Leu, is the most widely recognized center in the world for conducting research on the comprehension and learning skills associated with successful use of communication and information technology. The work of the New Literacies Research team is focused on identifying the new skills, strategies, and dispositions required for successful reading comprehension and learning on the Internet, and on discovering the best way to prepare students for these new literacies. Because of the considerable resources and numerous projects associated with the team, new information is published on the website on a regular basis. Periodic visits to this website will keep you informed of their groundbreaking research findings.

**http://www2.scholastic.com/browse/article.jsp?id=10216**
Wilburn, D. (2009). *What is leveled reading?: Helping kids become better readers by matching them to the right books at the right time.* New York: Scholastic.

## *Companion Website Resources*

The following resources to support and extend your learning with this chapter can be found on our companion website (waveland.com/Extra_Material/32979/): key vocabulary, concepts, and other terms; extended examples; updated resources specifically tied to information in the chapter; related websites; and other support features. The companion website also includes *Establishing Guidelines: Twenty Questions for Examining Textbook Reading Series Materials*, the Textbook Adoption Survey, and additional information on new developments and uses of technology.

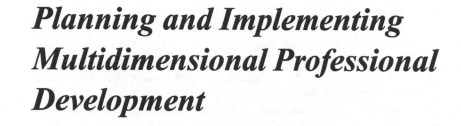

# Planning and Implementing Multidimensional Professional Development

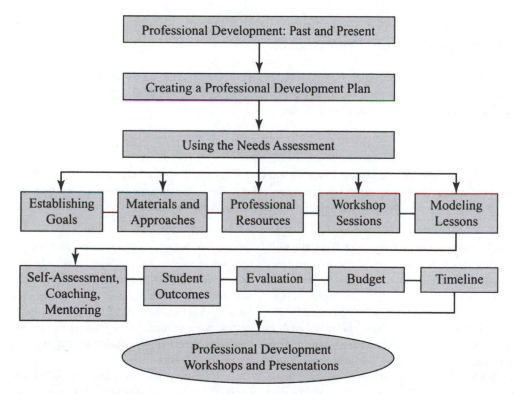

**FIGURE 11.1**   *Chapter Overview*

## *Learning Goals*

After reading, discussing, and engaging in activities related to this chapter, you will be able to:

1. Design a professional development plan for your school or district based on a needs assessment.

2. As a part of the professional development plan, create and deliver a literacy session or workshop for teachers.

3. Evaluate the effectiveness of the literacy in-service or workshop for teachers within the context of the professional development plan.

4. Prepare a list of book club selections aligned with your needs assessment findings. Provide a research base and rationale for each selection. Make a list of possible participants in the various groups and prepare a tentative schedule.

5. *Personal Learning Goal:* In a three-minute brainstorming session, share what you know about professional development. Write a goal or a question that reflects something you want to learn as we explore these topics. Share this with others in your group.

## Standards for Reading Professionals

This chapter provides focused support for current IRA Standards for Reading Professionals. See our companion website (waveland.com/Extra_Material/32979/) for a complete listing of the standards that align with this chapter.

### Two Vignettes

We begin this chapter with two vignettes, offering contrasting scenarios related to professional development. As you read them, think about your own experiences as a participant or presenter. We will revisit these vignettes throughout the chapter.

**Scenario 1 (Based on a true story from the not-so-distant past):** *Norma Chen was running late as she pulled her SUV up to Emerson Elementary School, piled a large bin of workshop materials onto her rolling cart, and walked quickly into the school. In the office, there was the usual end-of-the-day bedlam as children poured out of their classrooms. Norma spotted the principal talking on the phone. She introduced herself to Mrs. Waters, the principal's administrative assistant, and asked where she was supposed to be. Mrs. Waters gave a wave of her hand and replied, "You're in the cafeteria, down the first corridor. Let us know if you need anything." Luckily, a custodian directed her to the lunchroom. As Norma walked into the cavernous* room, she sighed. No overhead projector, no screen, no refreshments for teachers, and worst of all, cafeteria tables folded up along the wall. She also discovered that the handout she had sent the previous week was nowhere to be found. Looking at the clock, she realized that in fifteen minutes, she was to begin a mandatory reading workshop for sixteen primary teachers.

*Norma knew that the custodian and the principal's administrative assistant were her best friends in a time of crisis. As a faculty member at the nearby university, she was not a novice presenter and was often asked to be a featured speaker on professional development days. Realizing this was no time to panic, she sprang into action. As the custodian set up the tables, she hurried back to the office to ask about an overhead and screen, then quickly returned to the cafeteria to greet the teachers who were arriving with lesson plan books to complete and papers to grade. Things were not looking good.*

*When everything was in place and the teachers had settled in, the principal hurriedly entered the cafeteria. She said, "Thanks so much for being here today, Norma. Sorry that things were such a mess. Let's see . . . you're doing comprehension today, right? Could you also bring in something about spelling? Our spelling scores*

*are miserable right now and the teachers need help. Oh, and your handout is being duplicated right now. How would you like me to introduce you? Is there anything you'd like me to say? Do you have everything you need?"*

*With that, the principal introduced her quickly, and left. At the end of the two-hour session, with little said about spelling and marginal involvement from the attending teachers, Norma packed up her things, glanced over the so-so evaluations the teachers completed, and headed for her car. She thought to herself, "I'm not doing this again. Something's gotta change."*

## Thinking Points

Until recently, this was the classic "in-service" model. Professional development, as it is evolving today, has been transformed in the last decade. Thank goodness!

1. What are the elements in this scenario that make it an ineffective approach to professional development?
2. There are a number of people involved: Norma, the principal, the teachers, and perhaps even the office assistant and the custodian. What could each of them have done to ensure a better outcome?
3. Are there any individuals who are missing?

**Scenario 2 (Based on a true story from the very recent past):** *Norma Chen has an excellent relationship with the teachers and administration at Emerson Elementary School. As a faculty member at the nearby university, she has been consulting with the staff for years. Recently, Andrea Elaver, the school's literacy coach, called her and asked for help. "The teachers in grades 1–3 and I have been using your book in our study group to improve our evidence-based teaching of strategies related to informational text." Norma asked why they had chosen that goal. "Well, we noticed on our data retreat that there seem to be some gaps in our student's performance. We decided to make this an area of long-term focus, and it's part of our two-year plan. Your session with us will fit into our*

*ongoing process. Our group has been meeting for several months on a regular basis. Each month we choose another informational text strategy that needs attention and we incorporate it in our teaching. I've been helping teachers in setting personal goals, demonstrating lessons, finding resources, and coaching them both informally and formally. We also share ideas and peer coach when we can."*

*Norma could hear the enthusiasm in Andrea's voice. "Wow! I'm impressed," she said. "I'd love to come. Tell me more."*

*"We've been keeping a list of questions as we go and there are some things puzzling us. In particular, we struggle with how to assess our teaching. We wondered if you might be able to spend an interactive session with us, next month*

*after school, for about two hours. Maybe you can help us think things through. We keep logs of our meetings and that should give you a good idea of where we are and where we hope to be.*

*"If you're interested in doing this, I can send you our notes, and a list of specific things we'd like addressed. Then you and I can map out the session. You may have some ideas to add, or maybe you want to see some recorded lessons or other things before you come. Pat Murphy, our principal, has given us some ideas, too. We don't have much money, but we can talk about what you* *would need, and Pat promised to feed us. Tell us about the set up you need, and we'll take care of that. Oh, and let us know about any materials you'd like us to bring. I'm thinking teachers could meet in the media center and use those round tables. There are fourteen teachers and, of course, the principal and I will be there. After the session, we'd like to touch base with you from time to time about how we're doing."*

*Norma was excited. "Send me what you have and I'll get back to you and the group. We should probably talk in a week to share ideas."*

### Thinking Points

1. List three things in Scenario 2 that you think are most important for facilitating lasting change.
2. Analyze the roles of the people in Scenario 2. What do you notice about their participation?
3. What suggestions do you have for Andrea and Norma as they plan this session?

## Models of Professional Development

Until recently, the only component of professional development was the occasional conference or adrenaline-producing presentation. Once we "got those out of the way," we could go back to our teaching. We now know that professional development is multilayered and focused on both our shared long-term goals and our individual needs. These elements are part of a coherent Professional Development Plan (PDP). The PDP requires sustained administrative and staff support, shared ownership, adequate resource allocation, and ongoing assessment of progress toward goals. That is why the reading specialist and literacy coach are such key players in professional development.

It is no surprise that when IRA released its long-range strategic plan in January of 2010, the number one area of emphasis was professional development. The report called professional development "IRA's North Star" (Harvey, 2009/2010, p. 32) for achieving its overall mission to increase literacy around the globe (see http://www.reading.org/General/AboutIRA/Strategic.aspx).

### What Is Multidimensional Professional Development?

One of the most quoted definitions of professional development is from Guskey (2000). He defines professional development as "those processes and activities designed to enhance the professional knowledge, skills, and attitudes of educators, so that they might, in turn, improve the learning of students" (p. 1). The day-to-day sustained efforts to support school improvement have rightly taken center stage in professional development, and formal presentations, though still valuable, are used in much more context-specific and relevant ways.

In this chapter, we will focus on the components of a responsive Professional Development Plan (PDP), the school-based roles of the literacy professional, and the structure of workshops and presentations, so often the responsibility of the literacy coach, instructional coach, or reading specialist. We describe such a plan as *multidimensional*. What we mean by that is:

- It addresses shared goals, identified through the school's needs assessment.
- A focused set of support structures are planned for working toward each goal.
- The structures may include a few or all of the following: planning sessions, formal workshops and problem-solving, formal or informal observation, peer coaching, individual consultation, dissemination of resources, incorporation of specialized materials, self-evaluation, in-class support, or lesson modeling by reading specialists and literacy coaches—in short, whatever is needed to achieve the particular goal.
- Collaboration, communication, and feedback from all stakeholders is essential to ownership of the shared vision, in which educators see themselves as part of professional learning communities (PLCs) (Hord & Sommers, 2008).
- Periodic assessment is integrated into the plan so that progress toward the goal can be monitored and adjustments can be made to ensure that the goal will be met.
- Ways to support teachers' individual goals must be incorporated into the plan.
- Remember to keep in mind that *all of these components* comprise a comprehensive Professional Development Program (PDP).

## What Is the Difference between a Transmission Model and a Constructivist Model?

Schools used to spend thousands of dollars two or three days a year bringing in "big guns"—expensive, well-known educators and motivators. These experts would drive or fly in from somewhere, for an hour to a full day, to share ideas and methods in the hope that teachers would pick up one or two ideas that they could hurry back to the classroom to implement. These sessions, aimed at *training* teachers rather than *educating* them, had little benefit to teachers, other than to give them professional development hours or points tied to salary growth. As two people who have done our fair share of these types of "in-service" sessions, this is a bit hard to admit!

Palmer (1998) likens this transmission model of teaching to using an IV bottle: "When we teach by dripping information into their passive forms, students [or teachers] who arrive in the classroom alive and well become passive consumers of knowledge and are dead on departure when they graduate [or leave]" (p. 42). This description of some presenters and teachers we have seen at in-services is not that far off.

Single-event professional development experiences do have one benefit; particularly at the onset of a new initiative, *they can set the tone for change*. However, they have limited ability to transform beliefs or practice. Some of the reasons drive-through professional development (the fast food model) is not effective are:

- In a group of thirty teachers, there may be just a handful of individuals interested in the topic of the day.
- In most cases, the topic is selected because the principal or administrator decides the teachers *need* it.
- Attendance is mandatory.
- The idea, strategy, or theme has little to do with any larger, systemic plan, so sometimes it's hard to figure out where and how it *fits*.

In 1997, Ann Lieberman, a school reformer, argued for a "radical rethinking" of professional development. She suggested, "What everyone appears to want for students—a wide array of learning opportunities that engage students in experiencing, creating, and solving real problems, using their own experiences, and working with others—is for some reason denied to teachers when they are learners" (cited in Sparks & Hirsch, 1997, p. 591). Since she wrote those words, much has changed.

In hard times, one of the first budget items to be slashed is professional development. Some educators mistook the drastic cuts in funds for education caused by the recession of 2008–2009 as the final death knell for professional development. However, by that time, the old *in-service* model was already quickly disappearing. In the first decade of the new century, something incredible was happening in the arena of professional development. As a response to mandates for change and the need for teachers to improve their practice, schools started hiring literacy coaches. While there were many problems with role descriptions, qualifications, and standards that were not yet in place, as noted in previous chapters, evidence began to come in that systemic professional development, as facilitated by literacy coaches, not only improved teaching, but also had a positive effect on students' reading achievement. Suddenly, administrators and teachers began to realize that with the emergence of the literacy coach and teams of highly talented teachers and committed administrators, they had everything they needed to provide a much more effective kind of professional development, grounded in evidence and fueled by collaboration and ownership.

The new approaches to professional development embraced the evidence that a constructivist approach to student learning also applied to teachers. For those of you who may still be unclear as to just what constructivism is, that's exactly what Lieberman was describing. Within the working definition of *constructivism* is the belief that *students bring with them their unique knowledge and experiences which they use to make* (not "get") *meaning* (McLaughlin & Vogt, 1996). We agree with Sparks and Hirsch (1997), when they wonder how teachers can be expected to understand, embrace, and enact a constructivist orientation in their classrooms if we provide professional development via the old transmission model.

## Revisiting the Vignette: Thinking Points

1. Which elements of Scenario 1 involve a constructivist view of professional development?
2. Which elements of Scenario 2 involve a constructivist view of professional development?

As teachers, we have all been affected by swinging pendulums in the never-ending call for educational reform. (This happens almost as often at the university level as it does in K–12, lest you think we as professors no longer experience this phenomenon.) New initiatives are often purchased, mandated, and implemented before any of us understand what they're all about and, more importantly, whether they're grounded in research or appropriate for *our* students in *our* schools in *our* communities. That's why the basic assumption that educators use evidence-based practice is a compelling idea. Now, if we could all just agree on what constitutes evidence.

# Creating a Professional Development Plan (PDP)

## Understanding Teacher Development

Professional development is all about change. In order to talk about professional development, we need to understand how teachers change as they grow in their profession. Snow, Griffin, and Burns (2005) suggested that teachers progress through five stages: *preservice, apprentice, novice, experienced,* and *master teacher.* During each stage, the teacher goes through a cycle that involves learning, enactment, assessment, and reflection, which prepares them for the next stage. As they advance from stage to stage, they acquire a different type of knowledge: *declarative, situated, stable, expert,* and *reflective.* For example, preservice teachers' knowledge is *declarative.* They've taken classes, done a little observation, and worked a bit in classrooms. By and large, they have a collection of facts and ideas, things they "know," but haven't tried out or experienced. Beginning teachers are mainly in the *situated* stage in that they see how their preservice knowledge works in the immediate context of their classroom. When the novice teacher settles into a more comfortable set of practices, the *stable* stage emerges. As these teachers grow in confidence, professional knowledge, and effective practice, they enter into the *expert* stage of their professional lives. Finally, there are the master teachers, those who use much more *reflective* knowledge, that is, knowledge based on years of learning the profession, seeing what works, and witnessing the outcomes of thousands of decisions. They have the knowledge base to ask questions of themselves and others that move the thinking in the field forward. Understanding this progression can help both teacher and coach in examining the unique professional development needs of the teacher, establishing individualized goals, and accommodating individuals within the school's professional learning community (Hord & Sommers, 2008; Roberts & Pruitt, 2009).

## Using the Needs Assessment as a Guide for Professional Development

The professional development of the past often went something like this:

1. A teacher or administrator went to a workshop,
2. saw something "neat" and decided
3. WE should get someone in here to do a workshop on that and
4. then WE should *all* do it in our classrooms.

The good news: There's a better way. You can use the needs assessment and two-year plan for direction. You have the data to show you where you need help. Now you need to plan for the professional development to get you there. The professional development plan (PDP) is but one piece of the two-year plan, our action guide for school improvement. It is the enactment of the vision. It is directly linked to the needs you discovered. This makes sense, because you collected and analyzed the data together as a school. No doubt you found areas that needed attention. Some of these were minor, such as the lack of certain materials. But some were major, for example, finding that teachers were struggling to implement guided comprehension. Test results and teacher surveys confirmed that teachers need and want systematic, focused, multifaceted support in order to improve their teaching and help their students become more proficient readers. As the literacy coach, you are the one who coordinates all the pieces and provides support to groups and individuals, relying on the shared expertise of the stakeholders.

## Evidence-Based Professional Development

As you and the team select materials and approaches, you will need to prepare a short rationale for each. Write one or two meaty paragraphs indicating the underlying research base. This should be distributed to everyone and briefly reviewed at the following faculty meeting.

## Multilayered Professional Development

When we say that effective professional development is multilayered, we mean that it involves a constellation of activities and events, not just a study group, not just a series of presentations, not just modeling of lessons, not just *any* one thing. Rather, an effective professional development plan is a carefully orchestrated combination of supports, in which there are provisions for differentiation. Some teachers may need more support within the professional learning community. In effect, the needs of individual teachers can be addressed in much the same way we differentiate for students in Tier I of RtI.

## Sustained Professional Development

A great deal of this chapter addresses the idea of long-range support for change. Important initiatives and substantial changes in instructional methods and materials require an effort spanning months, maybe even a year or more in the case of a major program change.

The PDP will require a great deal of collaboration, commitment, time, and effort from the literacy coach and the staff, but also from principals and administrators to help establish a budget and timeline. Research shows that school reform is greatly dependent on the committed support and leadership of an administrator (Fullan, Hill, & Crévola, 2006; Lambert, 2002; Moxley & Taylor, 2006; Waddell & Lee, 2008). Don't be afraid to ask for your administrator's support from the outset. Administrators can take steps to follow up on professional development by classroom observation, literacy walk-throughs (dropping into classrooms), meeting with the literacy team and other teacher groups, and helping the participants assess and adjust goals. In other words, they need to do the kinds of things that display a physical presence so teachers know that their educational leader shares in their mission (Meltzer & Ziemba, 2006).

### Components of the Professional Development Plan (PDP)

**Goals.** The goals of the PDP are tied directly to the targeted needs. Because the needs are based on data from the needs assessment, they are already evidence-based. They should be prioritized, with the most important ones first. However, you need to proceed with caution. For example, it is unrealistic to think that everyone will be able to use guided reading within three months. Write three or four goals that can be implemented in increments, measured, then evaluated and adjusted periodically. There are two dimensions to professional development goals:

1. *Program Goals*: These are global goals shared by everyone in the school or district. They relate to the overall school vision. Such a goal might be to implement RtI as the school's intervention structure.
2. *Individual Teacher Goals*: These goals are differentiated. For example, if one teacher's goal is to learn to use certain screening instruments, professional development might include a set of readings, individual guidance, and self-evaluation. Usually, a small group of teachers share the goal. Study groups, book clubs, and shared tutorials would be appropriate.

**Materials and Approaches.** Because your needs assessment survey examined materials and methods teachers are using, you will have an accurate idea of what exists and what you need to purchase to reach the targeted goal. You can also estimate how much support teachers will need to become facile in using the new materials and approaches.

**Professional Resources.** As savvy as many teachers are today, as the literacy coach or reading specialist, you are often the one teachers come to when they need information. Among your responsibilities will be to work with your team to find a variety of resources. Whatever the need, there are articles, book, Internet sources, instructional videos, and human resources (people with expertise who can guide you). You don't have to buy every book on the subject. Your nearest university library is a great resource. Good places to look are professional organizations such as IRA, NCTE, and The Literacy Coaching Clearinghouse where you'll find articles, briefs, position statements, links to research, and books to purchase on their websites. Be careful to honor copyright guidelines. Some websites, such as the IRA's, stipulate limits on the number of single-use copies you can make. Keep in mind that your role is to build background knowledge and to ensure that everyone knows the research base underlying what they do. This may require creating study guides, maps, or summaries. You might also use the Jigsaw technique, a great way to cover a large amount of material. With Jigsaw, you will be able to assign parts of books or long articles for teachers to read and share.

**Study Groups.** What makes study groups so powerful as a catalyst for change is that they involve a high degree of choice and ownership. A group of teachers choose a book or set of articles that interests them and meet to exchange ideas (Toll, 2005; Walpole & McKenna, 2005). Goal orientation is already built in, and participants are active learners and collaborators. These are all things that lead to "buy in." As the literacy coach, your role in the group is participant and co-learner, but you will be actively involved in helping suggest and select a wide variety of materials that may be useful to the group. Sometimes coaches organize informal discussion study groups around topics of interest.

***Professional Development Presentations or Workshop Sessions.***    Before you begin any professional development planning, we suggest you obtain the LLC's *Coach Tool: Professional Development Setting Checklist* (2009), created by Catherine Rosemary and Naomi Feldman. This excellent tool leading you from initial planning through self-assessment is available at http://www.literacycoachingonline.org/briefs/tools/Rosemary_%26_Feldman_PD_setting_tool_4.5.09.pdf. As the literacy coach, you are not expected to be the sole creator, presenter, and facilitator of a series of large formal workshops, as we saw in past models. One of the hallmarks of a good leader is the ability to empower others. By sharing ownership of projects, others have the opportunity to grow in leadership. Here is your opportunity to honor that wonderful teacher who has tremendous skills, but who has never been asked to share them. You have a group of talented team members and teachers who can provide workshops for targeted groups, large or small, and you probably know experts you can invite in to lead workshops. There could be a kickoff activity, even if it's just a little after school get-together in the teachers' lounge with refreshments and a cake with your new logo on it. (Remember we suggested you develop a theme or logo that appears on everything the group hands out.) There are also local and state reading council meetings, opportunities from your district, county, or regional educational collaboratives and IRA. What's important is that every aspect of your professional development plan is tied to the targeted goal.

- As you prepare for these sessions, remember to include administrators and instructional assistants. You want to be certain that all stakeholders are involved and aware of what you hope to accomplish. It is also wise to have at least one meeting with parents at which you and the team discuss your goals. This could happen at one of the P.T.A. events that are normally scheduled throughout the year.
- Planning is the hallmark of successful professional development. You need to construct a grid or map outlining the purpose and all the elements: time, place, materials, participants (and what they will be expected to do). You are operating under a common goal: to improve teaching and increase student learning.
- Throughout this book we have emphasized that learning is social, so it should come as no surprise that we advocate a great deal of substantive discussion and collaborative problem-solving. You will also want to include a self-assessment element for participants to monitor their progress. And don't forget to assess yourself as well.

***Supporting Teachers as Coach, Mentor, and Classroom Guide.***    This part of the coach's role involves consulting with teachers, helping them set goals for themselves, and then providing the in- and out-of-class support they will need to reach that goal. As we mentioned in Chapter 2, excellent resources from the Literacy Coaching Clearinghouse (http://www.literacycoachingonline.org) include guides and checklists to help coaches in planning, observing, evaluating, and supporting teachers in the following:

- *Goal-Setting.* You will find that teachers are at different levels in the five stages of teacher development (Snow, Griffin, & Burns, 2005), and at different places within each level. Most will be operating in the last three stages: novice, experienced, or master teacher. What we know about goals is that the ones that most impel us to change are the ones we set for ourselves. Often, a person may want to do something, but have difficulty putting whatever it is into words. The literacy coach or reading specialist can help teachers establish and articulate their personal goals (tied to the target goal) and guide them in self-assessment.
- *Modeling.* This is an excellent way to scaffold knowledge. It is most effective when followed by giving the teacher the opportunity to try the new strategy or technique while the coach observes and later provides supportive feedback. MaryEllen recalls a time when she entered a classroom to model a lesson only to discover (after she started teaching) that all of the students were English learners. It was enough to convince her that even if you are just going into a classroom and modeling for one teacher, you should spend a few minutes getting to know the students. In other words, prepare yourself for the students and prepare them to work with you; otherwise you might end up modeling what *not* to do.
- *Co-Teaching.* This is a great way to help teachers develop skills. It can involve sharing different parts of teaching a lesson. Another interesting way to go about it is for you and the teacher to each take a reading group within the same classroom, working at side-by-side tables. This gives the teacher a chance to see the skill or process modeled, and the coach a chance to informally observe the teacher (Duessen, Coskie, Robinson, & Autio, 2007).
- *Consulting.* A less intrusive form of professional development is consulting. Here, the coach meets with the teacher outside of the classroom to discuss progress toward the goal, provide suggestions, and determine that the teacher is receiving the level of support needed. This hands-off approach is appropriate when a teacher is relatively skilled or comfortable in progression toward the goal, or is interested in exploring a new goal. Another consulting role might occur when the coach meets with those who are mentoring another teacher to give support or answer any of the mentor's questions (Costa & Garmston, 2002).
- *Observation and Feedback.* The coach has several roles in observation. While there are dozens of models of this process, almost all follow the same basic progression.

The first step involves the teacher and coach working together in *planning.* It includes

a. establishing clear objectives,
b. deciding on the student artifacts that demonstrate the success of the lesson,
c. outlining the specific steps in the progression of the lesson, and
d. establishing the criteria for feedback.

The second step is *observation,* using the tools that you created with the teacher. We suggest that you

**a.** concentrate on a particular aspect of the lesson, and

**b.** work out the parameters of how both of you will discuss it, observe it, and evaluate it.

The last step involves *feedback*. This includes

**a.** a debriefing, a joint reflection on what went well,

**b.** any insights that were gained, and

**c.** a plan for the future.

Observation and feedback is meant to be a trusting experience, goal-oriented rather than person-oriented. This kind of relationship between coaches and teachers is classic. According to Lyons and Pinnell (2001) the coach's goal is to support teachers in applying knowledge, developing skills, and deepening their understanding. We believe it is imperative.

***Self-Assessment.***    In Chapter 2, we touched on the importance of guiding teachers toward self-assessment. As you mentor the teachers with whom you work, involve them in reflective self-assessment, and be discrete and professional in all your interactions with faculty and administrators. In doing so, your coaching efforts are more likely to be perceived as helpful and geared toward implementation of professional development goals.

One of the most important things you can do is to assess yourself. The LLC's *Teacher Contact Form* is an excellent self-assessment tool for coaches. It will help you analyze how you are allocating your time and effort, and evaluate the successes and areas for improvement in your interactions with teachers. It is available at http://www.literacycoachingonline.org/briefs/tools/teacher_contact_form_tool_1.11.09.pdf.

***Student Outcomes.***    Improved student outcomes, after all, are why we engage in professional development, and it's important throughout the process to keep student performance at the center. Informal reading inventories and other assessments can provide data, as well as end-of-year standardized tests. Not all professional development efforts will yield data on student outcomes, but if you can gather data, do so.

***Evaluation.***    Your PDP must include a means for periodic evaluation of its success. Use the goals you established at the beginning of the planning process to guide your evaluation, and determine for each how you will collect and analyze data. For example, you may wish to include a survey of all participants or use field notes, interviews, and a report of student outcomes, if appropriate. Your data may be both quantitative (percentage of responses) and qualitative (written comments).

***Budget.***    After you have completed a draft of the professional development plan, list everything that you want to include that costs money—and we mean everything—the cost of books; duplication of articles; fees, travel, and expenses of speakers; conference fees; snacks or meals; and miscellaneous expenses. Obviously, budgeting for professional development must be done in consultation with your site and/or district administrators.

***Timeline.***    The final step in creating a PDP is to write a timeline, similar to what you did for the two-year plan, but with more detail. Keep in mind that the timeline can be somewhat flexible. We recommend that you set out the year, month by month, including the activities involved and the materials that are going to be read and shared, followed by workshops and/or conferences, the discussion and sharing of information from these, demonstration lessons, study groups, and peer coaching opportunities. See the PDP in Figure 11.2 for an example of a timeline, as well as the other components discussed in this section.

*Note:* A blank template for the completed Sample Professional Development Plan (Figure 11.2), including all components discussed in this chapter, such as resources, timeline, budget, assessment, workshops, study groups, and coaching, can be found on our companion website. It can serve as a starting point for developing your own format for a PDP.

---

**ABC Elementary School Professional Development Plan**
Created by Sonia Beagonea, Reading Specialist
The Literacy Team: (List Names and Grade Levels or Other Affiliation)

Targeted Need: Improving Students' Comprehension
of Narrative and Expository Texts, Grades K–6

***Goals of Professional Development***

1. Establish a research foundation for and understandings of the comprehension processes involved in proficient reading.
2. Provide all faculty and instructional assistants with relevant and effective professional development and follow-up support. Focus on instructional methods, materials, and approaches for teaching comprehension skills and strategies.
3. Use Informal Reading Inventories and other artifacts to assess students' fluency, comprehension, and word recognition.
4. Improve students' comprehension of narrative and expository texts as determined by a variety of formal and informal measures.

***Currently Used Instructional Materials and Approaches***

As a literacy team, we will survey all faculty about current methods, approaches, and instructional materials used for teaching comprehension. We will interview selected faculty about how they currently teach comprehension and assess students. Our findings will be summarized and then reported at the first weekly staff meeting in October.

***Professional Resources***

Purchase six copies (one for each grade level) of the following books:

 McLaughlin, M., & Allen, M. B. (2009). *Guided comprehension in grades 3–8* (2nd ed.). Newark, DE: International Reading Association.

 Opitz, M. F., & Ford, M. P. (2008). *Do-able differentiation: Varying groups, texts, and supports to reach readers*. Portsmouth, NH: Heinemann.

Purchase three copies (one for grades K–3) of the following book:

 Mere, C. (2005). *More than guided reading: Finding the right instructional mix*. New York: Stenhouse.

Purchase three copies (one for grades 3–6) of the following book:

 McLaughlin, M., & Allen, M. B. (2009). *Guided comprehension in grades 3–8* (2nd ed.). Newark, DE: International Reading Association.

*(continued)*

---

**FIGURE 11.2   *Sample Professional Development Plan***

Purchase one copy for each faculty member:

Johns, J. J. (2008). *Basic reading inventory* (10th ed.). Dubuque, IA: Kendall/Hunt.

Duplicate and have ready for checkout ten copies of an article from *The Reading Teacher* (note IRA policy regarding duplication for one-time use).

### Suggested Activities for Professional Resources

- During a school faculty meeting, review the Needs Assessment data related to comprehension instruction.
- Book-talk the new books the Literacy Team has selected.
- Invite staff members (including administrators and instructional assistants) to form grade-level discussion and study groups for the professional books.
- Offer a workshop on how to administer Informal Reading Inventories; include opportunities for teachers to analyze results; provide time for grade-level meetings to use findings to plan effective comprehension instruction.

### Professional Development, Workshops, and Presentations

- Offer a workshop on comprehension skills and strategies, to establish a foundation of current research.
- Offer at least one workshop (with district reading specialist) on how to administer and analyze results from an Informal Reading Inventory.
- Offer one or more workshops on how to use IRIs to assess comprehension, fluency, and word recognition.
- Survey faculty to determine if additional professional development is needed.
- Encourage and coordinate attendance at professional reading conferences, as budget will allow.
- Encourage teachers who have been implementing reciprocal teaching to share with other teachers during after-school workshop.

### Demonstration Lessons

- Offer and then schedule modeling of lessons on the following topics:
  - Administering an IRI
  - Teaching comprehension skills (e.g., critical reading, questioning, problem-solving)
  - Comprehension strategies with DRTAs for narrative text and SQP2RS* for information/expository text (or other processing strategies related to the needs assessment)
  - Reciprocal teaching/guided reading lessons
  - Others, as requested

### Self-Assessment/Peer Coaching/Mentoring

- Discuss possibility of recording comprehension lessons as opportunities for reflective self-assessment. Determine if anyone is interested in forming discussion groups to analyze and reflect on teaching effectiveness of comprehension lessons.
- Determine if any teachers are interested in or willing to establish peer coaching partners. If so, discuss how these might be organized and implemented.

**FIGURE 11.2** (*continued*)

*SQP2RS: An instructional framework for teaching comprehension strategies: Survey text; Generate questions; Make predictions of what will be learned; Read the text; Respond to the text, the questions, and predictions; Summarize key concepts. See Vogt & Echevarria (2008) for more information about SQP2RS.

- Establish mentors/coaches for teachers in years one to three of teaching.
- Assess your own professional development efforts.

### Student Outcomes

- Improvement in comprehension as measured by pre–post IRI passages, word recognition, and student artifacts.
- Improvement in comprehension as measured by pre–post standardized test scores.
- Increase in number of students who are able to read grade-level texts.
- Observation of student/classroom events.

### Evaluation

- Measures (IRI results) for evaluating comprehension growth in selected (from high-achieving, average, and low-performing) students for each grade level.
- Standardized test scores in comprehension for all students.
- Satisfaction measures (surveys, interviews) of teachers at end of first and second years.
- Evaluations collected at the end of all workshops.
- Comparison of pre–post reading logs of students in grades 2–6.
- Teacher journals/self-assessment.

### Estimated Budget

- Professional resources for teachers and administrators (books)     $   900.00
- Duplicating of journal article                                                                           30.00
- Materials for in-service                                                                                 170.00
- Honoraria for speakers                                                                                 1500.00
- Conference attendance fees for teachers                                                     500.00
- Total                                                                                                             $ 3100.00
- Each year's budget (years one and two)                                              $ 1550.00

### Tentative Timeline

*Year One*

*September–October:*

Distribute copies of books to grade-level teams. Organize study groups with team members, determine a schedule, and begin reading the books. Be sure at least one member of the literacy team is in each study group.

Schedule afternoon workshops on how to administer the Informal Reading Inventory.

*November–December:*

Schedule modeling for teachers wishing to see the administration of an IRI.

Schedule study groups for teachers wishing to discuss results and implications of IRIs they have administered.

Study group: Finish reading one or two books. At staff meeting, as a group, share main ideas and concepts from the books.

Literacy team: Offer an after-school session on comprehension strategies. Share copies of *The Reading Teacher* article.

*(continued)*

**FIGURE 11.2     (*continued*)**

*January–February:*

Schedule modeling of lessons on strategy instruction for any interested teachers.

Study group: Begin new book. Share ideas teachers have tried.

Model DRTA process for literacy team; encourage them to use it and discuss its effectiveness.

Schedule demonstration lessons on DRTA or another comprehension monitoring strategy using narrative text.

*March–April:*

Finish reading books. Share ideas teachers have tried. Discuss how the comprehension strategy instruction is working.

Schedule classroom observations for interested teachers.

Establish peer coaching for observations. Offer to take classes of those who will be coaching.

Schedule schoolwide (required) session for all teachers and administrators. Invite district reading specialist to assist literacy team in planning and implementing.

*May–June:*

Model lessons on SQP2RS or other fix-up strategies (for expository/informational texts) for interested teachers. Offer to cover classes so peer coaches can observe each other using SQP2RS or another comprehension monitoring strategy.

During staff meeting, have teachers complete evaluation of the year's efforts in improving comprehension instruction.

When standardized scores become available, spot-check them to see if there are any changes in comprehension scores.

Provide assistance in administering post-IRIs on selected students at each grade level (high-achieving, average, and low-achieving). Look for areas of growth.

Administer a needs assessment related to comprehension for the following year.

*Year Two*

*Fall Semester:*

Model lessons on comprehension processes. Implement peer coaching as necessary.

Review and revisit DRTA and SQP2RS or other monitoring strategies. Introduce QARs.

Schedule conferences as needed.

Involve literacy team in planning one or two afternoon sessions (as needed) on activities and strategies from the books previously read.

Target new teachers and those new to the school. Provide them with demonstration lessons, workshops, and copies of the books.

*Spring Semester:*

Assess overall comprehension plan toward the end of the school year.

1. What is working well? How do we know?
2. What still needs farther work? How do we know?
3. Which teachers are consistently and effectively teaching comprehension skills and strategies? How are their students performing?

Assess all students with IRIs, if time allows. If not, focus on struggling readers.

Compare IRI results with standardized test scores. Look for trends and any changes.

With literacy team, complete final evaluations of comprehension professional development plan.

With literacy team, conduct and evaluate results of new needs assessments.

With literacy team, establish a new two-year plan for professional development.

**FIGURE 11.2**   *(continued)*

# Planning and Leading Professional Development Workshops and Presentations

Now that you and the team have planned the topics and outlined the schedule for professional development workshops, it's time to discuss the steps necessary to create a dynamic workshop or presentation. Although it can be inspirational to have a well-known expert come into your school on occasion, it is essential for you to be able to conduct workshops and sessions, both big and small, as needed. We hope this "Beyond the Book" activity will get you started.

## BEYOND THE BOOK

### Chapter 11 Focus Issue: The Great Ones Make It Look EASY

We've all heard the saying, "Never let them see you sweat!" If there's ever a time when nerves are being tested, it's right before you give a presentation. We still experience that every time we lead a professional development session or give a research presentation to our peers. We all know people who manage to mesmerize, inspire, enlighten us with great information, and entertain at the same time. We need to ask what we can learn from them, because, in fact, when they are presenting, they are *modeling how to present*.

This exercise involves working in small groups.

1. For each question listed below, briefly brainstorm with your group.
   - What was the most interesting, worthwhile, and positive presentation or workshop you ever attended?
   - Who was the speaker? What was it about that person and/or what they did that was so effective?
   - Was the topic tied to a goal that you had in mind, something you wanted to learn? Did you have a choice in attending?
   - How did the presenter keep the audience active and engaged?
   - Did you change something about the way you taught or thought as a result of this presentation? If so, what kinds of additional things did you have to do (after the presentation) to implement the change?
2. Jot down ideas shared.
3. Using the insights from the sharing, make a group list of at least five things inspirational speakers do.
4. Setting goals: Have each individual in the group select the one thing he or she would like to improve and incorporate into his or her next presentation. This can be used as a personal goal.

### Preparing the "Package"

We know you have wonderful things to share with teachers. We are also betting that as reading professionals, you know how to teach and how to keep a group of students engaged. However, when it comes to working with adults, the bar is raised. In *The Presenter's Field-book,* Robert Garmston (2005) asks us to think about the types of people that are included in almost any group. You need to make sure your presentation has something for all of them. As you plan your session, be sure to keep these four types of people in mind, and be sure that the phrases you use reflect this. For example, according to Garmston, there are:

1. *The Professors:* They want mastery and competence. They like facts, evidence, and detail, so include phrases like, "Research tells us . . .," and "Did you know that . . ." You can easily spot these folks. They are taking detailed notes, and it's probably safe to bet that their writing is neat.

2. *The Scientists:* They want to examine and process data. They like to explore possibilities and hypotheses. You can engage them by using phrases like, "This is how it works . . .," "The processes involved are . . . ," and "Here is why . . . ." They are the ones who ask the best (and most challenging) questions. But be careful, they can derail you.

3. *The Inventors:* These are the creative folks. They want to rearrange, adapt, and reorganize information in novel ways. They love to explore and generate new solutions. It's as if they were born to brainstorm. They perk up when they hear phrases like, "I wonder if there are other ways to . . . ," or "What would happen if we . . . ?"

4. *The Friends:* As Barbra Streisand would say, these are the "people who need people." They love engaging with others, working in groups, participating in hands-on learning. They love time to share, and they respond to emotional hooks, personal stories, and metaphors. When you use phrases like, "I had a student who . . ." or "That reminds me of . . . ," they sit up straight.

We can all see parts of ourselves and our colleagues in these examples. And although our descriptions were light-hearted, we hope you are beginning to understand the importance of considering who is "out there" and what they need from you. After all, you want to reach people with your message and have them embrace your ideas. The first thing you need to do is figure out which category is most like you. Obviously we are all more complicated than any one-dimensional classification, but most of us have a "home base" in one of these types more than in others. Garmston (2005) explains that most of us present information in ways that characterize our type. If you are a "scientist" at heart, you probably adopt a more factually oriented presentation style. If you recognize that, you can make sure that in every major shift of topic, you plan to include phrases and response activities that engage both those who are like you and those who are not. Here's the big secret: All good presenters seem to know this intuitively, without ever having been told. Now you know it, too.

## Examining the Structure of the Professional Development Workshop

In the Beyond the Book exercise, you reflected on the relevant workshops you've attended that had a real impact on you and your teaching. Thinking about the opening, the organization, the speaker's skill at making transitions from one activity to the next, your engagement, your participation, and your collaborative work with others around you will help you plan effective opportunities for other teachers. While you plan and organize, we encourage you to consider each of the following:

1. *Prepare your opening:* Include the name of the school or district (even if it's your own) and, if possible, some anecdote about it. Make it personal. Thank those who have invited you and acknowledge any special assistance that you received from specific individuals.
2. *State your goals:* Clearly state your objectives and what you hope the teachers will take away from the session.
3. *Include an agenda:* We recommend that you provide a tentative agenda that allows flexibility (see Figure 11.3). Notice how this agenda lets participants know when the important things are going to happen (like breaks and lunch), but the topics allow the presenter to change plans as needed. After a break, briefly summarize what you've discussed in the previous session so that you can bridge to what is coming. Garmston (2005) suggests that the first break after lunch should come no later than one hour after you reconvene, because that's the most difficult time to engage an audience.

ABC Elementary School
Workshop Day
February 18, 2011

Sponsored by your Literacy Team
Presented by Sonia Beagonea, District Reading Specialist

| | |
|---|---|
| 8:30–8:45 | Registration and Coffee |
| 8:45–9:00 | Welcome, Introduction, and Plans for the Day |
| 9:00–10:30 | Administering an Informal Reading Inventory |
| 10:30–10:45 | Break |
| 10:45–12:00 | Analyzing the Results of Informal Reading Inventories |
| 12:00–12:45 | Lunch |
| 12:45–1:45 | Using Results for Planning Instruction |
| 1:45–2:00 | Break |
| 2:00–3:00 | Implications for Teaching Vocabulary and Comprehension |
| 3:00–3:30 | Sharing Ideas, Wrap-Up, and Evaluation |

**FIGURE 11.3** *Sample Workshop Agenda*

4. *Humor:* If there's one thing that's important to plan, it's humor. Cartoons, jokes (not shady or questionable), poems and stories about teachers' lives in the classroom, and anecdotes are fine. However, remember that forced humor is worse than none at all!

5. *Content:* Most novices plan much more than they can reasonably accomplish in an hour, half-day, or school day. It's almost guaranteed. It's best to overplan, but be prepared to let things go. Include what's crucial; then have other activities ready to go if you have a quiet group or teachers who are knowledgeable about the topic and can move more quickly.

   One other comment about content: Learn about your teachers and what they know about the topic you're presenting. Always provide a *brief* research background for what you're sharing, because you need to establish the evidence base for what you do.

6. *Activities:* Remember that many of the instructional techniques that work with students also work with adults, and you can scaffold their learning by building background, activating and reinforcing what they already know and do, reviewing what you've covered periodically throughout the day, and being very attentive to questions, puzzled faces, and the "aha's!" that you see. As in your classroom, vary the approaches and activities you use, and don't expect teachers to sit much more quietly than your kids!

   Remember that we all learn better by "participating and doing" than by "being told." Model the strategies you're teaching and take the audience through the various techniques as learners, so that when they try the activities in their own classrooms, they can feel successful.

7. *Conclusion, wrap-up, and evaluation:* Plan the ending of your session as carefully as you've planned the rest of it. Summarize your main points and leave time for questions. In your conclusion, give the teachers something they'll remember, and conclude on a positive note, reinforcing how important the job is that they are doing everyday. Leave a few minutes at the end for everyone to complete an evaluation, something that will help you become a better presenter and plan for subsequent workshops. See Figure 11.4 for a sample evaluation form for the workshop on how to administer and analyze results from an informal reading inventory.

For additional suggestions on creating useful handouts and effective visual presentations, visit our companion website.

## A Few More Hints for Success

Based on our experiences, we have a few more suggestions that may help you present a successful workshop.

1. Watch your time carefully. Don't try to cram everything into the last half hour of the workshop if you get off schedule. Speaking so fast that no one understands you and slamming one transparency after another onto the overhead (or flying through Power-Point slides) only results in frustration. As the session is winding down, mentally decide what to omit. With experience, you'll learn how much you can include in a one-hour, two-hour, three-hour, or all-day session.

ABC Elementary School
Workshop Day, February 18, 2011
Presented by Sonia Beagonea, District Reading Specialist

**IRI Workshop Evaluation**

Please respond to each of the following statements by circling the number that best represents your feelings. Use the following scale.

| Strongly Agree | Agree | No Opinion | Disagree | Strongly Disagree |
|:---:|:---:|:---:|:---:|:---:|
| 1 | 2 | 3 | 4 | 5 |

1. The rationale for today's workshop was made clear and is aligned with my personal goals and those of our school.
    1        2        3        4        5

2. This session met my expectations for the day.
    1        2        3        4        5

3. I feel confident about how to administer an Informal Reading Inventory.
    1        2        3        4        5

4. I feel confident how to analyze the results of an IRI.
    1        2        3        4        5

5. I feel I can begin to match IRI results to my comprehension instruction.
    1        2        3        4        5

6. It would be helpful to meet with my grade-level colleagues to do additional planning with the results of our students' IRIs.
    1        2        3        4        5

7. The pacing of today's session was appropriate.
    1        2        3        4        5

8. The activities in which we participated today were helpful.
    1        2        3        4        5

9. The handout will help me remember and implement today's key points.
    1        2        3        4        5

10. One idea I will remember and implement from today's workshop is:

11. One concept or idea that is still unclear to me is:

12. I would like more assistance in learning how to:

13. Overall I would rate this session as:

| Very Helpful | Helpful | Somewhat Helpful | Okay | Not Helpful |
|:---:|:---:|:---:|:---:|:---:|
| 1 | 2 | 3 | 4 | 5 |

Please write any comments you would like to share on the back of this survey or email them to me at sbeago@abcelem.edu.k12.

**FIGURE 11.4**   *Sample Workshop Evaluation*

2. You'll find in every audience three to four teachers who are with you every step of the way. You can tell by their reactions because they're nodding, smiling, engaged, and participating. Although it's important to watch for those who are looking bored and uninterested and try to enlist their participation, it's those who are engaged throughout the workshop who let you know that they've valued your time together. If you have the opportunity to thank them for their participation, do so—they'll appreciate that you noticed.

3. Last, be gentle with yourself. Even the most experienced and gifted speakers have "those days" when nothing seems to go right. Also, as you read your evaluations, even if you have 95 percent positive responses, you'll tend to dwell on the few negative comments that we all have received. If you can, read those first and learn from the remarks, if they're relevant. Then, focus on the positive comments you received because these, most likely, will be the ones that will help you improve the most.

### Conducting Workshops outside of Your District

At some point, you may find yourself in the position of being invited to give a workshop or presentation outside of your district and offered a fee for doing so. Although it is beyond the scope of this book to address the ins and outs of making such presentations, we have included a few resources for you on our companion website. There you will find information on compliance with district policy, signing contracts, and establishing fees.

## Revisiting the Vignettes

You have analyzed and compared both scenarios several times throughout this chapter. We are certain you had little difficulty identifying what went right and what went wrong in the scenarios. However, we would like to pose a third alternative to you. What if the school had not invited Norma, an outside "expert," to come in and conduct the workshop? What if, for example, you were the literacy coach or reading specialist and you and your team were planning professional development? Think about a topic related to comprehension or a strategy that fits the goals of your school.

1. How could the literacy coach or reading specialist (with the support of the team) plan and present this session?
2. List three professional development activities that might take place over the months that preceded the workshop and three professional development activities that might follow it.
3. What are the pros (there are some) and cons of having someone come in to give a focused workshop?

## Points to Remember

In the past, professional development for teachers consisted primarily of unrelated in-service sessions that were selected by principals or teachers based on availability and interest. There was little coherence within a school, and professional development opportunities often had little or nothing to do with the assessed needs of the teachers or their students. Today, professional development is considered part of a school's comprehensive plan for improving and sustaining effective literacy instruction and for recertification. Based on a comprehensive needs assessment, a professional development plan includes not only presentations and workshops, but also research, texts, discussion groups, demonstration lessons, mentoring, and coaching. Designing sessions, conducting workshops and demonstration lessons, and evaluating the effectiveness of professional development efforts represent a major responsibility of the reading specialist and literacy coach at both the school and district levels. Increasingly, stakeholders see themselves as part of a professional learning community.

## Portfolio and Self-Assessment Projects

1. Based on the needs assessment findings for your school, design a professional development plan according to the model presented in this text. Share it with your principal or other administrator.

2. Design, deliver, and evaluate the effectiveness of a one-hour workshop related to a need identified in your two-year plan. Conduct the workshop for others in your group of reading specialist candidates or for teachers in your school. Reflect on how everything went and suggest changes or additions for a future workshop on the same topic.

3. Plan and provide a demonstration lesson on a literacy topic for a teacher in your school. After you have finished the lesson, reflect on it with the teacher, both in terms of how he or she might use what you presented in his or her teaching and in terms of what you could do next time to make the lesson more effective. Also, solicit and include in your written reflections suggestions or a critique from the teacher.

## Recommended Readings: Suggestions for Book Clubs, Study Groups, and Professional Development

DuFour, R., Eaker, R., & Many, T. (2006). *Learning by doing: A handbook for professional development communities at work.* Bloomington, IN: Solution Tree Press. These authors were among the first to advocate for "the learning community" as an approach to professional development. The book demonstrates their continued commitment to educational reform as well as their continued pioneering efforts in the field.

Garmston, R. (2005). *The presenter's fieldbook: A practical guide* (2nd ed.). Norwood, MA: Christopher-Gordon. This is a wonderful resource, one that we heartily recommend. It includes all the nuts and bolts about becoming an effective presenter in the field of education.

Goldenberg, C. (2004). *Successful school change: Creating settings to improve teaching and learning.* New York: Teachers College Press. This book is about the process of changing schools by improving teaching and learning through professional development, administrator and teacher commitment, and parent involvement. It focuses on a Los Angeles elementary school in a Latino community and follows it for five years, with all the successes and frustrations. As Michael Fullan says in the Introduction, this is "a great book, which takes us far into the real dynamics of reform. It pushes the boundaries . . . and sets the stage for going to the next stage of lasting reform."

Roberts, S. M., & Pruitt, E. Z. (2009). *Schools as professional learning communities: Collaborative activities for professional development.* Thousand Oaks, CA: Corwin Press. The focus of this book reflects the new paradigms that are being embraced by educators and others who are interested in creating dynamic professional development programs. This is a particularly timely and useful book for literacy leaders, administrators, teachers, and literacy teams.

Rosemary, C. A., Roskos, K. A., & Landreth, L. K. (2007). *Designing professional development in literacy: A framework for effective instruction.* New York: Guilford Press. Written specifically for reading professionals by three highly regarded experts, this book provides comprehensive support for all components of dynamic, effective, collaborative, professional development in literacy. The evaluation section is particularly strong.

## Online Resources

**http://pdinfocus.ascd.org/LearnHow.aspx#leaders**
The official website of ASCD (formerly the Association for Supervision and Curriculum Development), an organization of over 175,000 educational leaders worldwide, has a wealth of resources. Among them you will find *Online Media and Tools for Powerful Professional Development,* a particularly helpful guide for school leaders.

**www.reading.org**
The IRA website contains resources, books, links to journal articles, and other valuable tools for professional development.

**http://www.literacycoachingonline.org/briefs/tools/Rosemary_&_Feldman_PD_setting_tool_4.5.09.pdf**
*Professional Development Setting Checklist: A Coach's Tool for Planning and Assessing Professional Learning Settings* by Catherine Rosemary and Naomi Feldman. This is one of the Literacy Coaching Clearinghouse website's Coach Tools, another well-developed resource for literacy and instructional leaders, teacher leaders, curriculum directors, and professional development facilitators.

## Companion Website Resources

The following resources to support and extend your learning with this chapter can be found on our companion website (waveland.com/Extra_Material/32979/): key vocabulary, concepts, and other terms; extended examples; updated resources specifically tied to information in the chapter; related websites; and other support features. The companion website for this chapter also includes a template for you to use as you follow the directions for completing the Sample Professional Development Plan, suggestions for creating effective handouts and visuals, and guidelines for conducting workshops and presentations outside of your district.

# Moving the Field Forward as Leaders and Literacy Advocates

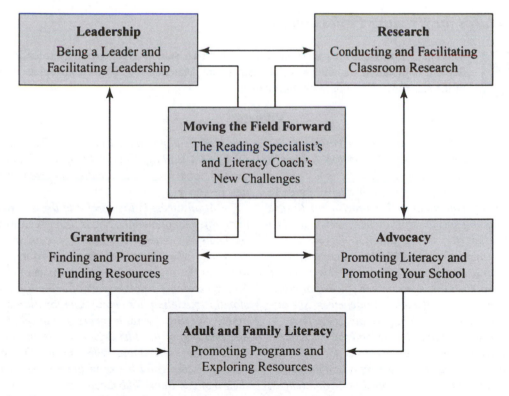

**Leadership**
Being a Leader and
Facilitating Leadership

**Research**
Conducting and Facilitating
Classroom Research

**Moving the Field Forward**
The Reading Specialist's
and Literacy Coach's
New Challenges

**Grantwriting**
Finding and Procuring
Funding Resources

**Advocacy**
Promoting Literacy and
Promoting Your School

**Adult and Family Literacy**
Promoting Programs and
Exploring Resources

**FIGURE 12.1**   *Chapter Overview*

## Learning Goals

After reading, discussing, and engaging in activities related to this chapter, you will be able to:

1. Define the characteristics of leadership as they apply to the reading specialist and literacy coach in school and community contexts.
2. Explain the importance of establishing and maintaining professional affiliations, and locate the professional resources and publications related to literacy.
3. Become familiar with the grant writing process, the sources of funding, and external support for school personnel engaged in grant writing.
4. Design and conduct classroom research and support teachers in research endeavors.
5. Understand the role of the reading specialist and literacy coach as literacy advocates.
6. Examine the issues surrounding adult literacy programs.
7. Discuss family literacy and its relationship to children's reading development.
8. *Personal Learning Goal:* Reflect on your current role as an educator. As a reading specialist and/or literacy coach, what is one goal you have for your future?

## Standards for Reading Professionals

This chapter provides focused support for current IRA Standards for Reading Professionals. See our companion website (waveland.com/Extra_Material/32979/) for a complete listing of the standards that align with this chapter.

### Vignette

When you walk into the office of Pat Ortiz, the reading specialist at Payne Elementary School in central Florida, you notice her diplomas on the wall near her desk. She has a master's degree in elementary education and a provisional license as a reading specialist while she finishes the last few classes for this additional degree. Pat is friendly and helpful to all of her colleagues, sharing ideas and support. She puts a weekly schedule of her work with students on her office door along with time slots available for conferences. She distributes a monthly literacy-related newsletter to all faculty and staff at Payne, and she has created a variety of forms that are used for referrals, assessment plans, and case reports. Pat notifies faculty about upcoming workshops, conferences, and local reading council meetings. She has established a lending library of books and journal articles, and keeps the faculty informed about new research.

At all times, Pat is careful to dress and act in a professional manner. She is never seen wearing jeans or sweatshirts to school, except on rare occasions when a special event warrants such attire. To Pat, this is an important aspect of being "a professional." Another part of being a professional is modeling her enthusiasm for literacy to others. She and several teachers, paraprofessionals, and one of the bus drivers share the latest novels they are reading with one another and openly discuss good books in the lounge during their monthly Book Club meetings.

### Thinking Points

1. What is your first reaction to Pat's ideas about professionalism?
2. If you were discussing professionalism with Pat, what would you ask her?
3. What would you share with her about your own views of being a professional?

## Expanding the Vignette: Exploring the Issues

*One Wednesday evening, in her graduate leadership, administration, and supervision class, Pat and her cohorts were discussing how rewarding it is to share their love of reading with their colleagues. They each talked about how they modeled this passion for their friends. However, Danielle appeared to be deep in thought as Pat described her beliefs about how her office should look and how she should dress while at work. Danielle was clearly disturbed and said, "You know, I'm reluctant to hang my diplomas or 'dress up' within the casual atmosphere of school. I don't want to be perceived as arrogant." Several others in the class nodded their assent and expressed similar concerns about appearing "too professional."*

### Thinking Points

1. How do you feel about Pat and Danielle's differences of opinion about "professionalism"?
2. Why might individuals perceive these issues differently?
3. What other factors might be important for Pat and her cohorts to consider?

## *Continuing the Professional Journey*

It appears we have come full circle, addressing some of the issues that concerned us as we began to write this book: What does it mean to be a reading specialist? What does it mean to be a literacy coach? What does it mean to be a professional? As individuals grow and change, they are forced to redefine their roles and their identities. Pat and her classmates are exploring these issues as they begin their careers as reading specialists and/or literacy coaches. They are asking themselves what it means to be a professional, an important question to raise. In this chapter, we will examine their concerns, emphasizing issues of leadership and professionalism. As you read the chapter, think about your responses to the questions in the vignette. We will revisit them at the end of the chapter.

The role of the reading specialist changed dramatically in the last quarter of the twentieth century; there were few if any literacy coaches. Although some aspects of the jobs remain much the same, such as working with groups of struggling readers or assisting teachers in implementing new strategies, other tasks have emerged since 2000 that require increased levels of expertise and professionalism. Mandates for high-stakes testing and calls for alignment with national, state, and local standards require reading specialists and coaches to focus beyond their schools and districts. This broadened perspective requires understanding the impact of external social and political forces on local instructional practices. The idea that the school is no longer isolated from the context of community gives rise to new awareness of our responsibility to advocate for adult and family literacy programs, too. As we discovered in Chapter 1, reading specialists and literacy coaches find themselves responsible for leading initiatives to change teacher beliefs and behaviors. In response to limited local resources and demands for accountability, they are asked to seek and obtain external funds to support literacy initiatives. The one-day workshop has been replaced by more extensive long-term professional development. Although this kind of professional support is consistent with lasting change, reading professionals are expected to be knowledgeable about all the new trends and strategies that teachers might want to learn. At the same time, the media fan the fires of dissent, perpetuating the myth that the schools don't teach enough phonics and that children in the United States cannot read. Often, teachers and administrators look to reading specialists and literacy coaches for leadership in situations involving the need for advocacy.

Today's reading professionals must, by necessity, form affiliations with networks of professionals and agencies that support the increased demands of the job. Instead of being able to answer all the questions—an impossible task—the reading specialist and/or literacy coach must know how to locate information and contact individuals with specialized expertise. The purpose of this chapter is to connect reading specialists and literacy coaches with the human, technological, and material resources needed to meet growing professional demands. We have asked experts in different areas to share their specialized knowledge. As you read this chapter, you will hear from John Brekke, a corporate consultant and an expert in leadership; Connie Erickson, an educational grant writing consultant; and Michael Ford, Professor of Reading Education at the University of Wisconsin, Oshkosh and nationally recognized expert in literacy advocacy. We have included web sources and links to professional organizations. It is our hope that you will continue to seek new ways to connect with other professionals and to support those dedicated to increasing literacy levels in our schools and communities.

We've also included an overview of issues surrounding adult literacy and family literacy. In Chapter 9 we noted that schools have intensified their attention to workplace literacy, attempting to stem the tide of students leaving our schools unprepared to meet the literacy demands necessary for employment. These initiatives resulted in heightened awareness of the enormous problems faced by the adults already out there whose literacy skills are inadequate. In addition, new initiatives for preschool children have drawn attention to the need for much greater support for family literacy programs. One of the best ways to support children's literacy development is to ensure that their parents have the skills necessary to support their families and to act as partners with the school. We realize that most teachers have little knowledge about and experience in dealing with adult and family literacy. Our purpose here is to provide a broad overview of the issues, trends, and resources available and to invite literacy professionals to become informed advocates for adult and family literacy.

## The Reading Specialist and the Literacy Coach as Leaders

Reading specialists and coaches are increasing their visibility as leaders. They are on the front lines, implementing the changes mandated by others, but also shaping the future by fostering changes from within. If they attempt to coerce teachers, even in well-intentioned and pedagogically sound initiatives, they are doomed to fail. Today's definitions of leadership involve shared goals and collaboration. The leader is the one who invites and inspires others to "buy in" to a vision. A true leader seeks to help individuals discover their leadership potential and finds ways to foster those qualities. Often, this means "leading from behind" or "guiding from the side": mentoring, supporting, and encouraging others.

### OTHER VOICES: John L. Brekke

*The following excerpts are from a taped interview on leadership given by corporate consultant John L. Brekke for inclusion in this book. John's clients include the CEOs of a handful of the largest corporations in the United States. As a former educator and administrator in higher education, John draws on his experiences in the corporate and academic worlds to share his expertise with us.*

## On the Five Qualities of Effective Leaders

Leadership is one of those terms that I will not attempt to define, but I'll talk about the qualities of leadership, as I understand them. Years ago, leadership was defined in terms of competencies. I think *management* is defined in terms of competencies, and I think *leadership* has to do with qualities or characteristics of the people who are followed. I'm going to mention five of these qualities. They are certainly applicable to the world in which I work.

The five qualities I am going to talk about are derived from a variety of collated sources, including those firms that spend their lifetimes studying leadership, some academics who study this, and firms that specialize in placing leaders in senior management positions.

The first is *strategic thinking*. Strategic thinking, from my standpoint, simply means the ability to step back and take a look at the large picture; and, as a result of seeing that larger picture, to create a vision for the future of the organization. People who are strategic often talk about "implications thinking." If they are addressing a decision or trying to solve a problem, they readily ask, "What are the implications of the solution, of this decision, of this reorganization?" I think being strategic assumes the ability to act on the strategies that have been put in place.

The second quality or characteristic is *people-relatedness*. For many years we've heard of "management by walking around" within organizations whereby the bosses touched the lives of the individuals on a regular basis. And that's even more important today. What employees are really saying is, "I want to be recognized as a person who is contributing to the organization," or "I want to be seen as somebody who's valued by my boss and I want that boss, that person, to come to my area and have a conversation with me there."

The third quality or characteristic is really two words that have been, in the last few years, paired: *urgency and accountability*. I'm convinced these attributes are inextricably linked. The fast-paced nature of the workplace demands that decisions be made more quickly at the appropriate level. That is a very important qualifier—*decisions made more quickly, at the appropriate level, by people who are then held responsible*. It's a pretty simple formula. But it can get messed up rather quickly if decisions become too much of a deliberative thing or if bosses assume that they should be making all of the decisions. As long as people feel they have that authority to be making those decisions, regardless of where they are in that organization, then they expect that they will be held accountable.

Number four is what is called *cultural attention*. Employees are looking to the leadership in organizations to create organizations that are focused, provide opportunities for personal growth, demand personal excellence, and are employee-friendly. People understand that culture is constantly emerging and it's not haphazard. As organizations are being restructured today, cultures will emerge, even if you don't give attention to it. In time, you will be able to define the behaviors that support the culture of the organization. The challenge, of course, is to make sure that the behaviors are appropriate behaviors. Therefore, the cultural creation process is a very conscious and continuing effort by leaders within an organization.

The last attribute, or quality, is *coaching*. I am convinced that the most important thing leaders can do in this day and age is to devote themselves to coaching others. A couple of magical things happen. One is not unlike the process of teaching. I went to college and I went to graduate school and I supposedly learned some things for which I was qualified to teach. But, I really didn't learn that material until I was put into a position to teach. That's when it dawned on me that I better know this stuff. I better know this stuff at least well enough to be asking the provocative question in the classroom that would lead to the students learning. In like manner, those people who put themselves in the role of a coach—coaching others—much more consciously understand what leadership is all about.

■ *Group Inquiry Activity*  The five principles of leadership John Brekke described were presented in the context of the corporate world although they are relevant to the world of the reading specialist/literacy coach. In your group, for each of the five principles, describe a situation in which a reading specialist or literacy coach could apply it in a specific school setting.

1. Strategic thinking
2. People-relatedness
3. Urgency and accountability
4. Cultural attention
5. Coaching

John's ideas about leadership demonstrate that leaders in corporations, too, recognize the role of cultures within organizations. Our perspective moves us away from the rigid definitions and boundaries we draw around concepts such as leadership. New views of mentorship are more egalitarian, often involving shared support in identifying and attaining goals. An outgrowth of these ideas is that, increasingly, compromise is no longer viewed as the best way to solve problems. When two people compromise, both sacrifice a portion of their goals. In effect, it's a lose–lose proposition, such as when teachers have to lose part of their teaching identities in order to adopt a new strategy being imposed on them. No wonder they resist.

Newer forms of leadership stress approaching seemingly contradictory goals by finding ways to produce win–win situations. Reading specialists and coaches who understand this stop trying to "get" teachers to do things their way. They sit down with the teachers and find ways to support what goes on in the classroom and find compatible strategies that foster change in nonthreatening ways, much like the secondary literacy coach we described in Chapter 9. Smart leaders start with a shared goal. They understand that what impels a person to change is the desire to find a better way to reach a goal he or she already embraces. That's a win–win situation.

## ■ *Author Connections: Brenda and MaryEllen*

### *The Role of the Reading Specialist/Literacy Coach as a Professional*

Historically, a course in leadership, administration, and supervision is taken at the end of the master's degree or advanced certification program. Through the years, both of us noticed that something important happened as our students in this course progressed through the semester: They became professionals in ways that were readily apparent but difficult to describe. These individuals changed their perceptions of themselves and crossed a threshold from literacy teachers to literacy professionals. If ever there were proof that identity is socially constructed, it occurred in this class. As the weeks passed and students engaged in passionate discussions involving real-life problems that were situated in their schools and communities, their sharing took on deeper dimensions. The group developed cohesiveness as the teachers became more and more willing to take risks with their peers by sharing problems that occasionally elicited tears and by confiding what they still didn't know or understand. We found these to be the teachable moments; living vignettes that provided us with the kinds of authentic group problem-solving that can make or break a reading specialist or literacy coach. Many of these inspired the vignettes and examples in this book.

When we were students in our graduate supervision course in the old days, we discussed professionalism as "trait theory." "A professional is an extrovert." "A professional is confident." Our textbooks even reminded us about good grooming, including perfume, hair, and makeup! We never even questioned the assumption that reading specialists were all women. If you had asked us to define professionalism, we would have rattled off a set of attributes with a fair degree of confidence. How ironic that the more we learn about social constructivism, the less we are able to define professionalism as a static construct. We are not so sure we know what it means to be a professional because it (like so much else) seems to depend on the context.

So the question, "What is a professional?" depends on who's asking and who's answering. Each person will answer the question based on a variety of culturally and socially constructed beliefs and values, further shaped by life experiences and the context of the school and community in which the person teaches. Is it possible that Pat, in this chapter's vignette, will be perceived as a professional in one school or community and as an elitist in another? We suspect that it is more helpful to define a professional by what the person does in a given setting than by what the person *is*.

■ ***Group Inquiry Activity*** *Think–Pair–Share:* On your own, write your answers to the following questions. Share your ideas with a partner and create a Venn diagram comparing and contrasting your ideas.

1. Describe how you would model "professionalism" in your school and community.
2. How would you describe what the reading specialist or literacy coach (as a professional) does within this context?
3. What are the beliefs and cultural influences from your childhood and adulthood that influenced your answer?
4. Which attitudes, beliefs, and needs of your school influenced your answer?
5. Which aspects of your university experiences shaped your answer?

As you negotiated ideas and definitions of professionalism, you may have found these questions limited in scope, dealing with external and superficial aspects of professionalism. To assist you in reflecting on what a literacy professional does, we developed a few questions. We hope you will consider them with regard to your particular social, cultural, and professional context.

*Questions for the Reading Professional*

1. How does a literacy professional interact with administrators? With colleagues?
2. In what ways is a reading specialist and/or literacy coach like and unlike other classroom teachers?
3. What are the obligations of a professional with regard to dissemination and implementation of ideas and strategies? Is there any difference between the ways peer teachers interact in a shared lesson and the way a reading specialist or literacy coach might interact in a shared lesson?
4. Is there a kind of "professionalism" that distinguishes reading specialists and literacy coaches from their peers?
5. What is the obligation of the professional with regard to:
   • remaining current in literacy-related research and practice;
   • assisting teachers' use of technology to enhance literacy and content learning;
   • the balance between working with students and helping teachers;
   • engaging in advocacy for literacy for students, adults, and families;
   • belonging to professional organizations and developing presentations;
   • sharing expertise with teachers and in what manner;
   • securing external funds;
   • reading, understanding, and disseminating journal articles, website lists, and other resources;
   • leading professional development; and
   • engaging in community outreach and service?

We hope you will add to the list of questions over the course of your career. Because professionalism is not a static concept, you need not be so concerned about defining the word *professionalism*. It is more helpful for you to ask, "How did the idea of *professionalism* come to mean what it does to me?"

As reading specialists and literacy coaches, we believe that we should be engaging in each of the behaviors listed in the previous section. Therefore, what follows are some suggestions for how to become involved in professional organizations and professional endeavors.

## Involvement in Professional Organizations

As a reading specialist and literacy coach, you have the right to be served by professional organizations, but, as a professional, you also have the *obligation* to serve your chosen association. Membership in local councils, state associations, and IRA provides reading specialists and literacy coaches with the opportunity to participate in what Gee (2001a, 2001b) describes as "affinity groups." Recall that affinity groups are formed by individuals who share a common goal, culture, or interest, and have a common discourse or way of using language when they interact within the group. Especially in small communities, reading specialists and literacy coaches often feel like isolates. Active membership in literacy organizations allows for sharing of problems and insights that advance the collective expertise. Large associations such as the International Reading Association and many state

reading associations provide a wealth of online information, access to res
tioner journals, and opportunities to attend outstanding conferences.

Opportunities for service and leadership within local, state, and
plentiful. We hope you will feel an obligation to serve these organizations by assuming
leadership roles, engaging in committee work, and sharing your ideas and innovative teaching strategies through presentations and journal articles. Reading specialists and literacy
coaches often volunteer for special events such as Reading in the Mall, Books for Babes
(for new mothers in the hospital), Book Drives, or Young Authors' Conferences—all of
which are regularly sponsored by various local and state reading associations. Both of us
have served as presidents of our local and state reading associations and in 2004–2005,
MaryEllen served as IRA president. We mention this not only because we want to reinforce
or encourage your participation, but also because we have found that it's virtually impossible to "burn out" when you're involved with other professionals who remain committed to
improving literacy. Professional organizations are important and effective support groups.
We hope you will investigate the opportunities for professional affiliation and growth
offered by the literacy-related organizations listed in the next section.

## Professional Organizations for Educators

***International Reading Association (IRA).*** This professional organization, with a membership of over 90,000 literacy professionals, serves as a clearinghouse for reading research
and provides information through conferences and publications. The goal of IRA is to
improve the quality of literacy instruction for all and to promote lifelong literacy learning
throughout the world. The International Reading Association serves as the parent organization for over 1,200 local and state reading councils with over 300,000 affiliate members in
more than 100 countries. On the IRA website (www.reading.org) you will find information
on how to become involved in your state associations and local reading councils. Publications of IRA include *The Reading Teacher, The Journal of Adolescent and Adult Literacy,
Reading Research Quarterly,* and the quarterly news magazine, *Reading Today.* IRA also
has a large publishing division and each year it introduces a wide variety of new book titles
related to reading and language arts. You also might find the IRA position statements to be
of use in your school and district.

***National Reading Conference (NRC).*** This important research organization has as its
members university researchers and teacher educators, graduate students, and reading specialists, all of whom share an interest in and commitment to conducting and disseminating
the results of cutting-edge literacy research. NRC's website (www.nrconline.org) has links
to white papers that synthesize research addressing key topics in literacy. NRC publications
include the annual *Yearbook of the National Reading Conference* and *Journal of Literacy
Research.*

***National Council of Teachers of English (NCTE).*** This organization is dedicated to
improving the learning of English and language arts in all areas of education, and its members include elementary and secondary English teachers, reading specialists, and others
interested in English education. On the website (www.ncte.org) there are many opportunities available to teachers for professional growth and a forum to discuss issues related to the

teaching of English. There is also a free weekly newsletter of ideas, articles, and connections for those who teach reading/language arts on the NCTE website (www.ncte.org). Among the publications of NCTE are *Language Arts, Voices from the Middle, The English Journal,* and *Classroom Notes Plus.*

***American Library Association (ALA).*** Members of ALA include teachers, reading specialists, media specialists, and librarians. The organization addresses areas of diversity, professional development, literacy programs, equal access, and protecting intellectual freedom (www.ala.org). ALA also honors outstanding children's book authors and illustrators each year with the Newbury and Caldecott Awards.

***ASCD (formerly the Association for Supervision and Curriculum Development).*** The members of this organization are professionals with the common goal of providing excellence in education and creating success for all learners (www.ascd.org). The primary journal of ASCD is *Educational Leadership,* and the association is known for its videotapes and books, which are available through its publishing division.

***National Middle School Association (NMSA).*** This organization (www.nmsa.org) serves professionals, parents, and others who are interested in the educational and developmental needs of young adolescents (ages 10 to 15). Its publications include *The Middle School Journal* and a monthly magazine entitled *Middle Ground.* The organization holds an Annual Literacy Leaders Institute.

***National Staff Development Council (NSDC).*** This is the largest organization dedicated to ensuring the academic success of students through staff development and school improvement. The organization is a resource for high-quality staff development programs and instructional materials (www.nsdc.org).

***Teachers of English to Speakers of Other Languages, Inc. (TESOL).*** The mission of TESOL is for its members to be able to communicate effectively in diverse settings and respect the language rights of others (www.tesol.org).

It is important that reading specialists and literacy coaches remain informed of the current research and practice in literacy through the major publications in the field, particularly *The Reading Teacher* (elementary), *Journal of Adolescent and Adult Literacy* (adolescent through adult), *Reading Today,* and *Reading Research Quarterly,* all publications of the International Reading Association (IRA). Sharing articles and current news about literacy issues with colleagues is an essential role of all reading specialists/literacy coaches.

## *Writing Successful Grant Proposals*

Securing outside funding for special literacy projects is becoming a commonplace task for reading specialists. Numerous websites support teachers in locating funds for specific purposes and guiding them through the writing process. We list a few of these sources for you at the end of this chapter. We also urge you to read Jim Burke and Carol Prater's (2000) very informative book on grant writing. You can locate other resources through organizations such as the International Reading Association, your state Department of Public Instruction, or agencies such as the Cooperative Educational State Agencies (CESA).

## OTHER VOICES: Connie Erickson

*Because of her expertise at writing grants and assisting teachers and schools in securing funds, we asked Connie Erickson to share her best advice about successful grant writing. Connie began writing grants almost twenty years ago as a young media specialist right out of college. Within the last few years, she left her school district in rural Wisconsin to become a full-time educational grant consultant for CESA #11 and has since become Director of Instructional Services.*

A number of years ago, I was in the grocery store with my then 5-year-old son, Daniel, and was just ready to pay our bill when I realized that I had forgotten my checkbook. As I dug through my purse, looking for my credit card or cash, Daniel declared to the young cashier "Oh, that's OK. My mom will just write you out a grant." If only it were that easy!

It is no secret that writing grant proposals can be a time-consuming and complicated process. Successful grants are most often done in a collaborative manner, involving as many of the stakeholders as possible. Gathering people together and meeting deadlines requires organization and patience at the same time. Although this may be enough to deter the average person from stepping into the grant writing arena, most educators have a leg up on the process from the start: Teachers work like this each and every day!

Grants are so much more than money. Learning how to develop and write successful grant proposals can provide opportunities for your students and school districts that traditional funding cannot afford. Many schools have historically looked for grant funding to support "things" such as computers, books, and facilities. In fact, more and more funding sources are awarding grants to projects that strengthen professional development, provide new learning experiences for teachers and students, and promote a stronger relationship between school and community resources.

Despite the fact that each grant program will have its own guidelines, these useful hints should help get your proposal started:

1. Determine Your Outcomes
   - What problem or need do you hope to address in the grant? Design the project backward from these outcomes.
2. Begin with Data; End with Data
   - What data do you have to support your need?
   - Find current research to support your project idea. You do not have to reinvent the wheel, but you can't simply jump on someone else's bandwagon either.
   - Assess everything, using a variety of methods that will provide feedback on your project's objectives and goals.
3. Do Your Homework
   - Attend workshops and contact people who have worked on grants before to gather information on the process.
   - Learn about funding sources and guidelines.

- Ask for last year's winning grant proposals.
- Create a timeline with deadlines.

4. Gather District Support for the Project
   - Make sure that key administrative personnel are aware of your proposal. Invite and encourage help from district leaders in the beginning: You may need their support during the implementation phase.
   - Many grants require matching or "in kind" funds from your district. Depending on the grant, items such as volunteer time, transportation expenses, and even facility costs may be used.
   - Circumstances can exist where districts are limited to the number of federal and state grants for which they can apply. Be sure to ask.

5. Follow the Rules
   - Warning: About one-third of all grant proposals are thrown out because they do not follow directions. Review the guidelines and have others do the same.
   - Do not assume anything about the grant evaluators: Spell everything out for them.
   - Do not edit your own work. Have outside people read and evaluate your proposal. If they do not understand it, chances are the grant evaluators will probably have questions as well.
   - Stay true to your goals. Do not stray.
   - Do not send anything extra. Keep it concise.

## *Role of the Reading Specialist/Literacy Coach in Supporting Classroom Research*

It has only been within the last twenty years that large numbers of teachers have begun to see themselves as researchers. Until that time, research was seen as the province of the university, not the school. When teachers began to recognize research as a process with four basic components—asking a compelling question, gathering data systematically, analyzing the data, and translating their insights into classroom practice—they realized research was at the heart of reflective practice. Good "kid watchers" do it every day. The difference is that systematic data gathering around a specific question transforms reflective practice into inquiry.

The reading professional has the potential to be a catalyst in the process of fostering classroom research too, collaborating with a teacher or a group on research planning, and conducting research together. The process might start during a casual conversation in which a teacher mentions a new project, strategy, or question. The reading specialist/literacy coach might reply, "What an interesting idea. What do you think about conducting classroom research together to investigate this?" The ideal is when a group of teachers share an interest in a common question and decide to engage in a group research project. Topics for classroom research might arise from teacher study groups formed during the implementation of the two-year plan. Just as we are on the alert for the "teachable moment" with our students, we must be aware of the "researchable moment" when we can foster classroom research.

Reading specialists and literacy coaches collaborate with teachers by:

- Developing a clear research question, one that can lead to data collection, and defining terms used to frame the research. The question can be open-ended and need not require statistical data. For example, a teacher might ask, "How will daily sustained silent reading increase the amount of voluntary recreational reading I observe in my classroom?"
- Locating related research and providing a rationale for the study; explaining why the research is important; and sharing publications such as *The Reading Teacher* to locate information on the topic.
- Selecting and developing systematic observational and performance data that are appropriate to the question and preserving the integrity of complex, situated classroom events. For example, if you want to find out whether a certain strategy will improve children's story writing, but you are only measuring spelling and grammar, your methods are inadequate for answering your question. Collecting writing samples from a child over time and comparing patterned elements in them is a much more authentic and informative approach to the question. In the case of our question about the effects of sustained silent reading (SSR) on voluntary reading, the teacher could designate one day a week in which she or he counts the number of books being read during times of free choice.
- Analyzing the data. In our SSR example, perhaps the teacher finds that recreational reading has increased dramatically, and has the data to prove it.
- Asking "So what?" Now that the teacher knows the impact of SSR on amounts of recreational reading, what will the teacher do in the classroom? The choice seems clear. She or he will most likely continue with the practice of SSR.

The process may end when "So What?" is answered, but we suggest you invite teachers to go one step further and publish their findings. The reading specialist or literacy coach can help a teacher or group start by writing an article about the research project for the local council newsletter. However, we suggest you attempt to write for your state reading journal or a similar publication. We also suggest you study articles from the publication to which you will submit your work. What is the structure of these articles? What kinds of discourses are used? What kinds of articles and topics seem to "fit" in this publication? The two of you or the study group can meet weekly to work on the writing project. We have witnessed how thrilling it is for a teacher to see his or her name on that first article. The process changes individuals and the way they view themselves as professionals. This sort of mentorship by the reading specialist is very much in the spirit of leadership advocated by John Brekke in his advice to us.

## *The Reading Specialist and Literacy Coach as Literacy Advocates*

As political forces and various constituency groups attempt to advance their agendas for school reading programs, IRA has recognized the need for literacy educators to develop a strong collective voice to explain and defend their practices. State and local literacy organizations acknowledge that these debates often take place in local arenas. Therefore, it is essential to join local and state literacy groups that collect and disseminate research, information, and materials that can be used to address school boards, politicians, and the media.

## OTHER VOICES: Michael Ford

*Michael Ford, Professor of Reading Education at the University of Wisconsin Oshkosh, is a nationally recognized leader in issues related to advocacy. Michael received a grant from the Gertrude Whipple Professional Program through the International Reading Association to compile* Advocacy for Best Practice: Resource Materials for Reading Educators. *This rich resource contains research-based information to defend sound practice, transparencies and other materials to aid educators in making presentations, and a variety of supportive resource material. We asked Mike to share some ideas about advocacy with you. You can find this and other advocacy resources at http://www.wsra.org/committees/advocacy.php.*

It wasn't until their local school district threatened to eliminate the Reading Recovery program they had helped to secure and implement that three teachers, Barbara Keresty, Susan O'Leary, and Dale Wortley, found the need to become political. They came together, organized, prepared, and successfully fought for the survival of the program in which they believed deeply. They reminded many of us that when teachers become activists, they can influence policy decisions. They wrote of their story and strategies in *You Can Make a Difference: A Teacher's Guide to Political Action* (Keresty, O'Leary, & Wortley, 1998). Their message is still relevant.

This battle, like most others, reminds reading specialists that the most important advocacy efforts take place at the local level. Even when proposed policy changes at the state and federal levels have the power of impacting local reading programs, advocacy through local representatives may be the best way to influence decisions being made beyond the building or district level.

With increasing public and political scrutiny of reading programs, many reading specialists find themselves defending practices as often as they do implementing them. It is important to be reminded of a few key guidelines for effective local advocacy efforts.

- First, pick your battles wisely. Some critics are more interested in arguing than they are in the arguments. Save your time and energy for those families and stakeholders who have genuine concerns about local reading programs. Respond to critical issues with receptive audiences to maximize the impact of your efforts.
- Second, be able to anticipate what the opposing side is going to say and then prepare your response accordingly. When critics choose to indict local programs using aggregated data and generalized information indicting programs everywhere, local advocates must clearly respond with accurate local data, program descriptions, and specific documentation.
- Finally, network with others. Join local and state organizations that bring you into contact with material and human resources that can assist local advocacy efforts. When frustrated by how your single voice is marginalized, join with others to help turn up your volume.

### ■ *Group Inquiry Activity*

1. What, if any, groups or individuals have tried to influence reading instruction in your own district, community, or states? Who are these people and what is their agenda? What is their background? Why are they trying to influence reading instruction? Who has their ear?

2. What has been the response to these individuals of your school board? Of your local reading council? Of your local and state politicians?

3. If you are involved in your local reading council, do you have a legislative or advocacy chairperson? If not, what can you do to help establish such a position? If you are not involved in your local reading council, get involved! This is *your* professional organization!

Mike Ford has assembled a wealth of information on the Wisconsin State Reading Association (WSRA) website (http://www.wsra.org/committees/advocacy.php). The materials can be easily adapted to address specific local issues. If you need materials to use in a presentation to your school board or a parent or community group, Mike's materials are essential.

One of the goals of the International Reading Association is *Advocacy,* and we encourage you also to take advantage of the publications, the assistance from the Division of Governmental Relations, and the wide variety of position statements and standards (e.g., the Standards for Reading Professionals, Standards for Secondary Literacy Coaches, and the Standards for Reading/Language Arts). Particularly if you have an interest in advocacy but perhaps not the "know-how," these resources can be very helpful.

A very practical book on advocacy published by the IRA is titled *Educators on the Frontline: Advocacy Strategies for Your Classroom, Your School, and Your Profession* (Lewis, Jongsma, & Berger, 2005). As literacy professionals and leaders who may ask, "Why me?," the authors respond: "The answer is simple: You have knowledge and experience that you need to share, You have information that no one else can give. It is easy for the naysayer or the skeptic to sit back and say that the opinions of individuals do not count and that no one will pay attention to an individual's interests or concerns . . . [but] your conversations with local officials, business leaders, and school board members can make a difference" (pp. 15–16).

In addition, Allen Berger (1997) suggests we write editorials and articles and send them to mainstream publications *before* we are under attack. This makes so much sense to us that it is surprising we often fail to think about it. His advice on how to write an article for a newspaper is to turn the usual journal article upside down. A journal article doesn't present *findings* until near the end. It starts by describing what happened in the past, followed by what is happening in the present, and giving suggestions for the future. Berger suggests you begin your article for the public by telling what you found out and then telling how it connects with past research (p. 8).

He also recommends that teachers read and edit one another's drafts. In addition to articles, the reading specialist or literacy coach can suggest writing a joint or collaborative editorial. Projects such as these transform teachers into advocates and published professionals. They transform and energize reading specialists and literacy coaches, too. Good advice seems to stand the test of time.

### Revisiting the Vignette: Thinking Points

1. Think about how you addressed Pat's struggle with defining herself as a professional.
2. Are there any additional insights you gained as you read and discussed the ideas in this chapter?
3. What advice would you give Pat if you were in her graduate course in leadership, administration, and supervision?

## *Adult Literacy and Family Literacy*

### *Adult Literacy*

According to the U.S. Department of Education (USDE), National Center for Education Statistics (2007) Report, *The Condition of Education 2007* (NCES 2007–064), the literacy level of 60 million adults in the United States places them at the *Below Basic* level, indicating they possess no more than the most simple and concrete literacy skills in:

- *Quantitative literacy* (the knowledge and ability to perform computations, either singly or sequentially);
- *Prose literacy* (the knowledge necessary to comprehend, search, and understand information in connected text, such as paragraphs); and
- *Document literacy* (the knowledge and ability to read and understand nonconnected text such as information on medicine bottles or bills, directions for assembling that new bookshelf, or applying for a passport).

The official USDE definition of the term *literacy* is: "using printed and written material to function in society, to achieve one's goals, and to develop one's knowledge and potential." Every year the U.S. government provides basic literacy services to more than a million adults, defined as "people age 16 or older living in households or prisons."

Few would argue that we have an enormous amount of data at our fingertips to indicate the literacy achievement levels of *school-age children*. (You need only pick up a newspaper or turn on the television to hear the latest grade-by-grade, school-by-school, and state-by-state comparisons of the standardized test scores of our nation's children.) The same is not true for adults. At the time of this writing, the latest statistics that were derived from a large-scale assessment of adult literacy proficiency were collected in 2003 by the National Assessment of Adult Literacy (NAAL). Similar data had last been gathered in 1992. The initial report of findings on these data came from *A First Look at the Literacy of America's Adults in the Twenty-First Century* (Kutner, Greenberg, & Baer, 2005) and was followed by a USDE Institute for Education Sciences (IES) report titled *Trends in Adult Literacy* (2007), which further analyzed the results against comparable data from 1992. The full report is available at http://nces.ed.gov/programs/coe/2007/section2/indicator18.asp.

Adult literacy is one of the few areas in which instruction is provided almost exclusively by volunteers. Despite the gains made in knowledge about effective methods of literacy instruction, training qualified volunteers remains a challenge. There appears to be strong momentum for increasing professional development in adult literacy education programs, just as there is in our schools. The National Institute for Adult Literacy and other organizations are devoting more attention to professional development, and there are grant opportunities available for research and program development.

At first it is surprising to find that research cited on studies related to adult literacy is often more than a decade old. However, this makes sense. Think about how hard it must be to identify whom you should include, to have them agree to allow you to use their data, and then to gather sample data on individuals who are scattered throughout society. How would you assess them? How would you get a representative sample? How would you ensure uniform data gathering procedures? How would you measure *prose* literacy, *document* literacy, and *quantitative* literacy? It is difficult to imagine the costs in terms of dollars, time, and human resources associated with such an undertaking. If you are interested in the methodology used or a breakdown of the statistics along lines of gender and ethnicity, you can obtain the full report on the Condition of Education in 2007 at http://ies.ed.gov/pubsearch/pubsinfo.asp?pubid=2007064.

There are issues and challenges with regard to adult literacy practices and programs and areas in need of research. They include:

- A general lack of awareness on the part of the public and educators about the scope and seriousness of the state of adult literacy.
- The ability to respond to the ever-growing numbers of adult English learners.
- The need for improved core training and continued professional development for teachers.
- The absence of full-time career path literacy teachers.
- A lack of client-specific records or management data in many local programs, needed to analyze and improve their effectiveness.
- Waiting lists for those attempting to get adult literacy services.
- The high degree of teacher turnover. (Smith, H. V., & Hofer, D., 2003)

We have long known that:

1. Pedagogical methods and materials that are effective for children may be quite inappropriate for adults.
2. The majority of adults in a literacy program stay for no longer than six months before terminating the program, even though this amount of time is almost always insufficient for meeting academic and personal goals.
3. Many adults reenter programs, a cycle that prolongs the duration of literacy acquisition over a long period of time. (Venezky, Sabatini, Brooks, & Carino, 1996)

## BEYOND THE BOOK

### *Chapter 12 Focus Issue: Adult Literacy*
We are not surprised that adults have a difficult time remaining in these adult literacy programs. To get an understanding of how difficult this might be, choose a partner and briefly answer the following questions:

1. Have you ever started an exercise program or any other lessons and not followed through?
2. What's one thing you do poorly or with which you have always struggled?

3. Do you enjoy doing it? Why or why not?
4. How has it made you feel every time you had to do it?
5. How difficult would it be to work on that activity for at least an hour every day?
6. Do you think you could sustain it for one full year? Why or why not?

---

We hope this Beyond the Book activity provides you with new insight and compassion for adults who struggle to survive with inadequate literacy skills. In times of economic hardship, we realize they are among the first to suffer the loss of employment. The IRA website (www.reading.org) is a wonderful source of information on both adult and family literacy.

A generation ago, most people associated adult literacy with helping an individual learn to read well enough to secure a General Education Diploma (GED). Although this continues to be an important component of adult literacy programs, the field has greatly broadened its mission. Programs today reflect the complex and changing demographics of society, the increasing literacy demands brought about by advances in technology, the health-related issues surrounding inadequate literacy, the needs of English learners, and the importance of developing critical literacy skills that require technical, social, and mathematical reasoning. Government and private agencies are also incorporating measures to enhance accountability and improve professional development.

***The USDE National Institute for Adult Literacy.*** The National Institute for Adult Literacy (NIAL) is the official government adult literacy organization. In 2009, NIAL identified the key issues defining its mission as follows:

The Institute seeks to strengthen literacy across the lifespan, including for adults. It has also played an important role in bringing research to the forefront of the government's efforts to strengthen adult literacy services and reading instruction. The Institute:

- Identifies scientifically based research findings to support responses and answers to questions about adult literacy.
- Disseminates those findings to educators, families, and caregivers in plain language in publications such as its Teaching Adults to Read Summary of the five essential components of reading.
- Examines professional development practices that support adult literacy instruction.
- Identifies topics to be studied in future research on adult literacy.

The institute's website (http://www.nifl.gov/adult/adult.html) provides full access to comprehensive government information, resources, program locations, grant opportunities, support networks, professional development materials, and more.

***ProLiteracy.*** State agencies, public and privately supported literacy centers, and technical and community colleges are at the forefront of adult literacy programming and instruction. One of the largest and best-known international nonprofit organizations is ProLiteracy (www.proliteracy.org). ProLiteracy was formed when Laubach Literacy International, one of the pioneers in adult literacy, merged with Literacy Volunteers of America, Inc. in 2002.

ProLiteracy assumes a more global stance toward literacy. Its mission statement reflects a strong commitment to advocacy, promoting the power of literacy to end poverty, injustice, discrimination, and violence. It is dedicated to empowering adults to make a better life and world for their families, thus enabling them to support the literacy development and school performance of their children. The following statement from the ProLiteracy website encapsulates the organization's mission: "We know that literacy helps families be healthier, support themselves through work, be better citizens, and create a more fair and just society" (ProLiteracy, 2008).

If you are interested in learning more about adult literacy programs or would like to become more involved through advocacy or volunteerism, visit any of the sites discussed in this chapter, or visit our companion website for links to adult literacy organizations.

## Family Literacy

What is *family literacy?* According to the National Center for Family Literacy (NCFL), it's a practical solution that addresses the root of devastating social problems: low literacy rates and poverty. The goal of family literacy programs is to develop literacy and life skills for every member of the family (http://www.famlit.org/ncfl-and-family-literacy/what-is-family-literacy). The foundation of such programs is the premise that both parents *and* their children learn best when they learn together—building essential skills for success in school and for competing in today's global economy. Critics of family literacy programs argue that a research vacuum exists in relation to the most effective ways for programs to work with families and children (Yaden & Paratore, 2003). Although family literacy programs claim to have the power to break the destructive cycle of poverty, unemployment, poor health, and inadequate housing, research is needed to determine which elements of such programs work. Some of the best evidence we have (Hannon, 2003) focuses on their ability to enhance the achievement of children enrolled in early childhood programs such as Even Start and Head Start. Family literacy programs work hard to provide families with the skills they need today as well as those that will be needed for tomorrow's generations. For these parents or caregivers, family literacy programs may provide an important link to school.

The current Adult Education and Family Literacy Act suggests that family literacy programs integrate (1) interactive literacy activities between parent and child, (2) training in parenting activities, (3) literacy training that leads to economic self-sufficiency, and (4) age-appropriate education to prepare children for success in school and life experiences. These family literacy programs generally work with both individuals and the family as a unit. Participants include parents, children, single parents, and other close family members.

Sharon Darling and Laura Westberg (2005) of the National Center for Family Literacy found that systematic training of parents in how to engage with their children while they are learning to read (e.g., teaching reading strategies rather than just listening to children read) resulted in greater academic gains for the children. Further, it was found that when parent involvement activities incorporated information about their children's literacy development, parents supported their children's reading acquisition while improving their own.

We are interested in discovering whether the increasingly significant role parents are assuming in RtI will lead to a greater focus on family literacy in our schools. Family involvement seems to have the greatest benefits for children from the poorest families. Heather Weiss, Director of the Harvard Graduate School of Education's Family Research Project, and her colleagues (Weiss, Dearing, Mayer, Kreider, & McCartney, 2005) found that high levels of family involvement were more strongly associated with average literacy performance between kindergarten and fifth grade for children whose mothers had less than a high school education compared with children whose mothers had relatively higher levels of education. It seems almost inevitable that if we expect parents to become our partners, we will have to provide them with the support they need to do so. This is particularly relevant for the large number of children and adults who are English learners. Family literacy may well be one of the next frontiers for research followed by action. Although we have a strong base on which to build, resources have fallen far behind need.

The structure of family literacy centers and programs is much like those established to address adult literacy. In fact, many public and private foundations and literacy centers have programs for both adult literacy and family literacy. In addition, many work closely with affiliated government and privately funded agencies that share the mission. Two high-profile nonprofits are the National Center for Family Literacy (NCFL) and the Barbara Bush Foundation.

***National Center for Family Literacy (NCFL).*** Among the best-known national nonprofit organizations supporting family literacy is the National Center for Family Literacy (NCFL), dedicated to building a more literate and prosperous nation by helping parents and children learn together. NCFL's reputation for pioneering and refining various family literacy models is built on years of helping to improve the lives of our nation's most at-risk children and families. The organization's work is cited frequently in news and research venues because of its innovative, high-quality programs and its impressive results. The NCFL website is http:www.famlit.org.

***The Barbara Bush Foundation for Family Literacy.*** The Barbara Bush Foundation has been a powerful force for promoting both adult and family literacy. As the wife of President George Herbert Walker Bush, Barbara Bush was able to use her leverage with the media and her access to those with power to bring literacy issues into the spotlight. Literacy advocates discovered, in Barbara Bush, one of their most passionate and devoted activists and champions. Since 1989, the foundation she helped create and that bears her name has provided millions of dollars to almost 500 family literacy programs in practically every state as well as Washington, D.C. For information on the work of the foundation, visit http://www.barbarabushfoundation.org.

Many of the initiatives for family and adult literacy and family literacy are supported and sponsored by business. This is not a coincidence. As we have seen, illiteracy is expensive. We know it costs industry millions, and it fills our prisons. If you need any convincing about the importance of family literacy initiatives, this powerful statement by the National Center for Family Literacy says it all:

Time and again, family literacy proves to break down other barriers to success, such as poverty, unemployment, poor health and inadequate housing. When parents struggle with literacy and basic life skills, their children have fewer chances for success. Family literacy reverses this destructive cycle by giving families the tools they need to thrive today, and most importantly, by helping them educate generations of tomorrow. (www.famlit.org/ncfl-and-family-literacy/what-is-family-literacy)

## Opportunities in Adult and Family Literacy

Obviously we are barely able to scratch the surface of issues related to adult and family literacy in a book such as ours. However, our website will direct you to numerous sources of information, especially if you are interested in exploring opportunities to become involved in adult or family literacy programs in your area. Both of these closely related fields are in need of research conducted by passionate, bright, informed literacy experts looking to forge promising career paths. We hope this brief overview will pique your interest and lead you to explore our companion website and other resources.

If you or members of your literacy team are interested in learning more about family literacy programs or would like to become more involved through advocacy or volunteerism, visit any of the sites discussed in this chapter, or visit our companion website for links to family literacy organizations.

■ *Final Author Connection: Brenda and MaryEllen* Writing the final paragraphs in a book such as this is an emotional experience, and as you read these final words, we hope that you now share our commitment to developing responsive and responsible literacy programs. Few would argue that our students need to be lifelong learners, able to read, evaluate, and navigate through a variety of communication symbols and systems. One can only guess at the changes the 15-year-olds of today will encounter in their lives and work. There are many challenges for the reading specialist and literacy coach in addition to creating the kind of schools that will prepare these students for the future.

We are pleased to leave you with the thoughts of our friend and colleague, Martha Rapp Ruddell, past president of the National Reading Conference and Professor Emerita of Reading Education at Sonoma State University.

### OTHER VOICES: Martha Rapp Ruddell

*On Literacy, Teaching, and Changing the World*

Many years ago, while at the IRA World Congress in Australia, I had dinner with Ed Fry [a respected and long-time reading expert] and some advanced graduate students in reading. In the course of the conversation, Ed turned to the graduate students and asked them, "In your career as a reading educator, how do you plan to move the world forward by a quarter of an inch?" He then commented that when we're young we all want to "Change the World," when in fact the most any of us can do is move it forward in very small increments.

I remember thinking at the time how *right* he was, and how profoundly optimistic and hopeful. Every time I think of it, his comment reminds me of the lessons I learned as a new teacher, and which have been reinforced throughout my teaching career: (1) I could *not* save every child that needed saving; (2) I could not make every teacher in the school good and fair and reasonable; (3) I could not make negative influences and circumstances of my students' home lives go away; (4) I was not always the perfect teacher; (5) I did not like all students equally; (6) I could not make fear and hate and other bad things go away; and on and on and on. On the other hand, I could save *some* kids. I could do everything possible to help all my students become fluent, avid readers and learners. I could make my classroom an oasis of tolerance and respect, where all students were sheltered from fear and hate and meanness. I could maintain my commitment to being a good teacher and my staunch belief that kids really do want to learn. I could hold firmly to the high academic and personal standards I set for my students and myself in my classroom. And I could continue my own learning throughout my career.

That's my "quarter of an inch"; that's how I have "Changed the World."

I now challenge you. How, in your career as a reading specialist and literacy coach, do you plan to move the world forward by a quarter of an inch?

## Points to Remember

This chapter explored some other expanding and emerging roles of the reading specialist and literacy coach. Some of the challenges inherent in trying to define what it means to be a professional and a leader in social constructivist terms were discussed. John Brekke offered thoughts on leadership congruent with the collaborative models of problem solving and learning we advocate for the schools. Connie Erickson provided valuable, practical guidance on grant writing. Reading specialists and literacy coaches were given a list of professional organizations and publications, and Mike Ford delivered a compelling argument for becoming locally active in advocacy initiatives for children, adults, and families. This chapter contains a variety of resources that are valuable to reading specialists and literacy coaches. They can be shared with colleagues. Finally, Marty Ruddell issues a challenge for your future as a professional literacy leader—as a *reading specialist* and *literacy coach*.

## Portfolio and Self-Assessment Projects

1. Think about how you would define the terms *professional* and *leader.* Consider your experiences, the cultural contexts that influenced you, your beliefs, and your current school culture. How do these factors shape your definitions? Choose one of the two terms and map it relative to the factors above.

2. Think about one of the needs you identified in your needs assessment. Is there a need for which you might write a grant? Find a small grant through one of the information sources listed and write a summary of a grant proposal.

3. Think about a classroom problem or question you have in your teaching. Using the steps from this chapter and referring to one or more of the resources listed, write a two- to three-page classroom research proposal you plan to carry out in the future.

4. What are the social and political issues related to literacy in the community and the state? Develop a plan outlining the steps you will take to become a knowledgeable and active advocate for literacy.

5. Create a brochure promoting involvement in adult and/or family literacy. Include local and regional programs and their contact information.

6. Reflect on the goal you set prior to reading this chapter. For your portfolio, create an action plan for meeting the goal.

 Visit our companion website for additional portfolio and professional development projects related to adult and family literacy.

# Recommended Readings: Suggestions for Book Clubs, Study Groups, and Professional Development

## Advocacy Featured Resource

Wisconsin State Reading Association: Advocacy Committee website. http://www.wsra.org/committees/advocacy.php. This committee, chaired by Michael Ford, University of Wisconsin Oshkosh, has won national awards for its work on advocacy related to NCLB/ESEA/Race to the Top, assessment, research-based instruction, RtI, and other issues. The site includes position papers; PowerPoint presentations for you to use with teachers, parents, and school boards; and much more. It is the first place to look for practical advice and advocacy support.

## Family Literacy Featured Resource

Sapin, C., Padak, N., & Baycich, D. (2008). *Family literacy resource notebook.* Kent, OH: The Ohio Literacy Resource Center. http://literacy.kent.edu/Oasis/famlitnotebook/ This is one of the highly practical resources available through the Ohio Family Literacy Center's website. We recommend you visit this site, because it will give you an idea of what you can find on similar comprehensive websites. Most act like clearinghouses. They collect, analyze, and report data related to adult literacy and family literacy, so you will find similarities among many of them. They provide articles and resources; discuss effective methods, programs, and models for those interested in working in the area of family literacy; and include connections and links to other agencies, grant sources, and materials. This site and others like it are updated periodically. Connie Sapin, Nancy Padak, Dianna Baycich, and Kent State University are to be commended for developing this resource and for their efforts on behalf of family literacy.

## Other Recommended Readings

Cooperative Children's Book Center (CCBC), 4290 Helen C. White Hall, 600 N. Park Street, Madison, WI 53706. This center for children's literature annually reviews and recommends thousands of children's books from around the world. It is also an excellent resource for intellectual freedom and provides resources for dealing with censorship issues (www.education.wisc.edu/ccbc). From this site, you can also link to "Read, Write, Think," a wonderful evolving collection of resources, including lesson plans written by teachers from across the country. The website is sponsored by NCTE, IRA, and Marco Polo.

Grant Update. Free newsletter sends grant announcements directly to your email. Tips on grant writing for beginners (www.grantupdate.com).

The International Reading Association has published a number of very helpful resources that are also quite inexpensive. We've included them here and encourage you to share them with parents and families.

International Reading Association. (2000a). *Beginning literacy and your child: A guide to helping your baby or preschooler become a reader.* Newark, DE: Author.

International Reading Association. (2000b). *"Books are cool!" Keeping your middle school student reading.* Newark, DE: Author.

International Reading Association. (2002). *Family–school partnerships: Essential elements of literacy instruction in the United States.* Newark, DE: Author. This IRA position statement suggests that teachers and other school personnel must receive appropriate training in how to work effectively with families to support their children's learning. Specific suggestions for maintaining active school–family partnerships are included for teachers, teacher educators, and administrators.

International Reading Association Literacy Links. Visit the IRA website (www.reading.org), and click on the Literacy Links for Adult Literacy and Family Literacy. Both will yield a large number of journal articles, books, websites, and other resources that you will find helpful.

The IRA also offers a series of brochures for parents. Single copies are free on request by sending a self-addressed stamped envelope to 800 Barksdale Rd., P.O. Box 8139, Newark, DE 19714–8139. These are also available in bulk. The titles include:

*Get Ready to Read! Tips for Parents of Young Children*
*Explore the Playground of Books: Tips for Parents of Beginning Readers*
*Summer Reading Adventure! Tips for Parents of Young Readers*
*Making the Most of Television: Tips for Parents of Young Viewers*
*See the World on the Internet: Tips for Parents of Young Readers—and "Surfers"*
*Library Safari: Tips for Parents of Young Readers and Explorers*

The American Library Association (ALA) also has a very helpful website (www.ala.org) that has a number of useful resources, including a Parent Outreach Toolkit to help parents become advocates for school libraries. It can be found at http://www.ala.org/ala/mgrps/divs/aasl/aaslissues/toolkits/toolkits.cfm.

Weiner, E. J. (2005). Keeping adults behind: Adult literacy education in the age of official reading regimes. *Journal of Adolescent and Adult Literacy, 49*(4), 286–301. The author presents a compelling argument for moving beyond research findings on children's literacy development (such as the Report of the National Reading Panel). He advocates, instead, focusing on the very different needs of adults. Weiner discusses two successful adult literacy initiatives that merge the technical and contextual—"critical integrative literacy"—in the service of social change and individual power.

## *Companion Website Resources*

The following resources to support and extend your learning with this chapter can be found on our companion website (waveland.com/Extra_Material/32979/): key vocabulary, concepts, and other terms; extended examples; updated resources specifically tied to information in the chapter; related websites; and other support features. Also included on the companion website for this chapter are additional resources, connections, and information on adult and family literacy programs and advocacy opportunities. There are also suggestions for additional portfolio and professional development projects, especially those related to adult and family literacy.

# Appendix A

# *Literacy History Prompts*

If you have never created a literacy history, we urge you to do so. You'll be amazed at what you learn about your own literacy development, and how it influences you today as a reader and writer. The following updated literacy prompts may assist you in remembering, reflecting, and creating the literacy history (McLaughlin & Vogt, 1996).

- What are your earliest recollections of reading and writing?
- Were you read to as a child? By whom? What do you remember about being read to?
- Did you read or write with siblings or friends?
- Did you have books, newspapers, and/or magazines in your home? Did you subscribe to any children's magazines? Did your parents or other family members maintain a personal library? Did they read for pleasure?
- Can you recall seeing family members making lists and receiving or sending mail? Did you send or receive mail (e.g., birthday cards, thank-you notes, letters) when you were a child?
- Did you go to the library as a child? If so, what do you remember about going to the library? When did you get your first library card?
- Do you remember your earliest experiences using technology? Were they positive? How did technology influence your literacy development?
- Can you recall teachers, learning experiences, or educational materials from elementary, middle, and secondary school? How did these influence your literacy development?
- Do you remember the first book you loved (couldn't put down)? Do you remember reading/writing as a pleasurable experience? If so, in what ways? If not, why not?
- How did you feel about reading in elementary school? Junior high? High school? Did your reading/writing ability influence your feelings about yourself as a person? If so, how?
- Did you read a certain type of book (i.e., mysteries, biographies) at a particular age? Why do you think you made such choices?
- What is your all-time favorite children's book? Novel? Nonfiction work?
- Are you a reader/writer now? If so, describe yourself as a reader; if not, why do you suppose this is so? What are you currently reading? Writing?
- In what ways do you use technology for information, communication, social or professional networking, or entertainment?

# Appendix B

## Examples of Two Schools' Vision Statements

The first example is the vision statement of Bret Harte Elementary in the Long Beach (California) Unified School District.

### Vision Statement

We believe that all students can learn and want to learn. They come to school with their own special experiences and knowledge. Students become literate by building on these experiences and knowledge and by receiving developmentally appropriate instruction. This provides the basis for students' progress from emergent to fluent readers and writers. In order to become members of a literate community, students need:

- A print-rich environment
- Modeling of proficient reading, writing, listening, and speaking
- Opportunities for daily practice: independent, directed, and collaborative
- An environment that encourages risk-taking and accepts approximations
- Opportunities to publish, share, and respond to writing
- Access to technology, which enhances communication

The second example was written by Christine Wright, a graduate student at the University of Wisconsin, Oshkosh.

### Vision Statement

We believe that the primary purpose of reading is comprehension. The major goal of reading instruction is the development of strategic readers who understand the reading process and who can construct meaning and apply the necessary strategies to learn from a variety of print and nonprint materials including technology. It is a developmental process in which students progress at their own rates.

An effective reading program is determined by the district curriculum, which is aligned with the state standards, evidence of effective practice, and the school's long-term literacy goals. It is student centered. Teachers are professionals who recognize multiple literacies and multiple communities and honor these in their approaches toward instructional goals. It is crucial, however, that family members, the wider community, and students themselves take active roles in the students' reading development.

Reading instruction encompasses the entire curriculum across all content areas, and effective lessons include pre-reading, reading, and post-reading activities as well as opportunities to engage in critical reasoning and to make personal connections with text. Evaluation of reading growth can be assessed through a variety of objective and subjective methods. It should be emphasized that teacher judgment based on daily observation and analysis of reading behaviors is a very important aspect of assessment. For an effective reading program to occur, professional development is essential. An effective reading program develops readers who can and will read. Reading is a lifelong activity that will enrich students' understanding of themselves and the world. Reading is the best practice for learning to read.

# Appendix C

## Standards-Based Curriculum Framework

| | | | | | |
|---|---|---|---|---|---|
| **Wisconsin Reading/Language Arts Standard A 4.1, Grade Three** | | | | | |
| *Complete Standard* | *Benchmark Expectations at Grade 3* | *Assessments to Demonstrate Competency* | | *Sample Activities and Strategies* | *Resources to Support Implementation* |
| *A 4.12* Infer the meaning of unfamiliar words in the context of a passage by examining known words, phrases, and structures | *First Semester* Infer the meaning of unfamiliar words in the context of a passage with support<br><br>*Second Semester* Infer the meaning of unfamiliar words in the context of a paragraph independently | *Formal* WI Gr. 3 test | *Informal* IRI<br><br>Teacher Notes<br><br>Vocabulary Self-Selection | *All Year* Infer word meanings Implement SIOP® Model for English learners Group discussion of possible meanings Affixes Synonyms Antonyms Homonyms Homophones Multiple meanings Figurative language Expand/enrich personal vocabulary Storylords strategies #2, 3, and 4 Ask a neighbor Read on Context clues | Spell Checker Dictionary Thesaurus Glossary |
| How often will this standard or benchmark be tested on the fourth-grade state-mandated test?<br>0 = Not tested      ✓ = 1 to 2 items on test      + = 3 to 4 items on test      * = 5 or more items on test<br>This will help you determine areas that are emphasized on the test. | | | | | |

# Appendix D

## Sample Needs Assessment Survey

This is a survey created by a graduate student for her course in leadership and supervision. Note that you will want to tailor your survey statements for your own school context. Also, you may find you get a higher return rate if you can have your colleagues complete the survey during a faculty meeting. Remember to get approval from your principal before you distribute the survey to teachers!

Dear Teachers,

I am currently in the reading specialist credential program at CSULB. One of my assignments is to conduct a schoolwide needs assessment of our reading/language arts instructional program. With your help I will be able to do my homework! This is an anonymous survey, but I would like to know some information about you. Also feel free to add comments.

Please return the completed survey to my box by April 21. Thanks in advance for your support!

Kristen Jones, Room 33

I am a:     ☐ Teacher          Grade level: 1 2 3 4 5 6
            ☐ Specialist
            ☐ Administrator

I have been teaching for:     1–2 yrs.     3–5 yrs.     6–8 yrs.     9–12 yrs.     13+ yrs.

***Reading/Language Arts Needs Assessment Survey***
***Barton Elementary School***

*Directions:* Please circle the number that reflects your feelings about the following statements. Note that "5" represents Strongly Agree.

| | *Strongly Disagree* | *Unsure/Unknown* | | | *Strongly Agree* |
|---|---|---|---|---|---|

**Instructional Materials**

| | | | | | |
|---|---|---|---|---|---|
| I have access to relevant district and state materials (e.g., standards/frameworks). | 1 | 2 | 3 | 4 | 5 |
| Appropriate texts, technology resources, and support materials are available to me. | 1 | 2 | 3 | 4 | 5 |
| The school media center is sufficiently stocked with print and nonprint resources my students need. | 1 | 2 | 3 | 4 | 5 |
| I have an adequate number of books and nonprint resources in my classroom library. | 1 | 2 | 3 | 4 | 5 |
| Our adopted reading series is appropriate for my students' needs, including English learners. | 1 | 2 | 3 | 4 | 5 |

**Reading Assessment and Instruction**

| | | | | | |
|---|---|---|---|---|---|
| I have adequate access to assessment instruments that I can use with my students. | 1 | 2 | 3 | 4 | 5 |
| I feel confident when using assessment instruments for screening, monitoring, and evaluating students. | 1 | 2 | 3 | 4 | 5 |
| I feel confident about how to align my instruction with district standards. | 1 | 2 | 3 | 4 | 5 |
| I feel confident in managing differentiated literacy instruction. | 1 | 2 | 3 | 4 | 5 |
| My students have adequate opportunities to read independently. | 1 | 2 | 3 | 4 | 5 |
| My students have adequate opportunities to write independently. | 1 | 2 | 3 | 4 | 5 |
| Our instructional block of time for reading and language arts is adequate. | 1 | 2 | 3 | 4 | 5 |
| I'm able to use a variety of instructional methods and approaches for teaching reading, including technology. | 1 | 2 | 3 | 4 | 5 |
| I feel confident in my ability to provide differentiated instruction to meet the literacy needs of my students. | 1 | 2 | 3 | 4 | 5 |
| We have adequate parent involvement and support at our school. | 1 | 2 | 3 | 4 | 5 |
| Our grade level team has adequate planning time. | 1 | 2 | 3 | 4 | 5 |

I would benefit from professional development in the following areas:

_____ Differentiating instruction
_____ Phonological processes (phonemic awareness/phonics)
_____ Comprehension skills and strategies
_____ Spelling and vocabulary development
_____ Curriculum and standards alignment
_____ Improving reading in the content areas
_____ Writing and district rubrics
_____ Selecting, administering, and evaluating results from assessments
_____ Flexible grouping and management
_____ Working with English learners (SIOP model)
_____ Incorporating multiliteracies and instructional technology
_____ Other

Comments (use other side if you wish):

# Appendix E

# Sample Needs Assessment Summary

| Jefferson Elementary School Literacy Program | | |
|---|---|---|

**Summary of Strengths:**
- Students exceed the target growth points on the state test by 68 points.
- Teachers continually attend workshops and engage in professional development to improve their literacy instruction.
- The school has adequate resources to meet objectives.
- Teachers are committed to literacy program improvement.
- Teachers conduct numerous assessments to determine students' literacy abilities.

**Summary of Needs:** The teachers, including special educators, agree or strongly agree that they have the ability to teach comprehension strategies, to identify students' needs through running records, and to read aloud to the students daily. The majority of the teachers feel that the school needs to find ways to increase parent support for literacy in the classroom. This is an area that needs significant attention. Other areas that need to be addressed include the reading series, intervention, English learners, technology, and classroom libraries.

| Goal | Strengths | Needs |
|---|---|---|
| The adopted reading series matches the needs of our students. The reading program interventions are effective. | The majority of the teachers indicated the series does match the needs of the student population. The majority also feel that program interventions are effective. To examine further how the series is meeting the needs of all students and how interventions are applied, additional information is needed. | Forty percent feel that the series does not meet the needs of the students. This may indicate that many student needs are not being met by the reading series. Many of these teachers stated they often need supplemental materials or other alternatives because their students' needs are not being met through the reading series. |
| Instructional materials used for intervention for struggling readers and writers are effective. | The majority of the teachers feel that they have sufficient materials needed to meet students' needs. Further investigations are needed to determine the effectiveness of the materials. | Thirty-nine percent feel that they need additional materials to assist struggling readers and writers. We need to identify materials teachers need to differentiate instruction for these students. |

| *Goal* | *Strengths* | *Needs* |
|---|---|---|
| The current reading program meets the needs of English learners. | Thirty-eight percent feel that the needs of English learners are being met in the classroom. | The majority of the teachers do not feel that the reading program meets the needs of ELs. The school's population consists of 68 percent ELs. |
| Collaborations among grade levels are frequent and productive. | Many first-grade teachers expressed the need for more collaboration. The other grade levels were inconsistent with their responses or felt their grade level needed to collaborate more consistently. | The majority of teachers felt the need to meet more consistently. We need to determine how to meet more frequently and more productively. |
| The needs of special education students are met with our current literacy program. | Thirty percent feel that they are meeting the needs of special education students and 17 percent had no opinion. This area needs to be investigated to determine if the question was fully understood and to examine how the needs are being met. | The majority believe the reading series isn't meeting the needs of special education students. We need to determine the skills and strategies that need to be implemented for these children. |
| Additional reading strategies for social studies and science texts are needed. | Many teachers report they need additional reading strategies for social studies/science, but have adequate strategy knowledge during language arts instruction. | Thirty-two percent report they need to learn additional strategies; the majority had no opinion. The question needs clarification to determine why so many have no opinion. |
| Providing students with adequate technology instruction and support. | Thirty-nine percent feel comfortable using technology in the classroom. These teachers need to provide assistance to those who feel inadequate teaching with technology. | The majority of teachers need support using technology in their rooms. Professional development is needed for helping teachers implement technology and access the Internet. |
| Classroom libraries have a sufficient number and variety of books. | The majority of teachers feel they have a sufficient number of books in their classroom libraries. | Thirty-eight percent indicated the need for more books in their classroom libraries. Some teachers may not be aware of how many books are sufficient for meeting students' reading needs. |
| Parent support for literacy is adequate. | | The majority of teachers feel the need for greater parent support. The faculty needs to discuss ways to help parents become more involved and comfortable in the academic environment. |

**Conclusion:** The results of the Needs Assessment Survey indicate there is little consensus regarding some of the areas of strength. The areas of need identified in this report are those in which approximately one-third or more of the teachers expressed concerns. There were a large number of responses that indicated "No Opinion." For these survey items, more detailed investigation is needed. Professional development is needed to assist teachers and administration in regard to the perceived lack of parental involvement in the literacy program.

# Appendix F

## Sample Two-Year Plan/Grid

### MacDonald Elementary School's Two-Year Literacy Improvement Plan: Year 1

MacDonald Elementary School is dedicated to designing, implementing, and evaluating a research-based literacy program that promotes academic success of students at all achievement levels.

> —from MacDonald Elementary Literacy Vision Statement
> by Autumn Stief, University of Wisconsin Oshkosh graduate student

| Targeted Need: Implementation of School Vision | Year 1 Quarter 1 | Year 1 Quarter 2 | Year 1 Quarter 3 | Year 1 Quarter 4 |
|---|---|---|---|---|
| **Goal 1:** Establish a literacy team that functions as representatives of their units | Educate staff on the purpose of a literacy team<br><br>Assemble literacy team based on guidelines suggested in the Needs Assessment<br><br>Establish group norms to allow for a cohesive, productive team | Adopt/revise suggested school vision<br><br>Communicate vision to staff, parents, and district via newsletters, updates at meetings, informal conversations, and the Internet | Provide staff with updates on current research findings at staff meetings | Share research findings with staff, parents, and district administrators |
| | *Assessment:* The formation of a literacy team based on the suggested criteria. | *Assessment:* An adopted vision statement is posted in the school. | *Assessment:* Communication of research is documented in staff meeting minutes. | *Assessment:* Communication of findings is documented in staff meeting minutes, curriculum committee minutes, and PTA meeting minutes. |

| Targeted Need: Implementation of School Vision | Year 1 Quarter 1 | Year 1 Quarter 2 | Year 1 Quarter 3 | Year 1 Quarter 4 |
|---|---|---|---|---|
| **Goal 2:** Design a research-based reading program that promotes academic success of students at all achievement levels | | Research best practices in reading by consulting professional texts, area experts, and the Internet | Continue research of best reading practices<br><br>List possible observation trips for teachers | Compile research by common themes and approaches<br><br>Summarize research findings<br><br>Observe and confer with other teachers in the area<br><br>Compile a list of references |
| | | *Assessment:* Research is gathered using sources representing various perspectives.<br><br>The team engages in a sharing time at the end of each research session. | *Assessment:* Research is gathered using a variety of sources.<br><br>The team engages in a sharing time at the end of each research session. | *Assessment:* Research summary and references are linked to vision statement.<br><br>The summary and reference documents are used when communicating with staff, parents, and district administrators. |
| **Goal 3:** Implement the research-based literacy program | | | | Assist teachers in planning for an extended block of reading instruction in Year 2<br><br>Select and order a professional book that supports a readers' workshop approach so the teachers have the option of reading over the summer<br><br>Order *The Literacy Coach's Survival Guide* for the literacy team to read over the summer, focusing on the peer coaching section<br><br>*Assessment:* Books are ordered and distributed, and teachers have turned in tentative copies of their schedules to the principal. |

## *MacDonald Elementary School's Two-Year Literacy Improvement Plan: Year 2*

MacDonald Elementary School is dedicated to designing, implementing, and evaluating a research-based literacy program that promotes academic success of students at all achievement levels.

*—from MacDonald Elementary Literacy Vision Statement*

| *Targeted Need: Implementation of School Vision* | *Year 2 Quarter 1* | *Year 2 Quarter 2* | *Year 2 Quarter 3* | *Year 2 Quarter 4* |
|---|---|---|---|---|
| **Goal 1:** Establish a literacy team whose members function as representatives of their instructional units | Allow time for members to reorient and review last year and refocus on this year<br><br>Review the vision statement and the goals of the literacy team with one another and then with the staff<br><br>Review and adjust the group norms to facilitate functioning as a cohesive, professional team<br><br>*\*Assessment:* The team is able to function in a professional, goal-driven manner. | Report team progress to staff via email, staff and unit meeting updates<br><br><br><br>*\*Assessment:* Updates are included in meeting minutes and email communication is documented. | Report team progress to staff via email, staff and unit meeting updates<br><br><br><br>*\*Assessment:* Updates are included in meeting minutes and email communication is documented. | Report team progress to staff via email, staff and unit meeting updates<br><br><br><br>*\*Assessment:* Updates are included in meeting minutes and email communication is documented. |
| **Goal 2:** Design a research-based reading program that promotes the academic success of students at all achievement levels | Review research summary and add any recent findings<br><br>Schedule additional classroom observations focusing on primary and intermediate implementation of readers' workshop | Continue reading professional books and articles to maintain and enhance knowledge of current research | Continue reading professional books and articles to maintain and enhance knowledge of current research | Continue reading professional books and articles to maintain and enhance knowledge of current research |

| *Targeted Need:* *Implementation of* *School Vision* | *Year 2* *Quarter 1* | *Year 2* *Quarter 2* | *Year 2* *Quarter 3* | *Year 2* *Quarter 4* |
|---|---|---|---|---|
| **Goal 2:** (continued) | Send a primary, intermediate, and administrative representative to a workshop conference | | | |
| | *\*Assessment:* Team members are able to verbally demonstrate an understanding of the research. Observations and conference notes are processed by the group and added to the comprehensive research. | *\*Assessment:* Additional references are added to the reference list. Personal classroom goals are changing and growing as a result of additional research. | *\*Assessment:* Additional references are added to the reference list. Personal classroom goals are changing and growing as a result of additional research. | *\*Assessment:* Additional references are added to the reference list. Personal classroom goals are changing and growing as a result of additional research. |
| **Goal 3:** Implement the research-based literacy program | Schedule monthly grade-level book discussions to be facilitated by the principal focusing on the initial procedures and structures of a workshop<br><br>Devote ten minutes at each staff meeting for teachers to discuss readers' workshop in small, multiple grade-level groups<br><br>Establish peer coaching relationships within the literacy team to reflect on each other's teaching and to assist in instructional goal-setting | Solicit interested individuals to participate in peer coaching with assistance from literacy team members<br><br>Devote professional development time to peer coaching, facilitated by select members of the literacy team<br><br>Schedule two follow-up sessions facilitated by the reading specialist to set expectations and goals for peer coaching relationships | Continue grade-level book discussions with a focus on conferencing; compile a list of prompts and record sheets to share with staff<br><br>Continue peer coaching relationships, having all involved teachers meet at the end of each month to discuss progress and support each peer coaching team<br><br>Extend another invitation to other staff members to join the peer coaching process | Continue grade-level book discussions with a focus on assessment<br><br>Continue peer coaching relationships, having all involved teachers meet at the end of each month to discuss progress and support each peer coaching team<br><br>Extend another invitation to other staff members to join the peer coaching structure |

*(continued)*

| *Targeted Need: Implementation of School Vision* | *Year 2 Quarter 1* | *Year 2 Quarter 2* | *Year 2 Quarter 3* | *Year 2 Quarter 4* |
|---|---|---|---|---|
| **Goal 3:** (continued) | | Continue grade-level book discussions with a focus on mini-lessons; compile a collection of texts to be used in mini-lessons along with anchor strategy lessons

Videotape a mini-lesson to show and discuss at a staff meeting | Support staff by showing a video at a staff meeting of a teacher having a conference with a student | Review survey results and begin developing implementation goals for the next two years |
| | *\*Assessment:* Communication is documented in minutes from grade-level and staff meetings. Copies of classroom schedules are submitted to the principal. Peer coaching response sheets are signed by participants. | *\*Assessment:* The majority of staff are able to write mini-lessons that reflect the needs of their students and the curriculum by the end of the quarter.

The majority of staff have agreed to engage in the peer coaching model. | *\*Assessment:* A growing number of staff members are participating in peer coaching relationships.

Informal conference records are reviewed at book study meetings and show that teachers are meeting with students to discuss text. | *\*Assessment:* A growing number of staff members are participating in peer coaching relationships.

Surveys of staff show growth in knowledge and implementation of best practices in reading. |

# References

Adams, M. J. (1990). *Beginning to read: Thinking and learning about print.* Cambridge, MA: MIT.

Afflerbach, P. (2007). *Understanding and using reading assessment, K–12.* Newark, DE: International Reading Association.

Allington, R. L. (2006). *What really matters for struggling readers: Designing research-based programs* (2nd ed.). New York: Addison-Wesley Longman.

Allington, R. L. (2008). *What really matters in fluency: Research-based practices across the curriculum.* Boston: Allyn & Bacon.

Allington, R. L., & Johnston, P. H. (2002). *Reading to learn: Lessons from exemplary fourth grade classrooms.* New York: Guilford Press.

Allington, R. L., & Shanahan, T. (2006). *Effective reading instructional policies: A search for common ground.* Featured session at the Fifty-First Annual Convention of the International Reading Association, Chicago, IL.

Allington, R. L., & Walmsley, S. (2007). *No quick fix: The RtI edition.* New York: Teachers College Press.

Alvermann, D. E., Smith, L. C., & Readence, J. E. (1985). Prior knowledge activation and the comprehension of compatible and incompatible text. *Reading Research Quarterly, 20,* 420–436.

American Library Association (ALA)/American Association of School Librarians (AASL). (2009). *Parent outreach toolkit.* Chicago, IL: American Library Association.

Anderson, R. C., & Pearson, P. D. (1984). A schema-theoretical view of basic processes in reading comprehension. In P. D. Pearson (Ed.), *Handbook of reading research* (pp. 225–295). White Plains, NY: Longman.

Anderson, R. C., Hiebert, E. H., Scott, J. A., & Wilkinson, I. A. G. (1985). *Becoming a nation of readers: The report of the Commission on Reading.* Washington, DC: National Institute of Education.

Anderson, V., Chan, C., & Henne, R. (1995). The effects of strategy instruction on the literacy models and performance of reading- and writing-delayed middle school students. In K. A. Hinchman, D. J. Leu, &

C. K. Kinzer (Eds.), *National Reading Conference Yearbook* (Vol. 44, pp. 180–196). Chicago: National Reading Conference.

Atwell, N. (1998). *In the middle: New understandings about writing, reading, and learning* (2nd ed.). Portsmouth, NH: Heinemann.

Atwell, N. (2007). *Lessons that change writers.* Portsmouth, NH: Heinemann.

Au, K. H. (1993). *Literacy instruction in multi-cultural settings.* New York: Harcourt Brace.

Au, K. H. (2000). A multicultural perspective on policies for improving literacy achievement: Equity and excellence. In M. L. Kamil, P. B. Mosenthal, P. D. Pearson, & R. Barr (Eds.), *Handbook of reading research* (Vol. III, pp. 835–851). Mahwah, NJ: Erlbaum.

Au, K. H., & Raphael, T. E. (2000). Equity and literacy in the next millennium. *Reading Research Quarterly, 35*(1), 170–188.

August, D., & Shanahan, T. (Eds.). (2008). *Developing literacy in second-language learners: A report of the National Literacy Panel on language-minority children and youth.* Mahwah, NJ: Erlbaum.

Ayres, L. R. (1998). Phonological awareness of kindergarten children: Three treatments and their effects. In C. Weaver (Ed.), *Reconsidering a balanced approach to reading* (pp. 209–255). Urbana, IL: National Council of Teachers of English.

Bandura, A. (1993). Perceived self-efficacy in cognitive development and functioning. *Educational Psychology, 28,* 117–148.

Banks, J. A. (1994). *An introduction to multicultural education.* Boston: Allyn & Bacon.

Barone, D., & Xu, S. H. (2008). *Literacy instruction for English language learners Pre-K–2.* New York: Guilford Press.

Barton, D., Hamilton, M., & Ivanic, R. (Eds.). (2000). *Situated literacies.* New York: Routledge.

Bean, R. (2009). *The reading specialist: Leadership for the classroom, school, and community* (2nd ed.). New York: Guilford Press.

Bean, R. M., Cassidy, J., Grumet, J. E., Shelton, D. S., & Wallis, S. R. (2002). What do reading specialists do? Results from a national survey. *The Reading Teacher, 55*(8), 736–744.

Bean, T. W. (2001, December/January). An update on reading in the content areas: Social constructivist dimensions. *Reading Online 4*(11). Available at www.readingonline.org/article/artjndex.asp?HREF=/handbook/bean/index.html.

Bear, D. R., Helman, L., Templeton, S., Invernizzi, M., & Johnston, F. (2007). *Words their way with English learners: Word study for phonics, vocabulary, and spelling instruction.* Upper Saddle River, NJ: Merrill Prentice-Hall.

Bear, D., Invernizzi, M., Templeton, S., & Johnston, F. (2004). *Words their way* (3rd ed.). New York: Prentice-Hall.

Bear, D. R., Invernizzi, M., Templeton, S., & Johnston, F. R. (2007). *Words their way: Word study for phonics, vocabulary, and spelling instruction* (4th ed.). Boston: Allyn & Bacon.

Bear, D., Templeton, S., Helman, L. A., & Baren, T. (2003). *Orthographic development and learning to read in different languages.* In G. G. Garcia (Ed.), *English learners: Reaching the highest level of English literacy* (pp. 71–95). Newark, DE: International Reading Association.

Beck, I. L., & McKeown, M. G. (2001). Text talk: Capturing the benefits of read-aloud experiences for young children. *The Reading Teacher, 55,* 10–20.

Beck, I. L., McKeown, M., & Kucan, L. (2002). *Bringing words to life: Robust vocabulary instruction.* New York: Guilford Press.

Berger, A. (1997). Writing about reading for the public. *The Reading Teacher, 51,* 6–10.

Bernhardt, V. L. (2009). *The school portfolio toolkit: A planning implementation and evaluation guide to continuous school improvement.* Larchmount, NY: Eye On Education.

Biancarosa, G., Bryk, A., & Dexter, E. (2008, March). *Assessing the value-added effects of literacy collaborative professional development on student learning.* Paper presented at the annual conference of the American Educational Research Association, New York, NY.

Biancarosa, G., & Snow, C. (2004). *Reading next: A vision for action and research in middle and high school literacy.* New York: Carnegie Corporation.

Biancarosa, G., & Snow, C. E. (2006). *Reading next—A vision for action and research in middle and high school reading: A report to Carnegie Corporation of New York* (2nd ed.). Washington, DC: Alliance for Excellent Education.

Blachman, B. A. (2000). Phonological awareness. In M. L. Kamil, P. B. Mosenthal, P. D. Pearson, & R. Barr (Eds.), *Handbook of reading research* (Vol. III, pp. 483–502). Mahwah, NJ: Erlbaum.

Blachowicz, C., & Fisher, P. J. (2002). *Teaching vocabulary in all classrooms* (2nd ed.). Upper Saddle River, NJ: Merrill Prentice-Hall.

Blachowicz, C., & Ogle, D. (2008). *Reading comprehension: Strategies for independent learning.* New York: Guilford Press.

Blevins, W. (1998). *Phonics from A–Z.* New York: Scholastic.

Block, C. C., & Pressley, M. (Eds.). (2002). *Comprehension: Research-based practices.* New York: Guilford Press.

Bond, G. L., & Dykstra, R. (1967a). The Cooperative Research Program in first-grade reading instruction. *Reading Research Quarterly, 2,* 5–142.

Bond, G. L., & Dykstra, R. (1967b). *Coordinating center for first-grade reading instruction programs.* (Final Report of Project No. X-001, Contract No. OE5-10-264). Minneapolis: University of Minnesota.

Bong, M. (2004). Academic motivation in self-efficacy, task value, achievement orientations, and attributional beliefs. *Journal of Educational Research, 97*(6), 287–298.

Boscolo, P., & Mason, L. (2001). Writing to learn, writing to transfer. In G. Rijlaarsdam, P. Tynjala, L. Mason, & K. Lonka (Eds.), *Studies in writing: Writing as a learning tool: Integrating theory and practice* (Vol. 7, pp. 83–104). Dordrect, The Netherlands: Kluwer.

Brozo, W. G., & Gaskins, C. (2009). Engaging texts and literacy practices for adolescent boys. In K. D. Wood & W. E. Blanton (Eds.), *Literacy instruction for adolescents: Research-based practice.* New York: Guilford Press.

Bruner, J. (1983). *Child's talk: Learning to use language.* New York: W. W. Norton.

Buckner, A. (2005). *Notebook connections: Strategies for the reader's notebook.* New York: Stenhouse.

Buckner, A. (2005). *Notebook know how: Strategies for the writer's notebook.* New York: Stenhouse.

Buehl, D. (2009). *Classroom strategies for interactive learning* (3rd ed.). Newark, DE: International Reading Association.

Burke, J., & Prater, C. A. (2000). *I'll grant you that: A step-by-step guide to finding funds, designing winning projects, writing powerful grant proposals.* Portsmouth, NH: Heinemann.

Byers, G. O. (2001). *Daily oral language.* Greensboro, NC: Carson Dellosa.

Caldwell, J., & Ford, M. (2002). *Where have all the bluebirds gone? How to soar with flexible grouping.* Portsmouth, NH: Heinemann.

Calkins, L. M. (1983). *Lessons from a child: On the teaching and learning of writing.* Exeter, NH: Heinemann.

Calkins, L. M., & Teachers College Reading and Writing Project. (2006). *Units of study bundle: Units of study for primary writing and Units of study for teaching writing, grades 3–5.* Portsmouth, NH: Heinemann.

Cambourne, B. (1988). *Learning and the acquisition of literacy in classrooms.* Portsmouth, NH: Heinemann.

Carlson, C., & Christenson, S. L. (2005). Evidence-based parent and family interventions in school psychology: State of scientifically based practice. *School Psychology Quarterly, 20,* 525–528.

Carnegie Foundation on Advancing Adolescent Literacy. (2010). *Time to act: An agenda for advancing adolescent literacy for college and career success.* New York: Carnegie Corporation.

Carnicelli, T. A. (2001). *Words work: Activities for developing vocabulary, style, and critical thinking.* Portsmouth, CT: Heinemann.

Carr, D. (2007). Other Voices. In M. E. Vogt & B. A. Shearer, *Reading specialists and literacy coaches in the real world* (2nd ed., pp. 167–169). Boston, MA: Allyn & Bacon.

Center One. (1998). *The needs assessment.* Washington, DC: ORBIS Associates.

Chall, J. S. (1967). *Learning to read: The great debate.* New York: McGraw-Hill.

Chall, J. S. (1983). *Stages of reading development.* New York: McGraw-Hill.

Chomsky, N. (1999). *Profits over people: Neoliberalism and global order.* New York: Seven Stories Press.

Clay, M. (1985). *The early detection of reading difficulties: A diagnosis survey and recovery procedure.* Portsmouth, NH: Heinemann.

Clay, M. (1991). *Becoming literate: The construction of inner control.* Portsmouth, NH: Heinemann.

Clymer, T. (1963). The utility of phonic generalizations in the primary grades. *The Reading Teacher, 16,* 252–258.

Cobb, C. (2005). Literacy teams: Sharing leadership to improve student learning. *The Reading Teacher, 58*(5), 472–474.

Cochran-Smith, M. (1995). Uncertain allies: Understanding the boundaries of race and teaching. *Harvard Educational Review, 65*(4), 541–570.

Cole, A. G. (2007). Expanding the field: Revisiting environmental education principles through multidisciplinary frameworks. *Journal of Environmental Education, 38*(2), 35–45.

Collins, E. (2008). RtI: Special education administrators' hopes and concerns. Arlington, VA: Council for Exceptional Children. Available from http://www.cecblog.typepad.com/rti/2008/08/rti-special-edu.html.

Colvin, C., & Schlosser, L. K. (1997/1998). Developing academic confidence to build literacy: What teachers can do. *Journal of Adolescent and Adult Literacy, 41,* 272–281.

Comber, B. (2001). Critical literacies and local action: Teacher knowledge and a "new" research agenda. In B. Comber & A. Simpson (Eds.), *Negotiating critical literacies in classrooms* (pp. 271–282). Mahwah, NJ: Erlbaum.

Condon, M. W. F., & Harrison, C. (2009, May). *Conversations around digital picture books by children.* Presentation at the International Reading Association Convention, Minneapolis, MN.

Conley, M. (2008). Cognitive strategy instruction for adolescents: What we know about the promise. *Harvard Educational Review 78*(1), 84–106.

Cook-Gumperz, J. (2006). *The social construction of literacy.* Cambridge, UK: Cambridge University Press.

Cooper, J. D., & Pikulski, J. J. (2000). *A research-based framework for Houghton Mifflin Reading: A legacy of literacy.* Boston: Houghton Mifflin.

Cooper, J. D., & Pikulski, J. J. (2002). *Houghton Mifflin Reading.* Boston: Houghton Mifflin.

Costa, A. L., & Garmston, R. J. (2002). *Cognitive coaching: A foundation for Renaissance schools.* Norwood, MA: Christopher-Gordon.

Crawford, G. B. (2008). *Differentiation for the adolescent learner: Accommodating brain development, language, literacy, and special needs.* Thousand Oaks, CA: Crawford Press.

Csikszentmihalyi, M. (1997). *Finding flow: The psychology of engagement with everyday life.* New York: Basic Books.

Culham, R. (2003). *6 +1 Traits of writing: The complete guide for grades 3 and up.* New York: Scholastic.

Cummins, J. (1979). Linguistic interdependence and the educational development of bilingual children. *Review of Educational Research, 49*(22), 51.

Cummins, J. (1981). The role of primary language development in promoting educational success for language minority students. In California State Department of Education, *Schooling and minority students: A theoretical framework* (pp. 3–49). Los Angeles: National Dissemination and Assessment Center.

Cummins, J. (1984). *Bilingualism and special education: Issues in assessment and pedagogy.* San Diego, CA: College-Hill.

Cummins, J. (2000) *Language, power and pedagogy: Bilingual children in the crossfire.* Clevendon: Multilingual Matters.

Cummins, J. (2003). Reading and the bilingual student: Fact and fiction. In G. G. Garcia (Ed.), *English learners: Reaching the highest level of English literacy.* Newark, DE: International Reading Association.

Cummins, J. (2006). How long does it take for an English language learner to become proficient in a second language? In E. Hamayan & R. Freeman (Eds.), *English language learners at school: A guide for administrators* (pp. 59–61). Philadelphia: Caslon Publishing.

Cunningham, J. W. (2001). The National Reading Panel report. *Reading Research Quarterly, 36*(3), 326–335.

Cunningham, J. W., & Fitzgerald, J. (2002). Balance in teaching reading: An instructional approach based on a particular epistemological outlook. *Reading and Writing Quarterly, 18*(4), 353–365.

Cunningham, P. M. (2009). Polysyllabic words and struggling adolescent readers: The morphemic link to meaning, reading, and spelling "big words." In K. D. Wood & W. E. Blanton (Eds.), *Literacy instruction for adolescents: Research-based practice* (pp. 307–327). New York: Guilford Press.

Cunningham, P. M., Hall, D. P., & Defee, M. (1998). Non-ability grouped, multilevel instruction: Eight years later. *Reading Teacher, 51*(4), 652–654.

Cunningham, P. M., & Smith D. R. (2007). *Beyond storytelling: Toward higher level thinking and big ideas.* Boston: Allyn & Bacon.

Daniels, H. (2002). *Literature circles: Voice and choice in book clubs and reading groups* (2nd ed.). Portland, ME: Stenhouse.

Darling, S., & Westberg, L. (2004). Parent involvement in children's acquisition of literacy. *The Reading Teacher, 57*(8), 774–776.

Darling-Hammond, L., & Berry, B. (1998, May 27). Investing in teaching. *Education Week,* 48.

De La Paz, S., & Graham, S. (2002). Explicitly teaching strategies, skills, and knowledge: Writing instruction in middle school classrooms. *Journal of Educational Psychology, 94,* 291–304.

Deal, T. E., & Peterson, K. D. (1999). *Shaping school culture: The heart of leadership.* San Francisco: Jossey-Bass.

Delpit, L. D. (1995). *Other people's children: Cultural conflict in the classroom.* New York: New Press.

Desimone, L. M. (2009). Improving impact studies of teachers' professional development: Toward better conceptualizations and measures. *Educational Researcher, 38*(3), 181–199.

Dickinson, D. K., & Smith, M. W. (1996). Long-term effects of preschool teachers' book readings on low-income children's vocabulary and story comprehension. *Reading Research Quarterly, 29,* 104–122.

Dillon, D. A. (2005). There and back again: Qualitative research in literacy education. *Reading Research Quarterly, 40*(1), 106–110.

Dillon, D. R. (2000). *Kid's insight: Reconsidering how to meet the literacy needs of all students.* Newark, DE: International Reading Association.

Dogan, B., & Robin, B. R. (2008). Educational uses of digital storytelling: Creating digital storytelling contests for K–12 students and teachers. Available at http://iteachworkshop.pbworks.com/f/site2009_dogan_robin.pdf.

Dolch, E. W. (1942). *Basic sight word test.* Champaign, IL: Garrard.

Dole, J. A. (2004). The changing role of the reading specialist in school reform. *The Reading Teacher, 57*(5), 462–471.

Dorn, L., French C., & Jones, T. (1998). *Apprenticeship in literacy: Teaching across reading and writing.* Portland, ME: Stenhouse.

Dorn, L., & Soffos, C. (2005). *Teaching for deep comprehension: A reading workshop approach.* York, ME: Stenhouse.

Downing, J. (1962). *Experiments with an augmented alphabet for beginning readers.* New York: Educational Records Bureau.

Duessen, T., Coskie, T., Robinson, L., & Autio, E. (2007). *"Coach" can mean many things: Five categories of literacy coaches in Reading First.* (Issues and Answers Report, REL 2007 No. 005). Washington, DC: U.S. Department of Education, Institute of Educational Sciences, National Center for Education Evaluation and Regional Assistance, Regional Educational Laboratory Northwest. Available at http://ies.ed.gov/ncee/edlabs/projects/project.asp?projectID=47&productID=22.

Duffy, G. G. (2002). The case for direct explanation of strategies. In C. C. Block & M. Pressley (Eds.), *Comprehension instruction: Research-based best practices.* New York: Guilford Press.

DuFour, R., Eaker, R., & Many, T. (2006). *Learning by doing: A handbook for professional development communities at work.* Bloomington, IN: Solution Tree Press.

Durkin, D. (1974–1975). A six-year study of children who learned to read in school at the age of four. *Reading Research Quarterly, 1,* 9–61.

Dyson, A. H. (1993). From invention to social action in early childhood literacy: A reconceptualization through dialogue about difference. *Early Childhood Research Quarterly, 8,* 409–425.

Dyson, A. H. (1994). Viewpoints: The word and the world—reconceptualizing written language development or, Do rainbows mean a lot to little girls? In R. B. Ruddell, M. R. Ruddell, & H. Singer (Eds.),

*Theoretical models and processes of reading* (4th ed., pp. 297–322). Newark, DE: International Reading Association.

Eccles, J. S., Wigfield, A., & Schiefele, U. (1998). Motivation to succeed. In N. Eisenberg (Ed.), *Handbook of child psychology: Social, emotional and personality development* (Vol. 3, 5th ed., pp. 1017–1095). New York: Wiley.

Echevarria, J., & Graves, A. (2011). *Sheltered content instruction: Teaching English language learners with diverse abilities* (4th ed.). Boston: Allyn & Bacon.

Echevarria, J., & Short, D. J. (2009). Programs and practices for effective sheltered content instruction. In D. Dolson & L. Burnham-Massey (Eds.), *Improving education for English learners: Research-based approaches*. Sacramento: California Department of Education.

Echevarria, J., Short, D. J., & Powers, K. (2006). School reform and standards-based education: An instructional model for English language learners. *Journal of Educational Research, 99*(4), 195–210.

Echevarria, J., & Vogt, M. E. (2011). *RtI for English learners: Making it work*. Boston: Allyn & Bacon.

Echevarria, J., Vogt, M. E., & Short, D. (2004). *Making content comprehensible for English language learners: The SIOP® model* (2nd ed.). Boston: Allyn & Bacon.

Echevarria, J., Vogt, M. E., & Short, D. (2008). *Making content comprehensible for English learners: The SIOP® model* (3rd ed.). Boston: Allyn & Bacon.

Echevarria, J., Vogt, M. E., & Short, D. (2010a). *Making content comprehensible for elementary English learners: The SIOP® model*. Boston: Allyn & Bacon.

Echevarria, J., Vogt, M. E., & Short, D. (2010b). *Making content comprehensible for secondary English learners: The SIOP® model*. Boston: Allyn & Bacon.

Ehren, B. (2008). Response to intervention in secondary schools: Is it on your radar screen? Washington, DC: RtI Action Network. Available at http://www.rtinetwork.org/Learn/Why/ar/RadarScreen.

Ehri, L. (1994). Development of the ability to read words: Update. In R. B. Ruddell, M. R. Ruddell, & H. Singer (Eds.), *Theoretical models and processes of reading* (4th ed., pp. 323–358). Newark, DE: International Reading Association.

Fisher, D., Flood, J., Lapp, D., & Frey, N. (2004). Interactive read-alouds: Is there a common set of implementation practices? *The Reading Teacher, 58*(1), 8–17.

Fisher, D., & Frey, N. (2004). *Improving adolescent literacy: Strategies at work*. Upper Saddle River, NJ: Merrill Prentice-Hall.

Fisher, D., & Frey, N. (2007). Implementing a schoolwide literacy framework: Improving achievement in an urban elementary school. *The Reading Teacher, 61*(1), 32–43.

Flanigan, K., & Greenwood, S. C. (2007). Effective content vocabulary instruction in the middle: Matching students, purposes, words, and strategies. *Journal of Adolescent and Adult Literacy, 51*(3), 226–238.

Flesch, R. (1955). *Why Johnny can't read*. New York: Harper.

Fletcher, R., & Portalupi, J. (2001). *Writing workshop: The essential guide*. Portsmouth, NH: Heinemann.

Flood, J., Lapp, D., & Fisher, D. (2005). Neurological impress methods plus. *Reading Psychology, 26*, 147–150.

Ford, M. (2005). *Differentiation through flexible grouping: Successfully reaching all readers*. Naperville, IL: Learning Point Associates.

Fountas, I. C., & Pinnell, G. S. (1996). *Guided reading: Good first teaching for all children*. Portsmouth, NH: Heinemann.

Fountas, I. C., & Pinnell, G. S. (1998). *Words matter: Teaching phonics and spelling in the reading and writing classroom*. Portsmouth, NH: Heinemann.

Fountas, I. C., & Pinnell, G. S. (2001). *Guiding readers and writers: Teaching comprehension, genre, and content literacy*. Portsmouth, NH: Heinemann.

Fournier, D. N. E., & Graves, M. F. (2002). Scaffolding adolescents' comprehension of short stories. *Journal of Adolescent and Adult Literacy, 48*(1), 30–39.

Fox, B. J. (2003). *Word identification strategies: Phonics from a new perspective* (3rd ed.). Upper Saddle River, NJ: Merrill.

Freeman, Y. S., Freeman, D. E., & Mercuri, S. P. (2005). *Dual language essentials for teachers and administrators*. Portsmouth, NH: Heinemann.

Frey, N., & Fisher, D. (2006). *Language arts workshop: Purposeful reading and writing instruction*. Upper Saddle River, NJ: Merrill Prentice-Hall.

Friend, M., & Cook, L. (2007). *Interactions: Collaboration skills for school professionals* (5th ed.). Boston: Allyn & Bacon.

Fries, C. C. (1963). *Linguistics and reading*. New York: Holt, Rinehart, & Winston.

Frost, S., & Bean, R. (2006). Qualifications for literacy coaches: Achieving the gold standard. Literacy Coaching Clearinghouse. Available at http://www.literacycoachingonline.org/briefs/LiteracyCoaching.pdf.

Fuchs, D., Fuchs, L. S., Mathes, P. G., & Simmons, D. C. (1997). Peer-assisted learning strategies: Making classrooms more responsive to diversity. *American Educational Research Journal, 34*, 174–206.

Fullan, M. (2005). *Leadership and sustainability: Systems thinkers in action*. Thousand Oaks, CA: Corwin Press and Ontario Principals' Council.

Fullan, M., Hill, P., & Crévola, C. (2006). *Breakthrough*. Thousand Oaks, CA: Corwin Press.

Gallagher, K. (2006). *Teaching adolescent writers*. New York: Stenhouse.

Gambrell, L. M., Morrow, L., Neuman, S. B., & Pressley, M. (1999). *Best practices in early literacy*. New York: Guilford Press.

Ganske, K. (2000). *Word sorts and more: Sound, pattern, and meaning explorations K–3 (Solving problems in the teaching of literacy series)*. New York: Guilford Press.

Garcia, O., & Baker, C. (2007). *Bilingual education: An introductory reader*. Tanawanda, NY: Multilingual Matters.

Garmston, R. J. (1997). Can collaboration be taught? *Journal of Staff Development, 18*(4). Available at http://www.markville.ss.yrdsb.edu.on.ca/mm/OISEAQ/Can_Collaboration_Be_Taught.pdf.

Garmston, R. J. (2005). *The presenter's fieldbook: A practical guide* (2nd ed.). Norwood, MA: Christopher-Gordon.

Gee, J. P. (1990). *Social linguistics and literacies: Ideology in discourses*. Philadelphia: Falmer.

Gee, J. P. (2001a). Identity as an analytic lens for research in education. *Review of Educational Research, 25,* 99–125.

Gee, J. P. (2001b, December). *Reading in "new times."* Plenary address presented at the National Reading Conference, San Antonio, TX.

Gee, J. P. (2004). *Situated language and learning: A critique of traditional schooling*. London: Routledge.

Genesee, F., Lindholm-Leary, K., Saunders, W., & Christian, D. (2005). English language learners in U.S. schools: An overview of research findings. *Journal of Education for Students Placed at Risk, 10*(4), 363–385.

George, P. (2005). A rationale for differentiating instruction in the regular classroom. *Theory into Practice, 44*(3), 185–193.

Gersten, R., Baker, S., Shanahan, T., Linan-Thompson, S., Collins, P., & Scarcella, R. (2007). *Effective literacy and English language instruction for English learners in the elementary grades: A practice guide* (NCEE 2007-4011). Washington, DC: National Center for Education Evaluation and Regional Assistance, Institute of Education Sciences, U.S. Department of Education. Available at http://ies.ed.gov/ncee.

Glickman, C. D., Gordon, S. P., & Ross-Gordon, J. M. (1998). *Supervision of instruction: A developmental approach* (4th ed.). Boston: Allyn & Bacon.

Goldenberg, C. (1993). Instructional conversations: Promoting comprehension through discussion. *The Reading Teacher, 46*(4), 316–326.

Goldenberg, C. (2008). Teaching English language learners: What the research does—and does not—say. *American Educator, 12*(2), 8–22. Available at http://www.aft.org/pubs-reports/american_educator/issues/summer08/goldenberg.pdf.

Goodman, K. (1986). *What's whole about whole language*. Portsmouth, NH: Heinemann.

Gordon, S. P. (2004). *Professional development for school improvement: Empowering learning communities*. Boston: Allyn & Bacon.

Goswami, U. (2000). Phonological and lexical processes. In M. L. Kamil, P. B. Mosenthal, P. D. Pearson, & R. Barr (Eds.), *Handbook of reading research* (Vol. III, pp. 251–265). Mahwah, NJ: Erlbaum.

Graff, Harvey J. (2007). Literacy, myths, and legacies: Lessons from the history of literacy. In H. J. Graff (Ed.), *Literacy and historical development: A reader* (pp. 12–37). Carbondale: Southern Illinois University Press.

Gray, W. S. (1915). Standardized oral reading test. *Studies of elementary school reading through standardized tests* (Supplemental Educational Monographs No. 1). Chicago: University of Chicago Press.

Greenwood, S. C., & Flanigan, K. (2007). Overlapping vocabulary and comprehension: Context clues complement semantic gradients. *The Reading Teacher, 61*(3), 249–254.

Guskey, T. R. (2000). *Evaluating professional development*. Thousand Oaks, CA: Corwin Press.

Guthrie, J. T. (2002). Motivation and engagement in reading instruction. In M. Kamil, J. Manning, & H. Walberg (Eds.), *Successful reading instruction* (pp. 137–154). Greenwich, CT: Information Age Publishing.

Guthrie, J. T., Van Meter, P., Hancock, G. R., Alao, S., Anderson, E., & McCann, A. (1998). Does concept-oriented reading instruction increase strategy use and conceptual learning from text? *Journal of Educational Psychology, 90,* 261–278.

Guthrie, J. T., & Wigfield, A. (2002). Engagement and motivation in reading. In M. L. Kamil, P. B. Mosenthal, P. D. Pearson, & R. Barr (Eds.), *Handbook of reading research* (Vol. III, pp. 403–422). New York: Erlbaum.

Haberman, M. (1996). Selecting and preparing culturally competent teachers for urban schools. In J. Sikula (Ed.), *Handbook of research in teacher education* (pp. 747–760). New York: Simon & Schuster.

Haggard, M. (1982). The Vocabulary Self-Collection Strategy: Using student interest and word knowledge to enhance vocabulary growth. *Journal of Reading, 21,* 203–207.

Hannon, P. (2003). Family literacy programmes. In N. Hall, J. Larson, & J. Marsh (Eds.), *Handbook of early childhood literacy* (pp. 99–108). Thousand Oaks, CA: Sage.

Hansen, R. A., & Farrell, D. (1995). The long-term effects on high school seniors of learning to read in kindergarten. *Reading Research Quarterly, 30,* 908–933.

Harris, T. L., & Hodges, R. E. (1995). *The literacy dictionary: The vocabulary of reading and writing.* Newark, DE: International Reading Association.

Harrison, C. (2004). *Understanding reading development.* Thousand Oaks, CA: Sage.

Harrison, C. (2007). Other voices. In M. E. Vogt & B. A. Shearer, *Reading specialists and literacy coaches in the real world* (2nd ed., pp. 181–182). Boston: Allyn & Bacon.

Harvey, S., & Daniels, H. (2009). *Comprehension and collaboration: Literacy circles in action.* Portsmouth, NH: Heinemann.

Harvey, S., & Goudvis, A. (2000). *Strategies that work: Teaching comprehension to enhance understanding.* York, ME: Stenhouse.

Harvey, W. B. (December 2009/January 2010). Strategic plan guides IRA's future efforts. *Reading Today, 27*(3), 32.

Heath, S. B. (1983). *Ways with words: Language, life, and work in communities and classrooms.* Cambridge, UK: Cambridge University Press.

Heath, S. B. (1983/1996). What no bedtime story means: Narrative skills at home and school. *Language and Society, 11,* 49–76.

Heath, S. B. (1994). The children of Trackton's children: Spoken and written language in social change. In R. B. Ruddell, M. R. Ruddell, & H. Singer (Eds.), *Theoretical models and processes of reading* (4th ed., pp. 208–230). Newark, DE: International Reading Association.

Hendron, J. G. (2008). *RSS for educators: Blogs, newsfeeds, podcasts, and wikis in the classroom.* Eugene, OR/Washington, DC: International Society for Technology in Education.

Hiebert, E. H., & Taylor, B. M. (2000). Beginning reading instruction: Research on early interventions. In M. L. Kamil, P. B. Mosenthal, P. D. Pearson, & R. Barr (Eds.), *Handbook of Reading Research* (Vol. III, pp. 455–482). Mahwah, NJ: Erlbaum.

Hiebert, E. H., Pearson, P. D., Taylor, B. M., Richardson, V., & Paris, S. G. (1998). *Every child a reader.* Ann Arbor, MI: Center for the Improvement of Early Reading Achievement (CIERA), University of Michigan.

Hinchey, P. (2001, May). Learning to read the world: Who—and what—is missing? *Reading Online, 4*(10). Available at www.reading.org/newliteracies/lit_index.asp?HREF=/newliteracies/hinchey.

Hinchman, K. A. (2005). Why qualitative research continues to thrive: Jason and the politics of representation. *Reading Research Quarterly, 40*(1), 100–105.

Hinchman, K. A., & Anders, P. L. (2009, May). *Paying attention to the school community: Designing a comprehensive all-school literacy program.* Presentation at the International Reading Association Convention, Minneapolis, MN.

Hinchman, K. A., & Sheridan-Thomas, H. K. (2008). *Best practices in adolescent literacy instruction.* New York: Guilford Press.

Hock, M. F., Deshler, D. D., & Schumaker, J. B. (2005). Enhancing student motivation through the pursuit of possible selves. In C. Dunkel & J. Kerpelman (Eds.), *Possible selves: Theory, research and applications* (pp. 205–221). Hauppauge, NY: Nova.

Hord, S. M., & Sommers, W. A. (2008). *Leading professional learning communities: Voices for research and practice.* Thousand Oaks, CA: Corwin Press.

Horn, M., & Giacobbe, M. E. (2007). *Talking, drawing, writing: Lessons for our youngest writers.* New York: Stenhouse.

Howard, M. (2009). *RtI from all sides: What every teacher ought to know.* Portsmouth, NH: Heinemann.

Huebner, C. E., & Meltzoff, A. N. (2005). Intervention to change parent–child reading style: A comparison of instructional methods. *Journal of Applied Developmental Psychology, 26*(3), 296–313.

Huey, E. B. (1908/1968). *The psychology and pedagogy of reading.* Cambridge, MA: MIT Press.

Hull, G. (2003). Youth culture and digital media: New literacies for new times. *Research in Teaching English, 38,* 229–333.

Institute for Educational Services (IES) National Center for Educational Statistics (2007). *Trends in adult literacy.* Washington, DC: Author. Available at: http://nces.ed.gov/programs/coe/2007/section2/indicator18.asp.

International Reading Association (1994). *Standards for the assessment of reading and writing: A position statement of the International Reading Association.* Newark, DE: Author. Available at www.reading.org.

International Reading Association & National Council of Teachers of English. (1996). *Standards for the English Language Arts.* Newark, DE: International Reading Association. Available at www.reading.org.

International Reading Association. (1997). *The role of phonics in reading instruction: A position statement of the International Reading Association.* Newark, DE: Author. Available at www.reading.org.

International Reading Association. (2000a). *Beginning literacy and your child: A guide to helping your baby or preschooler become a reader.* Newark, DE: Author.

International Reading Association. (2000b). *"Books are cool!" Keeping your middle school student reading.* Newark, DE: Author.

International Reading Association. (2001). *Integrating literacy and technology in the curriculum.* Newark, DE: Author.

International Reading Association. (2002a). *High stakes assessment in reading: A position statement of the International Reading Association.* Newark, DE: Author. Available at www.reading.org.

International Reading Association. (2002b). *What is evidence-based reading instruction? A position statement of the International Reading Association.* Newark, DE: Author. Available at www.reading.org.

International Reading Association. (2003a). *A call to action and a framework for change: A position statement of the International Reading Association.* Newark, DE: Author. Available at www.reading.org.

International Reading Association. (2003b). *The role of reading instruction in addressing the overrepresentation of minority children in special education in the United States: A position statement of the International Reading Association.* Newark, DE: Author. Available at www.reading.org.

International Reading Association. (2004a). *Standards for reading professionals.* Newark, DE: Author. Available at www.reading.org.

International Reading Association (2004b). *The roles and qualifications of the reading coach in the United States: A position statement of the International Reading Association.* Newark, DE: Author. Available at www.reading.org.

International Reading Association (2005). *Best practice brief: The reading coach. A position statement of the International Reading Association.* Newark, DE: Author. Available at www.reading.org/downloads/resources/BPBrief_reading_coaches.pdf.

International Reading Association. (2006). *Standards for middle and high school literacy coaches.* Newark, DE: Author.

International Reading Association. (2007). *Category descriptions of reading professionals.* Newark, DE: Author. Available at www.reading.org/downloads/standards/definitions.pdf.

International Reading Association & National Council of Teachers of English. (2009). *Standards for the assessment of reading and writing.* Newark, DE: International Reading Association. Available at www.reading.org.

Invernizzi, M., Justice, L., Landrum, T. J., & Booker, K. (2004/2005). Early literacy screening in kindergarten: Widespread implementation in Virginia. *Journal of Literacy Research, 36,* 479–500.

Jenkins, J. R. (2003, December). *Candidate measures for screening at-risk students.* Paper presented at the National Research Center on Learning Disabilities Responsiveness-to-Intervention symposium, Kansas City, MO. Available at http://www.nrcld.org/symposium2003/jenkins/index.html.

Jenkins, J. R., Graff, J. J., & Miglioretti, D. L. (2009). Estimating reading growth using intermittent CBM progress monitoring. *Exceptional Children, 75,* 151–163.

Jenkins, J. R., & O'Connor, R. E. (2002). Early identification and intervention for young children with reading/learning disabilities. In R. Bradley, L. Danielson, & D. P. Hallahan (Eds.), *Identification of learning disabilities: Research to practice* (pp. 99–150). Mawah, NJ: Erlbaum.

Jetton, T.A., & Alexander, P. A. (2007). Domains, teaching, and literacy. In T. A. Jetton & J. A. Dole (Eds.), *Adolescent literacy research and practice* (pp. 15–39). New York: Guilford Press.

Johns, J. J. (2008). *Basic reading inventory: Pre-primer through grade 12 and early literacy assessments* (10th ed.). Dubuque, IA: Kendall/Hunt.

Johnson, E. S., Pool, J. L., & Carter, D. (2009). Implementing a screening process within an RtI framework: A review of methods and instruments K–12. National Center on Learning Disabilities RTI Action Network. Available at www.rtinetwork.org.

Johnson, R. T., & Johnson, D. W. (1986). Action research: Cooperative learning in the science classroom. *Science and Children, 24,* 31–32.

Joyce, B., & Showers, B. (2002). *Student achievement through staff development* (3rd ed.). Alexandria, VA: Association for Supervision and Curriculum Development.

Kahoun, J., & Bjurlin, A. (2009, May). *Effective leadership teams.* Presentation at the International Reading Association Convention, Minneapolis, MN. Available at www.reading.org.

Kamil, M. L. (2010). *Adolescent literacy and textbooks: An annotated bibliography.* New York: Carnegie Foundation.

Katz, L. G. (1992). *What should young children be doing?* ERIC Digest. Urbana, IL: ERIC Clearinghouse on Elementary and Early Childhood Education, University of Illinois.

Keene, E. O. (2008). *To understand: New horizons in reading comprehension.* Portsmouth, NH: Heinemann.

Keresty, B., O'Leary, S., & Wortley, D. (1998). *You can make a difference: A teacher's guide to political action.* Portsmouth, NH: Heinemann.

Ketch, A. (2005). Conversation: The comprehension connection. *The Reading Teacher, 59,* 8–13.

Kirp, D. L. (2007). *The sandbox investment: The preschool movement and kids-first politics.* Cambridge, MA: Harvard University Press.

Kist, W., & Ryan, J. (2009). How can adolescent literacies outside of school be brought into the classroom? In J. Lewis (Ed.), *Essential questions in adolescent literacy: Teachers and researchers describe what works in classrooms* (pp. 58–76). New York: Guilford Press.

Klesius, J. P., & Griffith, P. (1996). Interactive storybook reading for at-risk learners. *The Reading Teacher, 49,* 552–560.

Klingner, J. K., & Edwards, P. A. (2006). Cultural considerations with Response to Intervention models. *Reading Research Quarterly, 41*(1), 117.

Knobel. M. (2001). "I'm not a pencil man": How one student challenges our notions of literacy failure in school. *Journal of Adolescent and Adult Literacy, 44,* 404–414.

Knobel, M., & Lankshear, C. (2005). New literacies: Research and social practice. In *Fifty-Fourth Yearbook of the National Reading Conference.* Oak Creek, WI: National Reading Conference.

Knobel, M., & Lankshear, C. (2009). Wikis, digital literacies, and professional growth. *Journal of Adolescent and Adult Literacy, 52*(7), 631–634.

Kos, R. (1991). Persistence of reading difficulties: The voices of four middle school students. *American Educational Research Journal, 28,* 875–895.

Krashen, S. D. (1985). *The input hypothesis: Issues and implications.* New York: Longman.

Kucan, L., & Beck, I. L. (1997). Thinking aloud and reading comprehension research: Inquiry, instruction, and social interaction. *Review of Educational Research, 67,* 271–299.

Kutner, M., Greenberg, E., & Baer, J. (2005). *A first look at the literacy of America's adults in the twenty-first century.* Washington, DC: U.S. Department of Education, National Assessment of Adult Literacy.

LaBerge, D., & Samuels, S. J. (1974). Toward a theory of automatic information processing in reading. *Cognitive Psychology, 6,* 293–323.

Ladenson, R. F. (2003). Inclusion and justice in special education. In R. Carren (Ed.), *A companion to the philosophy of education* (pp. 525–539). Malden, MA: Blackwell.

Ladson-Billings, G. (1995). Toward a theory of culturally relevant pedagogy. *American Education Research Journal, 32,* 465–491.

Lambert, L. (2002). A framework for shared leadership. *Educational Leadership, 59*(8), 37–40.

Lankshear, C., & Knobel, M. (2003). *New literacies: Changing knowledge and classroom learning.* Buckingham and Philadelphia: Open University Press.

Lapp, D., Fisher, D., Flood, J., & Frey, N. (2003). Dual role of the urban reading specialist. *Journal of Staff Development, 24*(2), 33–36.

Lazar, A. (2001). Preparing white preservice teachers for urban classrooms: Growth in a Philadelphia-based literacy practicum. In J. V. Hoffmann, D. L. Schallert, C. M. Fairbanks, J. Worthy, & B. Maloch (Eds.), *National Reading Conference Yearbook* (Vol. 50, pp. 558–571). Chicago: National Reading Conference.

Lee, C. D., & Spratley, A. (2010). *Reading in the disciplines: The challenges of adolescent literacy.* New York: Carnegie Foundation.

Lefever-Davis, S., & Pearman, C. (2005). Early readers and electronic texts: CD-ROM storybook features that influence reading behaviors. *The Reading Teacher, 58*(5), 446–454.

Leftwich, S. (2001, December). *Using the ABCs Model to help preservice teachers involved in a community reading project.* Symposium presented at the 51st Annual Meeting of the National Reading Conference, San Antonio, TX.

Lesaux, N., & Geva, E. (2008). In D. August & T. Shanahan (Eds.), *Developing reading and writing in second-language learners: Lessons from the Report of the National Literacy Panel on Language-Minority Children and Youth.* New York: Routledge. Copublished with the Center for Applied Linguistics and the International Reading Association.

Leu, D. (2005). *Literacy research for lives with literacy.* Presidential address given at the 55th Annual Meeting of the National Reading Conference, Miami, Florida.

Leu, D. (2010, March). *My ten basic ideas on how to integrate the new literacies of online reading comprehension into your classroom.* Keynote address at the Virginia State Reading Association Conference, Virginia Beach, Virginia.

Leu, D., & Castek, J. (2006). *What skills and strategies are characteristic of accomplished users of the Internet?* San Francisco: American Educational Research Association.

Levin, H. M., Catlin, D., & Elson, A. (2010). *Adolescent literacy programs: Costs of implementation.* New York: Carnegie Foundation.

Lewis, C. (2001). *Literacy practices as social acts: Power, status, and cultural norms in the classroom.* Mahwah, NJ: Erlbaum.

Lewis, C., & Fabos, B. (2005). Instant messaging, literacies, and social identities. *Reading Research Quarterly, 40*(4), 470–501.

Lewis, J. (Ed.). (2009). *Essential questions in adolescent literacy: Teachers and researchers describe what works in classrooms.* New York: Guilford Press.

Lewis, J., Jongsma, K. S., & Berger, A. (2005). *Educators on the frontline: Advocacy strategies for your classroom, your school, and your profession.* Newark, DE: International Reading Association.

Lipson, M. Y., & Wixson, K. K. (2003). *Assessment and instruction of reading and writing difficulty: An interactive approach* (3rd ed.). Boston: Allyn & Bacon.

Lipson, M. Y., & Wixson, K. K. (2008). *Assessment and instruction of reading and writing difficulties: An interactive approach* (4th ed.). Boston: Allyn & Bacon.

Literacy Coaching Clearinghouse. (2008). *Role of a reading specialist: Qualifications of a reading specialist.* Available at http://www.literacycoachingonline.org/aboutus/reading_specialist.html.

Lose, M. K. (2008, May). *Making RtI work for children, teachers, and schools.* Presentation at the International Reading Association Convention, Atlanta, Georgia. Available at http//:www.reading.org/downloads/53rd_conv_handouts/lose.ppt.

Luke, A., & Freebody, P. (1999, August). Further notes on the four sources model. *Reading Online.* Available at www.readingonline.orgpast/past_index/asp?HREF=/research/lukefreebody.html.

Lyman, F. T. (1981). The responsive classroom discussion: The inclusion of all students. In A. Anderson (Ed.), *Mainstreaming digest* (pp. 109–113). College Park, MD: University of Maryland Press.

Lyons, C. A., & Pinnell, G. S. (2001). *Systems for change in literacy education: A guide to professional development.* Portsmouth, NH: Heinemann.

Maeroff, G. I. (1993, March). Building teams to rebuild schools. *Phi Delta Kappan, 74*(7), 512–514.

Maeroff, G. I. (2006). *Building blocks: Making children successful in the early years of school.* New York: Palgrave Macmillan.

Mangin, M. (2009). Factors that influence a district's decisions about literacy coaches. The Literacy Coaching Collaborative. Available at http://www.literacycoachingonline.org/briefs/factors_district_decisions.pdf.

Marzano, R. J. (2007). *The art and science of teaching.* Alexandria, VA: Association for Supervision and Curriculum Development.

Marzano, R. J., Waters, T., & McNulty, B. (2005). *School leadership that works: From research to results.* Alexandria, VA: Association for Supervision and Curriculum Development.

Mazurkiewicz, A. J., & Tanyzer, H. J. (1966). *Easy to read i/t/a program.* New York: Initial Teaching Alphabet Publications.

McAndrews, S. (2008). *Diagnostic literacy assessments and instructional strategies: A literacy specialist's resource.* Newark, DE: International Reading Association.

McClelland, D. C. (1987). *Human motivation.* New York: Cambridge University Press.

McConnell, S., Carta, A., & Greenwood, C. (2008, February). *Bringing Response to Intervention (RtI) into preschool—Bridging research and practice.* Presentation at the Biannual Conference on Research Innovations in Early Intervention, San Diego, California. Available at http://www.crtiec.org/Documents/CRIEI RtI Intro and Challenges.pdf.

McDonald, T., Thornley, C., Staley, R., & Moore, D. W. (2009). The San Diego Striving Readers' Project: Building academic success for adolescent readers. *Journal of Adolescent and Adult Literacy 52*(8), 720–722.

McGill-Franzen, A., & Allington, R. L. (1993). Flunk 'em or get them classified: The contamination of primary grade accountability data. *Educational Researcher, 22,* 19–22.

McGlinn, J. (2009, May). *The Paperless SQ3R.* Presentation at the Content Area Reading SIG: 54th Annual International Reading Association Conference, Minneapolis, Minnesota. Available at http://www.reading.org/General/Conferences/AnnualConvention/MinneapolisMain/ProgramMN.aspx.

McKenna, M. C., & Walpole, S. (2008). *The literacy coaching challenge: Models and methods for grades K–8.* New York: Guilford Press.

McLaughlin, M., & Allen, M. (2009). Teacher-directed whole-group instruction. In *Guided Comprehension in Grades 3–8* (2nd ed., pp. 17–32). Newark, DE: International Reading Association.

McLaughlin, M., & DeVoogd, G. (2004). *Critical literacy: Enhancing students' comprehension of text.* New York: Scholastic.

McLaughlin, M., & Vogt, M. E. (1996). *Portfolios in teacher education.* Newark, DE: International Reading Association.

Medina, C. L. (2005). *Critical literacies through performative pedagogies: Intersections between identities, social imaginations and language.* Paper presented at the 2005 National Reading Conference, Miami, Florida.

Meek, M. (1983). *Achieving literacy: Longitudinal studies of adolescents learning to read.* London: Routledge & Kegan Paul.

Mehan, H. (1979). *Learning lessons: Social organization in the classroom.* Cambridge, MA: Harvard University Press.

Meltzer, J., & Ziemba, S. (2006). Getting schoolwide literacy up and running. *Principal Leadership (Middle School Edition), 7*(1), 21–26.

Mere, C. (2005). *More than guided reading: Finding the right instructional mix, K–3*. New York: Stenhouse.

Messick, S. (1989). Validity. In R. L. Linn (Ed.), *Educational measurement* (3rd ed., pp. 13–103). New York: Macmillan.

Moje, E. B. (2000). Critical issues: Circles of kinship, friendship, position, and power: Examining the community in community-based literacy research. *Journal of Literacy Research, 32*(1), 77–112.

Moje, E. B. (2006). Motivating texts, motivating contexts, motivating adolescents: An examination of the role of motivation in adolescent literacy practices and development. *Perspectives, 32*(3), 10–14.

Moje, E. B. (2007). Developing socially just subject-matter instruction: A review of the literature on disciplinary literacy teaching. *Review of Research in Education, 31*(1), 1–44.

Moje, E. B., & Hinchman, K. (2004). Culturally responsive practices for youth literacy and learning. In T. L. Jetton & J. A. Dole (Eds.), *Adolescent literacy research and practice* (pp. 321–350). New York: Guilford Press.

Moje, E. B., & Tysvaer, N. (2010). *Adolescent literacy development in out-of-school time: A practitioner's guide*. New York: Carnegie Foundation.

Mokhtari, K., Rosemary, C. A., & Edwards, P. A. (2007). Making instructional decisions based on data: What, how, and why. *The Reading Teacher, 61*(4), 354–359.

Moll, L. C. (1994). Literacy research in community and classrooms: A sociocultural approach. In R. B. Ruddell, M. R. Ruddell, & H. Singer (Eds.), *Theoretical models and processes of reading* (4th ed.). Newark, DE: International Reading Association.

Moon, T. (2005). The role of assessment in differentiation. *Theory into Practice, 44*(3), 226–233.

Moore, D. W., Bean, T., Birdyshaw, D., & Rycik, J. (1999). *Adolescent literacy: A position statement for the Commission on Adolescent Literacy of the International Reading Association*. Newark, DE: International Reading Association.

Moore, D. W. (1997). Questions of balance. *Reading Research Quarterly, 32*(2), 212–215.

Moore, M., & Wilson, H. B. (1927). *A peep into fairyland: A child's book of phonics games*. Moore-Wilson Readers. Boston: D.C. Heath.

Moran, M. C. (2007). *Differentiated literacy coaching: Scaffolding for student and teacher success*. Alexandria, VA: Association for Supervision and Curriculum Development.

Morrow, L. M., & Asbury, E. (1999). *Best practices for a balanced literacy program*. New York: Guilford Press.

Morrow, L. M., & Gambrell, L. B. (2004). *Using children's literature in preschool: Comprehending and enjoying books*. Newark, DE: International Reading Association.

Morsy, L., Kieffer, M., & Snow, C. E. (2010). *Measure for measure: A critical consumers' guide to reading comprehension assessments for adolescents*. New York: Carnegie Foundation. Available at http://www.carnegie.org/literacy/tta/pdf/tta_Morsy.pdf.

Mosteller, F., Light, R. J., & Sachs, J. A. (1996). Sustained inquiry in education: Lessons from skill grouping and class size. *Harvard Education Review, 66*(4), 797–842.

Moxley, D. E., & Taylor, R. T. (2006). *Literacy coaching: A handbook for school leaders*. Thousand Oaks, CA: Corwin Press.

Murphy, R., Penuel, W., Means, B., Korbak, C., & Whaley, A. (2001). *E-DESK: A review of recent evidence on the effectiveness of discrete educational software*. Menlo Park, CA: SRI International.

Nagy, W. (1988). *Teaching vocabulary to improve reading comprehension*. Urbana, IL: National Council of Teachers of English, and Newark, DE: International Reading Association.

National Association of Secondary School Principals. (2005). *Creating a culture of literacy: A guide for middle and high school principals*. Reston, VA: Author.

National Center for Education Statistics. (2002). *Internet access in public schools and classrooms*. Available at http://nces.ed.gov/pubsearch/pubsinfo.asp?pubid=2001071.

National Center for Educational Statistics. (2007). *The Condition of Education 2007* (NCES 2007–064). Washington, DC: United States Department of Education, Institute of Education Sciences. Available at http://www.nifl.gov/adult/adult.html.

National Council of Teachers of English. (1974). Students' rights to language. *College Composition and Communication* (pp. 2–3). Urbana, IL: Author.

National Council of Teachers of English. (2006). *NCTE principles of adolescent literacy reform: A policy research brief*. Urbana, IL: Author.

National Governor's Association (NGA) & Council of Chief State Officers (CCSO). (2010). *Common core state standards initiative (CCSSI)*. Available at http://www.corestandard.org.

National Reading Panel. (2000). *Teaching children to read: An evidence-based assessment of the scientific research literature on reading and its implications for reading instruction*. Washington, DC: National Institute of Child Health and Human Development, National Institutes of Health.

NCELA (National Clearinghouse for English Language Acquisition). Frequently asked questions. Available at http://www.ncela.gwu.edu/faqs.

NICHD Early Childhood Research Network. (2004). Multiple paths to early academic achievement. *Harvard Educational Review, 74*(1), 1–29.

Nieto, S. (1999, December). *Language literacy and culture: Intersections and implications.* Paper presented at the 49th Annual Meeting of the National Reading Conference, Orlando, Florida.

Noell, G. H. (2008). Research examining the relationships among consultation process, treatment integrity, and outcomes. In W. P. Erchul & S. M. Sheridan (Eds.), *Handbook of research in school consultation: Empirical foundations for the field* (pp. 323–342). Mahwah, NJ: Erlbaum.

North Central Regional Educational Laboratory (NCREL). (1995–Present). *Assessment.* Available at http://www.ncrel.org/sdrs/areas/issues/students/earlycld/ea500.htm.

O'Brien, D. (2001, June). "At-risk" adolescents: Redefining competencies through the multiliteracies of intermediality, visual arts, and representations. *Reading Online 4*(11). Available at www.readingonline.org/article//HREF=/newliteracies/obrien/index.html.

O'Brien, D., & Dubbels, B. (2009). Technology and literacy: Current and emerging practices. In K. D. Wood & W. E. Blanton (Eds.), *Literacy instruction for adolescents: Research-based practice* (pp. 472–493). New York: Guilford Press.

O'Brien, D. G., & Stewart, R. A. (1992). In E. K. Dishner, T. W. Bean, J. E. Readence, & D. W. Moore (Eds.), *Reading in the content areas: Improving classroom instruction* (3rd ed., pp. 30–40). Dubuque, IA: Kendall-Hunt.

O'Brien, D., Stewart, R., & Beach, R. (2009). Proficient reading in school: Traditional paradigms and new textual landscapes. In L. Christenbury, R. Bomer, & P. Smagorinsky (Eds.), *Handbook of adolescent literacy research* (pp. 80–97). New York: Guilford Press.

Oczkus, L. D. (2007). *Guided writing: Practical lessons, powerful results.* Portsmouth, NH: Heinemann.

Okagaki, L., & Sternberg, R. (1993). Putting the distance into students' hands: Practical intelligence for school. In R. R. Cocking and K. A. Renninger (Eds.), *The development and meaning of psychological distance* (pp. 237–254). Hillsdale, NJ: Erlbaum.

Olson, G. (2006). *New tools for learning.* Available at http://faculty.eicc.edu/golson/tools.htm.

Olsen, S. (2006). *Kids outsmart web filters.* Available at http://news.cnet.com/2009-1041_3-6062548.html.

Opitz, M. F., & Ford, M. P. (2001). *Reaching readers: Flexible and innovative strategies for guided reading.* Portsmouth, NH: Heinemann.

Opitz, M. F., & Ford, M. P. (2008). *Do-able differentiation: Varying groups, texts, and supports to reach readers.* Portsmouth, NH: Heinemann.

Pailliotet, A. W. (1998). Deep viewing: A critical look at visual texts. In J. L. Kincheloe & S. Steinberg (Eds.), *Unauthorized methods: Strategies for critical teaching* (pp. 123–136). New York: Routledge.

Palinscar, A. M., & Brown, A. (1982). *Reciprocal teaching of comprehension-monitoring activities* (Tech. Rep. No. 269). Champaign, IL: Center for the Study of Reading, University of Illinois.

Palinscar, A. M., & Brown, A. (1984). Reciprocal teaching of comprehension fostering and monitoring activities. *Cognition and Instruction, 1,* 117–175.

Palmer, P. J. (1998). *The courage to teach: Exploring the inner landscape of a teacher's life.* San Francisco: Jossey-Bass.

Pardo, L. S. (2004). What every teacher needs to know about comprehension. *The Reading Teacher, 58*(3), 272–280.

Parker, K. R., & Chao, J. T. (2007). Wiki as a teaching tool. *Interdisciplinary Journal of Knowledge and Learning Objects, 3,* 57–72. Available at http://www.ijklo.org/Volume3/IJKLOv3p057-072Parker284.pdf.

Patty, D., Maschoff, J. D., & Ransom, P. (1996). *The reading resource handbook for school leaders.* Norwood, MA: Christopher-Gordon.

Payne, S. (2001). *McGuffey readers.* Available at www.nd.edu/~rbarger/www7/mcguffey.html.

Pearson, J. W., & Santa C. M. (1995). Students as researchers of their own reading. *Journal of Reading, 38*(6), 462–469.

Pearson, P. D., Harvey, S., & Goudvis, A. (2005). *What every teacher should know about reading comprehension.* Portsmouth, NH: Heinemann.

Phillips, L. M., Norris, S. P., & Mason, J. M. (1996). Longitudinal effects of early literacy concepts on reading achievement: A kindergarten intervention and a five-year follow-up. *Journal of Literacy Research, 28,* 173–195.

Pikulski, J. J. (1995). Preventing reading failure: A review of five effective programs. *The Reading Teacher, 48,* 30–39.

Pinnell, G. S., Fried, M. D., & Estes, R. M. (1990). Reading Recovery: Learning how to make a difference. *The Reading Teacher, 43,* 283–295.

Pool, J., & Johnson, E. (2009). *Universal screening for reading problems: Why and how should we do this?* Washington, DC: RtI Action Network. Available from www.rtinetwork.org/Essential/Assessment/Universal/ar/ReadingProblems.

Pressley, M. (2000). What should comprehension instruction be the instruction of? In M. L. Kamil, P. B.

Mosenthal, P. D. Pearson, & R. Barr (Eds.), *Handbook of reading research* (Vol. III, pp. 545–562). Mahwah, NJ: Erlbaum.

Pressley, M. (2006). *Reading instruction that works: The case for balanced literacy.* New York: Guilford Press.

Pressley, M., Allington, R. L., Wharton-McDonald, R., Block, C. C., & Morrow, L. M. (2001). *Learning to read: Lessons from exemplary first grade classrooms.* New York: Guilford Press.

Progoff, I. (1975). *At a journal workshop: The basic text and guide for using the intensive journal.* New York: Dialogue House Library.

ProLiteracy. (2008). *Who we are: Mission statement.* Available at http://www.proliteracy.org/NetCommunity/Page.aspx?pid=303&srcid=555

Purcell-Gates, V. (2000, July). The role of qualitative and ethnographic research in educational policy. *Reading Online 4*(1) Available at www.readingonline.org/article/gates/HREF=/article/purcell-gates/index.html.

Quatroche, D. J., Bean, R. M., & Hamilton, R. L. (1998). *The role of the reading specialist: A review of research.* A Report of the Commission on the Role of the Reading Specialist. Newark, DE: International Reading Association.

Radencich, M. C. (1995). *Administration and supervision of the reading/writing program.* Boston: Allyn & Bacon.

Ramos-Ocasio, A. (1985). An interpretation of a theoretical concept and its applicability to an ESL classroom setting. *Facilitating transition to the mainstream: Sheltered English vocabulary development.* National Council of Bilingual Education, Web Document 300860069. Available at www.ncbe.gwu.edu.

Raphael, T. E., Highfield, K., & Au, K. H. (2006). *QAR now: Question answer relationship.* New York: Scholastic.

Rasinski, T. (2004). Creating fluent readers. *Educational Leadership, 61*(4), 46–51.

Rawls, W. (1961). *Where the red fern grows.* Garden City, NY: Doubleday.

Ray, K. W. (2006). *Study-driven: A framework for planning units in the writing workshop.* Portsmouth, NH: Heinemann.

Reiss, J. (2008). *102 content strategies for English language learners: Teaching for academic success in grades 3–12.* Upper Saddle River, NJ: Merrill Prentice-Hall.

Richardson, J. (2009). *The next step in guided reading: Focused assessments and targeted lessons for helping every student become a better reader.* Danbury, CT: Scholastic.

Richardson, W. (2009). *Blogs, wikis, and podcasts and other powerful tools for classrooms* (2nd ed.). Thousand Oaks, CA: Corwin Press.

Robb, L. (2000a). *Redefining staff development: A collaborative model for teachers and administrators.* Portsmouth, NH: Heinemann.

Robb, L. (2000b). *Teaching reading in middle school: A strategic approach to teaching reading that improves comprehension and thinking.* New York: Scholastic.

Roberts, S. M., & Pruitt, E. Z. (2009). *Schools as professional learning communities: Collaborative activities for professional development.* Thousand Oaks, CA: Corwin Press.

Robinson, H. A., & Rauch, S. J. (1965). *Guiding the reading program: A reading consultant's handbook.* Chicago: Science Research Associates.

Rosemary, C. A., Roskos, K. A., & Landreth, L. K. (2007). *Designing professional development in literacy: A framework for effective instruction.* New York: Guilford Press.

Rosenblatt, L. M. (1978). *The reader, the text, the poem: The transactional theory of literary work.* Carbondale, IL: Southern Illinois University Press.

Rosenblatt, L. M. (1994). The transactional theory of reading and writing. In R. B. Ruddell, M. R. Ruddell, & H. Singer (Eds.), *Theoretical models and processes of reading* (4th ed., pp. 1076–1092). Newark, DE: International Reading Association.

Rothenberg, S. S., & Watts, S. M. (1997). Students with learning difficulties meet Shakespeare: Using a scaffolded reading experience. *Journal of Adolescent and Adult Literacy, 40*(7), 532–539.

Routman, R. (2001). *Invitations: Changing as teachers and learners K–12.* Portsmouth, NH: Heinemann.

Routman, R. (2003). *Reading essentials: The specifics you need to teach reading well.* Portsmouth, NH: Heinemann.

Routman, R. (2005). *Writing essentials: Raising expectations and results while simplifying teaching.* Portsmouth, NH: Heinemann.

Ruddell, M. R. (2005). *Teaching content reading and writing* (4th ed.). New York: Wiley.

Ruddell, M. R., & Shearer, B. A. (2002). "Extraordinary," "tremendous," "exhilarating," "magnificent": Middle school at-risk students become avid word learners with the vocabulary self-collection strategy (VSS). *Journal of Adolescent and Adult Literacy, 45,* 352–363.

Ruddell, R. B. (2004). Researching the influential literacy teacher: Characteristics, beliefs, strategies, and new research directions. In R. B. Ruddell & N. Unrau (Eds.), *Theoretical models and processes of reading* (5th ed.). Newark, DE: International Reading Association.

Ruddell, R. B. (2006). *Teaching children to read and write: Becoming an effective literacy teacher* (4th ed.). Boston: Allyn & Bacon.

Ryan, R. M., & Deci, E. L. (2000). Self-determination theory and the facilitation of intrinsic motivation, social development, and well-being. *American Psychologist, 55,* 68–78.

Saddler, B., & Graham, S. (2005). The effects of peer-assisted sentence-combining instruction on the writing performance of more and less skilled young writers. *Journal of Educational Psychology, 97,* 43–54.

Samuels, C. (2009). High schools try our RtI. *Education Week, 23*(19), 20–22.

Santa, C. (1988). *Content reading including study systems.* Dubuque, IA: Kendall/Hunt.

Sapin, C., Padak, N., & Baycich, D. (2008). *Family literacy resource notebook.* Kent, OH: The Ohio Literacy Resource Center. Available at http://literacy.kent.edu/Oasis/famlitnotebook.

Schallert, D. L., & Roser, N. I. (1989). The role of reading in content area instruction. In D. Lapp, J. Flood, & N. Farnum (Eds.), *Content area reading and learning: Instructional strategies* (pp. 25–33). Englewood Cliffs, NJ: Prentice-Hall.

Schmidt, P. R. (1998a). The ABC model: Teachers connect home and school. In T. Shanahan & F. V. Rodriguez-Brown (Eds.), *National Reading Conference Yearbook* (Vol. 47, pp. 194–208). Chicago: National Reading Conference.

Schmidt, P. R. (1998b). The ABCs of cultural understanding and communication. *Equity and Excellence in Education, 31*(2), 28–38.

Schmidt, P. R. (1999). Know thyself and understand others. *Language Arts, 76*(4), 332–340.

Schmidt, P. R. (2000). Emphasizing differences to build cultural understandings. In V. J. Risko & K. Bromley (Eds.), *Collaboration for diverse learners: Viewpoints and practices* (pp. 210–230). Newark, DE: International Reading Association.

Schmidt, P. R. (Ed.). (2005). *The importance of family involvement: Preparing educators to communicate with families and communities.* Greenwich, CT: Information Age Publishing.

Schmidt, P. R., & Finkbeiner, C. (Eds.). (2006). *ABCs of cultural understanding and communication: National and international adaptations.* Greenwich, CT: Information Age.

Seligman, M. E. P. (1972). Learned helplessness. *Annual Review of Medicine, 23,* 407–412.

Senge, P. M., Cambron-McCabe, N., Lucas, T., Smith, B., Dutton, J., & Kleiner, A. (2000). *Schools that learn: A fifth discipline fieldbook.* New York: Doubleday.

Serafini, F. (2001). *The reading workshop: Creating space for readers.* Portsmouth, NH: Heinemann.

Serafini, F. (2006). *Lessons in comprehension: Explicit instruction in reading workshop.* Portsmouth, NH: Heinemann.

Shanahan, T. (2004). Overcoming the dominance of communication: Writing to think and to learn. In T. L. Jetton & J. A. Dole (Eds.), *Adolescent literacy research and practice* (pp. 59–73). New York: Guilford Press.

Shanklin, N. (2007, December). Literacy Coaching Clearinghouse a continually evolving resource. *Reading Today, 25*(3), 12.

Shannon, P. (1999). Every step you take. *The Reading Teacher, 53,* 32–35.

Shearer, B. A. (2001, December). *Oral history project of the National Reading Conference: Excerpts from an interview with Robert Dykstra.* Poster session presented at the National Reading Conference, San Antonio, TX.

Shearer, B. A., & Ruddell, M. R. (2006). Engaging students' interests and participation in learning. In D. Lapp, J. Flood, & N. Farnan (Eds.), *Content area reading and learning* (3rd ed.). Mahwah, NJ: Erlbaum.

Shearer, B. A., Ruddell, M. R., & Vogt, M. E. (2001). Successful middle school intervention: Negotiated strategies and individual choice. In J. V. Hoffman, D. L. Schallert, C. M. Fairbanks, J. Worthy, & B. Maloch (Eds.), *National Reading Conference Yearbook* (Vol. 50, pp. 558–571). Chicago: National Reading Conference.

Shearer, B. A., & Vogt, M. E. (2004). "Desperately deconstructing Susan . . ." The reading professional: Seeking the right questions. *The New England Reading Association Journal, 40*(2), 6–11.

Shepard, L. A., & Smith, M. L. (1990). What doesn't work: Explaining policies of retention in early grades. *Phi Delta Kappan, 68,* 121–164.

Short, D. J., Vogt, M. E., & Echevarria, J. (2010). *The SIOP® model for teaching history-social studies to English learners.* Boston: Allyn & Bacon.

Short, D. J., Vogt, M. E., & Echevarria, J. (in press). *The SIOP® model for teaching science to English learners.* Boston: Allyn & Bacon.

Simpson, A. (1996). Critical questions: Whose questions? *The Reading Teacher, 50,* 118–127.

Slavin, R. E., Madden, N. A., Dole, L. J., & Wasik, B. A. (1996). *Every child, every school: Success for all.* Newberry Park, CA: Corwin Press.

Smagorinsky, P. (Ed.). (2006). *Research on composition.* New York: Teachers College Press.

Smith, H. V., & Hofer, D. (2003). *Review of the teacher turnover research in 2003 in the NCSALL report "The Characteristics and Concerns of Adult Basic Education Teachers"* (pp. 6–7). Available at at http://tinyurl.com/zxbkd.

Smith, M. W., & Wilhelm, J. D. (2003). *Reading don't fix no chevys: Literacy in the lives of young men.* Portsmouth, NH: Heinemann.

Smith, M. W., & Wilhelm, J. D. (2006). *Going with the flow: Making literacy in school more like life*. Portsmouth, NH: Heinemann.

Smith, N. B. (2002). *American reading instruction* (Special Edition). Newark, DE: International Reading Association.

Snow, C. E. (2005). From literacy to learning. In D. H. Bowman, From literacy to learning: An interview with Catherine Snow on vocabulary, comprehension, and the achievement gap. *Harvard Educational Letter, 21*(4), 21. Available at http://www.hepg.org/hel/article/290.

Snow, C. E., Burns, S., & Griffin, P. (1998). *Preventing reading difficulties in young children*. Washington, DC: National Academy Press.

Snow, C. E., & Goldfield, B. (1982). Turn the page, please: Situation-specific language acquisition. *Journal of Child Language, 10,* 559–569.

Snow, C. E., Griffin, P., & Burns, M. S. (2005). *Knowledge to support the teaching of reading: Preparing teachers for a changing world*. San Francisco: Jossey-Bass.

Soriano, F. I. (1995). *Conducting needs assessments: A multidisciplinary approach*. Thousand Oaks, CA: Sage.

Southall, M. (2007). *Differentiated literacy centers*. Danbury, CT: Scholastic.

Sparks, D., & Hirsh, S. (1997). *A new vision for staff development*. Alexandria, VA: Association for Supervision and Curriculum Development.

Spear-Swerling, L. (2004). A road map for understanding reading disability and other reading problems: Origins, prevention, and intervention. In R. B. Ruddell & N. J. Unrau (Eds.), *Theoretical models and practices in reading* (5th ed.). Newark, DE: International Reading Association.

Spindler, G., & Spindler, L. (1987). *The interpretive ethnography of education: At home and abroad*. Hillsdale, NJ: Erlbaum.

Stahl, S. A., & Nagy, W. E. (2005). *Teaching word meanings*. Mahwah, NJ: Erlbaum.

Stanovich, K. (1986). Matthew effects in reading: Some consequences of individual differences in the acquisition of reading. *Reading Research Quarterly, 21,* 360–407.

Steinkuehler, C. A., Black, R. W., & Clinton, K. A. (2005). Researching literacy as tool, place, and way of being. *Reading Research Quarterly, 40*(1), 95–100.

Stevens, E. (1995). The design, development, and evaluation of literacy education: Application and practice (LEAP). An interactive hypermedia program for English/Language Arts teacher education. Available at http://www.coe.uh.edu/~lizs.

Street, B. V. (2005, December). *Literacy, technology and multimodality: Implications for pedagogy and curriculum*. Plenary presidential address given at National Reading Conference 55th Annual Meeting, Miami, Florida.

Sturtevant, E. G. (2006). *The literacy coach: A key to improving teaching and learning in secondary schools*. Washington, DC: Alliance for Excellent Education.

Sullivan, M. W., & Buchanan, C. D. (1963). *Programmed reading series*. New York: McGraw-Hill.

Sulzby, E. (1994). Children's emergent reading of favorite storybooks: A developmental study. In R. B. Ruddell, M. R. Ruddell, & H. Singer (Eds.), *Theoretical models and processes of reading* (4th ed., pp. 244–280). Newark, DE: International Reading Association.

Sutherland, E. (1988). *Simpson's contemporary quotations*. Boston: Houghton Mifflin.

Tatum, A. W. (2009). *Reading for their life: (Re)building the textual lineages of African American adolescent males*. Portsmouth, NH: Heinemann.

Tatum, B. (1997). *Why are all the black kids sitting together in the cafeteria?* New York: Basic Books.

Taylor, B. M., Graves, M. E., & van den Broek, P. (Eds.). (2000). *Reading for meaning: Fostering comprehension in the middle grades*. Newark, DE: International Reading Association and Teachers College Press.

Taylor, B. M., Short, R. A., Shearer, B. A., & Frye, B. (1995). First–grade teachers provide early reading intervention in the classroom. In R. Allington & S. Walmsley (Eds.), *No quick fix: Rethinking literacy programs in America's elementary schools* (pp. 159–176). New York: Teachers College Press.

Teale, W. H., & Martinez, M. G. (1996). Reading aloud to young children: Teachers' reading styles and kindergarteners' text comprehension. In C. Ponticorvo, M. Orsolini, B. Berge, & L. B. Resnick (Eds.), *Children's early text construction* (pp. 321–344). Mahwah, NJ: Erlbaum.

Templeton, S., & Morris, D. (2000). Spelling. In M. L. Kamil, P. B. Mosenthal, P. D. Pearson, & R. Barr (Eds.), *Handbook of reading research* (Vol. III, pp. 525–543). Mahwah, NJ: Erlbaum.

Thorndike, E. L. (1917). Reading as reasoning: A study of mistakes in paragraph reading. *Journal of Educational Psychology, 8,* 323–332.

Thorndike, E. L. (1921). *The teacher's word book*. New York: Teachers College Press.

Tierney, R. J. (1991). *Portfolio assessment in the reading-writing classroom*. Norwood, MA: Christopher-Gordon.

Tobin, J. (2005). Strengthening the use of qualitative research methods for studying literacy. *Reading Research Quarterly, 40*(1), 91–95.

Toll, C. A. (2005). *The literacy coach's survival guide: Essential questions and practical answers.* Newark, DE: International Reading Association.

Tovani, C. (2000). *"I read it, but I don't get it": Comprehension strategies for adolescent readers.* Portland, ME: Stenhouse.

U.S. Department of Education, National Center for Education Statistics. (2007). *The condition of education 2007* (NCES 2007–064), Washington, DC: U.S. Government Printing Office. Available at http://inces.ed.gov/pubsearch/pubsinfo.asp?pubid=2007064.

Valencia, S. W. (2004). Reading between the lines of test failure. In *Research that matters: Putting testing to the test: Issues in student assessment and school accountability* (pp. 14–15). Seattle: College of Education, University of Washington.

van den Broek, P., & Kremer, K. (2000). The mind in action: What it means to comprehend in reading. In B. M. Taylor, M. F. Graves, & P. van den Broek (Eds.), *Reading for meaning: Fostering comprehension in the middle grades* (pp. 1–31). Newark, DE: International Reading Association and Teachers College Press.

Van Sluys, K., Lewison, M., & Seely-Flint, A. (2006). Researching critical literacy. *Journal of Literacy Research, 38*(2), 197–233.

Vaughn, S., Klingner, J. K., & Bryant, D. P. (2001). Collaborative strategic reading as a means to enhance peer-mediated instruction for reading comprehension and content-area learning. *Remedial and Special Education, 22*(2), 66–75.

Venezky, R. L., Sabatini, J. P., Brooks, C., & Carino, C. (1996). *Policy and practice in adult learning: A case study perspective* (Technical Report No. TR96-07). Philadelphia: University of Pennsylvania, National Center on Adult Literacy.

Vogt, M. E. (1989). *The congruence between preservice teachers' and inservice teachers' attitudes and practices toward high and low achievers.* Unpublished doctoral dissertation, University of California, Berkeley.

Vogt, M. E. (1997). *Intervention strategies for intermediate and middle school students: Three models (that appear) to work.* Paper presented at the Research Institute of the Annual Conference of the California Reading Association, Anaheim, CA.

Vogt, M. E. (2005). Health and social factors on literacy development: Implications for teachers and teacher preparation. In P. Anders & J. Flood (Eds.), *The contexts of literacy in urban schools.* Newark, DE: International Reading Association.

Vogt, M. E., & Echevarria, J. (2008). *99 ideas and activities for teaching English learners with the SIOP® model.* Boston: Allyn & Bacon.

Vogt, M. E., Echevarria, J., & Short, D. (2010). *The SIOP® model for teaching English language arts to English learners.* Boston: Allyn & Bacon.

Vogt, M. E., & Nagano, P. (2003). Turn it on with Light Bulb Reading: Sound-switching strategies for struggling readers. *The Reading Teacher, 57*(3), 214–221.

Vygotsky, L. S. (1978). *Mind in society.* Cambridge, MA: Harvard University Press.

Waddell, G., & Lee, G. (2008). Crunching numbers, changing practices: A close look at student data that turns the tide in efforts to close the achievement gap. *National Staff Development Council, 29*(3), 19–21.

Wade, S. E., & Moje, E. B. (2000). The role of text in classroom learning. In M. L. Kamil, P. B. Mosenthal, P. D. Pearson, & R. Barr (Eds.), *Handbook of reading research* (Vol. III, pp. 609–627). Mahwah, NJ: Erlbaum.

Wagstaff, J. M. (1999). *Word walls.* New York: Scholastic.

Walker-Dalhouse, D., & Dalhouse, A. D. (2001). Parent-school relations: Communicating effectively with African American parents. *Young Children, 56,* 75–80.

Walpole, S., & McKenna, M. (2005). *The literacy coach's handbook: A guide to research-based practice.* New York: Guilford Press.

Walpole, S., & Blamey, L. (2008). Elementary literacy coaches: The reality of dual roles. *The Reading Teacher, 62*(3), 222–231.

Watson Pearson, J., & Santa, C. (1995). Students as researchers of their own learning. *Journal of Reading, 38*(6), 462–469.

Watts-Pailliotet, A. (2000, July). Welcome to the New Literacies department. *Reading OnLine, 4*(1). Available at www.readingonline.org/newlitera-cies/lit_index.asp?HREF.wattspailliotetl/index.html.

Weiner, E. J. (2005). Keeping adults behind: Adult literacy education in the age of official reading regimes. *Journal of Adolescent and Adult Literacy, 49*(4), 286–301.

Weiss, H., Dearing, E., Mayer, E., Kreider, H., & McCartney, K. (2005). Family educational involvement: Who can afford it and what does it afford? In C. R. Cooper, C. T. García Coll, W. T. Bartko, H. M. Davis, & C. Chatman (Eds.), *Developmental pathways through middle childhood: Rethinking context and diversity as resources.* Mahwah, NJ: Erlbaum.

Wellins, R. S., Byham, W. C., & Wilson, J. M. (1991). *Empowered teams: Creating self-directed work groups that improve quality, productivity, and participation.* San Francisco: Jossey-Bass.

Wepner, S. B., & Seminoff, N. (1995). Evolving roles and responsibilities of reading personnel. In S. B. Wepner, J. T. Feeley, & D. S. Strickland (Eds.), *The administration and supervision of reading programs* (2nd ed., pp. 22–38). Newark, DE: International Reading Association and Teachers College Press.

Wepner, S., & Strickland, D. (Eds.). (2008). *Administration and supervision of reading programs* (4th ed.). New York: Teachers College Press.

Whitehurst, G. J., Falco, F. L., Lonigan, C. J., Fischel, J. E., DeBaryshe, B. D., Valdez-Menchaca, M. C., & Caulfield M. (1988). Accelerating language development through picture book reading. *Developmental Psychology, 24*(4), 552–559.

Wilburn, D. (2009). *What is leveled reading? Helping kids become better readers by matching them to the right books at the right time.* New York: Scholastic. Available at http://www2.scholastic.com/browse/article.jsp?id=10216.

Wilhelm, J. (2001). *Improving comprehension with think-alouds: Modeling what good readers do.* New York: Scholastic.

Wilhelm, J. (2007). *Engaging readers and writers with inquiry: Promoting deep understanding in language arts and the content areas with guiding questions.* New York: Scholastic.

Wilkinson, A. G., & Bloome, D. (2008). Research as principled, pluralistic argument. *Reading Research Quarterly, 43*(1), 6–8.

Wilkinson, L. C., & Silliman, E. R. (2000). Classroom language and literacy learning. In M. L. Kamil, P. B. Mosenthal, P. D. Pearson, & R. Barr (Eds.), *Handbook of reading research* (Vol. III, pp. 337–355). Mahwah, NJ: Erlbaum.

Wolfram, W. (1991). *Dialects and American English.* Englewood Cliffs, NJ: Prentice-Hall.

Wong-Fillmore, L. (1991). *The classroom as a setting for social learning.* Paper presented at the Celebrating Diversity Conference, Oakland, CA.

Wood, K. D., & Blanton, W. E. (2009). *Literacy instruction for adolescents: Research-based practice.* New York: Guilford Press.

Wood, K. D., & Harmon, J. M. (2001). *Strategies for integrating reading and writing in middle and high school classes.* Westfield, Ohio: National Middle School Association.

Wood, M., & Prata Salvetti, E. (2001). Project story boost: Read-alouds for students at risk. *The Reading Teacher, 55,* 76–83.

Worthy, J., Broaddus, K., & Ivey, G. (2001). *Pathways to independence: Reading, writing, and learning in grades 3–8.* New York: Guilford Press.

Xu, H. (2000). Preservice teachers in a literacy methods course consider issues of diversity. *Journal of Literacy Research, 32*(4), 505–531.

Yaden, D. B., & Paratore, J. R. (2003). Family literacy at the turn of the millennium: The costly future of maintaining the status quo. In J. Flood, D. Lapp, J. R. Squire, & J. M. Jensen (Eds.), *Handbook of research on teaching the English language arts* (2nd ed., pp. 546–565). Mahwah, NJ: Erlbaum.

Yaden, D. B., Rowe, D. W., & MacGillivray, L. (2000). Emergent literacy: A matter (polyphony) of perspectives. In M. L. Kamil, P. B. Mosenthal, P. D. Pearson, & R. Barr (Eds.), *Handbook of reading research* (Vol. III, pp. 425–454). Mahwah, NJ: Erlbaum.

Yarrow, F., & Topping, K. J. (2001). Collaborative writing: The effects of metacognitive prompting and structured peer interaction. *British Journal of Educational Psychology, 71*(2), 261–273.

Yeaton, W. H., & Sechrest, L. (1981). Critical dimensions in the choice and maintenance of successful treatments: Strength, integrity, and effectiveness. *Journal of Consulting and Clinical Psychology, 49,* 156–167.

Yinger, R. (1985). Journal writing as a learning tool. *Volga Review, 87*(5), 21–33.

Yopp, H. K. (1992). Developing phonemic awareness in young children. *The Reading Teacher, 45,* 696–703.

Zemelman, S., Daniels, H., & Hyde, A. (2005). *Best practice: Today's standards for teaching and learning in America's schools* (3rd ed.). Portsmouth, NH: Heinemann.

Zimmerman, B. J., Bandura, A., & Martinez-Pons, M. (1992). Self-motivation for academic attainment: The role of self-efficacy, beliefs, and personal goal-setting. *American Educational Research Journal, 29*(3), 663–676.

Zirkel, P. (2006). *The legal meaning of specific learning disability for special education eligibility.* Available at http://www.cec.sped.org.

Zwiers, J. (2008). *Building academic language: Essential practices for content classrooms.* San Francisco: Jossey-Bass.

# *Index*